Black Bartholomew's

MANCHESTER
1824

Manchester University Press

Politics, culture and society in early modern Britain

General Editors

PROFESSOR ANN HUGHES
PROFESSOR ANTHONY MILTON
PROFESSOR PETER LAKE

This important series publishes monographs that take a fresh and challenging look at the interactions between politics, culture and society in Britain between 1500 and the mid-eighteenth century. It counteracts the fragmentation of current historiography through encouraging a variety of approaches which attempt to redefine the political, social and cultural worlds, and to explore their interconnection in a flexible and creative fashion. All the volumes in the series question and transcend traditional interdisciplinary boundaries, such as those between political history and literary studies, social history and divinity, urban history and anthropology. They thus contribute to a broader understanding of crucial developments in early modern Britain.

Black Bartholomew's Day

Preaching, polemic and Restoration nonconformity

DAVID J. APPLEBY

Manchester
University Press
Manchester and New York

distributed exclusively in the USA by Palgrave

The right of David J. Appleby to be identified as the author of this work has been asserted by him in accordance with the Copyright, Designs and Patents Act 1988.

Published by Manchester University Press
Oxford Road, Manchester M13 9NR, UK
and Room 400, 175 Fifth Avenue, New York, NY 10010, USA
www.manchesteruniversitypress.co.uk

Distributed in the United States exclusively by
Palgrave Macmillan, 175 Fifth Avenue,
New York, NY 10010, USA

Distributed in Canada exclusively by
UBC Press, University of British Columbia, 2029 West Mall,
Vancouver, BC, Canada V6T 1Z2

British Library Cataloguing-in-Publication Data is available

Library of Congress Cataloging-in-Publication Data is available

ISBN 978 0 7190 8780 6 paperback

First published by Manchester University Press in hardback 2007

This paperback edition first published 2012

Printed by Lightning Source

FOR DAD
'KEEP GOING!'

Contents

ACKNOWLEDGEMENTS—ix
CONVENTIONS—xi
ABBREVIATIONS—xiii

Introduction   I

1   The context of Restoration nonconformity   18

2   Preaching, audience and authority   55

3   Scripture, historicism and the critique of authority   92

4   The public circulation of the Bartholomean texts   131

5   Polemical responses to Bartholomean preaching   171

6   Epilogue   211

7   Conclusion   218

BIBLIOGRAPHY—227
INDEX—247

Acknowledgements

I would like to thank Ann Hughes for her unstinting support, advice and encouragement throughout this project. I would like to thank all the academic and administrative staff in History, English and the Humanities Research Institute at Keele University for their help. Particular thanks go to Roger Pooley, Ian Atherton, Kate Cushing, Philip Morgan, Alannah Tomkins, Christopher Harrison, Malcolm Crook, Peter Jackson, David Amigoni, Simone Clarke, Jim MacLaverty, Kath McKeown, Amanda Roberts, Beryl Shore and Julie Street. I am very grateful to Peter Lake for many useful conversations during his tenure as Leverhume Visiting Professor at Keele. I have also benefited enormously from the help and advice generously given by Richard Cust, John Spurr, John Walter, Ted Vallance, Michael Mendle, Julie Sanders, Patricia Clavin, Elizabeth Clark, Jens-Wilhelm Wessels, Ian Green and Andy Fear, as well as the friendship and support of the Keele postgraduate community, including Geoff Baker, Clive Bradbury, Kelly Hignett, Clark Colman, Jon Denton, Ann McGruer, Natasha Grayson, Hitomi Yamanaka, Minako Ichikawa, Andy Barnicoat, Cath Yarwood and Graeme Smart. Thanks are also due to Erik Geleijns of the Koninklijke Bibliotheek, and David Wykes of Dr Williams's Library, and to staffs of the British Library, the Bodleian Library, Dr Williams's Library, the National Archives (Public Record Office), the John Rylands Library, Essex Record Office, Lichfield Record Office, Stafford Record Office, Shropshire Record Office, and Keele University Library. I am grateful to all at Manchester University Press for guiding me through the publishing process. Finally, I am very conscious of the debt owed to my family, particularly my father and late mother, for their encouragement and support over many years. This book is as much their achievement as it is mine.

Conventions

The old-style dating has been used throughout the book, except that the year has been calculated from 1 January rather than from Lady Day, 25 March.

Original italicisation, capitalisation, spelling and punctuation have been retained in contemporary quotations, except where these have been taken from subsequent sources and calendars. On isolated occasions when an explanation of a contemporary term or an apparent misspelling has been considered necessary, the explanation has been inserted within the quotation in square brackets.

The titles of contemporary published works have been left in their original form. Biblical quotations have been taken from the King James Version unless otherwise indicated.

In view of the fact that in many cases several editions exist of individual farewell sermons and particularly of the Bartholomean compilations, the Wing catalogue number of the precise edition referred to has been included where it has been deemed necessary to the better understanding of the text.

Abbreviations

Titles of books, articles and manuscripts have been cited in full in the first instance in each chapter, and abbreviated thereafter. In the case of original early modern texts, titles have been cited in short title format in the first instance, and abbreviated thereafter. The following abbreviations have been used for the sources or institutions most frequently cited in the footnotes:

Abridgement	E. Calamy (1671–1732), *An Abridgement of Mr Baxter's History of his Life and Times. With an Account of Many Other of those Worthy Ministers who were Ejected,* (London, 1702)
Account	E. Calamy (1671–1732), *An Abridgement of Mr Baxter's History of his Life and Times. With an Account of Many Other of those Worthy Ministers who were Ejected,* (2nd edn, 2 vols, London, 1713)
BL	British Library, London
Bodl.	Bodleian Library, Oxford
Continuation	E. Calamy (1671–1732), *A Continuation of the Account of the Ministers . . . Who were Ejected and Silenced* (2 vols, London, 1727)
CR	A. G. Matthews (ed.), *Calamy Revised: Being a Revision of Edmund Calamy's Account of the Ministers and Others Ejected and Silenced, 1660–2* (Oxford, 1934)
CSPD	M. A. E. Green (ed.), *Calendar of State Papers, Domestic Series, 1619–62* (London, 1858–93)
CSPV	A. B. Hines (ed.), *Calendar of State Papers, Venetian, 1661–1664* (London, 1932)
DNB	*Dictionary of National Biography from the Earliest Times to 1900,* ed. G. Smith (22 vols, Oxford, 1921–22)
DWL	Dr Williams's Library, London
ERO	Essex Record Office

Exact collection	*An Exact Collection of Farevvel Sermons, Preached by the Late London-Ministers* (1662), Wing E3632
HMC	Historical Manuscripts Commission
ODNB	*Oxford Dictionary of National Biography from the Earliest Times to the Year 2000*, ed. H. C. G. Matthew and B. H. Harrison (60 vols, Oxford, 2004); www.oxforddnb.com
Pepys, *Diary*	*The Diary of Samuel Pepys*, ed. R. Latham and W. Matthews, 11 vols (10 vols, 1970)
PRO	Public Record Office (National Archives)
Rawl.	Rawlinson MSS, Bodleian Library, Oxford
SP	State papers
s.v.	*sub verbo* (pl.: *s.vv.*)

Introduction

————◆————

A t 8 o'clock, on the morning of Sunday 17 August 1662, the diarist Samuel
Pepys elbowed his way through the crowd that had gathered around the
back door of St Dunstan's church. Despite the fact that the main doors had
not yet been opened, most of the pews were already full.[1] Like Pepys, tens of
thousands of people were jostling into churches across England and Wales
to witness an event of historic significance: the final sermons of hundreds of
clergy preparing to quit their Church of England livings.

It has often been noted that moderate Puritans facilitated the restoration
of the British monarchy without providing themselves with constitutional protection against a vengeful and neurotic Cavalier gentry.[2] If these individuals
– largely, but by no means exclusively, Presbyterian – felt secure in their
numerical and political significance, or trusted Charles II to deliver promises
to indulge tender consciences, they were seriously mistaken. Over the previous decade, mutual concerns over the perceived excesses of radical sects had
prompted increasing cooperation between Presbyterian and Independent
congregations. The return of the Long Parliament in January 1660, following the collapse of the Protectorate, had given hope to those who aspired to
the establishment of a disciplined state church organised along moderate
Presbyterian lines. The prospect of a restored monarchy had reinforced this
hope: negotiations between the exiled Charles Stuart and a delegation of
moderate divines sent out to the Netherlands were cordial not least because
the range of Puritan opinion there represented was generally prepared to
countenance a church overseen by a reduced episcopacy. But the optimism
engendered by these negotiations dissipated rapidly after the Restoration.
At the Savoy Conference of 1661 the disorganised and demoralised Puritan
delegates found themselves decisively outmanoeuvred and marginalised.
The intransigence of the bishops was, if anything, surpassed by allies in the
House of Commons: immediately after assembling in May 1661, activists

within the 'Cavalier' Parliament embarked upon a quest to secure church and state by implementing a rigid and exclusive Anglican orthodoxy in local government and the parish pulpit. The Corporation Act of 1661 was designed to cleanse local authorities of any vestigial Presbyterian elements. Its central requirement, willingly to participate in Anglican communion, was intended as a test of political loyalty. Within a year came even more proscriptive legislation in the shape of the Act of Uniformity.

The Act of Uniformity received the royal assent on 29 July 1662. The Act imposed detailed requirements on all Church of England clergy, as well as masters and fellows of Oxford and Cambridge, schoolmasters and private tutors. Such people were to acknowledge the illegality of armed resistance to the Crown or its representatives. They were required to disavow that pivotal document of the late rebellion, the Solemn League and Covenant. Ministers wishing to officiate within the Church of England were to affirm that their future liturgy would adhere precisely to the forthcoming Book of Common Prayer. They were required to provide proof that they had been ordained by a bishop or otherwise receive such ordination. The deadline by which to comply, subscribe in writing and publicly declare unfeigned assent and consent to these provisions lay less than one month ahead, on 24 August.[3] Ironically, given its significance in the Protestant calendar, this was St Bartholomew's Day. Those who refused to abide by the legislation in its entirety were to be ejected from their livings and barred from public ministry.

Almost seven hundred clergy had already been displaced by the Act for Confirming and Restoring of Ministers (1660). Some were victims of circumstance, displaced by the superior claim of a loyalist cleric to their particular living, whilst others had been targeted because of political or religious radicalism.[4] However, most Puritan clergy, particularly those of a Presbyterian persuasion, remained within the state Church until, as their antagonists intended, many found themselves unable in conscience to fulfil all the obligations demanded by the Act of Uniformity. Even then, the grumbles of bishops and Cavalier journalists suggest that several undesirables remained in their livings. William Mew, rector of Eastington, and some of his Gloucestershire neighbours attempted to outwit the authorities by using the exact form of words in the statute whilst reading their assent out in church, deliberately failing to replace the standard 'A. B.' with their own names.[5] Inadequate surveillance by a number of diocesan authorities meant that disaffected clergy such as Ralph Josselin in Essex, and John Angier in Lancashire were able to continue their ministry provided they did so quietly enough to avoid notice. Almost one thousand ministers, however, refused to conform, and made their dissent too obvious to ignore: 'Let us pity the Instruments', preached Robert Atkins, rector of St John's, Exeter, 'justify God, and condemn our selves.'[6]

Given the numbers of clergy involved, especially in London, many besides Pepys feared the consequences should the expulsions meet with resistance. The Privy Council received increasingly insistent reports of Presbyterian conspiracies as Bartholomew's Day approached, whilst the Venetian ambassador likened events to those that had presaged civil war twenty years earlier.[7] The Lord Lieutenant of Ireland was warned by a correspondent on 23 August that 'the nonconformist ministers are grown so insolent that I cannot assure my self you will not sooner than you imagin make use of your army ther'.[8] Military preparations in London and elsewhere throughout July and August 1662 gave the impression that many Cavaliers expected, or even desired, confrontation. The belief that Bartholomew's Day would see uprisings became so pervasive that even Clarendon began to give them credence.[9] It was in this volatile political atmosphere that hundreds of ministers began to declare and explain their nonconformity by preaching farewell sermons. Unsurprisingly, their expositions were followed with intense and widespread interest, and dissected for indications of future intent.

There was huge relief when it became apparent that the Great Ejection had passed with remarkably little trouble. However, this optimism was soon confounded by the appearance of pamphlets featuring the farewell sermons of several leading ministers. These were quickly followed into print by collections of farewell sermons and related material, unlicensed publications that grew weightier with each edition. As the authorities struggled to contain the literary tide, individuals such as Joseph Cooper, the curate of Moseley, Worcestershire, continued to offer noisy resistance. Despite having delivered his valediction in August, Cooper occupied his pulpit for a further three months, until he was seized by troopers and thrown into prison.[10] Soon after this, on 28 December, Edmund Calamy reoccupied his old pulpit at St Mary's Aldermanbury in London to deliver (as he claimed) an extempore sermon deprecating the times and warning of divine retribution. Calamy's open defiance of the law, and his subsequent incarceration in Newgate, gave the nonconformist press a *cause célèbre*. His actions were widely debated in print, and his sermon given prominence on the frontispieces of subsequent Bartholomean compilations.[11] The Aldermanbury incident, together with a growing influx of Bartholomean texts from the provinces, further swelled the torrent of print, provoking heated exchanges between nonconformists and their detractors. Far from considering the texts the inconsequential musings of a defeated faction, contemporaries of all persuasions clearly took them very seriously.

The fluidity of the Restoration political landscape, with its shifting factions, networks and (in the loosest seventeenth-century sense of the word) parties, has given rise to an equally fluid catalogue of definitions and appellations. Of all these terms, none has caused more debate than that of 'Puritan'. Peter

Lake has identified three principal approaches that have hitherto been taken to define Puritanism: as a movement committed to completing the reformation of the liturgy and government of the English Church; as a 'distinctively zealous or intense subset of a larger body of reformed or protestant doctrines or positions' (in other words, a tendency rather than a party); and lastly, as a rhetorical image created by enemies. Lake, in proposing a combination of the latter two definitions, argues that 'our concern should not be so much to list and delimit a group of telltale Puritan opinions so much as to pull together a sense of the central core of a Puritan style or tradition or world view'.[12] It could be argued, however, that in order to do this it is necessary to note the frequency and intensity of telltale Puritan opinions held by a given individual or network. Consequently, the term 'Puritan' is used here to indicate a godly individual who believed in moral conduct and worship according to Scripture, who resisted human innovation in worship, who believed in Providence and in a godly elect saved by Grace rather than good works. After the Restoration, Puritans, whatever their hue, were repeatedly associated with antimonarchism and regicide, despite the fact that the events of 1649 had exposed divisions within their ranks. Many of those affected by the Act of Uniformity were too young to have participated in the civil wars, and several had suffered for the royalist cause. There were many who remained desirous of a political compromise, albeit not necessarily willing to accommodate a doctrinal one. As the bishops suspected, many of those who remained within the ministry of the Church of England after 1662 were as much Puritans as those ejected from it.

In the political climate of the Restoration, particularly after the Act of Uniformity, Puritanism would be defined, in Patrick Collinson's words, 'not by the contentions of its adherents, but by the assessments of its observers'.[13] However, both John Spurr and Sears McGee have warned that despite the fact that Puritans would be 'legally defined and systematically recorded as dissenters', it would be wrong to assume that Puritanism was synonymous with Dissent. Many nonconformists would subsequently object to being labelled Dissenters because they had no wish to be associated with radical groups of whom they themselves disapproved.[14] The term most often applied to these conservative individuals is 'Presbyterian', a name which also implies a desire for a disciplined Calvinistic national church run by elders or, conceivably, a primitive episcopacy. However, this term was hijacked after the Restoration by Cavalier journalists and Anglican preachers for their own purposes – rendering the appellation 'Presbyterian' even more problematical than that of 'Puritan'.

The delineating of religious groupings caused by the Act of Uniformity allows historians who favour the term 'Anglican' to feel slightly less anxious about the pitfalls of anachronism than would be the case with earlier periods.[15]

The term as it will be used here will encompass members of the Church of England who worshipped according to the Book of Common Prayer and espoused episcopal government. However, whilst (like the alternative term 'episcopalian') this could equally refer to conformist Puritans, the most vociferous Anglican viewpoint within the Church of England was that promoted by the aggressively anti-Puritan Sheldon and his allies. The appellation 'Anglican' does not, however, adequately encapsulate the character of those who equated religious conformity with absolute political loyalty to the monarchical system of government. The activities of individuals such as Roger L'Estrange and John Berkenhead reveal a political heritage of ultra-royalism fused with the tenets of the restored state Church. This overtly political and secular strain of Anglicanism has been indicated in the following chapters by the use of the term 'Cavalier-Anglican'.

In 1727 Edmund Calamy III described Job Tookie, an ejected minister from Yarmouth, as 'a Bartholomean sufferer'.[16] The term 'Bartholomean' (which grew in popularity among later writers) is a useful one; more accurate than describing ministers as 'ejected clergy' before they had actually been ejected, and differentiating *post facto* between Puritan clergy who remained in Church of England livings and those who did not. The phrase 'Black Bartholomew's Day' has an even older provenance, as it was clearly already current by the time Richard Baxter came to write his autobiography. Calamy used the terms 'Black Bartholomew' and 'Fatal Bartholomew' interchangeably. That such terminology gave the impression of a discernible corpus was not lost on John Walker, who complained in his survey of Anglican sufferers that a particularly disagreeable character of his acquaintance had been canonised in Calamy's 'Bartholomew Legend'.[17]

The surviving Bartholomean oeuvre includes the texts of some seventy-seven farewell sermons, delivered by fifty ejected ministers, plus eight sermons by Joseph Cooper amalgamated into one publication.[18] Diaries and near-contemporary accounts contain information on several other valedictions. It seems likely that most ministers who anticipated ejection preached farewell sermons, including several destined to survive the purge: William Mew gave what he believed to be his farewell sermon on Sunday 17 August, as did Ralph Josselin the following Tuesday.[19] The urge to leave a lasting mark was particularly strong in individuals such as Joseph Cooper of Moseley and Richard Fairclough of Mells, Somerset, who devoted the final weeks of their official ministry to composing and preaching a coordinated series of lectures.[20] Such extraordinary efforts, together with the presence of many practised note-takers within the various congregations, ensured that a substantial number of valedictions became available to the book trade.

Five sermons have survived in manuscript form. The same hand transcribed the valedictions of Thomas Ford, Lewis Stucley and Thomas Powel, delivered in Exeter between 13 and 19 August 1662, and now preserved in the Rawlinson MSS in the Bodleian Library.[21] Two sermons preached by Matthew Newcomen from his pulpit in Dedham, Essex, on 17 and 19 August also survive: an endorsement on the covering page of the bound manuscript in Doctor Williams's Library affirms that it is Newcomen's own handwritten record, together with his introduction to the first farewell sermon and concluding prayers, given to a Robert Winter shortly after the event.[22] The lecture of 19 August was published – almost certainly from a different manuscript – in a number of printed collections.

The overwhelming majority of printed Bartholomean works were published between late 1662 and 1664. At least nineteen different pamphlets circulated during this period, varying from quartos and octavos featuring one or two sermons to a duodecimo containing Richard Fairclough's valedictory series of fourteen lectures. However, Cavalier journalists were far more alarmed by the appearance of compilations. The first of these, published in late 1662, featured London-based ministers, but within weeks valedictions began to arrive from the provinces. At least sixteen compilations were produced between August 1662 and 25 March 1663, by which time some had swollen into huge collections of forty-two sermons. Soon afterwards, L'Estrange, the Surveyor of the Press, calculated that there were around thirty thousand copies in circulation, with at least one edition printing in Dutch. A copy of *Versameling van Afscheytspredicatien*, published by Joannes van Someren of Amsterdam in 1662, is preserved in the Provincial Library of Friesland in Leeuwarden.[23]

A collection of sermons emerged from the East Midlands, entitled *England's Remembrancer* (1663), featuring a set of ejected ministers who appeared in no other compilation. The editors chose not to name the ministers involved, but it is clear that their identities were known within nonconformist circles. In his *Abridgement*, published in 1702, Edmund Calamy III disclosed that Robert Porter, the ejected vicar of Pentrich in Derbyshire, had featured in the collection. He was more forthcoming in the *Account* (1713), ascribing each of the valedictions to ministers ejected from livings in Nottinghamshire, Derbyshire and Staffordshire.[24] John Whitlock had already been revealed as the author of two sermons in the collection when the information was volunteered at his funeral by a fellow Bartholomean, John Barrett.[25] Given Calamy's privileged access to contemporary nonconformist networks, and in view of the fact that several of those identified were still alive in 1713, there is every reason to trust his attribution.

England's Remembrancer differed in another respect from other Bartholomean compilations in that it consisted solely of farewell sermons. Every other compilation included additional items, such as the funeral sermons for Simeon Ashe and James Nalton, ministers' prayers, Thomas

Lye's morning exercises, Thomas Watson's sermon against popery, and even Robert Wilde's poem on Calamy's imprisonment.[26] It is apparent from the construction of the various compilations, and from the writings of hostile journalists, that editors considered these extra texts intrinsic to the Bartholomean message. Thus, far from being mere marginalia, these supplementary items provide additional perspectives on the process of compilation and the historical context.

It is when we remember that the surviving Bartholomean oeuvre, voluminous as it is, represents a small fraction of the outpourings from hundreds of pulpits during August 1662 that the contemporary significance of the farewell sermons begins to emerge. Several items, among them the farewell sermons of William Jenkyn and Calamy's funeral sermon for Simeon Ashe, were printed on at least eleven separate occasions between 1662 and 1663. Even the attacks on the farewell sermons published by Cavalier journalists indicate that the Bartholomean texts had an impact far beyond the private bookshelves of the literate godly. By sheer weight of ink and paper alone, the Bartholomean corpus would appear to be an important resource for the study of early nonconformity, and a useful point of entry into the political and religious culture of the Restoration.

Since the 1980s the Restoration period has begun to attract the attention of a new generation of historians.[27] Scholars such as Tim Harris have challenged earlier conclusions that religion ceased to be an important national issue after 1660. To counter the preoccupation with high politics evident in works such as those of J. R. Jones and J. H. Plumb, Harris and others have called for a renewed scrutiny of political and cultural issues within the local communities.[28] But there is a more fundamental problem at work here than a lingering obsession with high politics: at root, the arguments for the diminution of religion as a political force appear to rely heavily on the preconception that historical significance should be measured in terms of structural change, or political or intellectual innovation. As far back as 1950, the ecclesiastical historian G. R. Cragg wrote that most religious controversy after 1660 was 'intolerably trivial, and in retrospect appears as sordid and inconsequential as an ale-house brawl', because 'many of the influential figures were second-rate in their ability, and made no striking contribution because they had no original thought'.[29] Similar attitudes appear to have inspired M. G. Finlayson to deny the significance of nonconformity in seventeenth-century politics, and John Miller to argue that 'few politically "seditious" works appeared before 1679'.[30]

Judged against such criteria, it is hardly surprising that the farewell sermons have hitherto been discounted; these valedictions did nothing to save their authors from ejection, and it would be easy to assume that they did not possess the potential to forestall or precipitate political change. This might explain why Mitchell's 1932 study of early modern preaching failed to include any Bartholomean valedictions in a forty-one page survey of 'representative' seventeenth-century sermons.[31] It might also explain why in his 1957 work on the Restoration settlement, Robert Bosher could describe the *embarras de richesses* of contemporary documents pertaining to the Great Ejection without referring to a single farewell sermon – an oversight still evident in John Hetet's influential thesis on the nonconformist literary underground in Restoration England thirty years later.[32] In histories where the farewell sermons have been cited at all, the impression has often been given that their authors were quietist. Just as L'Estrange's biographer wrote in 1913 that 'these pathetic discourses have very little in them beyond an exhortation to comfort', so John Spurr has argued that 'in their farewell sermons before "Black Bartholomew" and their circumspect behaviour after their "legal death" or ejection, these peaceable ministers strove to avoid offence'.[33] As we shall see, however, although most Bartholomeans certainly strove to avoid prosecution, this did not prevent their farewell sermons from causing considerable offence.

Perceptions of the farewell sermons and their authors appear hitherto to have been predicated on a relatively limited selection of the available texts. In some respects this is understandable; the amount of Bartholomean material to survive is voluminous and its rhetoric complex and problematical. As Lois Potter comments in her study of Interregnum royalist literature, 'the territory where literature and history meet is frightening enough as it is without the added hazards created by the existence of more material . . . than any one person can assimilate'.[34] The study of the farewell sermons echoes the dilemma encountered by Lori-Anne Ferrell during her research on Jacobean court sermons: 'faced with an overwhelming mass of words and an underwhelming number of deeds, how does the historian assess the significance of political language?'[35]

Writing in 1987, Neil Keeble contrasted the neglect of post-Restoration nonconformist writing with the enthusiasm shown by historians for the radical literature of the English Revolution.[36] Keeble attributes this bias largely to the influence of Christopher Hill, but in fact such predilections were already evident in the earlier work of W. F. Mitchell and G. R. Cragg. Restoration nonconformists were seen as stragglers in the footsteps of more charismatic Puritan forebears, whilst authors such as Milton were portrayed as brilliant anomalies marooned in an otherwise barren wilderness of aimless prolixity.[37] In more recent times, however, the writings of Greaves and Keeble have reflected a deepening interest in the politics of late seventeenth-century Dissent, together with a growing awareness of the richness and vibrancy of its literature.[38] Nevertheless, the embarrassment of riches represented by the Bartholomean oeuvre has yet to receive commensurate attention.

The comparative neglect of the Bartholomean corpus is surprising in view of the rising profile of preaching in recent debates on the nature and function of religion in early modern society. Increasingly, academics have begun to appreciate that sermons can offer valuable insights not only into the theological issues of the day, but also into the relationship between religion, politics and culture.[39] The challenges posed by postmodernism and the linguistic turn have forced a general reappraisal of the material, together with a dramatic improvement in the methodology of reading and interpretation, if only in order to respond to revisionist arguments fuelled by 'the sheer knock-out power of texts more closely read'.[40] Scholars such as Tony Claydon and Lori-Ann Ferrell now argue that the sermon was a principal arena of early modern public debate.[41] In contrast to the situation which impelled Mary Morrissey to lament the neglect of the subject in 1999, there is now less cause to complain, and increasingly less excuse to plunder sermons in ignorance.[42] In the midst of this progress, however, Restoration sermons have remained relatively unexplored. Just as Ferrell and McCullough's *The English Sermon Revised* (2000) contains no essays on the period, so studies of Restoration preaching have been conspicuous by their absence. But given the renewal of interest in the Restoration period, and the burgeoning enthusiasm for studies of early modern preaching, this would seem the ideal time to reintroduce the farewell sermons of 1662.

The proposal that the Bartholomean oeuvre is central to the study of the Restoration religious settlement, and provides a suitable entry point through which to explore the interaction between religion and politics, carries with it theoretical and methodological implications. Like Lois Potter's research, this present study is located at a point where literature and history meet. Ferrell, McCullough and Morrissey have all emphasised that considerable work is still needed in order to develop a methodology that will reveal 'a sermon's full engagement with its historical moment'.[43] A necessary part of this development – implicit in the chapters that follow – is an acknowledgement that the 'historical moment' (itself a complex and elastic structural concept) engaged with the sermon as much as the sermon with it. For this reason, this study will resist Morrissey's inclination to separate ideological and political considerations from theological criteria, and hold instead with her earlier call to examine sermons 'in a way that utilises both their rhetorical artfulness and their political significance'.[44] It will be argued here that politics and ideology were intrinsic to the construction of early modern English sermons – including those generated by the supposedly internalised faith of the Puritan. Even the desire to avoid giving offence presupposes a calculation based upon political and ideological criteria. It will be shown that spiritual and secular concerns were often consciously synthesised in the farewell sermons, a discourse which serves to demonstrate that religion remained a central element of political culture after 1660.

It is in the nature of things that our attempts to reconstruct this past discourse must be almost completely dependent upon the texts available to us. In the case of the farewell sermons the fact that most of the texts have survived only in printed form necessitates an awareness of the nature and historiography of print culture. Such theoretical studies have abounded since the 1980s, nurtured by sustained and healthy debate in the various fields of bibliographical study.[45] The message that has emerged is that whilst texts have the potential to reveal much about the mentalities of the societies in which they circulate, the issues surrounding their production, dissemination and reception are complex. Just as Chartier once declared that books do not make revolutions, 'but the ways they are made, used and read just might', so texts do not make histories – but the ways in which they are recovered, interpreted or ignored just might.[46] We must be ever more sensitive not only to nuances hidden in the contemporary use of phrases such as 'private' or 'tender conscience', but also to what Adrian Johns terms the historical specificity of reading practices.[47]

At the heart of the current interest in early modern print culture lie the issues of authorship and reception. Reports of the death of the author, so famously fashioned by Roland Barthes, have been somewhat revised since the 1990s.[48] Barthes' entire polemic, Sean Burke writes, 'is grounded in the false assumption that if a magisterial status is denied the author, then the very concept of the author becomes otiose'.[49] In the context of the early modern sermon, any assumption that magisterial status is a requirement of authorship is itself otiose. Barthes' Author-God and Foucault's distinctly modern perception of individualism are both anachronistic preoccupations in the context of seventeenth-century England. More than any other early modern author, the preacher functioned within his community. The text of the sermon was, and is, given meaning by its recipients, but those recipients did not, and do not, have a monopoly on meaning. When publishers sought to establish the veracity of the printed farewell sermons, and when readers presented wildly differing interpretations of them, both invariably attempted to do so in terms of authorial intention. Having said this, it will become evident that the author's intentions are not assumed here to fix the meaning of a given text, especially as having deliberately introduced ambiguity into their works the Bartholomeans were manifestly unable to control it. A continuing regard for authorship does not require a belief in the fixity of the text, simply an acknowledgement that the author's role in its creation remains important. As the following chapters will demonstrate, much of the meaning imputed to the farewell sermons by recipients proceeded from an ongoing preoccupation with the identity, status and aspirations of the ejected ministers. By contrast, ministers such as Roger Seddon of Kirk Langley, Derbyshire, frequently sought to deny themselves authorial primacy, repeatedly declaring their desire to exist only as a conduit of God's will, relaying the Word strictly as revealed in Scripture.[50] In the event, this desire to purge their preaching of subjectivity was doomed primarily because it was impossible to disentangle 'internal' spirituality from 'external' politics and ideology. Ironically, nothing was more deliberately designed to preserve the continuing agency of the author than when the text of a farewell sermon declared that its author was 'civilly dead'. As John Oldfield declared in a farewell sermon given just before his ejection from the living of Carsington, Derbyshire, 'though we are dead, *we yet speak*'.[51]

The evocation of dead voices is a rhetorical device so ingrained in the writing of history that it would be easy to overlook the significance of contemporary distinctions between the spoken, written and printed word. Recent scholarship has begun to acknowledge the desirability of retrieving the physical moment, even if many historians, such as Bryan Crockett, believe that 'any attempt to reconstruct accurately the original audiences' experience of Reformation sermons (or Renaissance plays) will fail'.[52] However, even Crockett has conceded that this does not preclude the possibility of translation altogether. Ferrell and McCullough note that early modern sermons were 'instruments of policy, documents of religious change and expressions of public life: they were, in short, both historical texts and historical context. But since sermons survive only as the former, we must work carefully and creatively to reconstruct the latter'.[53]

Whilst acknowledging the obvious difficulties, therefore, it is important to consider the aural impact of the farewell sermons. Bruce Smith has pointed out that 'the disproportionate power of [a] literate minority in representing early modern England to posterity' obliges us to recover as much of the lost acoustic world as possible.[54] Any reconstruction of the nature and impact of the spoken word, however, must be grounded in written or printed texts. Adam Fox has recently argued against positing a 'crude binary opposition between "oral" and "literate" culture', offering many persuasive examples of the reciprocities between the two.[55] But at least one oral-literate dichotomy persists, and was recognised even in the seventeenth century, as the editor of William Bates' farewell sermons acknowledged in his preface to *The Peace-Maker* (1662):

> We need not mention the vast difference betwixt hearing and reading, or the lustre lost in Printing, which words had in delivering, neither how neatly they might have been cloathed if sent abroad by the Author; all that we shall say, is, thou hast them in such a dress as they were clad with in their first delivery.[56]

Restoration editors thus knew the same frustrations as those experienced by modern historians; that a fleeting facial expression, a tiny gesture, a momentary pause, a minute change in the speed, volume or tone of the preacher's delivery might easily have conveyed a message dramatically different from that which appears to present itself to us in print. Equally important and complex issues surround the questions of moral ownership, economics, state censorship and self-censorship. It is important to bear the motivation and method of the amanuensis in mind, whether this was the preacher himself, a member of his flock, a government spy or a mercenary scribe. We must consider whether the transcribers transcribed all that they heard and whether they heard everything, whether the printers printed all that they received and whether they received everything.

These questions return inexorably to the issues of audience and reception. Whilst the text of a sermon can often give clues as to how it was received, additional sources are needed to confirm whether listeners were hostile, sympathetic or heterogeneous, whether the sermon was heard in reverential silence or drowned out by jeers and catcalls. Seating or standing arrangements, church furniture and hangings – inevitably different from the physical acoustics of the same buildings today – would all have had an effect.

The issues of authorship, reception and provenance can all inform on the creation and survival of the farewell sermons, and provide a useful theoretical basis for their deconstruction. The intention here, however, is to join in the general movement towards considering sermons as rhetorical texts.[57] Historians may sometimes be guilty, as Johns has suggested, of taking 'at face value the persuasive power of printed material to affect the perception and actions of their readers', but few forget that whereas print is frequently a mediator of power, language is more often the arbiter of it.[58] There were few more skilled exponents of rhetoric than the ministers who appear in the following chapters. Their rhetoric was 'fixed' in the sense that they utilised rhetorical commonplaces that were widely understood, but many exploited a multivalent religious rhetoric that could be both pious and polemical at the same time. The rhetoric used in such exegesis was carefully constructed from the building blocks of sub-divided doctrines and applications to produce an intricately interconnected essay in epistemology – a house of cards as much as a deck of cards.[59] Assessing the significance of political language, opening up these texts to their historic meaning, and rescuing Black Bartholomew's Day from the condescension of history, therefore, requires careful navigation.

Chapter 1 analyses the societal and religious identities of the Bartholomean clergy, exploring their relationships within local communities, together with their fears and aspirations for a laity bereft of godly preaching. Building on this, chapter 2 considers the farewell sermons as physical performances, whose prevalence and intensity – both in exposition and reception – demonstrate that religion remained a prominent feature in the Restoration landscape.

Chapter 3 seeks to decode the rhetorical content of the Bartholomean texts, revealing how political comment was skilfully embedded in the exegesis, and how the apocalyptic epistemology which underpinned so many texts could hardly fail to produce highly charged political polemic. Chapter 4 reveals how this polemic was affected by the process of scribal and printed circulation, whilst chapter 5 explores the polemical responses of the Bartholomeans' detractors to that process. In particular, it will be argued that figures in the Restoration establishment exploited the texts not simply to pursue an anti-Puritan (particularly anti-Presbyterian) agenda, but often in order to promote factions at Court and further their personal careers. The transforming effects of such interventions are confirmed in chapter 6, which charts how the representation of the Bartholomean corpus has changed over the succeeding centuries to suit the times.

This study thus explores the farewell sermons and their authors from a variety of perspectives – historical, biographical and literary – and from various viewpoints within the Restoration establishment. It seeks to re-establish a sense of the enormity of the event of Black Bartholomew's Day, and the colossal risks involved on all sides. In doing this, the intention is to demonstrate that religion remained central to political affairs after 1660 not least because Puritans, despite their political eclipse, could not be painlessly or easily cut out of the body politic. Lori-Anne Ferrell, whilst noting the need to re-evaluate England's seventeenth-century wars of religion, has argued that historians need to consider 'how words in this period could operate in lieu of action, contradict current, verifiable events; and eventually re-script the assumptions of religio-political culture in such a way as to transform it entirely'.[60] In presenting a fresh view of the Bartholomean corpus, this study will similarly argue that although the Bartholomeans went peaceably (for the most part), the rhetoric from their pulpits was no mere exhortation to comfort: it was an obstacle to the complete restoration of monarchical and episcopal authority and, amplified by the process of publication, represented a serious challenge to the new political order.

NOTES

1 Pepys, *Diary*, iii, pp. 166–8.

2 E.g., N. Keeble, *The Literary Culture of Nonconformity in Later Seventeenth-Century England* (Leicester, 1987), p. 25.

3 14 Car. II, cap. 4; A. Browning (ed.), *English Historical Documents 1660–1714* (1966), pp. 377–82; *CR*, p. xii.

4 *CR*, p. xi.

5 *Account*, p. 332.

6 R. Atkins, *The God of Love and Peace with Sincere and Peaceable Christians* (Exeter, 1715), p. 6.

7 Pepys, *Diary*, iii, p. 183; *CSPD* 1661–2, pp. 418, 428, 488; *CSPV* 1661–4, p. 180; Keeble, *Literary Culture*, p. 32; A. Hopper, 'The Farnley Wood plot and the memory of the civil wars in Yorkshire', *Historical Journal*, 45, 2 (2002), p. 287; R. Greaves, *Deliver Us from Evil: The Radical Underground in Britain 1660–1663* (Oxford, 1986), pp. 87–91, 95–103.

8 Bodl. MS Carte 31, fo. 602 (Goring Rous to the Marquis of Ormonde, 23 August 1662).

9 *CSPD* 1661–2, p. 442; HMC, *Report on the Manuscripts of Allan George Finch Esquire*, 71st report, vol. 1 (1913), p. 206 (Sir John Nicholas to the earl of Winchelsea, 4 August 1662); Pepys, *Diary*, iii, p. 183; R. Hutton, *The Restoration: A Political and Religious History of England and Wales 1658–1667* (Oxford, 1985), pp. 178, 193; I. Green, *The Re-establishment of the Church of England 1660–1663* (Oxford, 1978), pp. 4, 183; Carte MS 47, fos 1, 3, and Clarendon MS77, fo. 340, quoted in Green, *Re-establishment*, p. 218; *CSPD* 1661–2, pp. 48, 428, 488, quoted in Keeble, *Literary Culture*, p. 32.

10 *Continuation*, II, p. 884.

11 E. Calamy (1600–66), *Eli Trembling for Fear of the Ark* (1662), Wing C231A; Calamy, *Eli Trembling for Fear of the Ark* (Oxford, 1663), Wing C231; Calamy, *Eli Trembling for Fear of the Ark* (Oxford, 1663), Wing C232; Calamy, *A Sermon Preached at Aldermanbury Church, Dec. 28, 1662* (Oxford, 1663), Wing C267; *Master Edmund Calamy's Leading Case* (1663).

12 P. Lake, 'Defining Puritanism – again?', in F. Bremer (ed.), *Puritanism: Transatlantic Perspectives on a Seventeenth-Century Anglo-American Faith* (Boston, MA, 1993), pp. 3–6. Cf. B. Hall, 'Puritanism: the problem of definition', *Studies in Church History*, vol. 2, ed. G. Cuming (1965), pp. 283–96; P. Collinson, *The Religion of Protestants: The Church in English Society 1559–1625* (Oxford, 1982); L. Ferrell, *Government by Polemic: James I, the King's Preachers and the Rhetorics of Conformity 1603–1625* (Stanford, CA, 1998), pp. 16–17; J. Miller, *After the Civil Wars: British Politics and Government in the Reign of Charles II* (Harlow, 2000), pp. 11–13.

13 P. Collinson, *The Puritan Character: Polemics and Polarities in Early Seventeenth-Century English Culture* (Los Angeles, 1989), p. 29, quoted in L. Ferrell and P. McCullough (eds), *The English Sermon Revised* (Manchester, 2000), p. 13.

14 J. Spurr, *English Puritanism 1603–1689* (1998), p. 131; S. McGee, *The Godly Man in Stuart England* (1976), p. 9.

15 For a discussion of the anachronisms implicit in the term 'Anglican', see J. Spurr, *The Restoration Church of England 1646–1689* (1991), p. xiii.

16 *Continuation*, II, p. 618.

17 R. Baxter, *Reliquiae Baxterianae*, ed. M. Sylvester (1696), sig. [d3v]; *Abridgement*, pp. 266, 298, 304, 318, 341; *Account*, pp. 110, 198, 224, 239, 269, 314, 476, 477, 585, 640, 685, 755, 803, 816; *Continuation*, II, pp. 593, 824, 834; J. Walker, *An Attempt Towards Recovering an Account of the Numbers and Sufferings of the Clergy of the Church of England* (1714), pt II, p. 207; *Continuation*, II, p. 714.

18 J. Cooper, *The Dead Witnesse yet Speaking to His Living Friends* (1663).

19 *Account*, p. 332; Ralph Josselin, *The Diary of Ralph Josselin 1616–1683*, edited by A. MacFarlane (Oxford, 1976), p. 491.

20 Cooper, *Dead Witnesse*; Fairclough, *Pastor's Legacy*.

21 Bodl. Rawl. MSS E93.

22 DWL CL MSS. I.h.35, frontispiece.

23 R. L'Estrange, *Considerations and Proposals in Order to the Regulation of the Press* (1663), sig. [A3v–A4]; *Versameling van Afscheytspredicatien, Gepredikt van Mr. Calamy* . . . (Amsterdam, 1662); a reference I owe to the kindness of Mr Erik Geleijns. I am indebted to Marina McKenna for confirming the translation.

24 *Abridgement*, p. 392; *Account*, pp. 164, 165, 168, 173, 179, 180, 436, 521, 524, 529, 531, 537, 631.

25 J. Barrett, *A Funeral Sermon, Preached at Nottingham, Occasioned by the Death of Mr John Whitlock, sen., December 8ᵗʰ, 1708* (1709), p. 27.

26 Wilde's poem was appended to *A Compleat Collection of Farewell Sermons* (1663), Wing C5638aA, sig. [Uu3–Uu4v].

27 T. Harris, 'Introduction: revising the Restoration', in T. Harris, P. Seaward and M. Goldie (eds), *The Politics of Religion in Restoration England* (Oxford, 1990), p. 1; Hutton, *Restoration*, p. 1; K. Sharpe and S. N. Zwicker (eds), *Politics of Discourse: The Literature and History of Seventeenth-Century England* (1987), p. 231; R. Faithorn, 'The survival of Dissent in Yorkshire 1660–1780', in Royle (ed.), *Regional Studies in the History of Religion in Britain Since the Later Middle Ages* (Hull, 1984), p. 95.

28 Harris, Seaward and Goldie, *Politics of Religion*, pp. 1–2, 4, 5. Note also the arguments for the continuing importance of religion in politics put forward earlier by D. Lacey, *Dissent and Parliamentary Politics in England 1661–1689* (New Jersey, 1969).

29 G. Cragg, *From Puritanism to the Age of Reason* (Cambridge, 1950), pp. 10–11.

30 M. Finlayson, *Historians, Puritanism and the English Revolution: The Religious Factor in English Politics Before and After the Interregnum* (1983), pp. 7–8; Miller, *After the Civil Wars*, p. 56; Harris, Seaward and Goldie, *Politics of Religion*, pp. 4–5. Harris touches on this problem when he argues against the notion that the Restoration brought in a new brand of politics; *ibid.*, p. 2.

31 W. Mitchell, *English Pulpit Oratory from Andrewes to Tillotson: A Study of its Literary Aspects* (1932), pp. 411–52.

32 R. Bosher, *The Making of the Restoration Settlement* (1957), p. 254; J. Hetet, 'A Literary Underground in Restoration England: Printers and Dissenters in the Context of Constraints 1660–1689' (unpublished University of Cambridge PhD thesis, 1987).

33 G. Kitchin, *Sir Roger L'Estrange* (1913), p. 109; Spurr, *Restoration Church*, p. 44. See also Spurr, *English Puritanism* p. 133; N. Keeble, *The Restoration: England in the 1660s* (Oxford, 2002), p. 144.

34 L. Potter, *Secret Rites and Secret Writing: Royalist Literature 1641–1660* (Cambridge, 1989), pp. xi–xii. See also M. Morrissey, 'Interdisciplinarity and the study of early modern sermons', *The Historical Journal*, 42, 4, 1999, p. 1112.

35 Ferrell, *Government by Polemic*, p. 1.

36 Keeble, *Literary Culture*, preface, p. 20. A notable exception was Geoffrey Nuttall (see bibliography).

37 E.g., C. Hill, *The World Turned Upside Down* (1975), pp. 370–9; C. Hill, *Some Intellectual Consequences of the English Revolution* (1980), p. 55, quoted in Keeble, *Literary Culture*, p. 20. Cragg, *From Puritanism to the Age of Reason*, pp. 10–11, *passim*; G. Cragg, *Puritanism in the Period of the Great Persecution 1660–1688* (Cambridge, 1957), pp. 2–3, *passim*; Mitchell, *English Pulpit Oratory*, p. 17, *passim*.

38 R. Greaves and R. Zaller (eds), *Biographical Dictionary of British Radicals in the Seventeenth Century*, 3 vols (Brighton, 1982–4); R. Greaves, *Saints and Rebels: Seven Nonconformists in Stuart England* (Macon, GA, USA, 1985); Greaves, *Deliver Us from Evil*; Keeble, *Literary culture*, preface.

39 Ferrell and McCullough, *English Sermon Revised*, p. 2. See also M. Todd (ed.), *Reformation to Revolution: Politics and Religion in Early Modern England* (1995).

40 L. Ferrell and P. McCullough, 'Revising the study of the English sermon', in Ferrell and McCullough, *English Sermon Revised*, p. 12.

41 A. Claydon, 'The sermon, the "public sphere" and the political culture of late seventeenth-century England', in Ferrell and McCullough, *English Sermon Revised*, pp. 208–34; Ferrell, *Government by Polemic*, pp. 10–11.

42 Morrissey, 'Interdisciplinarity', pp. 1112–13; Ferrell, *Government by Polemic*, p. 18.

43 Morrissey, 'Interdisciplinarity', p. 1123.

44 M. Morrissey, 'Scripture, style and persuasion in seventeenth-century English theories of preaching', *Journal of Ecclesiastical History*, 53, 4 (2002), p. 705; Morrissey, 'Interdisciplinarity', p. 1111.

45 Johns, *The Nature of the Book: Print and Knowledge in the Making* (1998); R. McKerrow, *An Introduction to Bibliography for Literary Students* (Oxford, 1928); P. Gaskell, *A New Introduction to Bibliography* (Oxford, 1972); E. Eisenstein, *The Printing Press as the Agent of Change* (Cambridge, 1979); R. Darnton, 'What is the history of books?', *Daedalus*, 3 (1982), pp. 65–83; R. Chartier, *Cultural Uses of Print in Early Modern France*, trans. L. G. Cochrane (New York, 1987); R. Chartier (ed.), *Culture of Print: Power and the Uses of Print in Early Modern Europe*, trans. L. G. Cochrane (Cambridge, 1989). W. Williams and C. Abbott, *An Introduction to Bibliographical and Textual Studies* (New York, 1985) has been a useful guide – a reference I owe to the kindness of Jim McLaverty.

46 R. Chartier, *The Cultural Origins of the French Revolution* (Durham, 1991), pp. 85–7, quoted in A. Johns, *Nature of the book*, p. 57.

47 Johns, *Nature of the Book*, pp. 623–5.

48 R. Barthes, 'The death of the author', in *Image-Music-Text*, trans. S. Heath (1984), pp. 142–8.

49 S. Burke, *Death and Return of the Author* (Edinburgh, 1992), p. 27.

50 *England's Remembrancer*, p. 227. Maurice Biriotti has pointed out that 'a tradition of textual exegesis that does not depend on a monolithic authorial source has existed for centuries, particularly in Biblical scholarship'; M. Biriotti and N. Miller (eds), *What Is an Author?* (Manchester, 1993), p. 2.

51 *England's Remembrancer* (1663), p. 265; Hebrews 11:4.

52 B. Crockett, "Thomas Playfair's poetics of preaching", in Ferrell and McCullough, *English Sermon Revised*, p. 61.

53 Ferrell and McCullough, 'Revising the study of the English sermon', in Ferrell and McCullough, *English Sermon Revised*, pp. 7–8.

54 B. Smith, *The Acoustic World of Early Modern England* (1999), p. 24.

55 A. Fox, *Oral and Literate Culture in England 1500–1700* (Oxford, 2000), pp. 6, 43.

56 W. Bates, *The Peace-Maker* (1662), sig. [A]. An identical passage appears in the preface to M. Mead, *The Pastor's Valediction* (1662), sig. [A2v].

57 See Morrissey, 'Interdisciplinarity', p. 1116.

58 Johns, *Nature of the Book*, p. 623.

59 The 'deck of cards' metaphor appears in J. Caudle, 'Measures of Allegiance: Sermon Culture and the Creation of a Public Discourse of Obedience and Resistance in Georgian Britain 1714–1760' (unpublished PhD thesis, Yale University, 1995), quoted in Morrissey, 'Interdisciplinarity', p. 1116.

60 Ferrell, *Government by Polemic*, p. 6.

Chapter 1

The context of
Restoration nonconformity

The nonconformist hagiographies penned by Edmund Calamy III have always been such familiar features in the historical landscape that the character and motivation of those ejected in 1662 have often been taken for granted. The perception of a moderate, essentially Presbyterian, nonconformist community, politically docile and desirous of religious comprehension has dovetailed neatly into suggestions that early modern English Protestantism was, despite all appearances, underpinned by theological consensus. As a consequence, studies of Restoration ecclesiology have habitually been preoccupied with apportioning blame for the religious divisions of the period, with the Act of Uniformity variously portrayed as an instrument of vindictive duplicity or as the cornerstone of a code which, whilst confirming Cavalier-Anglican possession of the state Church, arbitrarily defined a community of religious outcasts.[1] At the same, however, although the early Stuart period (not to mention the events of the Regicide and Interregnum) had bequeathed something of a legacy of anti-clericalism and a distrust of religious enthusiasm, it is evident that the ministers threatened with ejection in 1662 enjoyed the support and sympathy of a sizeable constituency. Just as Ann Hughes has demonstrated that there was such a thing as 'popular' Presbyterianism in the 1640s and 1650s, so it will be argued here that many of those preparing to quit their public ministry in 1662 had a considerable following, and their sermons spoke to a ready and receptive audience.[2]

This chapter seeks to analyse the character of the Bartholomean cohort, considering both the ministers' backgrounds and who and what they had come to represent by 1662. In many ways, the information contained within the farewell sermons presents a set of intimate Restoration tableaux, revealing much about the existence of clerical networks, as well as the preachers' perception of the political issues at stake and their sense of religious identity. The second half of the chapter discusses the nature and role of the laity, using the farewell sermons as an entry point through which to investigate the Bartholomeans' often ambivalent relationships with patrons and parishioners, and their hopes and fears for a people facing an uncertain future without a godly public ministry.

Preaching from the pulpit of Batcombe for the last time, Richard Alleine left his listeners in no doubt as to the choice facing ministers who could not in conscience comply with the requirements laid out in the Act of Uniformity: they could either retain the benefits and trappings of ministerial authority within the established Church or eschew them in order to maintain the purity of their spiritual authority as messengers of God.[3] The explication of this choice in their farewell sermons moved the Bartholomeans to examine how they saw themselves, their godly constituents, and the profane world ranged against them.

I

The ministers ejected from the Church of England in 1662 may, in many cases, have associated with one another during the Interregnum, but these informal networks did not amount to an organised party within the Church, nor were they united by a common manifesto. Even those older Bartholomeans who had signed one of the *Testimonies* of 1648 or participated in a regional *classis* during the Interregnum varied enormously in their response to the political and religious questions posed by the Restoration. But there is no doubting that the authors of the Act of Uniformity had a certain type of individual in mind when they had drawn up its provisions, and Anglican preachers certainly aimed at a specific target when they attacked 'our modern Puritans (call them Presbyterians if you will)' in their sermons.[4] As David Underdown has observed, 'royalists could identify a Presbyterian when they saw one, even if we cannot, and for them the name evoked a much more powerful emotional response than the word "moderate" would have aroused'.[5] Despite their heterogeneity, the individuals and networks at the receiving end of this emotional response had enough in common to realise that they were the object of abuse. In as much as their enemies portrayed them as an organised force, and not least because of their mutual resolve to dissent from the Act of Uniformity, the Bartholomeans were (at least temporarily) a recognisable body, whose status, opinions, aspirations and influence could not easily be dismissed.

Neil Keeble is right to point out that the social standing of nonconformist ministers and authors 'was not high in an age when even the clergy of the Church of England were only doubtfully gentlemen', although few historians would now agree with W. F. Mitchell, who in his survey of early modern preaching in 1932 dismissed the intellectual capacities of such clergy with the comment that they had been 'in a good many cases of limited if not slight education'.[6] Even a cursory survey of the ministers ejected between 1660 and 1662 reveals that at least 85 per cent had received a university education.[7] The largest portion of the Bartholomeans had been educated at Cambridge – a trend even more clearly represented among the authors of the published farewell sermons. A hotbed of Puritanism, Emmanuel College figured in the background of at least eighty-seven Bartholomeans. Given that it was the policy of godly tutors to introduce promising students to one another it is likely that individuals such as Ralph Venning, George Swinnock and John Whitlock (all of whom had graduated from Emmanuel in 1646) had known each other as teenagers, and had met like-minded students from other Cambridge colleges.[8] Although proportionately fewer of the future ejected ministers had attended Oxford, four colleges (Exeter, Magdalen, New Inn Hall and Wadham) had produced at least 111 Bartholomeans between them. However, of these only Wadham and Exeter, each with three alumni, stood out among the ranks of the published authors.[9]

As a result of their education, most Bartholomeans were therefore trained rhetoreticians, able to impart the Word illuminated not only by Beza, Augustine and Melanchthon, but also by Aristotle and Pliny. They were able, and often eager, to employ Latin, Greek and occasionally Hebrew in explicating the finer points of doctrine. Even Bartholomeans who did not boast a formal university education, such as Richard Baxter and John Oldfield, were manifestly well read. Educationally, therefore, the authors of the published farewell sermons were typical of the Bartholomeans as a whole, and indeed typical of earlier generations of Puritan lecturers, whose London contingent had always been 'very much part of the educated elite of the Church of England'.[10] Far from being inferior, the ejected ministers of 1662 were at the very least the intellectual equals of the conformist clergy.

If the influence of godly tutors and the debates organised by colleges such as Emmanuel provided an introduction to professional networks, postgraduate training often took the form of an apprenticeship. Household seminaries were run by experienced ministers, where many a godly candidate acquired their mentor. Conferences of godly alumni had been a regular feature since Elizabeth's reign, and some, such as that at Dedham, had become famous. O'Day has argued that these godly networks functioned in much the same way as a modern professional association, facilitating introductions between peers and continuity between generations.[11]

By the early seventeenth century the average clergyman began his ministry in his mid-twenties, most usually as a deacon or a curate, and could anticipate a career of at least thirty years. This longevity might well account for Seaver's observation that between 1640 and 1662 the average age of a parish incumbent rose to 42 years.[12] A survey of 700 Bartholomeans listed in *Calamy Revised* (being those whose ages are known or can be estimated from university records) shows them to have had an average age of 41.9 years at the time of the Great Ejection, whilst a survey of those authors of surviving farewell sermons whose ages can be determined with reasonable confidence reveals an average age of 39.6. The ten Midland authors featured in *England's Remembrancer* had an average age of 32.7. Far from being past their prime, therefore, Bartholomean ministers were, if anything, slightly younger than the average Church of England incumbent. Even veterans such as Richard Fairclough (aged 41 at the time of his ejection) could demonstrate considerable physical and intellectual stamina. Fairclough's weekly routine included lengthy daily prayers, religious services, intense literary study, catechising, pastoral visits, long mid-week lectures and at least two hour-long sermons each Sunday. He habitually rose at 3 a.m. in order to squeeze his heavy workload into each day.[13] The relative youthfulness of the dissenting ministers – compared with the many elderly bishops and royalist clergy who had so recently been restored to their former livings – explains why so many would continue to preach (albeit illegally) decades after Black Bartholomew's Day had passed. The numbers of Bartholomeans who were actually too young to have participated in the Civil Wars or the framing of the Solemn League and Covenant has already been noted. Given that they were consequently less fettered by the past than their older colleagues, the fact that so many young clergy proved to be disaffected further fuelled Cavalier-Anglican insecurities.[14]

At the same time as they were presented with an energetic nonconformist ministry, the Restoration authorities faced the prospect that religious dissent was everywhere in evidence. Richard Greaves has observed that Presbyterians (a group he divides into radicals and moderates) were strongly represented in Northumberland, Lancashire, Cheshire, Devon, Somerset (particularly Bristol) and Carmarthenshire, whilst Congregationalists proliferated in southern and central Wales, the Midlands, Essex, Hertfordshire and Suffolk. A. G. Matthews' survey of the regional distribution of those ejected in 1662 suggests that the heaviest concentration of nonconformist ministers per capita was in the West Country, followed by Essex, Suffolk and Lancashire, with a fairly even distribution elsewhere relative to the local population.[15] The correlation between this geographical distribution and the printed farewell sermons will be discussed later, but suffice to say that whilst London is, predictably, hugely over-represented in the surviving printed works, the prominence of the West Country authors is also noticeable. Just as Cavalier-Anglicans feared, nonconformist ideas circulated in every county, through networks fostered by education, conference, kinship and commerce. These channels of communication could be remarkably efficient: in 1661 government spies observed Ralph Venning to be in weekly correspondence with ministers in the West Country, via the Exeter carrier.[16] In January 1663, ministers in Lancashire heard of James Nalton's death within seventy-two hours of his burial, and almost as quickly received news of Calamy's release from prison.[17]

Networks during the summer of 1662 also materialised in mutual support at local level, as can be seen from the evident collusion of two near-neighbours in Somerset. Not only did Richard Fairclough and Edward Hancock have a mutual acquaintance among the local gentry in the form of one Sir George Horner, but the structure of Hancock's single published sermon is strikingly similar to the fourteenth sermon in Fairclough's series. Whereas Fairclough urged his congregation to 'have the mark of mourners on your forehead' and to beware of God's wrath, Hancock told his to 'have the mark of mourners, rather than the Devil's mark'. Both ended their sermons with an almost identical flourish, inspired by Psalms 121:8, bidding their listeners to fare well in their shops and fields. Similarly, just as Fairclough declared, 'may my *enemies* be all well; though I have known but a few', Hancock proclaimed 'may mine enemies do well, though I know but of few'.[18]

Apart from endeavouring to synchronise the message of the farewell sermons, there is good reason to suspect that networks in certain localities were often responsible for coordinating the Bartholomean response. Although they had previously been embroiled in a dispute between Presbyterian and Congregationalist worshippers at Exeter Cathedral, Thomas Ford and Lewis Stucley had worked together to achieve a reconciliation between the two congregations. These same two ministers preached their farewell sermons on successive days in neighbouring pulpits, managing to ensure that neither clashed with the sermons of Robert Atkins and Thomas Powel, two more ministers who had been involved in the dispute. Atkins in turn delivered his valediction at St John's, Exeter, the day after Powel's sermon.[19] The effect was to present a unified front against the Act of Uniformity. This collusion was taking place, it should be remembered, at the same time as William Mew and fellow ministers in Gloucestershire were coordinating efforts to circumvent the public declaration of assent required by the Act.[20]

Mutual cooperation was also evident in London. John Herring, having been ejected from his living prematurely, was taken in by William Bates at St Dunstan's, and on the day of his host's farewell sermons delivered the preparatory readings. Thus, when Bates stated that he did not intend to discuss the political implications of the Great Ejection, he did so in the knowledge that Herring had already prefaced his valediction by recounting the story of Ananias and Sapphira (Acts 5:1–11), a married couple who had perished because they had engaged in idolatry and lied to God. Herring had added the comment that, 'This is just the case of England at present. God he bids us to preach, and men bid us not to preach; and if we do, we are to be imprisoned and further punished.'[21] The cooperation between Bates and Herring made their mutual position plain. This was not the only partnership to emerge as a result of Fatal Bartholomew: the Lancashire minister John Angier showed similar hospitality to Oliver Heywood after the latter's ejection.[22]

Larger nonconformist networks had even more significant effects on the Bartholomean message – such as the close-knit circle of ministers in the East Midlands that manifested itself in *England's Remembrancer*. Joseph Whitlock's biography of his fellow Bartholomean William Reynolds later described the friendships which had driven this particular network even before the summer of 1662. In several cases acquaintances had arisen from participation in the Nottingham and Derbyshire Associations during the Interregnum, although Reynolds and Whitlock had been friends since their undergraduate days.[23] Whilst preaching a funeral sermon for Reynolds in 1698 (he would preach at Whitlock's funeral ten years later), John Barrett lamented the passing of so many godly ministers in the locality 'who were all except three or four of them my intimate friends and acquaintances'.[24] Barrett's list included nine of the thirteen clergy whose farewell sermons had appeared in *England's Remembrancer*. Of the remaining authors in the collection, Joseph Moore had already been named as a member of the circle in Robert Porter's *Life of John Hieron* (1691), whilst Thomas Bladon and Samuel Shaw had been contemporaries at Repton.[25] When *England's Remembrancer* was first published in 1664, however, the identity of the authors and the extent of the network were carefully concealed. Nowhere in the copious text of *England's Remembrancer* is there any reference to local places or living persons. An active and cohesive network is only alluded to tangentially with vague expressions of solidarity and exhortations to the godly to pray for all distressed ministers.[26] This reluctance to name living colleagues was still evident in Porter's writing three decades later.[27] If the Midlands network had any plans to coordinate their farewell sermons after the manner of their brethren in Exeter, however, they were confounded when Reynolds, Whitlock and Barrett were all forced from their respective pulpits a month before Bartholomew's Day.[28]

The prospect of mass ejection engendered something of a national sense of solidarity among the threatened clergy. Matthew Newcomen spoke of '*those many Ministers that at this time have been forced to leave their stations*', whilst in the Midlands Robert Seddon alluded to the legislation which was 'shutting the mouths of so many hundreds of *learned, conscientious Ministers*'.[29] However, such sentiments do not substantiate the organised Presbyterian conspiracy frequently depicted in spies' reports and alarmist Cavalier-Anglican polemic. There were certainly leading lights among these 'modern Puritans' – many of whom would feature in the compilations of farewell sermons – but they were leaders by reputation more than anything else. Invitations to represent Presbyterian or other Puritan interests in the various conferences of 1660–61 owed as much to an individual's contacts and reputation within the political establishment as it did to the acclamation of any godly constituency.

Such niceties were lost on opponents who perceived a larger organised movement the various networks and correspondences. A month after Bartholomew's Day, one bishop's correspondent wrote that he had heard that most of the ousted Presbyterian clergy were heading for London to a general rendezvous, 'where they will endeavour to rally again after this Rout'.[30] The events of the 1640s and clandestine royalist and Presbyterian networks during the Interregnum had demonstrated how readily religious dissension could be translated into political action. Painfully aware that Presbyterian support had been instrumental in bringing about the Restoration, and mindful of the strong Presbyterian showing in certain areas during the elections of March 1661, Cavalier-Anglicans worried interminably that opposition to the religious settlement might at any moment transform itself into something more dangerous. 'If some pretend tenderness of conscience against that law', wrote a supporter of the Act of Uniformity, 'some might pretend tenderness of conscience against any law.'[31] An Act to Preserve the Person and Government of the King (otherwise known as the Treason Act) had come into force on 24 June 1661. The preamble laid the blame of the late troubles 'in very great measure' upon 'seditious sermons, pamphlets and speeches, daily preached, printed and published'.[32] As they composed their farewell sermons, many of the older Bartholomeans would have been acutely aware that they themselves had authored some of the works alluded to. Sermons published during the previous twenty years now appeared embarrassing, and, at worst, treasonable. Even those preachers who had been too young to participate in the Civil Wars would have been mindful of the ease with which they could fall foul of the new Treason Act, by imagining the death of the king, questioning his legal status, or stirring up disaffection towards his government. Indeed, the earl of Clarendon, like many in authority, suspected that the departing ministers' purpose in delivering their farewell sermons was 'to infuse murmur, jealousy and sedition in the heart of their several auditories'.[33] Thus, in preparing to deliver the sermons which marked their refusal to obey the will of Parliament, each Bartholomean had to tread a fine line between their personal conscience and the political legislation.

The most pressing problem for the dissenters was how to plead political loyalty whilst explaining their nonconformity. One solution was to declare for Charles II in preliminary prayers, and separate this exhortation from the farewell sermon itself. Seven of the thirteen prayers in the compilation entitled *A Compleat Collection of Farewell Sermons* (1663) lavish considerable attention on the royal family, with phraseology far more explicitly loyalist than in any of the surrounding farewell sermons. At the same time, however, even the most obsequious of these prayers contained a political moral: whilst praying at Aldermanbury on behalf of the King and his officials, Edmund Calamy found space to insert the declaration that the departing ministers could not 'sin at so cheap a rate as others do'.[34] Thomas Watson prefaced his farewell sermon at St Stephen's by entreating God to shower down His blessings upon the head of Charles II, but expressed the hope that God would also 'let him see wherein his chiefest interest lies; let him count those his best subjects, that are Christ's subjects'.[35] Six other prayers in *A Compleat Collection*, moreover, made no reference to the monarch at all.[36] If ministers such as Calamy and Nalton, having interceded for Charles II, risked accusations that they had undermined his royal status in their farewell sermons by referring to Christ as the 'King of Glory', a greater hazard was run by individuals such as Crodacot and Annesley, who conspicuously crowned Christ without making any loyal reference to Charles whatsoever.[37]

At least thirteen ministers featured in the London compilations had had official parliamentary fast sermons published during the 1640s and 1650s, and at least six had served as parliamentary army chaplains.[38] In the eyes of detractors such as William Assheton, such past activities placed these ministers in the same category as firebrands such as William Dell and Hugh Peter (who had been publicly executed in October 1660).[39] Given the accusations levelled at them by hostile writers, the reluctance of most Bartholomean authors to defend themselves is puzzling: whereas several ministers with similar backgrounds, such as Nathaniel Hardy and Samuel Kem, and even future Bartholomeans such as Henry Newcombe and Richard Eedes had all delivered loyal sermons immediately after the Restoration – and despite the fact that several ejected ministers observed the royalist anniversaries of 30 January and 29 May privately – no author of a printed farewell sermon appears to have made any effort to publicise their loyalty in print.[40] Thomas Case had delivered more parliamentary fast sermons than most, had served as a chaplain in the earl of Essex's army and had been a vociferous proponent of the League and Covenant. But he had also been publicly associated with the memory of Christopher Love, that paradigmatic Presbyterian martyr for the royalist cause, and had been imprisoned by the Commonwealth in 1651.[41] In the turmoil following Cromwell's death, Case had become a leading advocate for the restoration of the monarchy. Little of this new-found royalism seeped into Case's farewell sermon of 1662, however, where his regret at the missed opportunity for reformation was balanced by a scathing criticism of contemporary society:

> Religion never suffered the like, as it hath done these latter dayes, by the *pride* and *hypocrisie* of some *Pretenders* to it; Gods name hath been thereby blasphemed by an evill and hypocritical generation; the people of God have lien under the greatest reproaches and contempts that ever any did under the heavens.[42]

Thomas Case was not the only Bartholomean who declined to mention his suffering for the royalist cause. Christopher Love was absent from the farewell sermons of Edmund Calamy and Thomas Manton, who had not only known him, but had published funeral sermons in his honour.[43] In similar fashion, several Presbyterian clergy had supported Booth's uprising in 1659, and many more of them had refused publicly to declare Booth a traitor. One of the Midland authors, Robert Seddon, had been active for the King in 1659, for which he had been 'threatened to be carried to London to be tried for his life'.[44] But no mention of these adventures appeared in Seddon's farewell sermon. Thomas Watson was, however, less reticent, declaring in his farewell sermon that, despite accusations of disloyalty and sedition, 'what my actions and sufferings for his Majesty hath been is not unknown to a few of you'.[45]

Another departing minister, George Thorn counselled against rebellion, fearful of the consequences of challenging the power even of wicked and oppressive earthly rulers. 'Had Zimri peace that slew his Master?' he asked.[46] But Bartholomeans were nevertheless prepared to argue that their duty to God now forced them to resist royal authority. 'We are terrified by the threats of the great King', said John Collins, describing the sufferings of the holy men under Nebuchadnezzar, 'and we are likewise terrified by the threats of the great God.'[47] Citing Matthew 6:24 ('No man can serve two masters'), John Barrett declared that the godly could not give their hearts both to God and to the world.[48] Most Bartholomeans fell back on the tried and tested nonconformist position of delineating a distinction between transient carnal authority and God's eternal rule – a device which had been used by both Puritans and recusants in the past. Many Bartholomean preachers attempted to square the circle of loyal nonconformity, a concept summarised by Richard Fairclough as the 'tryal of Obedience' versus the 'tryal of our Faith'.[49] As Robert Atkins put it,

> We may be imprison'd as *Traitors*, condemn'd to die as *Traitors*: But let us abhor all *Treasonable Practices*, and then we may rejoice in the Testimony of our own Consciences, that we have approv'd our selves faithful Servants to God, and obedient Subjects (if not *Actively*, then *Passively*) to our Sovereign.[50]

'Sirs, we will do any thing for His Majesty, but Sin' said Atkins; 'we could even dare to Die for him, only we dare not be Damn'd for him.'[51] This was a theme echoed by John Oldfield: 'I acknowledge it my duty to obey passively, and suffer patiently, where I cannot with a good Conscience yeeld active Obedience.'[52]

In many cases, however, such irenic, if carefully qualified, expressions of loyalty were compromised when published in compilations that included much less guarded language. Thomas Lye, for example, after repeated exhortations to the godly to stand fast, invited his listeners to '*Come and set your feet upon the necks of these Kings*' (Joshua 10:24).[53] This insensitive reference to the public beheading of captured monarchs was compounded by a warning to Charles II, that when Alexander reached India he was defied by holy men who informed him that there were many that 'cannot be made by all your powers to change their mindes'.[54]

The fact that the Act of Uniformity had bound together several religious and political requirements into one declaration gave dissenting ministers room for manoeuvre. Individuals were able to declare that they could not in conscience assent to the Act without specifying which clauses they balked at. This ambiguity was particularly useful with regards to the issue of the Solemn League and Covenant, a document of huge symbolic significance to the Cavaliers; 'what state can prefer those who have sworn to overthrow it and its constitutions, and will not renounce that Oath, which is their case that come under the stroke of that Act?' wrote David Lloyd, of the Act of Uniformity.[55] Even before the Restoration, loyalty to the Solemn League and Covenant had invariably been the heaviest burden carried by the Presbyterians. Many had refused to sign the Engagement in 1650 because they considered that the Solemn League and Covenant obliged them to defend the person and authority of the king. But by the Restoration, when the Covenant again became a touchstone of political loyalty, the Cavaliers' re-writing of history had come to equate it with regicide.[56] In 1660, the future Bishop of Hereford, Herbert Croft, even felt emboldened to berate Charles II to his face for having taken the Covenant in 1650, alleging in his sermon that this act had moved God to chastise the Church of England and decree royalist defeat at the battle of Worcester.[57] Seeing the King forced to endure such public excoriation, the Bartholomeans can have been in no doubt as to the sensitivity of their position, not least because many had been closely associated with the original subscription in 1643 and subsequent renewals. In 1643, Joseph Caryl had declared himself 'resolved never to be withdrawne or divided by whatsoever terrour or perswasion from this blessed union and conjunction'.[58] In 1646, Edmund Calamy had described the Covenant as an oath of supremacy in allegiance to God. He considered that the nation was bound by the document, making disavowal 'a land-destroying sin'.[59]

Such statements underline the fact that the moral obligations of the Solemn League and Covenant had long since shaped Presbyterian attitudes towards the State. In 1650 many Presbyterians, among them Thomas Case, had flatly refused the Engagement precisely because it required them to forswear the Covenant.[60] To the argument put forward by supporters of the Engagement that the obligation to honour oaths depended on circumstance, those loyal to the Covenant replied that sworn bonds were non-reciprocal and indissoluble. This was entirely consistent with traditional Protestant casuistry, which, as Ted Vallance has found, 'denounced the use of tactics of equivocation and mental reservation in taking oaths'.[61] The question as to whether it was permissible to engage in equivocation and mental reservation when refusing to *disavow* oaths was a different matter. On the face of things, although non-conformist ministers did not have to specify which clauses of the Act of Uniformity they could not accept, preachers who had been so publicly associated with the League and Covenant as Case, Caryl, Calamy and Watson ostensibly had little alternative but to address the issue. It was, theoretically, possible to reconcile adherence to the Covenant with loyalty to the King: firstly, Presbyterians had refused the Engagement precisely because the Solemn League and Covenant contained an obligation to protect the monarchy, and, secondly, Charles II had taken the Covenant himself. The mood of the authorities, however, made such mitigation impracticable if not downright dangerous. Consequently, the word 'covenant' did not appear in the published farewell sermons of Watson, Calamy and Case, nor in Calamy's funeral oration for Simeon Ashe. Joseph Caryl used the term only once, and then only in an abstract sense.[62] In no published farewell sermon was adherence to the Solemn League and Covenant declared as a reason for defying the Act of Uniformity. Only Thomas Lye mentioned the document directly, when comparing 1662 to an earlier ejection:

> Beloved, I do well remember that upon the 24th of this moneth, 1651, I was then under the sentence of banishment that very day I preached my farewel Sermon to my people, because I would not swear against the King, having taken the Covenant to maintain his just power; then I could not forswear my selfe.[63]

This explicit reference to the Covenant in Lye's *The Fixed Saint Held Forth* was, however, not included when the same sermon came to be published in a subsequent compilation.[64] Although no other minister addressed the subject of the Covenant as directly as Lye, there are indications that the oath remained very much in Presbyterian ministers' thoughts. William Cross's farewell sermon included the phrase 'God hath given his People an interest in himself, and he hath confirmed this by Oath and Covenant.'[65] But although Cross (or his editor) implied that the phrase had been taken from Jeremiah 31:33, it does not, in fact, feature in the verse itself. Instead, Jeremiah 31:33 describes the children of Israel taking the Covenant of the Old Testament into their hearts. Caution is needed when plucking isolated sentences from such a carefully crafted and intricately interlaced rhetorical construction as a Restoration sermon – but it is precisely because such sermons were so carefully constructed that the use of such a loaded phrase seems deliberate and significant. William Bates's sermon similarly carried several innocuous instances of the word 'covenant', but concluded with a description of the bond between God and His children:

> It is a Covenant of *Peace* and *Friendship*; for now we stand upon tearms of amity with God, *Those who were strangers and enemies, are now reconciled.* And there is between God and us perfect peace, there is a League (as the Scripture speaks) between God and the Creature. It is a Covenant of *Trade*, there is now a way opened to Heaven, we may now ascend to God in duties of holiness.[66]

The juxtaposing of the words 'League' and 'Covenant' seem an obvious invitation to read between the lines. In the same way, Edmund Calamy's lecture of 28 December 1662 angered opponents not merely because it broke the law, but because his subject matter – Israel's loss of the Ark of the Covenant – was so obviously laced with meaning.[67] In view of his previously published views on the Solemn League and Covenant, and given his silence on the issue in his farewell sermon, Calamy must have been well aware of the controversy his text would provoke. The publishers who then advertised the sermon so prominently surely did so in the knowledge that it would rapidly become as notorious as *A Phenix, or, the Solemn League and Covenant*, which had appeared shortly before.[68]

Descriptions in the farewell sermons regarding God's covenant with his chosen people should thus not always be taken at face value. Some Bartholomeans may genuinely have intended to refer to the covenants of the Old or New Testaments; but many undoubtedly exploited the ambiguity to indicate their continued adherence to the Solemn League and Covenant. All must have been aware that the term had become loaded with political meaning. Conformist clergy, particularly the reformed Presbyterian Samuel Kem, exhorted moderate Puritans to 'repent of your Solemn League and Covenant-Fraction', and railed against oaths and solemn covenants which had dethroned and beheaded both magistracy and ministry.[69] By using coded references, and by conspicuously failing to accept repeated invitations publicly to disavow the Solemn League and Covenant, the Bartholomeans' refusal to discuss the document in their farewell sermons suggests that most chose to keep faith with it.

Episcopal ordination, on the other hand, was openly discussed in several farewell sermons; ministers explained that they could not comply with this requirement because it carried the implication that their previous ministry had been unlawful or spiritually invalid. Thomas Bladon denied that the bishops had a monopoly of ordination: 'where Christ hath given no superiority of power and jurisdiction, let no man claim it, lest he be found a Usurper;

whom the Apostle calls in one place *Bishops*; in another place, he calleth *Presbyters*'.[70]

There seems to be no specific allusion to the Common Prayer Book in any of the surviving farewell sermons, possibly because few ministers had managed to obtain a copy before Bartholomew's Day. Several bishops expressed concern that many conforming ministers had consented implicitly to a book they had not read – suggesting that many of those who refused to conform without the sight of the revised Prayer Book were opposed to it in principle, rather than in detail. The perennial quandary whether or not to tolerate certain items of liturgical practice was of course a familiar debate; John Oldfield acknowledged in his farewell sermon that this had been 'a bone of Contention ever since the beginning of the Reformation'.[71] William Jenkyn argued that to consecrate mundane items such as vestments, tables and communion cups was a sinful and abominable superstition.[72] John Whitlock denounced human invention in religion as the work of Satan, whilst William Cross instructed his flock not to rely on human props, but on God alone.[73] George Swinnock declared that to worship according to men's prescriptions was an act of rebellion against God:

> All worship of God without warrant is like private coyning mony, *high Treason* against the King of Heaven. God (though men durst not) charged *Jeroboam* with this crime, *He offered upon the Altar which he had made, in the moneth which he had devised of his own heart.*[74]

Thus, in several farewell sermons condemnation of human innovation appears to have been linked with a discussion of the legitimate extent of Church government and even, in some cases, an exploration of the limits of political authority. John Moore noted that

> Whatever power a Church hath about *natural Circumstances*, they have none about the *substance* of worship, either to add or take away; by putting in or putting out. To add new Ordinances or parts of Worship is a breach of the second Commandment. The Pharisees erred on this hand.[75]

But in this, as in other matters, the stance among the Bartholomeans varied considerably. Whereas Richard Fairclough appeared willing to tolerate things indifferent, the London minister John Collins refused to see things indifferent as toys which might be used or discarded. Collins cautioned his flock not to compromise: 'the term of indifferent, I suppose 'tis devised as a pillar to rest the conscience on, which otherwise would startle'.[76] He mused that

> It's a sad thing, many Christians study to draw out the lines of obedience as far as the honesty of the times will given them leave, but no farther: that they would go on with the Lord Jesus to the High Priest's hall, and there deny him.[77]

Paraphrasing Paul, Collins concluded that '*You cannot be the Servants of Christ, if you strive to please men.*'[78] As the authors of the Act of Uniformity had surely intended, this crisis of conscience had exposed elements within the Church who were willing to challenge the legal authorities in order to defend the Solemn League and Covenant or resist the imposition of the liturgical adiaphora. But if this enabled Cavalier-Anglicans to identify their 'modern Puritans', most Bartholomeans were actually torn between the need to belong and the urge to reform. Unlike the Corporation Act, the Act of Uniformity had no provision to eject 'hollow-hearted' subscribers. Consequently, many moderate Puritans, even some who were technically nonconformists, remained in their livings. Some, such as Ralph Josselin, appear simply to have remained undetected, whilst others, such as John Angier, were indulged.[79] Many friendships endured between Bartholomeans and conformists, encouraging Thomas Watson to hope that the Great Ejection would only prove a brief interruption of the public ministry.[80]

Despite their dissatisfaction with the established Church, most nonconformist ministers had no wish to separate. Many ministers continued to attend Anglican services after their ejection, or at least those parts that they could stomach.[81] Separation was at odds with the Presbyterian taste for discipline – as a Presbyterian pamphlet had argued in 1649, confusion was worse than tyranny.[82] Nowhere within the extant farewell sermons is separation advocated. Some Bartholomeans equated the very idea with sedition; as Robert Porter declared in his farewell to his parishioners at Pentrich, Derbyshire,

> The errand of this Truth (my dear people) is not to alarm you into Sedition or to gather you into any unlawful Assemblies, upon the account of the account of the loss of your *Solemn Assemblies*. Of Conventicles (truly so called) *i.e.* Meetings to plot Disturbance to the State. I would say, and have every one of you to say, as *Jacob* (*Gen.* 49: 6, 7). *O my soul, enter not into their secret, and to their Assembly mine honour be thou not united.* If I may not be a Trumpet to call you to the Assembly, I will not be a Trumpet of Rebellion to sound an Alarm. If I may not call you to the Mountain of the Lord, I will not say, *To your Tents, O Israel.*[83]

Having said this, the Bartholomeans' urge to belong did not assuage their distaste for the direction in which the Church was being taken. Edward Hancock repeatedly urged his followers to keep themselves pure from the sins of the world, at one point quoting Revelation 18:4: 'I heard a voice from heaven saying, Come out of her my people, and be not partakers in her sin, lest you are partakers of her plagues.'[84] John Whitlock was more direct, albeit more measured, when he came to discuss the same subject:

> Though I dare not advise you actively to join in any thing that is in it self, or in your judgement evil, till you be satisfied about it; yet I must advise you to

take heed of separation from the Church, or from what is good, and God's own Ordinance.[85]

Some of the more optimistic Bartholomeans held out the hope that their successor might prove acceptably godly. Thomas Wadsworth admitted that the doctrine of some conformist replacements might be good, even if it came out of a stinking cask. Nevertheless, he warned his congregation that they should be prepared to exercise discretion, and if they were to keep 'tenderness of heart' they should endeavour to obtain the best ministry they could get.[86] More common was the fear that the successor might, through ignorance or deceit, steer the congregation into error and sin.[87] It was on this point that even Wadsworth came close to expressing explicit religious dissidence:

fly, shun, avoid an idle drunken Minister. If you would ask me, then what shall we do in such a case? I *Answer*, Keep such a one out of your Parish if you can; if you cannot, then I advise you to take heed how you hear him . . . Because such Ministers, are no Ministers at all.[88]

In certain circumstances, therefore, even moderate Puritans were prepared to countenance a distance between themselves and the state Church. Wadsworth, after balancing the dangers of bad doctrine against the penalties for recusancy, advised his congregation that if his replacement proved wicked or profane, he would be no minister of Christ, 'and in such a case you must rather hazard your purses than your souls'.[89] However, even whilst lamenting the eclipse of godly ministry and warning of the dangers of unsuitable replacements, the Bartholomean clergy continued to believe that their rightful place lay at the heart of organised Protestantism rather than at its margins. Thomas Lye, for one, declared that he had an orthodox ministry, and that for the most part he was leaving his parish an orthodox place.[90] Such convictions did not necessarily preclude a desire for comprehension, as Richard Alleine pleaded during one of his more pragmatic moments,

We need to have more to shew for our Christianity, than that we are Presbyterians, *Independents, Anabaptists, Episcopal,* or *Erastians*; and the Devil must have more to prove us no Christians, than this, that we are in union with either of these, or in separation from them.[91]

'No longer tie up Christ *to a party*', Alleine entreated his congregation, imploring them not to impose their consciences upon others.[92] Similarly, Thomas Jacombe declared that he censured 'none that differ from me, as though they displease God'.[93] As one of the objectives of the Act of Uniformity was to eradicate diversity from the pulpits it is instructive that the ejected minister John Howe would later reminisce that 'his latitude [had] made him a nonconformist, rather than allowed him to conform'.[94] William Bates thought it 'most sad, when *Religion* which should restrain and bridle our passions, is made fuel and incentives of them'. However, much as Bates abhorred the prospect of religious conflict, he blamed only one of the contending parties, 'if', he observed, 'I may call one Party *contending* which is only liable to Penalties and is resolved to bear them patiently'.[95] Such sentiments suggest an awareness that even if nonconformists did not care to define themselves their opponents would certainly do so. As Richard Baxter would later complain, 'We were called all by the Name of *Presbyterians* (the odious Name), though we never put up one Petition for Presbytery, but pleaded for Primitive Episcopacy.'[96] Baxter's unwillingness to be tied up to a party was evident in his application for a preaching licence in 1672, in which he would still only condescend to describe himself as a 'nonconformist'. Such deliberate obfuscation is but one reason why it would be unwise to consider declarations of denominational affiliation made under the auspices of the Indulgence to be a infallible guide to the divisions of the 1660s. It can be stated that some 45 per cent of the original 1662 cohort opted to be classified as Presbyterian in 1672, compared with 65 per cent of the authors of the printed farewell sermons, and that 7 per cent of the total cohort declared themselves to be Congregationalist, as opposed to 17 per cent of these authors – but the fact that a disproportionate number of the published authors remained alive and active in 1672 can hardly have failed to affect such figures. In any case, although it is possible to construct an argument that the majority of the Bartholomean ministers were 'Presbyterian', it should always be borne in mind that most Bartholomeans regarded themselves as opponents of the Act of Uniformity rather than an alternative to the Church of England.

The widespread desire to remain within the Church may account for the fact that very few farewell sermons attacked the bishops directly. Most Bartholomeans appear to have been willing to function under a primitive episcopacy, primarily to ensure that they remained in a position to continue the work of reformation. But this is not to say that the ministers were uncritical of bishops, even if their comments were routinely coded (for example, when Thomas Lye pointedly condemned the Jewish Elders of the Old Testament as hypocrites and inventors).[97] In response to Anglican preachers who regularly rebuked Presbyterians by name, the farewell sermons tended to allude to the failings of their opponents within the Church by referring obliquely to crypto-papists, Arminians, misguided dupes or worldly hypocrites going through the motions of religious ritual. Ralph Venning opined that it was not only manly, but the defining mark of a Christian to hold to the true doctrine 'which doth distinguish a true Christian from a Hypocrite and a Counterfeit'.[98] Richard Baxter, like many Bartholomeans, exhorted his congregation not to surrender to 'a *formal, heartless, seeming Religiousness, Customariness* without the life' when the godly ministers had gone.[99] Thomas Brooks was similarly contemptuous of the 'vain, sinfull and superstitious wayes, that men of a formall, carnall, lukewarm spirit walk in'.[100] Such polemic took on even greater significance when associated in print with utterances such as those of John Crodacot, for whom formalists were nothing less than 'Romish Teachers, Jesuits, Priests, and Seminaries, who so affect the outward pomp, as they neglect the inward power of it'.[101] Crodacot reminded his flock that God had threatened the church at Ephesus for their failure to arrest 'the unfruitfulness, formality, lukewarmness declining of God's own people'.[102] The term 'formalist' had long been used by English Protestants – and not only Puritans – to denote the enemy within.[103] Thus, even when regarding co-religionists, ministers such as John Barrett were moved to declare that 'It is not a thing indifferent, what Religion men are of, whether they be for God, or *Baal*.'[104] The ungodly – whom Robert Atkins described as bastards, rather than sons, of the Church – could insinuate themselves in the most godly of company.[105] The kind of consensus called for by individuals such as Alleine and Jacombe, therefore, does not appear to have been a desire for a general acceptance of doctrine so much as the wish for a consensual commitment to godliness.

The farewell sermons show that many Bartholomeans were preoccupied with reviewing religious identity within the Church of England, and that consideration of groups outside its jurisdiction was usually in order to inform such introspection. Matthew Newcomen stated that,

> I have not shunned to declare the truth of God unto you in points of controversy, either between us and the Papists, or between us and the Lutherans, or between us and the Arminians, or between us and the Socinians, or Quakers, or any others.[106]

Of all the Protestant sects outside the Church, those mentioned most often in the farewell sermons were the Quakers. Mutual antipathy between Presbyterians and Quakers intensified at the Restoration, manifesting itself in diatribes such as those published by the Norfolk minister John Horn between 1659 and 1660.[107] Throughout the summer of 1662 ministers found themselves repeatedly molested by Quakers, who disrupted at least one farewell sermon.[108] Bartholomeans responded with thinly veiled contempt. Thomas Lye, whilst discussing the dangers of false doctrine in the course of his farewell sermon, expressed pity for 'those poor souls that we call Quakers'.[109] Richard Baxter used the Quakers as a litmus test of godliness, demanding of his listeners, 'If thou standst shaking under small temptations for want of confirmation, what wilt thou do when a Papist, or Quaker, etc., shall so speak concerning Religion, which thou art not able to answer?'[110] Quakers had been portrayed as papists in disguise in the past, and would be again, but, although Baxter's outburst demonstrates that Quakers and papists were juxtaposed, nowhere in the surviving Bartholomean texts was this particular symbiosis emphasised – unlike the image of the Presbyterian-papist which was then being peddled by Cavalier-Anglican opponents.[111]

During the early seventeenth century it had become almost obligatory for Protestant sermons to include attacks on Catholicism. Thus, in his valedictory series, John Barrett dutifully denigrated Catholicism as a 'miserable lame religion', declaring that it was preferable to 'perish in a wilderness than return to this spiritual Egypt'.[112] Similarly, much as he had earlier pleaded in his valediction for toleration and understanding within Protestantism, Richard Alleine equated the Pope's conclave with that of the Devil.[113] Surprisingly, however, although a number of farewell sermons included sideswipes at Catholicism, anti-popish rhetoric was by no means to be found in every published text. Even where it was deployed, the rhetoric was often formulaic, showing little of the enthusiastic and inventive vitriol of earlier decades. George Eubanke's allegation that blind obedience to popish superiors made every Catholic a potential murderer was, in the context of the farewell sermons, unusually harsh.[114]

It is possible, therefore, that when Thomas Case grumbled that 'Time was when . . . popery was more hated than now; when the name of a Toleration would have made Christians to have trembled' he was speaking the literal truth.[115] Just as John Miller has observed that the anniversary of 5 November fell into relative obscurity after the Great Fire of London, and did not regain its former popularity until the anti-popish scares of 1673, so a survey of the Bartholomean corpus reveals that only one farewell sermon – that of Thomas Bladon – carried a direct reference to the 'popish gunpowder plot'.[116] In similar vein, although the Bartholomeans might have been tempted to present the Act of Uniformity and the Great Ejection as a popish conspiracy, only one published farewell sermon did so. Equating papists with the Pharisees who had made it a mortal sin to read God's Word and had corrupted worship with human inventions, John Crodacot averred,

> Now it is thought utterly to deny liberty; and can there be a more horrible, hellish plot assigned than this, to take from people their knowledge of salvation? And thus the Church of Rome, whether they have Church-snuffers or not, to be sure they have Church extinguishers, and various means to put out the light![117]

However, no other published Bartholomean openly subscribed to the suggestion that Black Bartholomew was a popish plot, just as none cared to be so precise in defining formalism as inherently papist. Even 'Mr Watson's Sermon against Popery', a notable inclusion in later Bartholomean compilations, carried no mention of conspiracy. Watson attacked Cardinal Bellarmine, 'that Goliath of the Papists' and deployed Pauline scripture to decry popish idolatry, but otherwise presented popery as a somewhat distant threat from an external political power. Apart from an isolated observation that the popish religion was defended by force rather than argument, none of Watson's farewell sermons even mentioned the subject.[118] In one valediction, Matthew Newcomen warned of a great increase in the numbers of papists and the consequent need to hold fast against the least popish innovation, but in another pointedly refused to condemn 'the poor people' who suffered under the impious spell of the Pope and his acolytes.[119] Thomas Lye told his congregation that he had more pressing objectives in the final hours of his public ministry than to warn them against popery.[120]

Christopher Hill has attempted to account for the perceived decline in anti-popish rhetoric by arguing that the fear of Catholicism had lessened by the Restoration, and that 'undiscriminating use of the concept of the Antichrist made it unacceptable to the respectable classes, some of whose best friends were Catholics'.[121] John Miller has estimated that by 1660 Roman Catholics accounted for just over 1 per cent of the population – far less numerous and even more scattered than nonconformists.[122] But whilst these hypotheses have some validity, they do not appear to take into account the fact that anti-popery re-emerged as a potent political force less than a decade later. As Peter Lake has demonstrated, far from being a simple matter of doctrine, anti-popery was politically, and polemically, ambiguous.[123] In the 1640s anti-popish rhetoric, diplomatically directed at 'evil counsellors', had been used by parliamentarians to challenge the legitimacy of royal government. Consequently, at the Restoration, the association of anti-popish rhetoric with anti-royalism had become a political liability for moderate Puritans. By proscribing any discourse which implied either that Charles II was a papist or would endeavour to introduce popery, the Act to preserve the person and government of the King (1661) not only enshrined the politicisation of anti-popish rhetoric but also served to curtail its use.[124] As the Bartholomeans' principal explanation of their nonconformity was predicated on a separation of political and religious imperatives, gratuitous use of anti-popery had the potential to undermine the very basis of their argument. Thus, although Bartholomean preachers had lost none of their distaste for Catholicism after 1660, legal considerations and political circumstances appear to have made them cautious in their utilisation of anti-popish rhetoric. This, and the more immediate concern to prepare godly congregations for temptation and persecution, had significant effects on the overall tone of the farewell sermons. Many Bartholomeans neglected to discuss popery in their valedictions, and most of those that did sought to provide a yardstick of godliness rather than to attack Catholics as such; contrasting uncritical, misguided superstition with the active heart-searching of the godly, highlighting the dangers of setting up clerics to preside over their brethren and urging Protestant rulers to respect the supremacy of divine and natural laws.[125] Above all, papists were used to illustrate the necessity of Protestant unity, as William Bates exclaimed, 'Doth not the *publick enemy* rejoice over us, I mean the *Papists?* do they not warm themselves at the sparks of our divisions: for you know the old Maxim of *Divide* and *Reign*.'[126] The same argument was being used in the 30 January sermons – except that Anglican preachers aimed their anti-popish rhetoric directly at moderate Puritans, arguing that just as the Regicide had divided English Protestants, so Presbyterians, by their continued resistance to legally constituted authority, were fermenting schism and thereby doing the work of Rome.[127] The Bartholomeans were unable to respond in kind not only because of the restraining influence of the 1661 Treason Act, but, more importantly, because they themselves feared schism. Having said this, their absolute belief in their own orthodoxy, and their resolute commitment to reformation meant that many hundreds of godly ministers would be ejected. Consequently, the salvation of the Church, perhaps even the Reformation itself, would depend upon the character and moral fibre of the laity.

II

The true extent of nonconformist feeling among the lay population in 1662 has always been a matter of conjecture. Bishop Compton's census of 1676 surmised that approximately 5 per cent of the population were nonconformist, whilst a survey in the 1700s calculated the proportion to be nearer 6 per cent.[128] Such figures retrospectively projected onto the population of 1662 would produce a putative estimate of around 250–300,000 people. However, the complex questions regarding the extent of lay support for the Bartholomean ministers cannot be resolved by a simple headcount. Firstly, as we have seen, this 'community' was far from being a cohesive party. It is for this reason that Compton's census (which only counted as nonconformist those who had left the established Church) has been argued by Tim Harris to have been an underestimation of the true extent of the dissenting community.[129] Secondly, it was not distributed evenly across England, being particularly concentrated in areas such as London, the Northwest, the West Country, the East Midlands and the northern Home Counties.[130] Thirdly, the struggle for the soul of the Church of England was won and lost in the parishes. It was a matter of no small importance how well each minister understood the cultural, social and economic currents of his parish, and how effectively he interacted with the confusing and often contradictory patchwork of loyalties, affiliations, alliances and rivalries that made up a local community.

The length of time the authors of the farewell sermons had been in their livings varied immensely. John Galpin, aged twenty-three at the time of his ejection, had been curate in Ash Priors, Somerset, for just two years, whilst George Newton had served his Taunton congregation for over thirty. Among

the more career-minded Bartholomeans, Thomas Manton and Elias Pledger
had both made a series of short-term moves between pulpits in and around
London. However, many ministers on delivering their farewell sermons took
the opportunity to emphasise a long and intimate acquaintance with their
local community. Samuel Slater, a particularly elderly Bartholomean, declared
in his valediction that he had laboured among his flock at St Katherine's,
London, for almost forty years.[131] Matthew Newcomen reminded his audience
that he had held his Dedham lectureship for twenty-six years; expressing
gratitude to the local people and neighbouring ministers for their support
during that time, he declared that it was 'no easie thing to speak, or think of
parting with such an Auditory, and Society: the like to which I never look to
have on Earth again'.[132]

On the other side of the country, Richard Fairclough expressed an equally
intense emotional attachment to the Somerset living he had held for fifteen
years: '*farewel* this house; and *farewel* this Seat forever: and (within a little
while) *farewel* your discourse, and your faces; *farewel* my pleasant habitation,
and this sweet air of Mells'.[133] In nearby Batcombe, Richard Alleine expressed
similar warmth for his congregation, whose minister he had been for twenty
years, musing that 'This Morning I had a Flock, and you had a Pastour; but
now behold a Pastour without a Flock, a Flock without a Shepheard.'[134]

Such empathy was often reciprocated: the preface to Philip Lamb's farewell sermon, featured in the pamphlet *The Royal Presence* (1662), bears all
the hallmarks of a community petition, declaring the sermon to have been
published by the acclamation of '*We, the Inhabitants of* Beere *and* Kingstone
in the county of Dorset, *who have lived under the Rich Droppings, Plentiful Soul-
searching, Enlivening and Refreshing Dews of Heaven.*' Describing the purveyor
of these droppings as an eminent and faithful messenger of the Gospel of
Jesus Christ, the parishioners lamented '*that we are now deprived of them
by his removal from us*'.[135] But respect and affection had first to be earned.
Bartholomean clergy – who, after all, took their religion seriously enough
to risk their livelihoods on a point of principle – invariably emerge from
anecdotal evidence as indefatigable workers within their communities. John
Hieron, for example, was energetic in disseminating the Word in Breadsall,
Derbyshire, making it his goal to teach in every home. Henry Newcombe
continued catechising and repeating sermons after his ejection, even when
threatened with legal recriminations for doing so. According to Calamy, the
Exeter minister Robert Atkins had found his previous living in Essex overrun
with sects at his arrival, 'but his solid Doctrine joyn'd with a free and obliging
Conversation so convinc'd and gain'd them, that after a while he had not one
Dissenter left in his Parish'.[136]

The presence of an effective minister, however, was not enough to guarantee the sympathies of the locality. Shortly after Bartholomew's Day, Bishop

Ward commented of the ejected ministers in his Exeter diocese that the people in many places were glad to be rid of them. He knew of at least one Presbyterian minister who, despite belatedly conforming, had been sub-sequently locked out of his church by his parishioners.[137] Several farewell sermons reveal that ministers elsewhere faced similar opposition. In his valediction at St John's, Exeter, Robert Atkins declared that he was distressed to be leaving a loving congregation which just two years earlier had given him such a free and cheerful welcome. He did not dwell on the fact that he had suffered considerable censure from other sections of the local commun-ity, including 'some rigid People', who believed him to be too accommodat-ing in matters of religion, and others who considered him a dangerous radical. Shortly before his ejection, a local gentleman had attempted to intimidate Atkins during one of his sermons, and not long afterward the minister found himself accused of libelling the antagonist and a number of his associates. The fact that local magistrates reacted within hours of these allegations being made public suggests that Atkins was being dogged by an unfriendly clique. However, the minister appears to have been on amicable terms with others on the Bench, and was favoured by Seth Ward's predecessor Bishop Gauden, who arranged his release from prison. That Atkins was as popular as the rhetoric of his farewell sermon would suggest is borne out by a later abortive attempt to imprison him for holding illegal meetings in his house. According to Calamy, the Mayor of Exeter and an accompanying Justice found to their frustration that not only did other magistrates refuse to endorse the prosecu-tion, but, despite the fact that a large crowd had gathered about Atkins's house, the erstwhile persecutors 'could not either by Promises or Threats, get any to carry him to Prison'.[138] Several, however, volunteered to pay the minister's fine.

In several parishes, similar instances of financial assistance for outgoing ministers provide clues as to the extent of local support. One reason that the deadline for compliance had been set for 24 August was that it would prevent dissenting clergy from receiving the half-yearly tithes due on that day. The case of Thomas Newnham, rector of St Lawrence, Isle of Wight, demonstrates that whilst some parishioners duly withheld their contribution, many others deliberately paid their tithe early in order to ensure that the departing minister would have the benefit of it.[139] In London, the vestry of St Lawrence Pountney ordered as late as December 1663 that their ejected curate Thomas Wadsworth should have his tithes paid retrospectively.[140]

It was anticipated that many of those facing the loss of their livelihoods after Bartholomew's Day would quickly be reduced to penury. In some instances the families of these unfortunate individuals were relieved by other ministers: John Angier noted in his diary entry for 16 February 1663 that he had sent ten shillings to the wife of a deprived minister.[141] However, as it had long been accepted practice to elicit funds from the lay community, a number of Bartholomeans used their farewell sermons to appeal on behalf of colleagues facing imminent ruin. Whilst preaching on the morning of 17 August, Thomas Watson described the plight of ministers who had already been reduced to penury, and asked the congregation to show their love by contributing to the 'household of Faith', saying 'I believe no heart here would be so hard as to deny Jesus Christ; Why, remember whatsoever you give Ministers, and to his Members, he takes it as given to himself.'[142] Thomas Case likewise urged his congregation, 'to those that have been the instruments of your Conversion, or Edification, set apart something extraordinary for their relief and supply'.[143]

Significant amounts of financial aid continued to be supplied by sympathisers among the gentry and aristocracy. Notable Puritan families, who retained considerable influence in many localities, were not only able to provide pensions and employment for indigent ministers, but could, in many cases, still offer a measure of political protection. Edmund Calamy, for one, owed his release from Newgate in January 1663 to the influence of the earl of Manchester.[144] Despite holding the office of Lord Chamberlain within the Restoration establishment, Manchester remained a solid Presbyterian, who even after Bartholomew's Day held regular meetings with ejected ministers at his London lodgings, and continued to press for an inclusive religious settlement. Thomas Horton, whose funeral sermon for Simeon Ashe would feature so prominently in the Bartholomean compilations, perhaps owed the continuance of his Church ministry to the fact that he was Manchester's chaplain. More tellingly, in June 1662 Manchester defended Thomas Manton against accusations of disloyalty laid against the minister in the House of Lords.[145] Another notable Puritan peer, Lord Wharton was to provide financial assistance for many ejected ministers in the years after Fatal Bartholomew, and remained a sponsor of John Whitlock and his circle.[146] Ministers such as Thomas Manton relied heavily on the continued support of aristocrats such as the earl and countess of Bedford and the earl of Clare.[147] However, in stark contrast to the effusive dedications which embellished other published works of the period, references to these aristocratic patrons were conspicuous by their absence from the published farewell sermons – a confirmation of their fragile political position. Even in the provinces, very few county gentry were publicly connected with any Bartholomean publication – George Eubanke's pamphlet, which named his patron as Sir George Narwood Bart., of Cleveland in Yorkshire, and George Swinnock's published valediction dedicated to the wife of John Beresford, Esq., appear to be the only extant examples.[148] Other references were as tangential as they were rare: John Whitlock acknowledged the encouragement and respect he had received 'from the honourable Patron of this Place', Richard Alleine praised certain gentry for their support, but neither minister cared to name their benefactors.[149] Having welcomed the restoration of order, most Puritan gentry had no stomach for protracted political conflict; as Bishop Morley commented at the time, the Presbyterian nobility were unwilling to hazard their great wealth to support a public challenge to the Restoration authorities.[150] In addition to facing moves to eradicate their influence from local and national government, the Puritan gentry were as beset by spies and informers as their erstwhile ministers. Those who had somehow survived as MPs and Justices were closely monitored and reluctant to hazard what they had managed to retain.[151] The frequent allusions in the farewell sermons to the need for order, together with a marked reluctance to advertise the support of their patrons amongst the gentry reveals that most Bartholomeans had a keen awareness of political reality. At the same time, however, the published farewell sermons were not always so restrained when discussing the religious and social duties of the common people.

Despite the fact that it cut across all social strata, nonconformity was frequently portrayed as a religion of the poorer sort. The Cavalier-Anglican trope that Puritanism encouraged social unrest allowed writers such as L'Estrange to contend that nonconformist preachers posed a threat to the natural order.[152] Many Bartholomeans, well aware that they were being stigmatised as rabble-rousers, took great pains in their farewell sermons to stress that they had no such intent. Due respect was demanded for social rank, and householders were advised to educate their families and servants accordingly. Daniel Bull advised his congregation to 'Do your duty to your Superiours, to those that God hath set over you, so carry your selves as it was in the case of *Daniel*, that they may find nothing against you save in the matter of your God.'[153]

However, for every Bartholomean who advocated deference, there were others who persisted in stressing the equality of all in the sight of the Lord; as William Jenkyn argued, 'this outward disproportion, as to birth and education, puts no difference at all in a spiritual respect, between believer and believer: a King and a Beggar all one in Christ'. He opined that 'not many noble, not many rich, but the poor hath God chosen'.[154] Similarly, when Thomas Bladon contended that 'God is no respecter of persons, he regards no man the more for his dignities, riches, nobleness of birth and pedegree', he concluded by quoting James 2:5: 'He hath chosen the poor of the world, rich in faith and heirs of a kingdom.'[155] The rhetoric of equality was reinforced by other Bartholomeans such as Thomas Lye, who stated that the highest officers in the Church were 'but brethren to the meanest saints'.[156] As Peter Lake has written, it would be a mistake 'to posit too sharp a division between the artifice and artificiality of the merely literary and the supposed reality of the social'.[157] Both Bartholomean pronouncements and Cavalier-Anglican anxieties should be taken seriously – because both contributed to a physical reality in which words had the capacity to inspire and direct physical action.

The Restoration authorities were alarmed by words, therefore, because of the ability of words to translate into action. Apart from violent incidents such as Venner's Rising in 1661, it was noticed that the state anniversaries of 30 January and 29 May were unevenly observed across the country, and that some provincial communities had even continued to commemorate local royalist defeats in the Civil War.[158] In 1663, when printed farewell sermons were circulating in great numbers, magistrates investigating the Farnley Wood plot would indicate their concern at the willingness of elements within the middling and poorer sort to restore the ejected ministers by violent means.[159] Such fears reflected those that had been prevalent in the weeks leading up to Black Bartholomew's Day a year before.

Despite widespread expectations of trouble, however, disturbances during August 1662 were mostly limited to localised demonstrations. At St Matthew's in Friday Street, a gang of youths gathered and shouted 'Porridge!' (a derisive colloquialism for the Common Prayer Book) at the replacement preacher, but Pepys reported such tumults to be 'nothing as bad as common fame represents them, though some disturbances the new preachers had by the boys, and by none else, in three or four churches'.[160] Daniel O'Neill believed that those ministers who had threatened trouble had been let down by the reluctance of their congregations to become involved in a fight.[161] However, there was clearly considerable anger in many parishes, and the Venetian ambassador and others reported more widespread outbreaks of disorder.[162] Far from encouraging this, preachers such as Thomas Bladon made strenuous efforts to persuade their followers to remain calm and peaceable, secure in the knowledge that 'God in his due time will revenge this dishonour done to his Servants'.[163] Richard Fairclough preached a similar message, charging his flock to 'take the way of Peace before Schism; Obedience, before disobedience; self-denial, before self-pleasing; avoiding of scandal, before using of liberty'.[164]

Admittedly, some Bartholomeans were less unambiguous: whilst he called for his congregation to show restraint, Richard Alleine warned that whilst he desired them to follow the way of peace, he did not expect them to submit to 'tearms dishonourable or prejudicial to *Truth*'.[165] Even ministers such as Alleine, however, had no desire to contest the streets with the Cavalier-controlled militia – much less provoke the recall of the Marquis of Ormonde's regiments from Ireland. Even if it had been possible to recruit and arm the demobilised veterans of the New Model Army, most still willing to fight were radicals who detested anything that smacked of Presbyterianism. Armed conflict was not a serious option; indeed, it was emphasised in the farewell sermons that such notions detracted from the battle which was now to be fought for the far higher cause of God against Satan. The struggle for which the Bartholomeans were now preparing their congregations was that between the godly and the profane.

Many farewell sermons emphasised that godly congregations were in imminent peril from encircling wolves, and, more importantly, that the laity were now entrusted with the duty of consolidating the work of reformation within the Church of England.[166] 'Ministers may be forcibly parted from you, and have their mouths stopt, as ours and many others are, and are like to be', said Joseph Whitlock, 'yet let not the Word of Truth depart out of your minds, when we are gone.'[167] Thomas Bladon informed his congregation that they were now the Lord's soldiers, and had battles to fight against Satan, and innumerable enemies to overcome before they could hope for a crown of glory.[168] The Bartholomeans wished the godly to remain within the Church of England; not to capitulate, but to continue the struggle for the ultimate victory ordained by Scripture. However, given that mutual recognition was vital if the godly laity were to overcome a hostile world without their pastors, it is significant that, for all the emphasis laid upon the spiritual superiority and predestined separation of God's chosen people from the rest of mankind, Bartholomeans failed to identify them in the farewell sermons. Indeed, George Thorne stated explicitly at the start of his valediction that he did not intend to spend time discussing who was or was not godly.[169] Thomas Powel told his Exeter parishioners that 'I would not have you to conclude yourselves to be saints if you are not such indeed.'[170] Edward Hancock was even more pessimistic whilst preaching in Bristol: 'Really, Brethren, I am afraid few of you are real Members of the Church.'[171] Margaret Spufford's suggestion that we should 'investigate and discard the distinction usually made between the self-styled "godly" and the multitude' is particularly apposite.[172] The extant farewell sermons generally agree on what it is to be a true child of God, but at the same time betray considerable uncertainty as to precisely who could claim to be such. Departing ministers offered generalisations rather than definitive answers, perhaps because even those of a Presbyterian mentality acknowledged that such revelation remained intensely personal, born of introspection and individual communion with God. Philip Lamb, whose sermon twice featured a gender-defying metaphor of the elect as the wives of Christ, described this intense intimacy: '*By night in her bed.* Jesus Christ hath her bed thoughts, in her Closet and private duties, of Prayer, serious Meditations, Spiritual Ejaculations, and secret felt Examinations.'[173] Thus, much as the departing ministers offered advice and encouragement to those who aspired to be chosen, they did not presume to know precisely who would be saved on the Day of Judgement. On the contrary, this uncertainty was used as an incentive for the congregation to hold fast what they had seen and heard.

The basic prerequisites for godliness were clear: an absolute adherence to God's Word as revealed through Scripture, an absolute love of Christ transcending any worldly concern, and an absolute trust in God rather than Man. The godly were exhorted to '*Love not the world, neither the things that are in the world*', because the lovers of the world were enemies of Christ.[174] Thomas Bladon affected to perceive the otherness of the godly by their unworldly demeanour: 'God's People in Scripture are called *Pilgrims* and *Strangers*. Whilst they are in this world they are in a strange Country.'[175] Many other Bartholomeans agreed that a lack of concern for the world was a mark of godliness. Congregations were urged to think often on death, even to long for it, and the life thereafter, rather than muse on earthly affairs.[176] Thomas Manton suggested that the godly could recognise themselves by measuring their conduct against examples of men and women who had endured temptation and affliction for God, whilst Robert Porter saw mourning for the loss of solemn assemblies as a true believer.[177] But more generally membership of the invisible church was considered to be a matter of faith and conscience. Ralph Venning asked his listeners

> Now what were we *before Faith*? Why truly, we were not a people: so the Scripture tells you, They that were not a people, are now the people of God: so that, if we are not the people of God, we are, as if we were not a people.[178]

John Moore told his flock to 'Labour for tender Consciences, such as will be afraid of committing the least known sin, or of omitting the least known duty. Outward Reformation, is nothing without inward Renovation.'[179] Similarly, George Thorne urged 'If therefore you would keep the Way of the Lord, do not despise Conscience; do not neglect the Light within; but make it not thy Rule. Make the Word of God thy rule.'[180]

For all these words of advice and encouragement, many departing preachers feared that evil lurked within their congregations. Thomas Lye believed that most of his flock were godly, but suspected that tares had been sown in the parish.[181] Richard Alleine suggested to his congregation that they were 'black'd and burthen'd with such miserable creatures.' He suspected that he had some before him who had the face of a Christian and the tongue of a Saint, but the heart of a beast within. It was as hard to convince a hypocrite, he concluded, as it was to detect hypocrisy.[182] Other Bartholomeans responded positively in the face of uncertainty: Richard Fairclough, for one, composed a series of farewell sermons aimed successively at the profane, the half-hearted and the truly godly.[183] Pessimism, however, could be cathartic: Richard Baxter's conviction that many would prove false when tested, and that 'a considerable part of our congregations should be carried away' suggested that such a scouring might better reveal the true saints.[184]

A growing siege mentality coloured the Bartholomeans' advice to their followers regarding relationships with their local communities. Some preachers advanced arguments which appeared to go against traditional ties of neighbourliness. Thomas Lye advised followers to, 'Take ye heed every one of his Neighbour, and trust ye not in any Brother; for every Brother will utterly supplant, and every Neighbour walk in Slanders.'[185] At the same time, the godly were assured of their spiritual superiority. William Jenkyn declared that 'The righteous is more excellent than his neighbour', portraying many neighbours as brutish Sabbath-breakers, drinking and whoring as the godly prayed in church. Whereas the company of saints was like warm living coals, he considered the company of swearers and drunkards to be 'a spiritual frozennesse'.[186] Robert Atkins, whilst exhorting his followers to live as good neighbours and peaceable subjects demanded that they shun ungodly company.[187] John Whitlock advised his congregation to be much in conference with one another instead.[188] William Jenkyn, whilst pleading for public ordinances where worship could be performed with decency, nevertheless exhorted his congregation to turn their houses into churches, assuring them that 'the Closet, or Dining Room, or Chamber, the Field, or the River side' could be equally as holy.[189]

Recent studies have challenged the idea that the godly were 'mentally and emotionally separated' from conventional society and that sects could dislocate traditional communities.[190] However, as a snapshot of nonconformist attitudes, the farewell sermons reveal a discernible tension between the need to avoid spiritual contamination and the instinct to integrate. The Bartholomeans upheld neighbourliness inasmuch as they advised their congregations to act peaceably and deal honestly. But they repeatedly asserted that the godly, as superior creatures, should consort only with their own kind, interacting with the profane only as and when necessary. The transmission of such attitudes into the local community may not have been enough to dislocate society, but it was often enough to antagonise and alienate.

III

In May 1661 Matthew Newcomen had written to Richard Baxter to propose a reprinting of the Grand Remonstrance. This, he argued, would show how things had begun decades before and 'who they be that are still what they were'.[191] Just over a year later, the language of the farewell sermons suggests that even ministers who still harboured such militant sentiments had become considerably less eager to broadcast them. Few Bartholomeans were willing to advertise the extent to which they were still what they were in matters such as the Solemn League and Covenant. In response to a hostile establishment which equated religious conformity with political reliability, the Bartholomeans could offer only 'passive', rather than 'active' obedience. But the political ambiguities evident in the farewell sermons were much more than a response to the events of August 1662; they were an articulation of the crisis of conscience that had begun for moderate Puritans with the Regicide and had acquired increased urgency at the Restoration. The Act of Uniformity, on the other hand, reflected Cavalier-Anglican impatience with those they loosely termed 'Presbyterians', perceiving such individuals not as sincere Protestants facing a genuine dilemma, but as hypocrites engaged in deliberate subterfuge.

Because it was impossible to define with precision the nature and extent of disaffection within the Church of England, the efficacy of the Act of Uniformity relied in large part on the readiness of dissidents to reveal themselves. The nonconformist community, that was ultimately to be shaped by ejection and legal persecution, began to take shape in the farewell sermons by which ministers publicly declared their dissent from the Act. Although there were many more valedictions delivered than those which have survived in print and manuscript, the authors of the extant sermons seem to have been typical of the Bartholomean cohort as a whole, both demographically and in the range of their political and doctrinal viewpoints. The farewell sermons reveal glimpses of personal networks, mostly located in clusters at local level, but also of wider, if looser, associations across the regions. These networks were, however, nowhere near as systematic as the more neurotic among the Cavalier-Anglicans imagined. The nonconformists certainly possessed a sense of solidarity, which in the farewell sermons manifested itself in a hardening of religious resolve and a shared anticipation of persecution, but it did not inspire the formulation of a party agenda.

Nonconformity was an issue not simply for the clergy, but also for their congregations. Robert Bosher's notion of 'ejection from below' has long since been challenged by evidence of popular support for nonconformist ministers, as well as by the experience of ministers such as Robert Atkins which show that official attitudes could vary considerably.[192] The Bartholomeans clearly enjoyed a significant amount of moral support, and financial assistance, but there were reasons why such backing was insufficient to save their public ministry. Firstly, the Puritan gentry had for the most part been neutered by the shift in political power represented by the Restoration. Control of Parliament, the magistracy and the county militias had passed into other hands. Secondly, the Bartholomean ministers themselves sought to restrain their supporters, urging them to keep the peace and to obey the authorities in all civil matters.

In matters of religion, on the other hand, the Bartholomean message was far less accommodating. Ministers exhorted their followers to remain within the Church of England, not to condone, but to resist prelacy and formalism, keeping the flame of Scripture-based worship alive until such time as God and political developments would permit the return of a truly godly ministry. Given such intransigence, the relative lack of anti-popish invective in the farewell sermons is surprising. If, as Peter Lake has written, 'the Protestants' negative image of popery can tell us a great deal about their positive image of themselves', it tells us that there was considerable uncertainty within the ranks of moderate Puritanism in 1662, both as regards their own self-identity and the nature of the threat they now faced.[193] However, as the studies of Christopher Durston and Jacqueline Eales have argued, Puritanism was not a party or even a community, but manifested itself variously as a culture, a social experience and a spiritual activity.[194] All three elements were channelled through the medium of preaching. Inasmuch as preaching could influence attitudes and precipitate action, it contained a fourth aspect which never failed to alarm Cavalier-Anglicans: Puritanism as a political force.

NOTES

1 The debate surfaces in P. Collinson, 'Protestant culture and the cultural revolution', in Todd, *Reformation to Revolution*, pp. 33–52; N. Key, 'Comprehension and the breakdown of consensus in Restoration Herefordshire' in Harris, Seaward and Goldie, *Politics of Religion*, p. 195; D. Underdown, *Royalist Conspiracy in England 1649–1660* (New Haven, CT, 1960), pp. 3–4; Spurr, *Restoration Church of England*, pp. 44–6; Spurr, *English Puritanism*, pp. 133–5; Keeble, *Literary Culture*, p. 112; Miller, *After the Civil Wars*, pp. 134, 174–6; I. Green, *Print and Protestantism in Early Modern England* (Oxford, 2000), preface, pp. 3, 200–1; Nuttall and Chadwick, *From Uniformity to Unity*, pp. 11–14; Greaves, *Deliver Us from Evil*, p. 13.

2 A. Hughes, '"Popular" Presbyterianism in the 1640s and 1650s', in N. Tyacke (ed.), *England's Long Reformation 1500–1800* (1998), pp. 235, *passim*. For discussions of anti-clericalism, see C. Hill, *Change and Continuity in Seventeenth-Century England* (1973), pp. 162–3; R. O'Day, *The English Clergy: The Emergence of a Profession 1558–1642* (Leicester, 1979), pp. 3, 190–1, 205–6, 244, 245; P. Seaward, 'Gilbert Sheldon, the London vestries and the defence of the Church', in Harris, Seaward and Goldie, *Politics of Religion*, p. 67; Keeble, *Literary Culture*, p. 162; Spurr, *Restoration Church*, p. 225.

3 R. Alleine, *The Godly Man's Portion and Sanctuary* (1664), p. 174. See also John Barrett, in *England's Remembrancer*, pp. 65–6.

4 W. Walwyn (1614–71), *God Save the King* (1660), pp. 7–8.

5 Underdown, *Royalist Conspiracy*, p. 3.

6 Keeble, *Literary Culture*, p. 144; Mitchell, *English Pulpit Oratory*, p. 371.

7 The demographic statistics presented here have been compiled from the biographical information in *CR*.

8 Others attending Cambridge in 1646 included Luke Cranwell, Henry Newcombe, John Barrett, Robert Seddon and Oliver Heywood.

9 Robert Atkins, Thomas Lye and Thomas Manton (Wadham); Joseph Caryl, John Galpin and George Newton (Exeter).

10 P. Seaver, *The Puritan Lectureships* (Stanford, CA, 1970), p. 181.

11 T. Webster, *Godly Clergy in Early Stuart England* (Cambridge, 1997), pp. 17, 21–2, 44–6; O'Day, *English Clergy*, pp. 2, 106.

12 O'Day, *English Clergy*, pp. 17, 20–2; Seaver, *Puritan Lectureships*, pp. 190, 196.

13 J. Howe, *A Funeral Sermon For the Faithful and Laborious Mr Richard Fairclough* (1682), pp. 51–3.

14 E.g., J. Berkenhead, *Cabala* (1663), pp. '28', '25' (mispaginated – pp. 34–5).

15 Greaves, *Deliver Us from Evil*, pp. 9–10; *CR*, xii–xiii.

16 BL Egerton MSS 2543, fo. 28.

17 O. Heywood, *The Life of John Angier*, ed. E. Axon (Manchester, 1937), vol. 97, p. 128.

18 Fairclough, *Pastor's Legacy*, pp. 127, 137, 138; E. Hancock, *The Pastor's Last Legacy and Counsel* (1663), sig. B2, D–[Dv], [Div]. Edward Hancock was reputed to have served as Horner's butler, whilst Horner had presented Fairclough to his living at Mells in 1647 (*CR*, *s.vv.*).

19 Greaves, *Deliver Us from Evil*, p. 63; *CR*, *s.vv.*

20 *Abridgement*, p. 332; *CR*, p. 349.

21 *CR*, *s.v*; Pepys, *Diary*, pp. 166–8. See also Bates, *Peace-Maker*, p. 32.

22 Heywood, *Life of John Angier*, p. 28.

23 J. Whitlock, *A Short Account of the Life of Mr. William Reynolds* (1698), p. 37; *CR*, *s.vv.*

24 Whitlock, *Short Account*, pp. 109–10; Barrett, *A Funeral Sermon, Preached at Nottingham* (1709).

25 R. Porter, *The Life of Mr John Hieron* (1691), p. 53; *CR*, s.v.

26 E.g., *England's Remembrancer*, pp. 21, 65–6, 257, 381–2, 389, 424, 425–6, 446.

27 E.g., Porter, *Life of John Hieron*, p. 17.

28 Whitlock, *Short Account*, p. 38.

29 M. Newcomen, *Ultimum Vale* (1663), p. 18; *England's Remembrancer*, p. 224.

30 Bodl. Tanner MS 48, fo. 43 (Letter from G. W. to ?, September 1662).

31 Thorndike, quoted in Nuttall and Chadwick, *From Uniformity to Unity*, p. 14.

32 13 Charles II. St I. Cap. I; Browning, *Documents*, p. 63.

33 E. Hyde, *The Life of Edward, Earl of Clarendon* (2 vols, Oxford, 1857), p. 571.

34 *A Compleat Collection of Farewell Sermons* (1663), sig. [Iiiiv].

35 *Ibid.*, sig. [Llllv].

36 Jenkyn, Crodacot, Annesley, Caryl, Venning and Newton; *Compleat Collection*, sig.[Iiii2v–Kkkk2v], [Llll2v–Llll4v].

37 *Ibid.*: Calamy (sig. [Iiiiv]); Nalton (sig. Iiii2); Crodacot (sig. [Iiii4v]); Annesley (sig. Kkkk2).

38 See J. Wilson, *Pulpit in Parliament* (Princeton, 1969), Appendix II; A. Laurence, *Parliamentary Army Chaplains* (Woodbridge, 1990), pp. 92–3, 109, 110, 114–15, 155, 127, 134.

39 W. Assheton, *Evangelium Armatum* (1663), frontispiece, *passim*.

40 N. Hardy, *A Loud Call to Great Mourning* (1661); S. Kem, *King Solomon's Infalliable Expedient for Three Kingdoms' Settlement* (1660); H. Newcombe, *Usurpation Defeated and David Restored* (1660); R. Eedes, *Great Britain's Resurrection* (1660). The private observations are noted by Spurr, *Restoration Church*, p. 45, citing MS Eng. Th. D. 71, fo. 64v.

41 See T. Case, *Correction, Instructions or a Treatise of Affliction* (1652), republished in 1671; McGee *Godly Man*, p. 33.

42 *Exact Collection*, p. 101.

43 E. Calamy, *A Sermon Preached by Mr Edmund Calamy at Aldermanbury London, August 24 1651* (1651); T. Manton, *A Sermon Preached at the Funerall of M. Christopher Love* (1651).

44 *CR, s.v.*

45 Watson, *Pastor's Love Expressed*, p. 6.

46 G. Thorne, *The Saint's Great Duty* (1664), p. 28.

47 *Exact Collection*, p. 382.

48 *England's Remembrancer*, p. 96.

49 Fairclough, *Pastor's Legacy*, p. 100.

50 Atkins, *God of Love and Peace*, pp. 15–16.

51 *Ibid.*, p. 21.

52 *England's Remembrancer*, p. 256. See also Atkins, *God of Love and Peace*, p. 21.

53 T. Lye, *The Fixed Saint Held Forth* (1662), p. 19.

54 Lye, *Fixed Saint*, p. 23.

55 D. Lloyd, *Cabala* (1663), p. 3.

56 Keeble, *Literary Culture*, p. 29; J. Sawday, 'Re-writing a revolution: history, symbol and text at the Restoration', *The Seventeenth Century*, 7, 2 (1992) pp. 171–99.

57 Harris, Seaward and Goldie, *Politics of Religion*, p. 194; Bosher, *Restoration Settlement*, pp. 155, 183.

58 J. Caryl, *The Nature, Solemnity, Grounds, Property, and Benefits of a Sacred Covenant* (1643), pp. 11–12.

59 E. Calamy, *The Great Danger of Covenant-Refusing, and Covenant-Breaking* (1646), sig. [A4], pp. 8, 13, 17, 23, 34.

60 C. Hill, *The English Bible and the Seventeenth-Century Revolution* (1994), p. 281; Seaver, *Puritan Lectureships*, p. 279.

61 E. Vallance, 'Oaths, casuistry and equivocation: Anglican responses to the Engagement controversy', *Historical Journal*, 44, 1 (2001), pp. 59, 73.

62 J. Caryl, *The White Robe* (1662), p. 12.

63 Lye, *Fixed Saint*, pp. 1–2.

64 *Exact Collection*, pp. 328–9.

65 *England's Remembrancer*, p. 157.

66 Bates, *Peace-Maker*, pp. 9–10.

67 *Mercurius Publicus*, 1 (1–8 January, 1663) p. 14; Berkenhead, *Cabala*, pp. '28', '25' (mispaginated, and in fact pp. 34–5).

68 Calamy's sermon featured in at least four different pamphlets (see bibliography), and in *Exact Collection, Farewel Sermons Preached by Mr. Calamy, Dr. Manton, etc.*, ed. L. R., and S. N. (1663), *Compleat Collection* and its variant Wing C5638A; R. Douglas, *A Phenix* (Edinburgh, 1662).

69 Kem, *King Solomon's Infallible Expedient*, p. 11; see also M. Griffith, *The King's Life-Guard* (1665), p. 18.

70 *England's Remembrancer*, pp. 298, 299.

71 *Ibid.*, p. 259.

72 W. Jenkyn, *The Burning Yet Un-consumed Bush* (1662), p. 30.

73 *England's Remembrancer*, pp. 7, 153.

74 G. Swinnock, *The Pastors Farewell* (1662), p. 62.

75 *England's Remembrancer*, p. 397.

76 Fairclough, *Pastor's Legacy*, p. 121; Collins, in *Exact Collection*, p. 385.

77 *Ibid.*, p. 384.

78 *Ibid.*; Gal. 1:10.

79 Green, *Re-establishment*, pp. 149, 177.

80 Watson, *Pastor's Love Expressed*, p. 6.

81 See Newcombe, *Diary* (5 September 1662), p. 119. See also Spurr, *Restoration Church*, pp. 44–6; P. Jackson, 'Nonconformists and Society in Devon 1660–1689' (University of Exeter PhD thesis, 1986); Keeble, *Literary Culture*, pp. 36–7.

82 *The Lawfulness of Obeying the Present Government* (1649), quoted in Hill, *English Bible*, p. 218.

83 *England's Remembrancer*, p. 452.

84 Hancock, *Pastor's Last Legacy*, sig. B3.

85 *England's Remembrancer*, p. 38.

86 *Compleat Collection*, sig. [Ffff3–3v].

87 *Ibid.*; *England's Remembrancer*, p. 37.

88 *Compleat Collection*, sig. [Ffff3–Ffff3v].

89 *Ibid.*, sig. [Ffff3v].

90 Lye, *Fixed Saint*, p. 16; cf. *Exact Collection*, p. 341.

91 Alleine, *Godly Man's Portion*, p. 140.

92 *Ibid.*, pp. 139, 140.

93 *Exact Collection*, p. '104' [mispagination, actually p. 94 in sequence].

94 Quoted in Keeble, *Literary Culture*, p. 34.

95 Bates, *Peace-Maker*, pp. 11, 17.

96 Baxter, *Reliquiae Baxterianae*, pt II, p. 373.

97 Lye, *Fixed Saint*, p. 28.

98 *The Second and Last Collection of the Late London Ministers Farewel-Sermons* (1663), p. 129.

99 *Exact Collection*, p. 166. See also Whitlock and Porter in *England's Remembrancer*, pp. 21, 471; M. Mead, *The Pastors Valediction* (1662), p. 23; Caryl, *White Robe*, p. 6.

100 *Second and Last Collection*, p. 66.

101 *The Third Volume of Farewel Sermons* (1663), p. 11.

102 *Ibid.*, p. 18; Revelation 2:4, 5.

103 J. Davis, 'Against formality: one aspect of the English Revolution', *TRHS*, 6th series, 3 (1993), pp. 277, 280.

104 *England's Remembrancer*, p. 67.

105 Atkins, *God of Love and Peace*, p. 7.

106 Newcomen, DWL MS. I.l.35, fo. 21r.

107 J. Horn, *A Breife Discovery of the People Called Quakers* (1659); *The Quakers Proved Deceivers* (1660); *Truth's Triumph Over Deceit* (1660).

108 *Account*, ii, p. 128.

109 Lye, *Fixed Saint*, p. 28.

110 *Exact Collection*, p. 150.

111 Berkenhead, *Cabala*, pp. 3, 6, 20, 23, 25; Lloyd, *Cabala*, p. 56; R. L'Estrange, *Toleration Discuss'd* (1663), p. 28.

112 *England's Remembrancer*, pp. 95–6, 104.

113 Alleine, *Godly Man's Portion*, p. 29.

114 G. Eubanke, *A Farewell Sermon Preached* (1663), p. 25.

115 *Exact Collection*, p. 110.

116 Miller, *After the Civil Wars*, p. 75; *England's Remembrancer*, pp. 338–9.

117 *Third Volume*, p. 4; see also p. 11.

118 *Compleat Collection*, sig. Hhhh2, Hhhh; I Corinthians 10:14; Watson, *Pastor's Love Expressed*, p. 15.

119 *Second and Last Collection*, pp. 153, 158; Newcomen, *Ultimum Vale*, p. 41.

120 Lye's second sermon, in *Compleat Collection*, sig. [Z3]. The phrase does not appear in the version of the sermon published as Lye, *Fixed Saint*.

121 Hill, *English Bible*, pp. 297, 322.

122 Miller, *After the Civil Wars*, p. 118; J. Miller, *Popery and Politics in England 1660–1688* (Cambridge, 1973), pp. 9–12.

123 P. Lake, 'Anti-popery: the structure of a prejudice', in R. Cust and A. Hughes (eds), *The English Civil War* (1997), p. 187.

124 Browning, *Documents*, p. 63.

125 E.g., Moore, in *England's Remembrancer*, p. 413; Lye, *Fixed Saint*, pp. 3, 5, 15; Slater, in *Exact Collection*, p. 132; Seaman, in *Second and Last Collection*, p. 12.

126 Bates, *Peace-Maker*, p. 18. See also Lye, *Fixed Saint*, p. 18.

127 E.g., A. Bury, *The Bow* (1662), pp. 25–6.

128 Miller, *After the Civil Wars*, p. 133.

129 T. Harris, *Restoration: Charles II and His Kingdoms 1660–1685* (2005), p. 28.

130 Greaves, *Deliver Us from Evil*, pp. 9–10.

131 *Exact Collection*, p. 135.

132 DWL I.h.35, fo. 19r.

133 Fairclough, *Pastor's Legacy*, p. 140.

134 Alleine, *Godly Man's Portion*, p. 174. Cf. Thomas Ford (Bodl. Rawl. MSS E93, fo. 13), John Barrett and Thomas Bladon (*England's Remembrancer*, pp. 66, 287–8).

135 Lamb, *Royal Presence*, sig. A2.

136 Porter, *Life of John Hieron*, p. 14; Newcombe, *Diary*, p. 120; *Account*, ii, p. 214.

137 Bodl. Tanner MS 48, fo. 48 (letter from Seth Ward to Gilbert Sheldon, 27 September 1662).

138 Atkins, *God of Love and Peace*, p. 5; *Account*, ii, pp. 215–16. Evidence of local hostility is also evident in the texts of Newcomen, *Ultimum Vale*, p. 73; Lye, *Fixed Saint*, p. 16.

139 *CR*, s.v.

140 *Ibid.*

141 Heywood, *Life of John Angier*, p. 128.

142 *Compleat Collection*, sig. T2.

143 *Exact Collection*, p. 113.

144 Calamy, *Master Edmund Calamy's Leading Case*, pp. 12, 16.

145 W. Harris, *Some Memoirs of the Life and Character of Thomas Manton* (1725), pp. 33–6.

146 Keeble, *Literary Culture*, p. 144; *CR*, s.v.

147 Bosher, *Restoration Settlement*, p. 152; Green, *Re-establishment*, pp. 16–20, 85, 163; Keeble, *Literary Culture*, p. 144; Hill, *English Bible*, p. 244.

148 Eubanke, *A Farewell Sermon Preached*, frontispiece; Swinnock, *The Pastors Farewell*, sig. A2.

149 *England's Remembrancer*, p. 42; Alleine, *Godly Man's Portion*, p. 81.

150 Bosher, *Restoration Settlement*, pp. 267–8; J. Cliffe, *Puritans in Conflict* (1988) p. 191; Cragg, *From Puritanism to the Age of Reason*, pp. 156–60. Keeble, *Literary Culture*, p. 187.

151 E.g., Bodl. MSS Add. c 302, fo. 26.

152 E.g., *The Intelligencer*, 3 (14 September 1663), p. 23; R. L'Estrange, *Considerations and Proposals* (1663), sig. [A3v-A4]; Assheton, *Evangelium Armatum*, sig. [A3v].

153 *Third Volume*, p. 72.

154 Jenkyn, *Burning Yet Un-consumed Bush*, pp. 7, 8.

155 *England's Remembrancer*, pp. 293–4.

156 Lye, *Fixed Saint*, p. 4.

157 Lake, 'Defining Puritanism – again?', p. 18.

158 Miller, *After the Civil Wars*, pp. 74–5.

159 Hopper, 'Farnley Wood plot', pp. 290–1.

160 Green, *Re-establishment*, p. 156; Pepys, *Diary*, iii, p. 210.

161 Bodl. Rawl. MS 109, fo. 87, quoted in Bosher, *Restoration Settlement*, pp. 266–7.

162 Hyde, *Life*, i, p. 571; *CSPV 1661–64*, p. 185; Bodl. Carte MSS 47, fos 381v, 365v, quoted in Greaves, *Deliver Us from Evil*, p. 103.

163 *England's Remembrancer*, p. 381.

164 Fairclough, *Pastor's Legacy*, p. 94.

165 Alleine, *Godly Man's Portion*, p. 144.

166 This image, taken from Acts 20:28, appears in the sermons of Bladon and Whitlock, in *England's Remembrancer*, pp. 6, 289; Swinnock, *The Pastor's Farewel*, p. 4; Thorne, *Saint's Great Duty*, p. 40; Collins, in *Exact Collection*, p. 368; Beerman, in *Compleat Collection*, sig. Qq4; Newcomen, *Ultimum Vale*, p. 6.

167 *England's Remembrancer*, p. 21.

168 *Ibid.*, p. 372.

169 Thorne, *Saint's Great Duty*, p. 4.

170 Bodl. Rawl. MSS E93, fo. 42.

171 Hancock, *Pastor's Last Legacy*, sig. C1.

172 Spufford, 'The importance of religion in the 16th and 17th century', in Spufford, *World of Rural Dissenters*, p. 1; see also E. Duffy, 'The godly and the multitude in Stuart England', *Seventeenth Century*, I, 1 (1986) pp. 31–49.

173 Lamb, *Royal Presence*, sig. B, [C3v]. Webster, *Godly Clergy*, p. 105, comments on the ambivalence of gender identity in sermons.

174 *England's Remembrancer*, p. 394; I John 2:15; Philippians 3:18.

175 *England's Remembrancer*, p. 287.

176 E.g., Richard Baxter, in *Exact Collection*, p. 171.

177 *Ibid.*, pp. 310–11; *England's Remembrancer*, p. 448.

178 *Second and Last Collection*, p. 121.

179 *England's Remembrancer*, p. 391.

180 Thorne, *Saint's Great Duty* p. 47.

181 Lye, *Fixed Saint*, p. 16.

182 Alleine, *Godly Man's Portion*, pp. 67–9, 71, 161. See also Newcomen, *Ultimum Vale*, p. 73.

183 Fairclough, *Pastor's Legacy*.

184 *Exact Collection*, p. 150.

185 Lye, *Fixed Saint*, p. 6. See also Thorne, *Saint's Great Duty*, p. 40.

186 Jenkyn, *Burning Yet Un-consumed Bush*, pp. 7, 35; Proverbs 12:26.

187 Atkins, *God of Love and Peace*, pp. 18, 19–21.

188 *England's Remembrancer*, pp. 38–9.

189 Jenkyn, *Burning Yet Un-consumed Bush*, p. 32.

190 Stevenson, 'The social and economic status of post-Restoration dissenters' in Spufford, *World of Rural Dissenters*, pp. 360–1, and P. Collinson, 'Critical conclusion', in Spufford, p. 391; For older ideas, see Collinson, *Religion of Protestants*, p. 268; C. Hill, *Society and Puritanism in Pre-Revolutionary England* (1991), p. 491.

191 DWL *Baxter Letters*, 5. 179, quoted in C. Fell Smith, 'The Essex Newcomens', *Essex Review*, 2 (1893) pp. 37–8.

192 Bosher, *Restoration Settlement*, pp. 164–5; Green, *Re-establishment*, pp. 42, 186, 188; *Account*, ii, pp. 215–16.

193 Lake, 'Anti-popery', p. 182.

194 C. Durston and J. Eales (eds), *The Culture of English Puritanism 1560–1700* (1996), pp. 16, 20, 31.

Chapter 2

Preaching, audience and authority

The 'matter of the ministry', as Thomas Horton described it, exercised the minds both of preachers and the Restoration establishment.[1] In 1661, Cavalier politicians framing the Treason Act had publicly laid the blame for the late rebellion 'in very great measure' upon seditious preaching.[2] Perversely, instead of neutering the pulpits, the Act of Uniformity served to emphasise the continuing centrality of preaching in public debate.

Most of the individuals the Cavalier-Anglicans described as Presbyterians detested extremist preaching, but would find that the authorities had a rather broader definition of extremism. Despite having ejected hundreds of radicals from the Church by the Act for Confirming and Restoring of Ministers (1660), it was a source of anxiety to Cavalier-Anglicans that many celebrated Puritan preachers remained in their livings; men whose opinions continued to find a ready public and whose past sermons had damaged the royalist cause. Circumstances had bestowed preachers with more than the task of purveying the Gospel and imparting moral advice: they were at the same time potential spokesmen for Authority, and potential figureheads of resistance to it. As the principal objective of the Act of Uniformity was to bring the pulpits of the state Church under state control, the farewell sermons, by their very existence, could hardly fail to register as an exposition of political as well as religious dissent.

Preaching was thus of enormous contemporary significance even before the farewell sermons began to appear in print, and impinged on the national consciousness ever more intensely as Bartholomew's Day approached. This chapter will consider how these self-conscious performances were planned and orchestrated, and what the texts reveal about the relationships between the Bartholomean preachers and their various audiences. As the content and delivery of sermons were manifestly affected by external political pressures, the chapter will examine what Michael Braddick, John Walter and others have termed the 'negotiation of power'.[3] It will be seen that parliamentary legislation and political action at local and national level impinged on the minds and actions of the nonconformist ministers, and helped shape the character of the farewell sermons.

I

One of the more unpleasant prospects Richard Alleine contemplated in his valediction was the fate of a godly people bereft of the benefit of preaching. '*Faith comes by Hearing*', Alleine declared, '*and how shall they hear without a Preacher?*'[4] This belief led him to conclude that the dearth of godly public ministry after the Great Ejection would not be redressed merely by private Bible-study.[5] John Crompton worried that private prayer could not maintain the sense of unity and power fostered by public assembly.[6] The largest proportion of scriptural citations in the published farewell sermons were taken from the Pauline epistles, not only because the nonconformists found in Paul's experience of persecution an insight into their own predicament, but also because the epistles emphasised the primacy of preaching.

The inclination of English Protestants to place their religion in the pulpit rather than on the altar was still noticeable in the late seventeenth century.[7] However, preaching was never the exclusive domain of Puritans; many conformists also valued the pulpit highly, to the chagrin of Anglican clerics, who complained of an unsophisticated laity who 'thought of going to church only to hear a sermon'.[8]

The revivified emphasis on liturgical worship represented by the revised Book of Common Prayer may not, therefore, have met with universal enthusiasm in a society which retained an appetite for sermons. Just as Margaret Spufford has noted, 'religion was "news", a matter for rowdy argument, emotional involvement, and anxiety, just as in extreme cases, it was dangerous', it is equally apparent that the catalyst for this intense public interest was the pulpit.[9] Far from losing its potency after the Restoration, preaching became, in Tony Claydon's words, a 'vital medium of political debate', with the consequence that control of the medium became a political imperative.[10] Edmund Calamy might have predicted that a sermon illegally delivered from his old pulpit on 28 December 1662 would result in imprisonment as well as public acclaim.

The popularity of preaching presented Puritan ministers with something of a conundrum, in that they frequently found themselves facing large audiences at the same time as they sought to portray the godly as a small and beleaguered elect. The paradox became acute during Black Bartholomew, although William Jenkyn argued that his huge congregation was 'but a handful in comparison of what are drinking in Alehouses, and whoring, and walking in the field'.[11] However, despite Jenkyn's gloomy assessment, popular preachers regularly drew more spectators than bear-pits or theatres. Gadding to hear a good preacher remained fashionable, but given that it invariably underlined the popularity of Puritan rather than Anglican exposition this was a source of anxiety to the bishops.[12] Such nervousness was evident in reports reaching the Privy Council, which, following the strong Presbyterian showing in the elections of March 1661, was disquieted to hear that well over 2,000 Londoners had gathered to hear Mr Graffen preach against bishops, that Crofton had 'the greatest auditory in London', and that Lazarus Seaman was 'mightily followed'.[13] In contrast, on 29 May 1663 – at a time when printed copies of the farewell sermons were circulating in their thousands – Samuel Pepys would note after a quick tour of the capital that some services held to commemorate Charles II's nativity and restoration had attracted 'hardly ten people in the whole church, and those poor people'. This was in marked contrast to August 1662, when he had observed William Bates deliver two farewell sermons to packed congregations.[14] The texts of other valedictions bear out Pepys' experience: John Collins and Edward Hancock both noted large congregations from their pulpits, whilst William Jenkyn's editor described such a great gathering at Christ Church, London, that many people were unable to hear.[15] The authorities deduced from the 'extraordinary concourse of people' who had witnessed Calamy's sermon on 28 December 1662 that it had been premeditated, surmising that the laity would not have appeared in such numbers otherwise.[16] That church attendance during the Uniformity crisis was significantly higher than normal is suggested by a wistful observation found in John Crodacot's farewell sermon, probably given at St Sepulchre's in London: 'Now indeed we cannot but observe, and approve, of your flocking to the Lords Ordinances, as Doves to the holes of a window; but did you do so some moneths ago?'[17]

Although the precise numbers of listeners who heard the farewell sermons during the period of Black Bartholomew will remain a matter of conjecture, it is reasonable to propose that most of the 936 Bartholomeans listed in *Calamy Revised* delivered at least one farewell sermon. Many Bartholomeans are known to have given more, whilst a number of ministers who would survive the purge gave valedictions in anticipation of ejection. On 17 August, therefore (the last Sunday on which the nonconformist ministers could legally preach) it is conceivable that something in the order of one thousand farewell sermons were delivered across the nation. Thomas Lye professed to know of thousands of congregations that were at that moment 'yet mingling tears with us, and especially as I hear in the *West* of *England*'.[18] Even small churches such as that of Boxted in Essex (where the incumbent Nathaniel Carr was ejected) could comfortably have accommodated a standing audience of several hundred people. The grander churches in nearby Colchester

– let alone those in London or Bristol – were considerably larger. Matthew Newcomen's predecessor in Dedham, John Rogers, had been known to attract as many as 1,200 people to his weekly Tuesday lecture, a figure which Newcomen, scarcely less renowned, was regularly able to match.[19] Given that the nonconformist population in 1662 probably amounted to well in excess of 300,000 people, it seems reasonable to suggest that at least this number, and in all likelihood considerably more, flocked to see the Bartholomeans' final performances. The farewell sermons of 1662, delivered within a narrow timeframe and all carrying the message of nonconformity, were therefore a powerful means of mass communication.

The political authorities were well aware that sermons given to mark a particularly poignant event could reach a large audience. Because of this, early modern governments had often treated such preaching, unless officially sanctioned, as a potential threat to the state. The significance of such discourse was widely understood not least because preachers of all persuasions had recourse to the same images and signifiers – many of which had acquired political currency during the Civil Wars. Thus, just as royalist and parliamentarian preachers had employed a similar structure and rhetoric to deliver mutually antagonistic but nonetheless mutually comprehensible messages in the 1640s, so, twenty years on, attacks on Presbyterians in Anglican sermons delivered to commemorate 30 January and 29 May shared a language of metaphor and scriptural interpretation with their intended victims. Aside from this, two episodes in particular during the Interregnum had set a precedent for the politicised farewell sermons of 1662. In 1651 a considerable number of Presbyterians – including many future Bartholomeans – had been suspended from their livings for refusing to endorse the Engagement. Thomas Lye, preaching his final sermon in August 1662, found it ironic that he had faced a similar situation precisely eleven years earlier, and had preached a farewell sermon on that occasion.[20] Similarly, in 1655, in the weeks leading up to 30 December, many future Anglican clerics delivered emotive valedictions to protest at the Cromwellian authorities' decision to ban the Book of Common Prayer. Evelyn, for example, recorded that he went to St Gregory's to hear Dr Wilde preach the funeral sermon of preaching.[21] However, apart from the furore surrounding Christopher Love's execution, these earlier politicised sermons appear to have caused far less problems for the authorities of the day than those delivered during Black Bartholomew. Firstly, a far greater number of clergy were threatened with ejection as a result of the Act of Uniformity than had been the case in either 1651 or 1655; secondly, the Bartholomeans' plight attracted far more publicity, and threatened far more serious consequences. Thus, in August 1662 preaching was firmly at the centre of the political stage.

The other sense in which the farewell sermons were 'on the stage' lay in the fact that most of the preachers involved were trained and experienced in rhetoric and gesticulation. But although their exposition was carefully marshalled and delivered with the expertise of a professional thespian, it is clear that preachers sincerely believed that the Word was transmitted all more effectively for a good performance. The events of Black Bartholomew made several individuals even more acutely aware of the theatricality of their profession. Just as Edward Hancock mused that he and his colleagues were 'but seeming Actors in a play in this world', so Robert Porter confided that 'It may be some of us are possessed with so dumb a Devil, that when we are off the stage, and have lost our set and stated Pulpit-work, we shall do little in occasional work [*viz.*] Preaching, Converse and Conversation.'[22]

References in the farewell sermons of Joseph Caryl and Matthew Newcomen indicate that the crowd-pleasing performances of the 'thundering preacher' remained popular with Restoration audiences.[23] Whereas it has been argued that the antics of radical demagogues during the civil wars and Interregnum had rendered such theatrics increasingly distasteful to the gentry, such exposition was still in evidence in 1662.[24] Thomas Wadsworth, for example, appears to have enlivened his valediction by using first-person characters, delivering an impression of God castigating London for killing his prophets and casting them into prison.[25] But, as the nonconformist clergy's dependence on their gentrified patrons must have increased after their ejection, it would have been natural for ministers to attend ever more closely to the sensitivities of their benefactors. Dramatic flourishes and deafening roars that had worked well in the expansive space of a public church would become less appropriate in the intimate and confined surroundings of a private house. There is good reason to propose, therefore, that the Bartholomean sermons not only heralded the birth of organised nonconformity, but also the eclipse of charismatic preaching.

Contemporary jibes about 'sweaty' Puritan preaching, meanwhile, possessed a kernel of truth; some preachers exerted themselves so much that they concluded their sermons drenched in perspiration.[26] Thomas Bladon told his congregation at the end of his farewell sermon that he had exhausted himself in delivering it, but asked for leave to continue a little longer.[27] A waspish detractor alleged that Thomas Lye had wept for a quarter of an hour at the end of his valediction, whilst Thomas Case had been encouraged by Bartholomean colleagues to 'cry two hours together' at St Giles-in-the-Fields.[28] Lye's own editor reported that the minister ended his farewell sermon with 'a weeping epilogue'.[29] Thomas Jollie, a Bartholomean from Lancashire, who reputedly never failed to soak two handkerchiefs during a sermon, believed in later years that such copious weeping had affected his eyesight.[30] Displays of extreme emotion seem to have been commonplace, judging from Thomas Horton's funeral sermon for James Nalton:

> It was the saying of one, that a good man is full of tears; so this good man was full of tears, not affected, but very real, and hearty, drawn from the fullness of his Spirit, as the Apostle *Paul* saith, he served the Lord in much humility and many tears.[31]

On many other occasions preachers demonstrated hot emotion. John Galpin's farewell sermon rose to a crescendo of emotional pressure when comparing the spawn of Satan with a child of God.[32] However, on the whole, the printed farewell sermons were notable for their emotional symmetry. By positing the picture of a bad minister who pulled down more than he built up, John Crodacot implied that a good sermon maintained a balance between rebuke and encouragement, 'quickening' Christian devotion by a symbiosis of fear and love.[33] Most Puritan preachers sought to deliver a quickening performance: Richard Baxter would psyche himself up before a sermon rather like an athlete preparing for a race – a sporting analogy expounded in Thomas Manton's valediction.[34] Henry Newcombe, after repeatedly describing in his diary how he had prepared himself for his weekly encounters with his public, dejectedly recorded just two weeks after his ejection that 'I was somewhat afflicted when the time came that I use[d] to go up to my study and prepare for the public, and now had not that work to do.'[35]

Sometimes 'quickening' the audience involved breathtaking juxtapositions; Thomas Lye avowed that he would believe that saints could intercede with God 'when I believe the *Whore* of *Babylon* to be *Christs Spouse*'.[36] However, in this, as in so many other aspects, no Bartholomean was completely alike. William Beerman exhibited almost total detachment throughout his last sermon, concealing his own emotion by substituting third-hand descriptions of Paul's feelings at parting from his flock.[37] It is hard to imagine Beerman indulging in the kind of theatrical role-playing that had moved other preachers to replicate the roars and screams of souls in Hell.

Unfriendly critics sometimes derided the 'nasal accents and strange delivery' of Puritan preachers (a notion perpetuated by the historians Mitchell and Cragg), but this does not appear to have been a complaint levelled at the most notable preachers.[38] The Anglican hagiographer John Walker was particularly eager to elicit and encourage unsympathetic accounts of Puritan demeanour, whilst his rival Calamy praised the 'natural and unaffected voices of Dr Bates and Dr Galpin'.[39] Baxter advocated passion, but was opposed to 'indecent' expressions and gestures whilst preaching.[40] Thomas Horton outlined the balance required between emotion and sobriety:

> Now as the matter of the Ministry must be powerful, so the expressions must be powerful; there should be suitableness of expression to the matter,

i.e. with gravity, sobriety, affection, &c. Strong lines make but weak preaching, and take away the efficacie; but delivering truths in the demonstration of the spirit and in power, that is most effectual: when we speak feelingly and from our hearts, it comes then (through the blessing of the Lord with it) with power.[41]

Cragg has written that Puritan preaching was characterised by its 'distinctive note of urgency', with each sermon 'regarded as a kind of moral crisis'.[42] The very real crisis in 1662 made the rhetoric of the farewell sermons particularly insistent, but did not prevent several ministers from injecting humour into their performances. George Eubanke quipped, 'That Epitaph would not become a Christians Tomb-stone, which was found Engraven upon a Misers Monument, *Here lies one against his will.*'[43] William Jenkyn advised his flock that, 'if a man takes the Picture of a man, he will not take it of his backside'.[44] A comparison of the manuscript and printed versions of Matthew Newcomen's final sermons suggest that Puritan lectures might have had more moments of levity than received wisdom would suggest. Between several grave pronouncements, Newcomen repeatedly used humour to underline his argument. After warning the congregation against the deadly peril of forgetfulness, he softened his tone to assure the less intellectually gifted among his listeners not to worry, because 'God will not impute thy forgetfulness to thee; for God will not require much where he hath given little.' But in case this might be mistaken for licence, Newcomen swiftly quoted Plato to note he had never heard of an old man forgetting where he had hidden his gold.[45]

Given the circumstances of ejection, it would be tempting to assume that the average Bartholomean would have acted like a condemned man and delivered an interminably long valediction from a pulpit which had, in a sense, become a public scaffold. However, all indications suggest that most farewell sermons were of normal duration for the times. Whereas Cragg has opined that sermons often lasted two hours or more, clues in the text of several Restoration sermons, not least those of Black Bartholomew, suggest that it was customary to preach for about an hour, often timed by an hour-glass displayed prominently in the pulpit.[46] George Eubanke described his farewell sermon as '*this hours discourse*', as did William Jenkyn, whilst John Clark stated near the end of his valediction, 'Well, my Glass is run, my time is short, and I have but a few more words to speak to you: I am now, for ought I know, preaching my last Sermon.'[47] Several farewell sermons, however, did stray over their planned time; Thomas Case's valediction being one which lasted over two hours.[48] But other Bartholomeans who exceeded their usual limit asked their congregations for forbearance. John Galpin of Ash Priors in Somerset, pleaded the exceptional circumstances of Black Bartholomew for exceeding his normal duration, and asked for 'leave to trespass a little more upon your patience, seeing this is like to be the last opportunity that I shall have to speak to you from this place'.[49] Daniel Bull offered a similar apology, infused with humour:

> It may be I have been too long already; but God knows that it may be the last time that I may trespass in this kind; and I have the Apostles example, who preached at *Troas* till midnight: but I promise to have done in a great deal less time.[50]

Some farewell sermons appear to have been meticulously prepared whilst others were hurriedly assembled. Ministers who found themselves unexpectedly threatened with ejection by local authorities well before 24 August were often forced to adapt sermons that they had to hand. Others may have relied on instincts honed by years of training to produce an extempore lecture. Such experience, his testimony would have us believe, enabled Edmund Calamy to deliver a full sermon at a moment's notice when he decided on the spur of the moment to reoccupy his old pulpit on 28 December.

We have already seen that ministers such as Richard Fairclough habitually prepared two or three sermons in the course of a normal working week. As the Act of Uniformity passed through Parliament on 19 May 1662 (receiving the royal assent on 29 July), the fifteen weeks leading up to Bartholomew's Day would have given most ministers ample time to prepare their response. Richard Baxter made up his mind within days, and preached publicly for the last time on 25 May. He did this, he later wrote, because a clause in the Act of Uniformity required itinerant lecturers (as he himself had become) to cease preaching immediately. Baxter wished to advertise that he intended to obey the authorities in all that was lawful, but at the same time broadcast his nonconformity well in advance of Bartholomew-tide in order to encourage others who were minded to dissent.[51]

Many who shared Baxter's foresight used their remaining weeks to construct a series of farewell sermons devoted to casuistry and moral advice. Some predicated their series on a single text, such as Mr Creswick, a clergyman of Hampshire, who 'discoursed through four successive services on the text, *And took joyfully the spoiling of your goods, knowing in yourselves that ye have in Heaven a better and enduring Substance*'.[52] Although in most cases only one or two of their farewell sermons have survived in print, many published Bartholomeans repeatedly referred back to points they had made in previous sermons, in terms which indicate that these were part of an interconnected valedictory series.[53] John Whitlock, who had initiated a series of lectures some weeks before Bartholomew's Day, found himself having to improvise his concluding address when his ministry was arbitrarily curtailed on 6 July.[54]

The length of some valedictory series are known from the full titles of published pamphlets – for example, Joseph Cooper's *The Dead Witness Yet*

Speaking to His Living Friends (1663) was declared on its frontispiece to be an abridgement of a series of eight farewell sermons, whilst Richard Fairclough's *A Pastor's Legacy to His Beloved People* (1663) was described as the substance of fourteen sermons. Fairclough's series of sermons (which were curtailed when he was ejected by the local authorities before Bartholomew's Day) were successively targeted at various sections of society, pronouncing in turn upon 'the poor and ignorant', 'the rich and worldly', 'the furiously voluptuous', 'the proud and contentious', 'young people', 'old people', 'the enlightened and convinced', 'the hypocritical and deceived', and, of course, the godly. Like many other Bartholomeans, Fairclough constantly reiterated ground covered in past sermons to reinforce points made in later ones, emphasising that all should be viewed as parts of a whole.[55] In this, as in many other aspects, there are close similarities between certain passages in Fairclough's text and that of his near neighbour Edward Hancock. Although only the last of Hancock's works has survived in print, it is clear from his text that he had also delivered a series of farewell sermons which ran over two months, during which he, like Fairclough, had spoken to 'the several sorts of people in my Congregation, and to shew unto every one his duty, and how each particular Man and Woman ought to behave themselves both towards God and Man'.[56] All of which adds to the impression that the two ministers had collaborated closely over a considerable period. Such evidence of coordinated valedictory programmes, as opposed to the coordination merely of individual sermons, suggests that some nonconformist networks were capable of complex advance planning.

The existence of several series of lectures and closely intertwined pairs of farewell sermons (of the morning-afternoon or Sunday-midweek variety) suggest that prepared delivery invariably prevailed over extempore preaching. It was common enough for a preacher to write out notes in order to memorise them for delivery. William Perkins's *The Arte of Prophesying* – a book which went through a number of editions after its first appearance in 1592 and still exerted a residual influence in the 1660s – recommended preparing and polishing the discourse before memorising it for delivery. It has been claimed that this form of sermon became characteristic of nonconformist preaching.[57] Palmer, in his preface to *The Nonconformists' Memorial*, refers to the 'memoriter' preaching of 'the outed clergy of the black Bartholomew-tide'.[58] Richard Baxter, for one, usually wrote his sermons in their entirety, before reading them aloud in a manner rather redolent of a modern day conference paper.[59] But extensive preparation did not preclude flexibility: George Eubanke chided himself for digressing during his final lecture.[60] John Clark mentioned that although preparation was important, he was nevertheless reorganising his last sermon as he spoke. Perhaps because of this, he was later necessitated to gloss over several issues which he had clearly intended to discuss.[61]

John Galpin betrayed similar time pressures when he indicated in his fare-well sermon that he had selected a particular observation to enlarge upon, 'not having time and liberty to insist on them all'.[62]

Most Bartholomeans, even the undistinguished and obscure, were experienced writers and performers as a result of their academic training. The sermons could incorporate spontaneity, flexibility and theatrical verve, but they were nevertheless closely scripted. Bartholomean pronouncements of a religious or political nature were therefore significant not least because they were widely assumed to be the result of careful deliberation. In the same way, the rhetorical style that conveyed these pronouncements was taken seriously because it was not deployed to impress so much as to convert.

Discussion of Puritan preaching during much of the twentieth century was predicated on the notion of the so-called 'plain style' of exposition – a description made fashionable by W. F. Mitchell – which subsequently led scholars such as J. F. Wilson to claim that a sharp dichotomy existed between 'witty' court preaching and a mechanistic Puritan 'plain style'. Mary Morrissey, however, has castigated the 'methodological laziness' of 'this easy association of styles and preaching philosophies', arguing that the notion of a 'plain style' has hampered the study of preaching rhetoric. Bremer and Rydell have likewise suggested that the pervasive influence of the 'plain style' theory has encouraged historians to discount the power and artfulness of the Puritan sermon.[63] However, by the time these criticisms had been voiced, Lois Potter and others had already commented on the difficulty of discerning between supposed 'royalist' and 'Puritan' styles, and were beginning instead to search for a differentiation along the lines of 'emotional polarities'.[64] A comparison of the Bartholomean farewell sermons with their contemporary Anglican counterparts bears out Potter's findings, revealing far more similarities than differences in rhetorical structure, and indicating that if a 'plain style' did exist, it was not inherently or exclusively Puritan.

Although the notion of 'plain style' has now largely fallen from favour, there remains a tendency to regard William Perkins's *Arte of Prophecying* as the template for Puritan exposition. The influence of Perkins's manual has consequently been heavily emphasised in scholarly studies, despite the fact that his directions regarding the management of style, voice and gesture, and his insistence that Scripture should not be defiled by human innovation, did little more than to confirm accepted practice. Perkins was mentioned in some farewell sermons, but certainly not as often as authors such as Thomas Hooker. Restoration preachers were clearly familiar with Perkins's manual, but the Bartholomean sermons more closely reflect the guidelines laid down in the *Directory for the Publique Worship of God* (1644), which had been republished in 1660. Perkins had recommended that terms of art, and Greek and Latin phrases should not be used in sermons because they distracted and hindered the understanding of listeners.[65] However, almost all the published Bartholomean sermons feature passages of Greek and Latin, and the structure of the texts indicates that these passages were delivered from the pulpit rather than added retrospectively. Indeed, Richard Alleine predicted that the nonconformist ministers' knowledge of the Classics would be sorely missed by their congregations, and proceeded to explicate a particularly problematical passage of Greek to prove that the Scriptures were hard to understand without a guide.[66] Similarly, Perkins had urged preachers to eschew 'the telling of tales and all profane and ridiculous speeches'.[67] But in addition to the examples of humour described earlier, folklore, homely analogies and phrases appear in almost every farewell sermon.[68]

The need to communicate effectively and intelligibly was argued by many writers other than Perkins. In 1646 John Wilkins had called for exegesis to be 'plain & naturall, not being darkened with the affectation of Scholasticall harshnesse, or Rhetoricall flourishes'.[69] Most Bartholomean preachers concurred with these sentiments; they were, as Perkins had been, opposed to ostentation, but not to eloquence or drama. William Bates deprecated 'the affectation of wit and flaunting eloquence', but praised his fellow Bartholomeans Manton, Baxter and Jacombe for their 'natural and free, clear and eloquent, quick and purposeful' style.[70] Richard Baxter's comments on preaching in his book the *Reformed Pastor* indicate that matter was more important to him than manner. But his call for men to speak 'so as to be understood' was a call for plain speaking, rather than a plain style.[71] George Eubanke wrote in his preface to *A Farewell Sermon Preached at Great Ayton* that he expected criticism for failing to include flourishes of rhetoric:

> *I consider'd my place, and Calling, which prompted me, to Act not the Orator in the Schooles, but as Preacher in the Church; and that God sent me not to Court, but to Convert; not to catch mens Ears, but their Souls: And therefore I was more studious of a sanctified than a silver Tongue, whereby I might accommodate you with Material, rather than Ornamental advantages.*[72]

However, the fact that Eubanke believed he might be criticised for a lack of rhetorical pizzazz suggests that he did place some value on such gestures, and hard on the heels of this disavowal of ostentation came eloquent descriptions of Seneca's writing, with tales of Caesar's guests shooting arrows at Jupiter only for the arrows to fall back to earth, mortally wounding them (Eubanke's moral being that Christians should not criticise God).[73] Thomas Lye supported his argument by presenting anecdotes from the life of Alexander the Great, Matthew Mead alluded to Homer's *Iliad*, Thomas Watson quoted Virgil, whilst George Swinnock cited a succession of classical authors including Euripides, Pliny and Seneca.[74] Although Adam Fox has recently suggested that Protestant preaching discouraged the telling of tales and the recounting of historical anecdotes such as the Golden Legend, these devices were still in evidence in the summer of 1662: at least two Bartholomeans, John Collins and John Hieron, referred to the wizard Simon Magus in terms which make it clear that the Golden Legend remained in common currency.[75] It might be expected that the farewell sermons would contain echoes of their authors' classical education at Oxford or Cambridge. W. F. Mitchell's opinion that the sermon was 'a highly finished rhetorical product' still holds true, but whether there was a distinctly Puritan genus is another matter.[76] Using Perkins' manual as his main inspiration, Mitchell argued that the paradigmatic Puritan sermon reduced the sermon into two parts: resolution and application. Perkins advised that the resolution be divided into doctrines, extracted from the text to and expounded in nine arguments: causes, effects, subjects, adjuncts, dissentaries, comparisons, names, distribution and definition. The application, meanwhile, was divided into four uses: mental application of doctrine (information to inform judgement), regardation (to guard against error), the first practical application (moral instruction) and the second practical application (to 'quicken', exhort and encourage and to detect and arrest misapprehensions and back-sliding). Mitchell noted differences of opinion between Puritan authorities over the appropriate proportion of the sermon to be devoted to 'doctrines' and 'uses', but believed doctrine to be pre-eminent.[77] G. R. Cragg noted that when the preacher introduced his theme it was in the form of a series of sub-headings, in the manner of a movie trailer, substantiated by a three-point structure of doctrine, explication and application. The use or application was further subdivided into three parts: instruction, comfort and exhortation.[78] However, a comparison between the Bartholomean oeuvre and contemporaneous Anglican sermons does not show a disparity in rhetorical structure so much as a greater readiness to expose that structure to the listener. In other words, whereas Anglican sermons customarily presented a seamless monologue, Puritan sermons proceeded painstakingly through successive divisions, with doctrines and uses clearly advertised. This may have been less apparent in oral delivery than on the printed page, but the readiness of Bartholomeans to show the workings of their sermon structure is evident from the internal dynamic of their texts. Many Puritan preachers had a habit of providing a running commentary on their progression through their doctrines and uses. William Jenkyn, commencing his final valediction, outlined his structure to the congregation: 'Here I shall handle it first doctrinally according to my constant method, then come to improve it by way of Application.'[79] Lewis Stucley announced in the middle of his exposition, that 'Having finished the Doctrinal part, my work this hour is to make application of it.'[80]

Such guidance was necessary because the rhetorical structure of the valedictions, far from being plain, was intricate and complicated. The typical farewell sermon lasted a considerable length of time, usually laced with Latin or Greek, and incorporated complex casuistry. The argument was made plain by painstaking rhetorical technique, which introduced the listener to the main scriptural text of the sermon, then explained clearly what it was to be about, and before outlining how the points were to be argued. The flow of the sermon was halted at regular intervals to allow the preacher to summarise and integrate past points, culminating in an itemised conclusion; as the editor of Thomas Watson's *A Pastor's Love* (1662) explained: '*The wisest Master Builder sees it sometime expedient to beat often upon one and the same truth, that they may nayl them not onely to the ears, but the hearts of their Auditors.*'[81]

Such pains were taken to ensure that the audience was able periodically to regain the thread of the text. Thus, Samuel Clark wrote that John Dod 'would not leave the text until he had it made plain to the meanest capacity'.[82] Similarly, before his ejection in 1660, Richard Fairclough's father, Samuel, 'sought to accommodate his expression to the capacity of his hearers, and would stoop to the weakest and lowest form of them'.[83] The *Directory for Publique Worship* charged the preacher to deliver his message painfully and plainly, 'that the meanest may understand'.[84] The ponderous delivery that often resulted sometimes taxed the patience of educated listeners, moving Samuel Pepys to write disparagingly of the dull 'Presbyterian manner' and to describe a lecture given by Thomas Jacombe at St Martin's in April 1661 as 'a lazy sermon, like a Presbyterian'.[85]

If this painstaking delivery enabled comparatively uneducated listeners to follow a complex rhetorical structure, repeated exposure to preaching and a lifelong familiarity with Biblical imagery facilitated an appreciation of the deployment of Scripture within the argument. As Scripture was the revealed Word it was unnecessary to persuade the audience of its significance. However, it was important to ensure that the preacher imparted the correct interpretation and delivered the desired message. Even the most devout Puritan preachers were not above picking and choosing sections of Scripture to suit their purpose: whilst delivering Simeon Ashe's funeral sermon, Edmund Calamy indicated that part of his main text (Isaiah 7:1) concerning the righteous man perishing was unsuitable, as Ashe, being one of the godly, was being gathered to God.[86] The way in which Scripture was presented was therefore almost as vital as the selection of verses themselves. Listeners were regularly invited to read around the actual verse cited. Christopher Hill notes this tactic in a sermon given in March 1643 by Joseph Caryl: after quoting the first part of Jeremiah 13:18, in which the prophet called on his king and queen to humble themselves, Caryl declared that he had no commission to add the remainder of the verse – which threatened that their crowns might otherwise fall.[87] In 1662 this ploy was still very evident: George Thorne, after citing Psalm 37:3, 4, 5, 7, 27 in his valediction, explained,

These words contain Advice and Counsel for the people of God, and tis considerable, either with respect to the troubles and temptations of the people of God in general; or with respect to that particular that is immediately touched on before the Text, *vers. 33*.[88]

In other words, Thorne intended his listeners to read around the verses cited, where they would find apocalyptic passages he did not dare highlight. Ralph Venning advised his flock, to 'consider a little further, as this the connexion between the Verse preceding the Text, and the Text'.[89] Thomas Jacombe in his forenoon farewell sermon cited John 8:28, but then suggested that the verse *before* the given text was significant.[90] Thomas Watson advised his listeners to study the context of his chosen text (Isaiah 3:10, 11) by reading the whole chapter.[91] In stating that he would 'look no further back to the precedent verses, than may give light to the present Text', John Hieron demonstrated an awareness that his audience would otherwise instinctively read around Scriptural references given in the sermon.[92]

Some Bartholomeans exploited such instincts, indicating a passage of Scripture but deliberately leaving it to the audience to discover the reason for the recommendation. John Crodacot having given a citation from John 12, offered no quotation or explication, but simply instructed his flock to 'read that'.[93] Philip Lamb urged his congregation to read the last chapter of II Chronicles, 'and at the 16 *verse*, and then you will see, when the wrath of *God* is like to break out upon a People without a remedy'.[94] He did not, however, quote or explicate the text of the sixteenth verse:

> But they mocked the messengers of God, and despised his words, and misused his prophets, until the wrath of the LORD arose against his people, till there was no remedy.[95]

Thomas Lye was equally adroit when lecturing those in authority, desiring them to read Luke 22:25 and Matthew 20:26, 27. He provided an explication of the verse from Matthew, but left that of Luke unexplained – very possibly because Luke 22:25–6 contrasts the inequity of kingly rule with the fraternal equality of the apostles[96] Thomas Bladon used a similar tactic, urging his congregation to read Isaiah 33:15–16 without advertising that the verses denounced oppression and promised heavenly reward for those that refused worldly inducements. Proceeding to cite James 1:22–5, Bladon left his listeners to read verse 25 by themselves:

> But whoso looketh into the perfect law of liberty, and continueth therein, he being not a forgetful hearer, but a doer of the work, this man shall be blessed in his deed.[97]

Bladons's paralipsis becomes clear when compared with the farewell sermon of Philip Lamb, who quoted James 1:25 in full, adding by way of explanation,

'Let it be the aim and intentions of our souls, when we come to hear, to turn hearing into doing.'[98]

Innocuous phrases with controversial associations featured in a number of farewell sermons: John Barrett and Thomas Ford both quoted inoffensive verses from Psalm 52, which many would instantly have recognised as the psalm which begins 'Why boasteth thou, thou man of power, that thou canst do mischief.' Ford, however, reminded the congregation that the context of the psalm concerned David's condemnation of Do'eg, the evil counsellor who had advised King Saul to slay his loyal priests.[99] Other passages of Scripture recalled the anti-royalist preaching of the 1640s, and it is plain that the notoriety of certain passages had lingered in the collective memory: Robert Porter did not need to explain the significance of his words when emphasising his distaste of separation from the Church, 'If I may not call you to the Mountain of the Lord, I will not say, *To your Tents, O Israel.*'[100] This, of course, was the verse that had echoed around London just before the outbreak of civil war in 1642.

It is entirely possible that many citations were as innocuous as they appeared; but Richard Baxter later admitted that passages of Scripture *had* been selected to be used against the times.[101] The manipulation of Scripture to convey politically contentious messages was clearly a response to increasing state censorship. In order to circumvent such censorship, the Bartholomeans needed to be confident that their coded messages would be received and understood by their audience.

II

The difficulty of reconstructing a lost acoustic world has often led to the assumption that Puritan preachers habitually overestimated the intellectual capacities of their hearers.[102] This, however, would underestimate the diligence of ministers who made it their business to know their parishioners and took great pains to ensure that their sermons were heard and received. The early modern sermon was designed to transmit on a variety of wavelengths in order to be understood by the widest possible audience; but whilst this was a response to the obvious disparities of the educational system, it would be unwise to dismiss the unlettered population as ill-informed simpletons. Margaret Spufford has found a widespread familiarity with religious discourse at all levels of the rural community, just as John Walter has noted a sophisticated knowledge of the law among early modern rioters.[103] The fact that Richard Baxter felt able to construct complex arguments abstracted from Scripture at the same time as he desired preachers to 'speak so as to be understood' suggests that he was confident that the implications of his arguments and scriptural references *would* be understood by the vast majority of his audience.[104] Ministers were sensitive to the heterogeneous mix of faces that looked up at them in the pulpit. The variety in content and tone across Richard Fairclough's series of farewell sermons demonstrates that he had a range of expectations for different audiences, for the sermons he aimed at the profane were neither as complex nor so heavily laced with scripture as those intended for the godly. Thomas Wadsworth did not have such a high opinion of the congregation at St Lawrence Pountney, feeling it necessary to explain the context of a metaphor from Revelation when several other ministers did not.[105] Thomas Case, on the other hand, assumed a wide familiarity with history and current affairs as well as religious doctrine when he berated Englishmen for their failure to lay the blood of Germany, Lithuania and Piedmont to heart.[106] Other Bartholomeans assumed that their audiences were familiar with the story of the apostate Francis Spira.[107]

There is much evidence in the farewell sermons to substantiate Bremer and Rydell's assertion that 'even the least educated parishioners were very familiar with the stories of the Bible'.[108] Unlike Richard Alleine, Daniel Bull was optimistic that Bible-study, private family worship and catechism could compensate for the lack of godly preaching, commenting 'I know no more likely means than setting up the worship of God in private families.'[109] Many Bartholomeans urged their listeners to study Scripture and other good books in lieu of sermons, in case the flock fell under the hand of a blind guide.[110] Thomas Bladon advised his listeners to read the Bible every day, believing that the more they read, the more they would understand and believe. He charged householders to instruct their families and servants in Scripture.[111] Thus, whilst a significant proportion of the congregation remained illiterate, most had access to the Bible through literate acquaintances. Robert Porter acknowledged that a minister was greatly helped, 'when Masters and Parents keep that in the eyes and ears of their Families all the week, that [which] he delivers on the Lord's Day'.[112] Petitions to the county Quarter Sessions indicate how well the illiterate coped with an increasingly literate culture, and familiarity with Biblical themes is evident in songs, ballads and even in pictures on embroidered jewel boxes.[113] Familiarity came not least from listening. A regular attendant at Dedham during Matthew Newcomen's twenty-six year tenure would, by the lecturer's own estimate, have heard almost three thousand sermons.[114] Consequently, when the Bartholomeans used Scripture as a coded argument against the times, it was in the expectation that most listeners would immediately grasp the significance of their words.

Whilst some preachers, most notably Richard Fairclough, directed their final sermons to particular social strata, they invariably argued that the important divisions were not social but spiritual. As the final division between the saved and the damned was known only to God, sermons had to speak to all. Thus, even those of a Presbyterian persuasion, who had little truck with the social radicalism of the Quakers, were required to believe in the equality of all in the sight of the Lord. Thomas Bladon, inspired by I Corinthians 1:26 declared that 'God hath chosen the foolish and weak things of the world to condemn the wise and strong.'[115] Matthew Newcomen drew attention to the fact that the Old Testament had originally been in Hebrew, which all Hebrews could understand, and that the New Testament had originally been in Greek, which most could then understand. 'And why', he asked, 'doth *John* write his *Canonical Epistle* to the *Elect Lady*, and to *Gaius*, a private Christian, if Ladies and private Christians might not read Canonical Scripture?'[116] Given our current perception of the early modern congregation as one where space was organised along hierarchical lines – to the extent that pew disputes between rival families were common – and given that many Bartholomeans were beholden to patrons among the gentry, the readiness of such preachers to humble the rich and laud the poor is striking. J. F. Wilson's assertion that Puritan rhetoric and logic, in promoting the notion of an 'intellectual priesthood of all believers', challenged 'a theory of communication associated with a traditional and aristocratic society' remains relevant, especially as the Bartholomean corpus confirms that even moderate Puritans persisted with such rhetoric well into the 1660s.[117]

The farewell sermons nevertheless also frequently betray tensions between this rhetoric of equality and the physical hegemony of the pulpit. Even Thomas Lye, having asserted in his valediction that the highest officers were 'but brethren to the meanest saints', related how Paul had loved the Thessalonians as children, and how his own congregation were 'his Benjamins'.[118] Such instinctive paternalism sat uncomfortably alongside sentiments that extolled the equality and fraternity of true Protestantism. Metaphors of the Bartholomeans' civil death were repeatedly framed in terms of a dying father's legacy to his children; an image emphasised in Edmund Calamy's funeral sermon for Simeon Ashe, when he informed the bereaved congregation that they had lost their spiritual father and shepherd.[119] Such phrases echoed a certain attitude in the *Directory for Publique Worship*, which pointed out that the minister was placed 'above the common sort of Beleevers' in Scripture.[120]

At least one Bartholomean appears to have valued such hegemony: Richard Baxter demonstrated more predilection for didacticism than most, expressing in his farewell sermon his desire that people should show 'humble submissiveness to their teaching'.[121] But the elevated position of the preacher in the pulpit and the conviction that they were relaying the revealed word of God does not mean that the farewell sermons can be discounted as a simple checklist of moral instruction. Although it is possible to agree with Adam Fox that much early modern preaching was didactic, the genius of Puritan exegesis – not least because of a belief in the equality of the godly – was dialectic.[122] It is naive to assume, as Barthes does, 'the arrogant listening of a superior, the servile listening of an inferior'.[123] The attitudes of individuals brought before early modern Quarter Sessions courts argue strongly against servility, be they maimed soldiers and war widows driven by a sense of natural justice, or iconoclasts emboldened by an assumption of godliness. In contrast to the Duke of Newcastle's belief that 'the Bible in English under every weaver's and chambermaid's arm hath done much harm', and even Baxter's preferences for a submissive audience, most Bartholomean authors did not expect or desire servility.[124] Just as Thomas Lye would assert that it was not for brethren to lord it over fellow-brethren, so Matthew Newcomen assured his listeners that 'We are not Lords over your Faith, but Helpers of your joy.' Citing Matthew 23:9, Newcomen advised them to '*Call no man your Father upon Earth; for one is your Father, which is in Heaven*', as ministers were, at the most, nursing-fathers to the godly.[125]

For Joseph Moore, Christianity was experimental. The godly could not seek the Lord or maintain their vigilance against corruption if they rested in 'a blind implicit faith'. The message of Matthew 23:9, Moore contended, was that it was 'for *Romanists* to believe as the Church believes; and what it is the Church believes, they understand not'.[126] Thomas Lye reminded his congregation during his morning farewell sermon on 17 August that, 'I have indeavoured to help your joy, but not to presse your faith, to cause you to believe this or that because I believe it. If so, you might turn Papist to morrow.' 'If I must believe with an implicite faith', he reiterated in the afternoon, 'I should turn Papist tomorrow.'[127] The perception that Catholics slavishly obeyed any doctrine presented to them was in contrast to the Puritan desire to encourage their congregations actively to engage with Scripture. Thus, John Barrett warned that 'an *ignorant Protestant* may soon turn a *confident Papist*', whilst William Beerman spoke scathingly of those who were too lazy to analyse what they heard, preferring to 'take all for truth the Minister tells them'.[128] Just as Beerman urged his audience not to adulate ministers, but to 'receive the person for the Word's sake', so Thomas Brooks advised his listeners to '*Take no truths upon trust, but all upon tryall.*'[129] Such pronouncements had a bearing on the reception of ministerial replacements. John Collins invited his congregation to exercise their own judgement of his successor by referring 'all Doctrines that are offered you to believe, and all Practices that are put upon you to practice to the Scriptures, the word of God: try them there, whether they be to be retained, or to be rejected'.[130]

Godly audiences, therefore, were expected to be active participants in the process of preaching. Thomas Bladon reserved his praise for doers of God's work, not mere hearers.[131] Philip Lamb enjoined his people to 'Hasten to do all that you have heard and learned', chiding those who listened but did not act.[132] Bombarded with demands for action, and goaded by salvoes of rhetorical questions, many congregations responded in kind.

We should therefore be sceptical of accepting at face value sixteenth-century woodcuts which contrast rapt and silent Protestant congregations with noisy and chaotic Catholic ones, although this image would appear to concur with John Evelyn's observation that English religion involved 'sitting still on Sundays'.[133] It should be remembered that such woodcuts were invariably an attack on popery whilst Evelyn's *Character of England* a century later sought to satirise Puritanism. Early modern congregations were far from passive. Years of listening, note-taking, discussing and catechising had 'produced a knowledgeable and critical laity with definite ideas about preaching and preachers'.[134] Listeners were quick to express their opinions, applauding or cat-calling whenever they agreed or disagreed with a particular point being made by the preacher.[135] Parishioners could often unite to support popular pastors: Philip Lamb's flock in Beere Regis, as noted earlier, were sufficiently motivated to see his farewell sermon through to publication.[136] That the valediction was apparently published against Lamb's wishes demonstrates that ministers could sometimes find themselves being swept along by their followers. Edmund Calamy's interrogator put it to him that his appearance in Aldermanbury's pulpit on 28 December 1662 had been at the behest of his former parishioners.[137] Thomas Vincent was coerced by his flock into continuing to preach after Bartholomew's Day, and subsequently encouraged other ejected ministers to do the same.[138]

The patchy observance of annual fast days on 30 January and 29 May indicates that Restoration congregations could be resistant to politically inspired initiatives. Many Bartholomeans encouraged their followers to persist in such resistance after their departure. John Collins advised his congregation to guard themselves by banding together. Thomas Brooks, in common with many Bartholomeans, praised those that had not defiled their garments, and called upon his people to come out of Sardis, in order not to partake in her sins. John Whitlock advised his congregation in considerable detail how they could expose corrupt doctrine, making it clear that he would then expect them to resist, telling the authorities that they had not so learned Christ.[139]

Ministers such as Whitlock had long encouraged an active and critical laity, with the result that there were many instances before and after Black Bartholomew of parishioners prepared to challenge doctrinal errors or sub-standard preaching. Edward Hancock's successor in Bristol, for example, struggled long and hard against an obdurate congregation.[140] But audiences' sympathies did not always lie with the departing ministers. Unfriendly parishioners and churchwardens frequently reported clergy who failed to use the Prayer Book, or, as John Crodacot had found in 1661, for neglecting to observe Christmas Day.[141] Congregations, particularly in London, were likely to contain not only the godly thirsting for salvation, but also connoisseurs such as Pepys desiring intellectual stimulation, Cavalier-Anglican opponents, spies and irreligious gawpers seeking free entertainment. John Crompton, however, declared in his farewell sermon that the godly should not shirk from praying in such mixed company because they could thereby be seen to serve God in public.[142] The verbal and physical iconoclasm that had disrupted sermons during the preceding decades meant that neither the persons nor the performances of Restoration preachers were inviolate. In Acton, Cheshire, Edward Burghal's farewell sermon was disrupted by Quakers.[143] Preaching during the final weeks of his public ministry in Devon, Robert Atkins was challenged by a prominent member of the local gentry, who stood before the pulpit and attempted to stare him out.[144] In Essex, a local weaver was apprehended for threatening to pull Matthew Newcomen out of the pulpit and roast him alive.[145]

Unsurprisingly, therefore, early modern preachers often took account of audience behaviour and adapted their exposition accordingly.[146] The Sunday sermon, invariably lighter in tone and argumentation than the midweek lecture, was usually aimed at a wider auditory than midweek lectures, which were predicated towards the educated godly; however, the huge public interest in the impending mass ejection suggests that both Sunday and midweek congregations were heterogeneous and volatile in the summer of 1662. Consequently, although the farewell sermons were structured by reasoned casuistry they were propelled by emotion in and out of the pulpit. George Thorne, interrupted by the sobbing of his audience, quoted Pauline scripture to chide, '*What mean ye to weep, and to break my heart?*'[147] Even in private prayer, emotion had always been a prominent feature of Puritan worship. Oliver Heywood recorded that his son Eliezer 'wept much' when praying, whilst another son used 'such expostulation as I wondered at, together with lively affections, many tears'.[148] The repeated imagery of the dying preacher indicates that many Bartholomeans actively exploited such emotional investment. Edmund Calamy reminisced that Simeon Ashe had not preached to tickle the ear, but to wound the heart.[149] A Dutch tourist, William Schellinks, witnessing Robert Atkins's final sermon in Exeter, observed that it was 'a fine sermon, moving to tears his hearers, young and old'.[150] Given that this manipulation of emotion was combined with exhortations to followers to be doers rather than mere hearers of the Word, Cavalier anxieties regarding the potentiality of the farewell sermons become increasingly understandable.

Whilst the population retained a huge appetite for sermons, and the godly clearly enjoyed hearing ministers preach, the physical and psychological demands on listeners should not be underestimated. Richard Baxter warned his final public congregation that the acquisition of grace involved diligent study, unwearied labour and patience.[151] Thomas Watson assured his listeners that they could drop into Hell with ease, but that it was all uphill to Heaven.[152] It required considerable mental stamina to sit (let alone stand) and listen to lectures so long and painstaking that even the godly occasionally nodded off. Philip Lamb advised his flock that they could better keep alert and attentive if they imagined that every word was being spoken to them personally.[153] Joseph Moore, on the other hand, feared that the thirst for sermons had, in some instances, detracted from the development of an active, critical Christianity:

> I think those Christians do much wrong themselves, who spend all the day in attending upon publick prayers and hearing: I would not have you strive to hear four or five Sermons a day, unless you can take so much times besides, as is necessary to *meditate of,* and *apply* what you hear. Two or three Sermons seriously heard, and ruminated upon in secret, do more good than ten Sermons heard, without meditation.[154]

But for other Bartholomeans the failure of so many listeners to last the course of a godly sermon had materially contributed to the predicament they now found themselves in. Edmund Calamy, after reminding his congregation of the years of painstaking ministry undertaken by his predecessors and himself, castigated the weary and bored he saw before him:

> Are there not some of you have itching ears, and would fain have Preachers that would feed you with dainty phrases, and begin, not to care for a Minister that unrips your Consciences, speaks to your hearts and souls, and would force you into heaven by frighting you out of your sins? Are there not some of you, that by often hearing Sermons, are become Sermon-proof, that know how to sleep and scoff away Sermons? I should be glad to say there are but few such; but the Lord knoweth there are too many that by long preaching get little good by preaching, insomuch that I have often said it, and say it now again, There is hardly any way to raise the price of the Gospel-Ministry, but by the want of it.[155]

Richard Alleine blamed the imminent loss of so many able ministers on a lazy and inattentive people.[156] Richard Fairclough warned that 'It's true, (what one expresses) in Hell there will be great Repetition of Sermons. Sermons, here heard unprofitably, will there be heard intollerably.'[157] In the midst of such gloom, however, Alleine perceived that the Great Ejection might be God's way of stimulating action and dispelling the lethargy of the godly, for, 'When they have no *Preacher,* their empty Pulpits shall preach to them; this most smarting of Rods will have its voice. If they have no longer the Light with them, their Darkness shall instruct them.'[158] John Whitlock came to the same conclusion, declaring that 'the very silence of so many Ministers, if blessed by the Lord, may prove the most powerful and effectual Sermon to People that they have had'.[159] He hoped that the vacuum left by the departing ministers would be filled by noisy lay activity: 'Yea, Ministers silence should cause People to speak the more, and louder to God in prayer for the continuance and restoring of Ministers and Ordinances to them.'[160] In saying this, the Bartholomeans surely anticipated that such vociferous appeals to God for restitution would also reach the ears of the political authorities.

III

The Restoration establishment's aspirations for parochial preaching were essentially those that had been articulated in *Directions for Preachers* forty years earlier; namely, that preachers should concentrate on providing spiritual comfort according to approved doctrine, and should not presume to question the authority of princes nor otherwise meddle in the affairs of state. However, just as the Elizabethan and Jacobean authorities had exploited 'the unique ability of religious language to shape political action', so the Caroline regime had required parish clergy to function as state propagandists, particularly on those occasions when the prescribed homily on obedience was ordered to be preached in all churches.[161] The pulpits were therefore thoroughly politicised by the outbreak of the Civil War, even before the Westminster Assembly's *Directory for the Publique Worship of God* (1644) began actively to encourage ministers to apply Scripture to contemporary affairs rather than rest in general doctrine.[162] The 30 January and 29 May sermons after the Restoration demonstrated that such application was not confined to Puritan pulpits, and underlined the extent to which preaching had become an integral element of general political discourse. Consequently, those Bartholomeans who declared their exegesis to be concerned solely with salvation were considered disingenuous, and to be fully aware that their valedictions had political capital. Thomas Bladon admitted as much when he described how preachers could escape persecution by acquiescing to the interests of the political establishment: 'If Ministers dare, and will comply with the sinful interests of great men, and become Court-flatterers and Parasites to Kings, either to preach up or not to preach down their State-Corruptions and Wickedness, they shall have peace and protection.'[163] Temporisers (and there were many in 1662) were regarded with contempt by John Crodacot:

> What would he not do rather than he would lose his Living? Which made me think Religion to be but a fancy. Wilt thou be able to say at the great Day, Lord, it was my sad lot and portion to live under the Ministry of such a one, who tuned his Fiddle to the times of every one?[164]

For many in authority, however, preachers who refused to tune their fiddle represented a clear and present danger. In May 1661 the earl of Clarendon urged Parliament to protect the king from such individuals, having had 'frequent information of seditious sermons in the city and in the country;

they talk of introducing popery, of evil counsellors and such other old calumnies'. Preaching treason from the pulpit, Clarendon opined, 'was worse than espousing it in the marketplace'.[165] But such accusations do not appear to have been aimed at the radicals who had been purged from the Church in 1660 so much as at the moderate Puritans who had remained within. In May 1662, as the Act of Uniformity was passing through Parliament, Sir Edward Nicholas complained that Presbyterian ministers 'preached very boldly' whilst Lord Mordaunt reported that Presbyterians in his locality 'preached nothing but rebellion'.[166] The Speaker's address to introduce the Bill warned of a 'Smectymnian plot' – an unmistakable reference to clergy such as Calamy and Newcomen, two of the original authors of *Smectymnuus*.[167] In many ways, such fears were understandable: the regime was only recently restored, and Presbyterian ministers had become notorious as political schemers (ironically, largely as a result of activities in support of Charles II during the 1650s).

But in the weeks before Black Bartholomew's Day, far from attempting to allay such anxieties, many Bartholomeans exulted in the revelation that their preaching had been so powerful as to worry the authorities. Images of prison surfaced repeatedly in the farewell sermons, with frequent allusions to the incarceration of those great preachers Paul and Silas.[168] George Eubanke assured his congregation, 'Nay, though I were sure to go to Prison as soon as I come forth of the Pulpit, yea I should think all well bestowed could I but see you begin to turn this Sermon into practice.'[169] During his valediction on 19 August, Matthew Newcomen, perhaps sensitive to threats posed by psychopathic weavers as much as by state-sponsored retribution, reminded his flock of the hazards of nonconformity: 'The Martyrs surely were not soe foolish and prodigall of their lives, but they knew what they did when they suffered, some of them for such matter, as some since have counted trifles.'[170]

This was no empty rhetoric; preachers were peculiarly vulnerable to charges of sedition and were often heavily punished. The prospect of martyrdom was real, but (as will become clear) not entirely unwelcome. However, such threats prompted most Bartholomeans to choose their words carefully. One reason why the farewell sermons invariably proved circumspect in their criticism of bishops may have been because it was common knowledge that William Strode had been charged with sedition in 1661 for that very act.[171] Nevertheless, John Crodacot sailed close to the wind when he declared during his farewell sermon that '*It is no breach of the Churches place, no argument of a contentious and unquiet spirit in a Minister, to speak vilely of vile Ministers and enemies of the Churches peace.*'[172] Crodacot knew better than most the consequences of speaking against the times: between 1660 and 1662, he, Matthew Mead and Elias Pledger had all been charged with offences arising from pronouncements made in the course of their preaching.[173] Charges of sedition could arise not simply from explicit political statements, but sometimes from the selection of contentious passages of Scripture. In 1660 some ministers were arrested for preaching on the text of Hebrews 12:4, 'ye have not resisted unto blood, striving against sin'. This, however, did not deter Elias Pledger from talking of resisting unto blood in his farewell sermon. Pledger's was a calculated act of defiance, not least because, in common with many London ministers, he must have known that his preaching had been under surveillance for some time.[74]

Charles II's secretaries of state had revived the government intelligence service in 1661. Most of the Post Office staff who had served Cromwell's spy-master John Thurloe had been retained, and by the spring of 1662 were intercepting Presbyterian correspondence.[75] In the London diocese, Bishop Sheldon had his own spies, and personal experience of having participated in clandestine Anglican activity during the Interregnum. There was menace behind the courteous interview afforded Baxter on the latter's applying to preach in London early in 1662, when Baxter, complaining of false and vague accusations against his character, was assured by Sheldon 'that if they had got any particulars that would have deserved it, I should have heard particularly from him'. Of his brief tenure in London, Baxter later reminisced, 'I scarce think that I ever preached a sermon without a spy to give them his report of it.'[76] Such surveillance had an effect even on the otherwise fearless Thomas Lye, who felt it prudent to declare, 'If there be any wicked catchers here, let them know I speak nothing but what is in the mind of the Text, and would not give occasion to be a greater sufferer than I am like to be.'[77]

Some ministers were shadowed long after their ejection, as demonstrated by the account of a London informer who reported that 'Mr Hancock of Bristol, lately a nonconformist and a pestilent fellow' had preached at the Lower Church in Bread Street on the morning of 27 November 1664, and in Ironmonger Lane in the afternoon.[78] On occasion, however, matters verged on the farcical: in 1664 Edmund Potter attempted to disguise the paucity of his intelligence by giving his employers the less than valuable news that Dr Wild was the ejected ministers' poet; an item almost certainly gleaned from one of the compilations of farewell sermons published some months earlier.[79]

Matters went beyond mere surveillance when local officials actively intervened in the process of preaching. The unfolding programme of legislation between 1660 and 1662 had given magistrates and bishops an array of instruments with which to intimidate, censor and ultimately silence recalcitrant preachers. In January 1661 the Privy Council had even banned the practice of gadding – a directive which, in his farewell sermon, Thomas Wadsworth tacitly encouraged his listeners to ignore, implying that the godly had a duty to search about for an acceptable ministry.[180]

In London, despite his beneficence towards Baxter, Gilbert Sheldon's resolve to eradicate dissent from the pulpits was made evident in a letter sent to Ormonde in Ireland: "'Tis only a resolute execution of the law that might cure this disease – all other remedies have and will increase it – and 'tis necessary that they who will not be governed as men by reason and persuasion should be governed as beasts by power of force."[181] Sheldon was alert to the dangers inherent in leaving the pulpits of ejected ministers to stand empty. By August 1662 he had assembled a pool of suitably qualified candidates in readiness to take over vacated livings. During the last week before Bartholomew's Day he held special services at St Paul's to ordain any ministers who might at the last moment decide to conform.[182]

Despite Sheldon's close attentions, however, Bartholomean ministers in London may often have been more daring in their valedictions precisely because they were more directly in the public eye than their brethren in the country. Ian Green has noted that the Cavalier Parliament contained more moderate and Puritan factions than has generally been realised, even if the majority of MPs were eager to pursue the cause of Uniformity.[183] Pulpits in London afforded more immediate access to the publishing media than country livings, and their occupiers had the ear of a significant Presbyterian element at Court. The farewell sermons delivered in the capital may have been delivered to heterogeneous audiences in churches full of bustle and noise, but for many Bartholomeans they were delivered in the knowledge that some measure of political protection was at hand, given by sympathetic courtiers, if not the London mob. This was well illustrated when Edmund Calamy was arrested on Sheldon's orders following the minister's illegal sermon in Aldermanbury on 28 December 1662, only for the earl of Manchester to engineer his release.[184] The fact that the prospect of martyrdom had quickly been exploited by the printing of *Master Calamy's Leading Case* (1663), and by the inclusion of the offending sermon in several Bartholomean compilations of farewell sermons, was not lost on those in power. Preaching to Irish MPs in May 1661, the Bishop of Down and Connor, whilst highlighting the dangers implicit in 'passive obedience', had already advised that it was impolitic to turn Presbyterians into 'little less than martyrs, and you no better than persecutors'.[185] Many in the English Parliament and Court clearly agreed, preferring not to risk public disorder or political discord by preventing departing London preachers from preaching their farewell sermons.

In the provinces, the willingness of local authorities to implement repressive parliamentary legislation varied. In the scenarios posited by Bosher and Green, the provincial gentry who sat in Quarter Sessions and commanded the county trained bands were overwhelmingly Cavalier and Anglican, predisposed to 'interpret religious discontent as political conspiracy' and always eager to unearth 'forces which challenged the ecclesiastical hierarchy and the existing order of society'.[186] Paul Seaward, by contrast, has argued that many moderate Puritan gentry remained in positions of authority, with the result that some authorities were 'relatively less eager to crush those groups – particularly Presbyterians – closer to the theological mainstream and political orthodoxy'.[187] There is evidence for both positions: local attitudes to non-conformity appear to have been heavily influenced by local factors, producing wide variations between, and within, regions. Local levels of Anglican activism, for example, might have been a reaction to local levels of Puritan activism: it is noticeable that the militant Anglicanism observed by Ian Green among the grand juries in the West Country occurred in a region which also saw an abnormally high incidence of published farewell sermons. By contrast, only one published farewell sermon originated in Essex – a county ruled by a relatively harmonious alliance of moderate Cavaliers and pragmatic ex-parliamentarians.[188]

Nonconformist preachers could find themselves harshly treated where local regimes were dominated by overbearing individuals such as Sir John Knight, MP for Bristol or by bishops such as George Morley or Seth Ward.[189] On the other hand, some Bartholomeans, as we have seen in the case of Robert Atkins in Exeter, found antagonistic magistrates restrained by friendlier elements.[190] The enforcement of the Act of Uniformity was, therefore, anything but uniform. The authorities in Manchester neglected to prevent Henry Newcombe preaching beyond Bartholomew's Day, as it was not until Sunday 31 August that he noted in his diary that he had made his last appearance in a pulpit. He was, however, cautioned by a Justice a few weeks later for repeating sermons.[191] William Durham preached his farewell sermon three weeks after his supposed ejection, whilst Philip Henry did not deliver his until October 1662, and the Worcestershire minister Joseph Cooper clung on until December.[192] Some ministers were able to escape ejection altogether: John Angier of Denton was not only allowed to continue in his living, but in 1665 brought in the ejected Oliver Heywood to assist him.[193] Given that such dissenters remained within the Church, it was fortunate for the authorities that the majority had advertised themselves by their farewell sermons and voluntarily vacated their livings. Occasionally, however, a Bartholomean who had advertised his anger too loudly was made to rue his imprudence: John Billingsley, in a farewell sermon preached in Chesterfield on 23 August, had alleged that whereas he knew of 'prelatical ministers' who had been removed from their livings for murder, drunkenness and whoring, he and his godly brethren were being ejected 'for being too holy and careful of religion'. In September, after the matter had been brought to the notice of John Hackett, Bishop of Lichfield, Billingsley was brought before a consistory court to answer a charge of slander. As a grimly satisfied Hackett related soon afterwards to Sheldon, 'In time many tears came down from him, and he hath given me a very humble confession of his Fault under his hand.'[194] Some officials maintained their vigilance long after Bartholomew's Day had passed: when Henry Maurice, who had initially conformed, succumbed to conscience and preached his farewell sermon in the late 1660s, he was formally charged with reflecting on the government of the Church and incarcerated in Shrewsbury jail.[195]

But even during Black Bartholomew some local ecclesiastical and secular authorities were very willing to intervene directly to assert control over their local pulpits. In the case of Richard Fairclough the intervention of the local Devon magistrates was justified. The minister had been under the erroneous impression that the Act of Uniformity allowed him to preach on Bartholomew's Day itself and had scheduled his programme accordingly. The frequency of sermons from Mells's pulpit increased as 24 August approached, until Fairclough was eventually preaching every day. But on 17 August he suddenly announced that, 'finding this week, by those that have judgement in the Law, that I have no more Sabbaths allowed me but this, I must contract my intentions for both days into this one and last'.[196]

If some Bartholomeans were required to curtail their ministry simply because they had misunderstood the terms of the Act, others found their valedictory preaching terminated prematurely by officials acting on dubious legal pretexts. On 1 July John Barrett and John Whitlock were summoned to appear before the Archdeacon of Nottingham, who ordered that from the next Sunday they were to conduct services wearing a surplice, using the liturgy laid down in the Common Prayer Book, or face immediate ejection. This action took both ministers completely by surprise. Whitlock's sermon of 27 June contained no inkling of the forthcoming crisis, but on 6 July, the Sunday on which both ministers were required to follow the Archdeacon's instructions, he informed his parishioners,

> Beloved, when I entered on this verse in my course of the *Friday-Lecture*, I little thought that I had so short a time to preach among you. I hoped I should have enjoyed some further opportunities for some few weeks, at least as long as the *Act of Uniformity* allowes. But it hath pleased God by his wise and holy Providence to order it otherwise, I being suspended from preaching here, from this day forward, for *Nonconformity*: how regularly or legally on mans part, I shall not dispute, but leave to the righteous God to determine.[197]

This was one tactic by which the authorities were able to disrupt what, in a matter of weeks, had grown into a dangerous and powerful expression of religious dissent which everywhere had the potential to destabilise the political order. Typically well educated, often well connected and invariably well informed, most Bartholomeans were well aware that many in political and ecclesiastical authority considered their sermons a threat. The testimony of Richard Baxter indicates that many Bartholomeans had obtained a legal opinion on the specific circumstances of their valedictory preaching before they ventured into the pulpit to deliver their farewell sermons.[198] Thus, whilst the Bartholomeans' negotiation of authority in their farewell sermons may have been underpinned by a sense of injured innocence and religious conviction, it was not conducted in ignorance.

IV

Preaching was central not just within English Protestantism, but also to the political culture of the Restoration. Ironically, in view of the fact that it was the intention of a particular Cavalier-Anglican grouping in Parliament to marginalise and neuter those they described as Presbyterians, this centrality was underlined by the widespread and intense public interest in the farewell sermons during the period of Fatal Bartholomew.

Departing ministers were not satisfied simply to present an explanation of their position and offer a message of comfort to their flock: many viewed their valedictions as calls to action, an opportunity to reflect on the role of preaching in revealing God's Word and to consider ways in which the know-ledge necessary for salvation could continue to be communicated after their ejection. These deliberations recognised the paramount importance of the pulpit in motivating audiences to carry the Word into everyday life. As trained and experienced orators, the Bartholomeans used a range of techniques to achieve this aim, deploying erudite casuistry and classically inspired rhetoric in one passage, and indulging in theatrical showmanship, earthy vernacular and sometimes crude manipulation of human emotion in the next. This fusion of reason and emotion, evident in so many farewell sermons, demonstrates that we cannot easily separate Puritan preaching along a fault-line marked by the anti-intellectualism of Bunyan at one extreme and the Aristotelian logic of Baxter at the other.[199] The evidence of the reception accorded the Bartholomean farewell sermons suggests that preaching could be both scholarly and populist, and provides an interesting starting point from which to answer Mary Morrissey's call for 'a full account of the reaction against "learned preaching" during the Civil War' – by questioning whether that reaction was necessarily negative.[200]

One reason to be cautious in positing a dichotomy between the scholarly and the populist is because it would offer a temptation to revive the stereotype of the 'plain style'. If there was such a concept as 'plain style' it arose from a determination to render exegesis comprehensible to the meanest in society – giving the godly hope of salvation whilst putting the fear of God into the rest. Despite Pepys's derision, preachers with Presbyterian leanings were not lazy or formulaic, any more than their prolific use of scripture led Puritans in general to pursue a mechanical argument. Much of the power of Puritan exegesis lay in the fact that it was dialectic in nature. For Presbyterians, as much as for any other Puritan, preaching was an invitation to an exploration of godliness rather than the regurgitation of didactic instruction. Tony Claydon has recently adapted Habermas's notion of the public sphere as a framework for testing theories regarding the power of sermons in the later seventeenth century, calling it 'a convenient shorthand for an apparent broadening of political participation'. Given the extent of the congregation's active participation in the process of preaching, it is possible that seventeenth-century sermons may be said to match the ideal of the public sphere even more closely than Dr Claydon has suggested.[201]

Bartholomean preachers were acutely aware that they existed in a political world in which they were necessitated to perform under increasingly intense moral pressure and legal constraint. The weight of legislation, government surveillance and the intervention of local secular and ecclesiastical officials all had a significant influence on the way in which the Bartholomeans conveyed their valedictory message, causing them to revert to tried and tested methods of self-censorship and evasion. To the Restoration establishment, however, preaching was not only a political activity, but one in which a complete and unambiguous expression of active loyalty was required. Consequently, the Act of Uniformity which rendered moderate Puritan ministers dissidents *de jure*, guaranteed that their farewell sermons would become *de facto* manifestos of political resistance. A complication for the authorities was that many thus put beyond the pale were famous and charismatic preachers. Their valedictions proved to be attended by huge crowds, providing an alarming comparison with the often threadbare congregations then attending services commemorating the royalist anniversaries of 30 January or 29 May. In addition, aside from the fact that the unprecedented number of farewell sermons being preached across the nation was politically significant in itself, it can be argued that the nature and extent of political repression (to which many Bartholomean preachers directed their hearers' attention) had the effect of bestowing considerably more *gravitas* on the farewell sermons than they might otherwise have had. In seeking to intimidate and silence dissident ministers, the authorities continually risked providing them with the oxygen of publicity and the potent aura of martyrdom. As it would seem strange that the authorities would do this in the absence of a genuine threat, we should question received assumptions regarding the political moderation of the Bartholomean ministers, and consider the implications and language of their dissent. As we will now see, these seemingly irenic ministers could often prove extremely provocative political and religious polemicists, with a critique couched in rhetoric and metaphor that was rarely explicit, but often explosive.

NOTES

1 T. Horton, *Rich Treasure in Earthen Vessels* (1663), p. 12.

2 Browning, *Documents*, pp. 63–5.

3 M. Braddick and J. Walter, 'Introduction', in M. Braddick and J. Walter (eds), *Negotiating Power in Early Modern Society* (Cambridge, 2001), p. 3.

4 Alleine, *Godly Man's Portion*, p. 51; Romans 10:13–14. See also Crodacot and Bull, in *Third Volume*, pp. 10, 51–2.

5 Alleine, *Godly Man's Portion*, p. 51.

6 *England's Remembrancer*, p. 199.

7 Halifax's phrase, quoted in Spurr, *Restoration Church*, p. 368; Cragg, *Puritanism in the Period of the Great Persecution*, p. 128.

8 Gaskarth, quoted in Spurr, *Restoration Church*, p. 367.

9 Spufford, 'The importance of religion in the 16th and 17th century', in Spufford (ed.), *World of Rural Dissenters*, p. 79.

10 T. Claydon, 'The sermon, the "public sphere" and the political culture of late seventeenth-century England', in Ferrell and McCullough, *English Sermon Revised*, pp. 211–12, 222.

11 Jenkyn, *Burning Yet Un-consumed Bush*, p. 35.

12 Privy Council Register 2/55, fos 48–50, quoted in Miller, *After the Civil Wars*, p. 183.

13 *CSPD* 1660–1, pp. 538–9.

14 Pepys, *Diary*, iv, p. 163, and iii, pp. 166–8.

15 *Exact Collection*, p. 367; Hancock, *Pastor's Last Legacy*, sig. [A3v]; Jenkyn, *Burning Yet Un-consumed Bush*, preface.

16 *Master Edmund Calamy's Leading Case*, p. 12.

17 *Third Volume*, p. 18.

18 *Compleat Collection*, sig. [Aav].

19 Bremer and Rydell, 'Performance art?', p. 52; J. Walter, *Understanding Popular Violence in the English Revolution* (Cambridge, 1999), pp. 175–6.

20 Lye, *Fixed Saint*, pp. 1–2.

21 Evelyn quoted in Spurr, *Restoration Church*, p. 15. The banning order had been issued on 24 November 1655.

22 Hancock, *Pastor's Last Legacy*, sig. [D4 v]; *England's Remembrancer*, pp. 466–7. See also Thomas Manton, in *Exact Collection*, p. 325.

23 Caryl, *White Robe*, p. 15; *Second and Last Collection*, pp. 161, 165.

24 Bremer and Rydell, 'Performance art?', p. 54; Morrissey, 'Scripture, style and persuasion', pp. 701–2.

25 *Exact Collection*, sig. [Ffff3].

26 Bremer and Rydell, 'Performance art?', p. 52.

27 *England's Remembrancer*, p. 378.

28 Berkenhead, *Cabala*, pp. 6, 7.

29 Lye, *Fixed Saint*, sig. A2.

30 T. Jollie, *The Note Book of the Rev. Thomas Jolly 1671–1693*, ed. H. Fishwick, (Manchester, 1894), p. 57, quoted in Cragg, *Puritanism in the Period of the Great Persecution*, p. 213.

31 Horton, *Rich Treasure*, p. 17.

32 *Third Volume*, p. 193.

33 *Ibid.*, p. 12; see also John Clark, in *England's Remembrancer*, p. 506.

34 *Exact Collection*, pp. 309, 315–16. See also Bladon, in *England's Remembrancer*, p. 374.

35 Newcome, *Diary*, p. 122.

36 *Exact Collection*, p. 358.

37 *Compleat Collection*, sig. [Qq3v], *passim*.

38 Mitchell, *English Pulpit Oratory*, p. 317; Cragg, *Puritanism in the Period of the Great Persecution*, p. 213.

39 Calamy, *Church and Dissent Compared*, p. 6, and *Account*, pp. 49, 155, both quoted in Cragg, *Puritanism in the Period of the Great Persecution*, p. 213.

40 R. Baxter, *The English Nonconformity* (1689), p. 15.

41 Horton, *Rich Treasure*, p. 12.

42 Cragg, *Puritanism in the Period of the Great Persecution*, p. 202.

43 Eubanke, *Farewell Sermon Preached*, p. 14.

44 Jenkyn, *Burning Yet Un-consumed Bush*, p. 11.

45 DWL MSS I. l. 35, fo. 30r.

46 Cragg, *Puritanism in the Period of the Great Persecution*, p. 213.

47 Eubanke, *Farewell Sermon Preached*, p. 28; Jenkyn, *Burning Yet Un-consumed Bush*, p. 20; Clark, in *England's Remembrancer*, p. 503.

48 Berkenhead, *Cabala*, p. 7.

49 *Third Volume*, p. 214.

50 *Ibid.*, p. 66.

51 Baxter, *Reliquiae Baxterianae*, p. 384. Several compilations, such as *Compleat Collection* erroneously date Baxter's farewell sermon to August 17.

52 *CR*, *s.v.*

53 E.g., Case (*Exact Collection*, pp. 5, 105); Watson (*ibid.*, sig. [S4]); Venning (*Second and Last Collection*, p. 117); Bull (*Third Volume*, p. 33).

54 *England's Remembrancer*, p. 17; *CR*, *s.v.*; Whitlock, *Short Account*, p. 38.

55 Fairclough, *Pastor's Legacy*, p. 32; see also the editor's preface (sig. [A2 v]).

56 Hancock, *Pastor's Last Legacy*, sig. A3.

57 Mitchell, *English Pulpit Oratory*, pp. 19–20, 22, 26.

58 Calamy, *The Nonconformist's Memorial*, ed. Palmer, i, preface, p. x.

59 R. Whitehorn, 'Richard Baxter – "Meer Nonconformist"', in G. Nuttall, R. Thomas, R. Whitehorn, and H. Short (eds), *The Beginnings of Nonconformity: The Hibbert Lectures* (1964) p. 67.

60 Eubanke, *Farewell Sermon Preached*, p. 41.

61 *England's Remembrancer*, p. 489.

62 *Third Volume*, p. 172.

63 Wilson, *Pulpit in Parliament*, p. 138; Morrissey, 'Interdisciplinarity', p. 1121; Bremer and Rydell, 'Performance art?', pp. 50–1.

64 Potter, *Secret Rites*, p. 208.

65 W. Perkins, *The Workes* (3 vols, Cambridge: 1616–18) II, 6706–30, quoted in Keeble, *Literary Culture*, p. 240.

66 Alleine, *Godly Man's Portion*, p. 51.

67 Perkins, *Workes*, ii, pp. 6706–30, quoted in Keeble, *Literary Culture*, p. 240.

68 E.g., John Clark, in *England's Remembrancer*, p. 487 [mispaginated as p. '486'].

69 Wilkins quoted in Keeble, *Literary Culture*, p. 241.

70 W. Bates, *The Works*, 2nd edn (1723), pp. 651, 707, 724, quoted in Keeble, *Literary Culture*, p. 242.

71 R. Baxter, *The Practical Works* (1707), iv, p. 358, quoted in Mitchell, *English Pulpit Oratory*, p. 104.

72 Eubanke, *Farewell Sermon Preached*, sig. A2.

73 *Ibid.*, p. 10.

74 Lye, *Fixed Saint*, p. 23; Mead, *Pastors Valediction*, p. 4; Watson in, *Exact Collection*, p. 57; Swinnock, *Pastor's Farewell*, sig. [A2v], pp. 1, 35, 58, 59.

75 Fox, *Oral and Literate Culture*, pp. 252–3; *Exact Collection*, p. 366; *England's Remembrancer*, p. 147.

76 Mitchell, *English Pulpit Oratory*, p. 396.

77 *Ibid.*, p. 369. See also Wilson, *Pulpit in Parliament*, p. 141.

78 Cragg, *Puritanism in the Period of the Great Persecution*, pp. 208–10.

79 Jenkyn, *Burning Yet Un-consumed Bush*, p. 3.

80 Bodl. Rawl. MSS E93, fo. 18v.

81 Watson, *Pastor's Love Expressed*, sig. A2–[A2v]. Cf. Eubanke, *Farewell Sermon Preached*, p. 2; Thorne, *Saint's Great Duty*, pp. 12–14; Caryl, *White Robe*, p. 1; Bladon and Crompton, in *England's Remembrancer*, pp. 199, 383–4, Bull and Galpin, in *Third Volume*, pp. 55, 181; Jacombe in *Exact Collection*, pp. 84–90.

82 S. Clark, *A General Martyrologie* (1660), p. 208, quoted in Keeble, *Literary Culture*, p. 241.

83 Quoted in Bremer and Rydell, 'Performance art?', p. 51.

84 *A Directory for the Publique Worship of God* (1660), Wing D1553A, p. 24.

85 Pepys, *Diary*, ii, p. 75.

86 *Exact Collection*, p. 390.

87 Hill, *English Bible*, p. 106. The remainder of the verse appeared in the published text.

88 Thorne, *Saint's Great Duty*, p. 3; Cf. the introduction of Psalm 37 by Daniel Bull, in *Third Volume* p. 46.

89 *Second and Last Collection*, pp. 133–4; Hebrews 10.

90 *Exact Collection*, p. 73. See also John Galpin, in *Third Volume*, p. 168.

91 *Exact Collection*, p. 51.

92 *England's Remembrancer*, p. 116.

93 *Third Volume*, p. 5. In John 12:35–6 Jesus instructs the godly to value the light, lest they suddenly be cast into darkness. Calamy used an identical tactic in his funeral sermon for Simeon Ashe; *Exact Collection*, p. 394.

94 Lamb, *Royal Presence*, sig. [F2] .

95 II Chronicles 36:16.

96 Lye, *Fixed Saint*, p. 4.

97 *England's Remembrancer*, p. 380.

98 Lamb, *Royal Presence*, sig. [B4, B4v].

99 *England's Remembrancer*, p. 99; Bodl. Rawl. MS E93, fo. 5.

100 *England's Remembrancer* p. 452; I Kings 12:16; II Chronicles 10:16.

101 Baxter, *Reliquiae Baxterianae*, p. 123.

102 Bremer and Rydell, 'Performance art?', p. 51; Cragg, *Puritanism in the Period of the Great Persecution*, p. 207.

103 Spufford, 'The importance of religion in the 16th and 17th century', p. 85; J. Walter, 'Grain riots and popular attitudes to the law: Maldon and the crisis of 1629', in J. Brewer and J. Styles (eds), *An Ungovernable People* (1980), p. 51.

104 Baxter, *The Practical Works*, iv, p. 358, quoted in Mitchell, *English Pulpit Oratory*, p. 104.

105 *Compleat Collection*, sig. Eeee.

106 *Exact Collection*, p. 100.

107 Caryl, *White Robe*, p. 14; Calamy, in *Exact Collection*, p. 7; Watson, *Pastor's Love Expressed*, p. 14.

108 Bremer and Rydell, 'Performance art?', p. 51.

109 *Third Volume*, pp. 54, 70, 71; cf. Alleine, *Godly Man's Portion*, p. 51.

110 *Exact Collection*, p. 173; Thorne, *Saint's Great Duty*, p. 49; *England's Remembrancer*, pp. 479–80, 507.

111 *Ibid.*, pp. 378–9, 381.

112 *Ibid.*, p. 465.

113 D. Appleby, 'The Culture and Politics of War Relief in Essex 1642–1662' (University of Essex, unpublished MA dissertation, 1996), chapter 3; G. Hudson, 'Negotiating for blood money: war widows and the courts in seventeenth-century England', in J. Kermode and G. Walker (eds), *Women, Crime and the Courts* (1994), pp. 148, *passim*; Fox, *Oral and Literate Culture*, pp. 9, 19, 22, 23; Brewer and Styles, *An Ungovernable People*, p. 27; Collinson, *Religion of Protestants*, pp. 197, 232–4; M. Spufford, *Contrasting Communities: English Villagers in the Sixteenth and Seventeenth centuries* (Thrupp., 2nd edn, 2000), pp. 320–34; M. Swain, *Embroidered Stuart Pictures* (1990).

114 DWL I.h.35, fo. 19r.

115 *England's Remembrancer*, pp. 293–4.

116 Newcomen, *Ultimum Vale*, pp. 42, 43.

117 Wilson, *Pulpit in Parliament*, pp. 139–40.

118 Lye, *Fixed Saint*, pp. 4, 7, 14.

119 *Exact Collection*, pp. 412–13.

120 *Directory for Publique Worship* (Wing D1553A), pp. 19–20.

121 *Exact Collection*, pp. 162–3.

122 Fox, *Oral and Literate Culture*, p. 235.

123 R. Barthes, 'Listening', in *The Responsibility of Forms*, trans. R. Howard, (Oxford, 1986), p. 259, quoted in B. Smith, *The Acoustic World of Early Modern England: Attending to the O Factor* (1999), p. 340.

124 A. Turberville, *A History of Welbeck Abbey and its Owners* (1938–39), i, pp. 173–4, quoted in Hill, *English Bible*, p. 47, and in Hopper, 'Farnley Wood plot', p. 301.

125 Lye, *Fixed Saint*, pp. 4, 5; Newcomen, *Ultimum Vale*, pp. 14, 21. See also Swinnock, *Pastor's Farewell*, pp. 10, 69; Thomas Watson in *Compleat Collection*, sig. T; Robert Seddon in *England's Remembrancer*, p. 227.

126 *Ibid.*, pp. 392, 413.

127 Lye, *Fixed Saint*, pp. 5, 26.

128 *England's Remembrancer*, p. 104; *Compleat Collection*, sig. [Ssv]; see also Lamb, *Royal Presence*, sig. [B4].

129 *Compleat Collection*, sig. Ss2; I Thessalonians 5:12–13; Brooks, in *Second and Last Collection*, p. 66. See also John Whitlock's advice in *England's Remembrancer*, pp. 18–19

130 *Exact Collection*, pp. 369, 370–2.

131 *England's Remembrancer*, p. 380. James 1:25.

132 Lamb, *Royal Presence*, sig. [B3v, B4]. See also Joseph Cooper, in *Compleat Collection*, sig. XXX, and Hancock, *Pastor's Last Legacy*, sig. [C4].

133 The interpretation in question is offered by Bruce Smith in *Acoustic World*, p. 262; J. Evelyn, *A Character of England* (1659), p. 16.

134 Seaver, *The Puritan Lectureships*, p. 43.

135 See *The Autobiography and Correspondence of Sir Simonds D'Ewes, Bart., During the Reigns of James I and Charles I*, ed. J. D. Halliwell (1845), I, pp. 219–20, quoted in Seaver, *Puritan Lectureships*, pp. 56, 326 (n. 6); Smith, *Acoustic World*, p. 269; Richard Baxter, quoted in Seaver, *Puritan Lectureships*, p. 31; Edmund Calamy, in *Exact Collection*, p. 408.

136 Lamb, *Royal Presence*, sig. A2.

137 *Master Edmund Calamy's Leading Case*, p. 12.

138 BL Sloane MS 4275, fo. 84.

139 Collins, in *Exact Collection*, pp. 380, 384; Brooks, in *Second and Last Collection*, p. 62 (Revelation 3:4 and 8:4); Whitlock, in *England's Remembrancer*, pp. 24–5.

140 T. Godwyn *Phanatical Tenderness or the Charity of the Nonconformists* (1684), cited in J. Barry, 'Politics of religion in Restoration Bristol', in Harris, Seaward and Goldie, *Politics of Religion*, p. 171.

141 Hutton, *Restoration*, p. 172; Crodacot's case appears in *CR, s.v.*

142 *England's Remembrancer*, p. 203.

143 *Account*, ii, p. 128.

144 *Ibid.*, p. 215.

145 Colchester Record Office D/B5, SB2/9, fos. 17, 116v; quoted in Walter, *Understanding Popular Violence*, p. 336.

146 J. Blench, *Preaching in England in the Late Fifteenth and Sixteenth Centuries: A Study of English Sermons 1450–1660* (Oxford, 1964), p. 72.

147 Thorne, *Saint's Great Duty*, p. 30; Acts 1:13.

148 O. Heywood, vol. III, p. 115, quoted in Cragg, *Puritanism in the Period of the Great Persecution*, p. 142.

149 *Exact Collection*, p. 408.

150 W. Schellinks, *The Journal of William Schellinks' Travels in England 1661–1663*, ed. M. Exwood and H. Lehmann, Camden 5th series, vol. 1 (1993), p. 129; a reference I owe to the kindness of Ian Atherton.

151 *Exact Collection*, p. 173.

152 Watson, *Pastor's Love Expressed*, p. 17.

153 Lamb, *Royal Presence*, sig. [B3v].

154 *England's Remembrancer*, pp. 399, 400.

155 *Exact Collection*, pp. 13–14.

156 Alleine, *Godly Man's Portion*, p. 53.

157 Fairclough, *Pastor's Legacy*, p. 65; see also Alleine, *Godly Man's Portion*, pp. 49–50.

158 *Ibid.*, p. 55.

159 *England's Remembrancer*, p. 42.

160 *Ibid.*, p. 43.

161 Ferrell, *Government by Polemic*, p. 19.

162 *Directory for the Publique Worship of God* (1644), Wing D1544, p. 31.

163 *England's Remembrancer*, p. 309.

164 *Third Volume*, p. 12.

165 Quotations from Bosher, *Restoration Settlement*, p. 178 and Greaves, *Deliver Us from Evil*, p. 60; see also Miller, *After the Civil Wars*, p. 176.

166 Miller, *After the Civil Wars*, p. 183; PRO SP29/41/49, quoted in Greaves, *Deliver Us from Evil*, p. 63.

167 G. Nuttall, 'The first nonconformists', in Nuttall and Chadwick, *From Uniformity to Unity*, p. 151.

168 E.g., Edmund Calamy and Thomas Watson in *Exact Collection*, pp. 5, 8, 55; Joseph Moore in *England's Remembrancer*, p. 396; Thomas Lye, in *Fixed Saint*, p. 2.

169 Eubanke, *Farewell Sermon Preached*, p. 21.

170 DWL MS I.h.35, fo. 46r.

171 Hutton, *Restoration*, p. 165.

172 *Compleat Collection*, p. 19.

173 Bosher, *Restoration Settlement*, p. 201; Greaves, *Deliver Us from Evil*, p. 96.

174 Hill, *English Bible*, p. 419; *Compleat Collection*, sig. [Fff3]; PRO SP29/56/18 (intelligence report on Pledger's sermon of 3 June 1662).

175 Hutton, *Restoration*, pp. 137, 164; Keeble, *Literary Culture*, pp. 80–1; Greaves, *Deliver Us from Evil*, pp. 63, 85.

176 Baxter, *Reliquiae Baxterianae*, ii, p. 302.

177 Lye, *Fixed Saint*, p. 3.

178 *CR*, s.v. Thomas Watson was another under surveillance during 1664–65.

179 *CSPD* 1664–5, p. 144. Wilde's poem was appended to *A Compleat Collection of Farewell Sermons* (1663) Wing C5638aA.

180 Privy Council Register 2/55, fos. 48–50, quoted in Miller, *After the Civil Wars*, p. 183; *Compleat Collection*, sig. [Ffff3].

181 Bodl. Carte MS 45, fo. 151, quoted in Bosher, *Restoration Settlement*, p. 265, and Spurr, *Restoration Church*, p. 47.

182 V. Sutch, *Gilbert Sheldon, Architect of Anglican Survival 1640–1675* (The Hague, 1973), p. 85.

183 Green, *Re-establishment*, p. 179.

184 *Master Edmund Calamy's Leading Case*, pp. 12, 16; *Mercurius Politicus* (1–8 Jan., 1663); Corporation of London, *Mayor's Waiting Book*, 2, 13 Jan.; SP28/67/39; 44/9, fo. 224, quoted in Hutton, *Restoration*, p. 194.

185 J. Taylor, *A Sermon Preached at the Opening of the Parliament of Ireland, May 8, 1661* (1661), p. 12.

186 Bosher, *Restoration Settlement*, p. 204; Green, *Re-establishment*, pp. 49, 180, 196–8.

187 P. Seaward, 'Gilbert Sheldon, the London vestries and the defence of the Church', in Harris, Seaward and Goldie, *Politics of Religion*, pp. 49–50.

188 Green, *Re-establishment*, p. 193; Appleby, 'Politics and Culture of War Relief in Essex', chapter 4.

189 See Barry, 'Politics of religion in Restoration Bristol', p. 169; Hutton, *Restoration*, p. 169.

190 *Account*, ii, pp. 215–16.

191 Newcombe, *Diary*, pp. 117, 126.

192 Nuttall, 'The first nonconformists', p. 180; *Continuation*, ii, pp. 884, 895. It has recently been written that Matthew Newcomen returned to his Dedham pulpit for one last farewell, although it could be argued that an encore from such a famous figure would have drawn as much publicity as Calamy at Aldermanbury; *ODNB*, s.v.

193 Heywood, *Life of John Angier*, p. 28.

194 Bodl. Tanner MS 48, fo. 49 (John Hackett to Gilbert Sheldon, 29 September 1662).

195 *Account*, ii, p. 568.

196 Fairclough, *Pastor's Legacy*, p. 119.

197 *England's Remembrancer*, p. 17.

198 Baxter, *Reliquiae Baxterianae*, ii, p. 384.

199 See Keeble, *Literary Culture*, p. 162.

200 Morrissey, 'Interdisciplinarity', p. 1113.

201 A. Claydon, 'The sermon, the "public sphere" and the political culture of late seventeenth-century England', in Ferrell and McCullough, *English Sermon Revised*, pp. 208–9, 220–1.

Chapter 3

Scripture, historicism and the critique of authority

Citing Matthew 10:16 in his afternoon farewell sermon at St Stephen's Walbrook on August 17 – 'Behold, I send you forth as sheep in the midst of wolves; be ye therefore wise as serpents and harmless as doves' – Thomas Watson advised the godly to join the serpent with the dove.[1] The Nottinghamshire minister William Cross assured his Beeston congregation that God was able to 'give the wisdom of the Serpent to such as have the Doves Innocency'.[2] The succeeding verses of Matthew 10 predicted that the godly would be taken before earthly authority for judgement and there persecuted for Christ's sake. Watson, however, had a more specific application:

> We must have the harmlessness of the dove, that we may not wrong others; and we must have the wisdom of the serpent that others may not abuse and circumvent us: Not to wrong the truth by silence, here is the innocency of the dove; not to betray ourselves by rashness, here is the wisdom of the serpent; O how rare is it to have these two united, the Dove and the Serpent; the Dove without the Serpent is folly, and the Serpent without the Dove is impiety.[3]

Watson's concern that he and his fellow nonconformists might 'betray' themselves was justified. In the volatile and fractious context of the Restoration, any message that criticised authority or justified political disobedience was one which had to be delivered carefully. However, not only was this message widely articulated, but many departing ministers expressed contempt for those who remained silent.[4] At the same time, even the most outspoken were usually careful when offering direct political comment, preferring to frame their argument with references to analogous Scripture. Metaphor, as several scholars have noted, frequently served as a mode of argument, contributing to an Aesopian language that had long been used as a rhetorical device in political literature. Annabel Patterson has discerned that since the mid-sixteenth century ambiguity had become 'a creative and necessary instrument, a social and cultural force of considerable consequence', with the resulting codes of communication employed by authors 'partly to protect themselves from hostile and hence dangerous readings of their work, partly in order to say what they had to publicly without directly provoking or confronting the authorities'.[5] Lois Potter has observed that this convention was so common that the terms 'encoding' and 'decoding' were habitually used in contemporary critical theory as synonyms for 'writing' and 'reading'.[6]

In order to decode the political message contained in the farewell sermons, therefore, it is necessary to unpick the intricate rhetorical structures through which it was communicated. Developing earlier propositions as to *how* Scripture was deployed, this chapter will analyse *what* was selected by the Bartholomeans and why. It will be shown that most of the extant farewell sermons rely heavily on the New Testament, in contrast to contemporaneous Anglican preaching, and even the parliamentary fast sermons of the Interregnum – which had, in many cases, been delivered by the same authors. A number of themes featured consistently in the farewell sermons: the eschatological significance of the ejection, memories of armed conflict, imminent persecution and the implications of 'civil' death. These themes were typically synthesised into an overarching thesis which challenged the moral hegemony of earthly authority.

At the same time that the Scriptural metaphor used in this valedictory preaching is to be considered as a mode of argument, it will be argued that it also functioned as a means of evasion. In common with royalist authors during the Interregnum, the Bartholomeans faced a conflict between the need to convey meaning at the same time as they were compelled to camouflage it. But Annabel Patterson, in suggesting that the prevailing codes of communication were in fact an 'implicit social contract between authors and authorities' (and a calculated, conscious and mutually intelligible one at that), implies that the convention of encoding was consensual rather than divisive.[7] Roger Pooley has noted that just before the Restoration there was 'a brief moment when both Anglicans and Nonconformists shared a language and experience of being embattled minorities', whilst Mary Morrissey has seen in the recent trend to consider sermons as rhetorical texts an emphasis on the significance of 'rhetorical commonplaces'.[8] The fact that much Bartholomean rhetoric did indeed involve the use of rhetorical commonplaces would appear, on the face of things, to have made the act of encoding futile. Nevertheless, the farewell sermons *were* encoded. Since the Reformation, the act of spreading God's word had always entailed a keen appreciation of political realities, if only for the fact that it was often necessary to anticipate and evade physical or legal restraints imposed by authority in order to ensure the pure transmission of divinely ordained Truth. The ability of Scripture to function on several different levels was often exploited to attain a useful ambiguity of signification.

The farewell sermons were certainly intended to inform, engage and comfort the godly. It is less obvious to what extent they were intended to inform, engage and influence the authorities. In the final analysis, the task of decoding the Bartholomean message involves a judgement of the extent to which their valedictions conformed to widely understood rhetorical conventions and how far they deviated by using rhetoric to evade censure – to what extent, in other words, the farewell sermons displayed the innocence of the dove, and the wisdom of the serpent.

I

Christopher Hill has written that if any book had power in early modern England, it was the Bible.[9] Not only did Scripture have an unrivalled claim to truth, but it also possessed a multivalence that enabled skilful preachers to frame arguments in such a way as to convey or conceal meaning at need. The citations and explications that proliferated in early modern sermons (particularly those of the Puritan variety) might not have encouraged elegant prose, but there was an overriding need to place contemporary events in a Biblical context. Consequently, texts were carefully chosen, scrupulously noted and hotly contested. Robert Porter's discussion during his farewell sermon concerning the omission of a single word from Psalm 84:4 illustrates how judiciously citations were deployed.[10] Thus, when George Thorne used an innocuous phrase from Psalm 37, he would have been well aware that more radical verses lurked nearby (and used one later in his sermon).[11] However, preachers did not simply collapse their argumentation into a series of Scriptural texts: the individual minister's gloss on his selection, his choice of translations and glossaries and, above all, his construction and application of doctrine could be highly individualistic. At the same time, similarities in the selection of texts and deployment of metaphor by nonconformist ministers reveal the extent to which cultural and societal mentalities, channelled through personal and institutional networks, resulted in overlapping epistemologies and shared responses to the political situation.

Surveys of earlier Puritan sermons have found a marked preference for Old Testament themes. J. F. Wilson, for example, has found that of the printed parliamentary fast sermons from the 1640s and 1650s a clear majority (162 out of 217) took their main text from this source. Within these a wide range of Scripture was utilised, whereas the sermons that took their theme from the New Testament used only thirteen of the twenty-seven books available – with very little recourse to the Pauline canon. Exodus was repeatedly cited, the escape of the Israelites from Egyptian bondage serving as a metaphor for England's release from royal tyranny. Wilson interprets this bias as 'confirmation that the Puritans, while reading their Old Testament in light of the New Covenant, yet were drawn back toward the earlier and richer materials in elaborating their conception of political and social life'.[12] The main Biblical texts chosen by the Bartholomeans, however, ran counter to this trend. Of the valedictions surviving in print and manuscript, only 13 derived their main text from the Old Testament, whereas 68 favoured the New. Fifty-one of the latter group, moreover, took their text from Pauline scripture or from Pauline anecdotes preserved in Acts.[13] The Old Testament texts came from a variety of sources, but only William Jenkyn took his theme from Exodus.[14]

Following the main text, each item of Scripture cited, explicated and applied added its own weight, direction and twist to the sermon. However, a quantitative survey of the incidence of Scripture in the farewell sermons is problematic: not only do the authors of the surviving farewell sermons represent a fraction of those ejected in 1662, but it is unlikely that the Scriptural texts cited during the farewell sermons were all recorded, much less accurately reproduced. This has produced a wide variety in the frequency of Scripture featured between one sermon and another. The 10 citations noted in the printed version of Bates's morning sermon, for example, seem sparse when set against the 235 items of Scripture cited in Bladon's afternoon sermon.[15]

Nevertheless, whilst acknowledging some heterogeneity in the frequency and deployment of texts, it is possible to posit some general indications of the Bartholomean use of Scripture. A survey of 76 sermons in the Bartholomean corpus reveals that each contained, on average, 49 citations of Scripture, of which some 60 per cent came from the New Testament. The 13 sermons in the corpus that used the Old Testament as their main text differed materially from the rest in that they featured a significantly higher average frequency of citations (67), only 40 per cent of which came from the New Testament. Even those preachers who took their main text from the Old Testament tended to use a relatively limited selection of material from books aside from the Psalms, most usually Proverbs or Isaiah. Several took their main text from the Old Testament only to explicate it by extensive recourse to the New.[16] Texts from books such as Deuteronomy, Jeremiah and Exodus were generally avoided. The isolated use of Jeremiah by Matthew Newcomen, for example, ran a risk in drawing attention to the conflict between that prophet and the ruling regime, and Israel's capitulation to Babylon: '*Hath a Nation changed their Gods, which are yet no Gods; but my People have changed their glory, for that which doth not profit.*'[17]

The most striking aspect of Scriptural citation in the Bartholomean corpus is the prevalence of texts taken from the epistles of Paul and Acts. These texts comprised, on average, 29 per cent of the citations. Even those preachers who had selected their main text from the Old Testament chose, on average, 20 per cent of their supporting texts from the Pauline canon. In those sermons which featured Pauline scripture as the main text there was an even greater emphasis, with an average of 42 per cent.

The overall character of the Bartholomean corpus was therefore overwhelmingly Pauline in nature, highlighting the nature of embattled Christian communities and truth claims implicit in images of persecution and death. However, despite this emphasis, the Old Testament was not entirely eclipsed. The particularity of images and metaphors, many closely associated with aggressive anti-royalist exegesis of the 1640s and 1650s, gave the Old Testament a disproportionate significance when quoted, making its deployment all the more deliberate because it was so obviously confrontational. Thus, whilst the Old Testament gave preachers the necessary tools with which to construct critiques of kings, kingship and political authority, it was used sparingly. The Book of Revelation, meanwhile, was rather more widely used as a main text, contributing to a sense of the historical moment in the farewell sermons which can best be described as apocalyptic.

II

Even in normal times, early modern religious culture ascribed immense significance to eschatological and historical cycles. But these were not normal times: Thomas Lye warned his congregation that a hurricane was coming.[18] Matthew Newcomen, who had chosen to discuss the implications of the Act of Uniformity openly in his sermon of 17 August, declared the next Tuesday that the day was at hand when he and many others would be though not naturally, yet civilly, dead. He invited his Dedham congregation to consider that it was not the laying by of one man, 'but of multitudes, fifty in one place, and threescore in another; and fourscore in another, and this not by a single Bishop, but by an Act of Parliament, which makes the wound the wider, and the more uncapable of cure; and shall not we be sensible of this?'[19] Just as God had killed all the firstborn of Egypt in one night, he continued in a subsequent sermon, so here 'God hath slain not *one* or a *few*, but *many* indeed of the *First-born* of *England* in one day.'[20] The great wailing that had been heard in Biblical Egypt would be echoed in England. John Whitlock pointed out that 'Had so many hundreds of Ministers dyed a natural death in one day, you would have looked upon it as a great judgement: And sure it is no less when so many shall dye a civil death.'[21] Thomas Case predicted a catastrophe to rank with the bloody events in Europe.[22]

Several ministers lamented on the wickedness of the times, and the fearful portents thereof. 'Now is the Ax laid at your roots', said Robert Seddon, warning that the removal of so many teachers was a sign that the godly should rouse themselves.[23] Samuel Slater wondered whether 'devils are come among us in the likeness of men', whilst Ralph Venning believed 'that there is a time a coming, the day will declare, whether it be best serving God or the Devil'.[24] John Whitlock perceived the fateful hour to be imminent, citing that chapter of Acts which prophesied that in that hour the faithful would be scattered. He advised the godly to prepare for the coming storm as Joseph had, laying up stores to protect himself and his family against the plagues of Egypt.[25]

The ministers were acutely aware that the day appointed for their ejection coincided with one of the most emotive dates in the Protestant calendar: the anniversary of the Bartholomew's Day massacre of French Huguenots in 1572. Richard Baxter's autobiography, printed thirty years after Black Bartholomew, recorded that 'this fatal Day called to remembrance the *French* Massacre, when on the same Day 30,000 or 40,000 Protestants perished by the religious *Roman* Zeal and Charity'.[26] Porter's *Life of John Hieron* (1691) also highlighted the poignancy of the anniversary of the Parisian massacre.[27] Gilbert Burnet recalled that in 1662 Presbyterians had not hesitated to compare the two events.[28] The surviving farewell sermons, however, suggest that few Bartholomeans referred to the massacre from their pulpits. Thomas Bladon was an exception:

> How dismal is the day of *St Bartholomew*! On this day was *Jerusalem*, once the Glory and Beauty of the world, sacked by *Titus* and *Vespasian*. On the Eve of this day, began that bloody Massacre in *Paris*. On this day is a great part of *Englands* Ministry slain; slain not in their persons, but in their Offices. The dismal transactions that have befallen the Church of God this day, deserve to be engraved in deep and indelible Characters on Pillars in the blackest Marble, that the Ages and Generations to come may reade, and weep showers of tears to quench Jerusalems flames, to wash and bath the Wounds of the poor massacred Christians, and bewail *Englands* loss.[29]

Among the other published Bartholomeans, only Edmund Calamy ventured to mention Vespasian's sack of Jerusalem, leaving the significance of the date unexplained.[30] Anglican clergy, by contrast, could be far less reticent: whilst preaching in 1660 James Warwell had asserted that the Engagement Oath instituted by the Commonwealth could have led to a slaughter of Protestants even worse than that of the Parisian massacre.[31]

Bartholomew's Day was not the only Protestant shibboleth requiring cautious handling. Over the preceding generations Foxe's *Acts and Monuments* had effectively become the third testament of the English Bible, creating powerful and emotive images imbued with highly sensitive political and religious connotations. Again, Anglican preachers were capable of exploiting such images to the full: delivering a sermon in memory of Charles I in Exeter on 30 January 1662, Arthur Bury had argued that the martyrs would have been disgusted by the Regicide, and would have martyred themselves again to defend traditional liberties and the Christian ideals Charles embodied.[32] Faced with this aggressive appropriation of the paradigmatic saints of English Protestantism, most Bartholomeans shied away from making direct comparisons between the martyrs and contemporary politics, although they remained willing to transmit their message by more circumspect means. Matthew Newcomen, noting ruefully that Foxe's book was no longer as prized as it had once been, suggested that his listeners 'read that part of it which containes the history of Queen *Maries* dayes; they will inform you of the great controversies that are between us and the Papists'. The Marian martyrs, Newcomen assured his flock, represented a pertinent example of godly resolve, which would help them face fears of suffering and death.[33] Thomas Lye, concerned lest consideration for families could lead to backsliding, warned 'Wives and Children were great temptations, the bloody Papists knew that, and therefore they caused them to be set before the Martyrs.'[34] Edmund Calamy and Philip Lamb warned their respective flocks that neglect of the Gospel during the time of Edward VI had facilitated papist persecution under Queen Mary, while Thomas Brooks invited his congregation to recall, 'what endeavours of old there hath been to darken this Sun, to put out the light of Heaven, in the *Marian* days'.[35] If such exhortations ran perilously close to implying a parallel between the persecuting Marian papists and the activities of the Restoration establishment, George Thorne compounded the hazard when combining an anecdote from Foxe with a description of Jehosaphat's corruption at the hands of King Ahab – an image which had been associated with Charles II during the time of his exile.[36] Calamy, in his December sermon, interwove the testimony of the martyred Mr Bradford into his argument that the Ark of the Covenant was in danger of being lost – an echo of his preaching during Black Bartholomew, when he had asserted that the civil death of so many ministers was a sign that God was angry with England.[37]

If few preachers were willing to discuss the political ramifications of the Great Ejection, most were ready to consider its eschatological significance. Robert Seddon, although dismayed by the turn of events, nevertheless saw the Great Ejection as part of God's grand design.[38] Richard Alleine reminded his flock that there was behind everything one great wheel still turning, and that one aspect of Providence was that God transformed kingdoms and governments, and removed and set up kings. He perceived in the unfolding crisis a battle between human scheming and God's will, taking comfort in the knowledge that the godly stood apart, and that Pharaoh's dream was for the Egyptians, not Israel: 'The lean Kine shall not devour the fat ones; there is a *Store-house* from whence they shall be supply'd.'[39]

Edward Hancock and Thomas Brooks quoted Revelation, reminding the godly that the voice from Heaven had ordered that they should 'come out of her my people, and be not partakers of her sin, lest you are partakers of her plagues'.[40] John Barrett surmised that the removal of so many ministers was God's judgement for the sins and shortcomings of preachers and their congregations, warning that they should show proper repentance as, 'it may be *the eleventh hour*'.[41] Daniel Bull asserted that in proposing to behead so many faithful ministers in one day, England had committed high treason against God. Such an unfaithful and ungrateful nation was clearly destined for a scourging.[42] George Eubanke, combining England's sin of past blood-guiltiness with a warning to those that dared touch the Lord's prophets, noted that,

> *Herod* did but cut one mans head off, and he is gone to Hell for it. Oh what an Hell mayest thou look for, who hast got so many heads, and drunk the blood of thousands of the Saints and faithful servants of the most High?[43]

Thomas Wadsworth called upon London to repent the killing and imprisoning of prophets, and delivered a rebuke on behalf of the Lord.[44] The seriousness of the loss of godly ministers was underlined by those preachers who alluded to the '*Chariots of Israel, and the Horsemen thereof*', a reference to the prophet Elijah, whose conduct had demonstrated that holy men had always been a more efficacious defence than military might.[45] Rather more optimistically, Samuel Shaw quoted Paul's epistle to the Philippians: '*I would ye should understand, Brethren, that the things which have happened to me have fallen out rather unto the furtherance of the Gospel.*'[46] Joseph Moore concurred, observing that although such misfortunes had previously only been suffered in Papist times, 'Extraordinary *eclipses* usually presage some extraordinary *Events*.'[47]

The Bartholomeans' sense of the historical moment was linked to their perception of the eschatological status of the English nation, confirming a historiographical thread which has posited that post-Reformation England was regularly considered the Israel of the New Covenant. Mary Morrissey has argued against this grain, asserting that England was not seen as a covenanted nation, and that Biblical Israel was an example, rather than a type.[48] However, the farewell sermons show that godly ministers did not automatically assume a covenanted nation to be a saved one. Although preachers such as Matthew Newcomen continued to argue that England was special in the eyes of the Lord, the failure to establish a rule of the saints had shaken Puritan perceptions of Providence.[49] As Edmund Calamy argued:

> *England* hath no Letters Patents of the Gospel; the Gospel is removable; God took away the *Ark* and forsook *Shilo*, and he did not only take away the *Ark*, but the Temple also; he unchurched the *Jews*, he unchurched the seven Churches of *Asia*, and we know not how soon he may unchurch us; I know no warrant we have to think that we shall have the Gospel another hundred years.[50]

Several preachers feared that God was about to remove his candlestick from England, a sign of which, according to John Crodacot, was the removal of those who were the 'Candles on the candlesticks of His Church'.[51] Such an Old Testament-style un-churching, coupled with other images such as the slaughtering of Saul's priests strongly suggests that Israel *was* regarded as a type, rather than a mere example.

The threat of un-churching had been a familiar refrain since at least the early years of the seventeenth century; nevertheless, Calamy warned his congregation not to pry into the Ark in an attempt to guess God's plan.[52] Daniel Bull admitted that even godly ministers could not predict the future, noting bleakly that 'our Troubles increase, and we have none to tell us how long'.[53] However, the prospect of the civil deaths of so many godly ministers gave millenarian instincts a renewed lease of life. The imminent civil deaths, alluded to in virtually every surviving farewell sermon, were perceived as unnatural. Some preachers recalled the slaughter of Saul's priests on the orders of Do'eg the Edomite.[54] Others reminded their congregations that Revelation predicted a killing of the Witnesses, a facet of the Apocalypse that had long been a central tenet of millenarianism.[55] In his morning farewell sermon, Thomas Bladon deepened the sense of doom prompted by his tableau of St Bartholomew's Day by affixing a montage containing Herod's massacre of the Innocents, the Pharisees' persecution of Christ and the martyrdom of John the Baptist. He reminded his flock of the prophecy that the Antichrist would make war against the Two Witnesses, which some took to be magistrates and ministers, but others ministers only: 'against these the Beast shall make war, and by a powerful prevailing of his interest, and of a prophane and corrupt party shall slay them; slay them not in their Persons, but in their Offices; it is not a natural but a civil death'. He surmised that this was a civil death because Revelation 11:9 specified that the dead would not be buried. The killings, inspired by the Antichrist in the shape of the Papacy, were to be followed by a civil resurrection 'that by enacted Laws shall give liberty and Authority to the slain Witnesses to re-assume the publick exercise of their Ministry and Magistracy of which they were before deprived'.[56] Several other published Bartholomeans alluded to the killing of the Witnesses prophesied in Revelation, and some to the cloud of witnesses in Paul's epistle to the Hebrews – although whether these witnesses were simply ministers or the whole invisible church was unclear.[57] Calamy in his December sermon took comfort from the certainty that God was even then pouring out his vials upon Antichrist. He was confident of ultimate victory, but warned that it might carry a high price:

> God may scourge all the reformed Churches before these Vials be poured out, and persecutions may go through them all; the which I call drops of these Vials, but the Vials are intended for Antichrist, and shall end in the ruin of

Antichrist: and whatsoever becomes of us, yet our children, and our childrens children, shall see the issue of the Vials poured out upon the Whore of *Babylon*.[58]

This prevalence of apocalyptic imagery and sentiment stands in stark contrast to Wilson's taxonomy of the parliamentary fast sermons of the 1640s and 1650s. For Wilson, apocalypticism (closely linked to millenarianism in his study) 'developed as a proclamation of hope in Israel's darkest hours', where 'God ruled the course of historical events and would bring out of the ominous present a glorious future quite independently of human agency'. Thus, whereas prophetic preaching was characterised by the invitation of human agency 'to respond to divine purposes' the apocalyptic outlook celebrated 'the independence of the divine from human agency'. Wilson perceived 'a fundamental differentiation' between Puritan clergy who adhered to a 'prophetic-reformist' outlook and their more radical brethren whose understanding of their times was 'apocalyptic-transformist'.[59] Predominantly Presbyterian in temper, most of the Bartholomeans who had given fast sermons during the Interregnum would appear to have been classified by Wilson as 'prophetic-reformists'. The fact that in 1662 these same preachers would display such strong apocalyptic tendencies therefore requires explanation. Logically, given the failure to establish the rule of saints on Earth and the imminent prospect of political eclipse, the only winning scenario remaining to the Bartholomeans was an apocalyptic one. The synthesis of apocalyptic and prophetic eschatology in the farewell sermons suggests that such discourse was, in fact, a response to a given political situation rather than a party badge.

III

The Act of Uniformity forced dissenting ministers to deny the right of the Restoration state to dictate individual conscience. By definition, the state was synonymous with royal authority, embodied in the person of Charles II; in reality it had many heads, and functioned on various levels, religious and secular, national, regional and local. The Bartholomeans were obliged by their calling to expose and confront ungodly iniquity, including – perhaps even especially – within the Establishment, and to exhort the sovereign and his officials to lead the nation in the ways of the Lord. But this spiritual war had to be waged in such a way as to avoid conceding any political advantage to would-be persecutors.

Most of these university-educated preachers would have been familiar with Quintillian's *Institutio Oratoria*, which held that, 'You can speak as openly as you like against ... tyrants, as long as you can be understood differently, because you are not trying to avoid giving offence, only its dangerous repercussions.'[60] Annabel Patterson believes that such 'oblique discourse' re-emerged in response to the growth of absolutism in early modern Europe.[61] Although in 1662 Charles II was (as yet) neither absolute nor tyrannical, it would have been rash to proffer direct criticism or qualification of royal authority from the pulpit. Ostensibly commenting on the repression and idolatry practised by the Biblical king Jeroboam, however, Thomas Bladon adumbrated a political landscape which was clearly intended to have contemporary resonance:

> Never was there any Interest of Great men so sinful and corrupt, nor any Religion owned, countenanced, and established by Authority, so superstitious, idolatrous and abominable, as to want Defenders and Promoters; some for favour, some for fear; some for secular advantages, to preserve and keep what they have, or to gain honours, preferments and riches by it.[62]

The Act to preserve the person and government of the King had rendered it treasonable to stir up discontent with the King's ministers, or even imagine his death.[63] At the same time, the anniversaries of Charles I's execution and the nativity and restoration of Charles II had been incorporated into the Church calendar.[64] Moderate Puritans (including some future Bartholomeans) had initially, attempted to participate in these events,[65] but by 1662 they were being used to rehearse Cavalier concepts of kingship and to demand unquestioning and absolute political loyalty for the regime. Anglican preachers continually drew attention to the disloyalty of Puritans in general and the perfidy of Presbyterians in particular. The martyred Charles I was repeatedly paralleled with Christ, whilst Charles II was rendered an embodiment of the Christ-type David. At the same time as they faced hostile Anglican exposition, many nonconformist ministers tempered their critiques of authority in the hope that the King could be persuaded to suspend the Act of Uniformity. John Miller has suggested that some Presbyterians even viewed Charles II (who had, after all, taken the Covenant) as a last opportunity to create 'a truly effective puritan national church'.[66] Given these factors, it is hardly surprising that the Bartholomeans were reluctant to comment directly upon the conduct of the King or the political authorities.

Some, however, did consider Charles II to be part of the problem – as Henry Newcombe wrote in his diary, 'It was not God, but the King who cast us down' – and even before the summer of 1662, moderate Puritans had found ways to voice criticism, carefully couched in Scriptural citation and metaphor.[67] Rhetorical devices (for example, bad kings such as Ahab and Rehoboam and good kings such as David and Josiah) were selected from a palette of iconography shared equally with Anglicans, meaning that the hermeneutics of such imagery would be widely understood. Thus, in 1660, whereas an Anglican might admit David's human failings in passing, the

Presbyterian Richard Eedes could both praise David and emphasise his scarlet sins, incorporating this into an argument that it was the duty of loyal subjects to conceal their prince's failings.[68] Similarly, another Presbyterian preacher, John Nelme, could remind his audience of David's imperfections in the course of observing that God could topple kings as easily as he could raise them.[69]

The Stuart kings who ruled England and Scotland were routinely paralleled with David, ruler of Biblical Israel and Judah. By the Restoration, in sermons, letters and private diaries across the Protestant spectrum, the metaphor was widely used to signify Charles II: as Robert Mossom preached in 1660, 'think we then David's person to be the King's, and Israel's condition to be England's'.[70] The repeated appearance of David in the farewell sermons was often, therefore, highly significant. Explicating the main text of his farewell sermon (II Samuel 21:14) Edmund Calamy presented the picture of David in 'a great strait', facing Divine punishment because he had counted his people and had taken an extra half-shekel in tax. David's sin, according to Calamy, was that he had done these things without a lawful reason. Calamy then referred directly to Charles II, reminding his flock that, 'our King and Soveraign was in a great strait in the dayes of his banishment', and expressing the hope that the nation would not begin to look back towards Egypt. The passage thereby became a warning of royal vulnerability as well as a subtle subversion of contemporary royalist imagery.[71] This vulnerability, together with the iniquity of evil counsellors, was the crux of John Barrett's message when he reminded his congregation of David's lament on learning that his lieutenant Joab had killed Abner in his name: '*I am this day weak, though anointed King.*'[72] Images of David as an imperfect king arose in several other valedictions. At the same time as Thomas Jacombe offered prayers for Charles II, he took pains to highlight David's failings, and the consequences of the King's infatuation with Bathsheba.[73] Naturally, the image of David could be applied in less controversial ways, enabling some departing ministers to parallel themselves with David the man, patiently awaiting God's will.[74]

Certain other images of kingship were less flexible and potentially far more dangerous, not least the iconography that had coagulated around the dead Charles I. By 1662, 30 January and 29 May sermons had consolidated the image of Charles the Martyr and were presenting regicide as a popish and Anabaptist doctrine condoned by Presbyterians.[75] Unsurprisingly, very few Bartholomeans alluded to the Regicide, or mentioned Charles I by name in their valedictions; to have done so might have drawn attention to sermons delivered during the late conflict. At the same time, however, many farewell sermons featured lengthy discussions on the mortality of kings, framed in such a manner that the audience can hardly have failed to make a connection. In one sermon, Thomas Lye supplemented Pauline exhortations to stand fast with an invitation taken from Joshua 10:24 to '*Come and set your feet upon the necks of these Kings.*'[76] By beheading the kings he had captured in battle, Joshua intended to make an example to his people, and deter other kings and magistrates from imitating their abominations, 'lest they should provoke God, who is no acceptor of persons'.[77] Soon after this insensitive reference to regicide Lye issued a coded warning to Charles II that despite the prowess of Alexander, there were many 'that cannot be made by all your powers to change their mindes'.[78] In Yorkshire, George Eubanke completed a warning to gentlemen to live godly lives, by asking,

> Suppose thou hadst a Crown on thy head, how long wouldst thou wear it? Suppose thou had'st a Scepter in thy hand, how long would'st thou hold it? They are sick at *Rome*, and dye in Princes Courts, as well as at the Spittle; yea, Kings themselves cannot keep their Crowns on their heads, *nor their Heads on their shoulders*, but must stoop when death strikes, *and go as naked to their Beds of Dust, as other men*; and in that day all their thoughts, their projects, and their pleasures perish with them; only the guilt of their sins, which were the Ladders, by which they did climb up to the top of their pleasures, the top of their honors, and preferments will dog them into another world. Hence said *Abner* to *Joab.*[79]

The human frailties of kings and the vulnerability of monarchies were observed in many farewell sermons. William Jenkyn noted that, unlike the ragged but godly John Baptist, the powerful Herod had become worm's meat when smitten by God.[80] 'A King in a Castle full of pleasures and incompast with powers, is not so secure and blessed, as is every sincere soul', remarked Richard Fairclough.[81] Jenkyn, using the prophet Nehemiah as an example, suggested that royal favour did not compensate for the suffering of the people of God.[82] The transience of human monarchies, described by ministers such as Barrett and derided by Eubanke using Isaiah 28:1 ('Woe to the Crown of Pride') was contrasted with the enduring righteousness of the godly, whom even the moderate William Bates alleged only God could judge.[83] Such observations served as a warning to those who sought to persecute the godly.

The Egyptians were seen as the archetypal persecutors and slave-masters, and Pharaoh the paradigm of tyranny. But such tyranny was not automatically equated with monarchy: many Anglican preachers, particularly when giving thanksgiving sermons for Charles II's homecoming in June 1660, portrayed the Interregnum as Egypt, and paralleled the Restoration with Israel's escape from bondage.[84] Gilbert Sheldon's sermon to the King on 28 June 1660 compared past resistance to the Stuart dynasty with the criticism Moses had suffered at the hands of his ungrateful and ignorant people.[85] By contrast, Exodus was sparingly deployed in the printed Bartholomean valedictions – not least because even isolated citations could be disproportionately powerful. The nonconformist preachers' use of Exodus has sometimes been interpreted as a passive acceptance of ejection, exemplified by Philip Henry's resolution to imitate the self-denial of Moses ('rather choosing to suffer affliction with the people of God, than to enjoy the good things of this world').[86] However, when other Bartholomeans used Exodus it was not simply to show the way to the Promised Land, but also to offer a coded critique of the regime being left behind. William Jenkyn's use of Paul's epistle to the Hebrews in his morning farewell sermon also likened the departing ministers to Moses, but ministers who 'chose rather to suffer affliction with the people of God, than to enjoy all the pleasure and preferment of Pharaoh's court'. Jenkyn supplemented this citation by contrasting the integrity of the godly with the obsequiousness of courtiers: 'Whom the King honours', he said contemptuously, 'they cringe to.'[87]

Richard Alleine made unusually extensive use of Egyptian imagery throughout his valediction, his refusal to participate in 'Pharaoh's dream' underlining his rejection of the Act of Uniformity. Later in the sermon, having called for peaceable behaviour, Alleine promptly introduced the most provocative piece of Exodus possible: the account of Pharaoh's demise whilst chasing the children of God across the Red Sea.[88] Joseph Cooper and Philip Lamb used the same episode to illustrate their belief that the godly would be protected from evil if they kept their faith.[89] This was a particular piece of Scripture that Roger L'Estrange, Surveyor of the Press, would soon declare to be nothing less than an invitation to armed resistance.[90] Even relatively innocuous allusions to Exodus could carry menacing undertones, as when John Clark stated that '*Jacob* told *Pharoah* that *the dayes of his life had been few and evil.*'[91] George Eubanke noted the 'fair and frequent warnings' Pharaoh had been given by Moses to change his ways before the events of the Exodus had unfolded.[92]

Biblical monarchs that had caused their people to turn from God, such as the corrupted Jehosaphat or idolatrous tyrants such as Jeroboam or Ahab, had clearly sinned more grievously than the heathen Pharaoh, and merited destruction. Since the Restoration, the Interregnum had routinely been paralleled with the worship of Baal's golden calves, and Cromwell as a latter-day Jeroboam.[93] The use of such imagery in the Bartholomean valedictions was rather more subtle. Thomas Brooks, speaking of the miseries suffered by an Israel bereft of the Gospel, informed his flock that there had still been priests, 'but they were *Jeroboam's* Priests'.[94] The implication, said Brooks, was that '*when the* Gospel *goes*, Civil Liberty *goes*', concluding 'Make not the example of great men a rule to go by; for who dare dye by, and stand by this, in the great day of accompt? Do not make any authority, that stands in opposition to the authority of Christ, a rule to walk by.'[95]

The image of King Ahab was a particularly perilous metaphor to use – not least because during the Interregnum he had often been paralleled with the exiled Charles II.[96] Nevertheless, John Barrett reminded his congregation that Ahab had persecuted Elijah and other godly prophets, with the intention of replacing them with the priests of Baal. In concert with several other Bartholomeans, Barrett reiterated Elijah's challenge to the children of Israel: '*If the Lord be God, follow him . . . if Baal, follow him.*'[97] Other preachers implied that Ahab's persecution of the godly might be attributed to the malign influence of his wife Jezebel (conceivably an allusion to Charles's mother Henrietta-Maria). Invariably, the use of Ahab was given a parenthesis: William Beerman turned a much-quoted verse from the Psalms ('Touch not mine anointed, nor do my prophets no harm') against Cavalier-Anglicans who habitually used it to demand political loyalty, whilst William Jenkyn added, 'I had rather have the prayers of *Paul*, then the preferments of the greatest Court on earth.'[98] Thomas Bladon noted that during Ahab's time those who bent the knee to Baal, 'had the security and protection of their Kings and Councils, when the others were oppressed'.[99]

Another avenue of criticism lay in the use of Biblical Sardis – a city whose people had turned from God. During his 29 May sermon in 1660, the Anglican John Douch had referred to Charles II as Cresus, King of Sardis.[100] Several contemporaneous sermons, including those preached by Bishop Parker, Clement Barksdale and Henry Newcombe linked Charles II firmly to his royal city.[101] Matthew Newcomen's sermon of August 17 1662 on the text of Revelation 3:3 made the link between these various elements explicit: in explaining that his text referred to Sardis, Newcomen stated that, 'it had been the chiefe City of the kingdom, as London is of England, therefore called the Royall City . . . a City full of Idolatry and uncleanness as the rest of the Heathen City'. Christ's warning to Sardis was thereby given immediate and menacing import by Newcomen: 'I will come upon thee as a thiefe, and thou shalt not know what houre I will come upon thee.'[102] Revelation 3:3 was cited in several other Bartholomean valedictions, with Joseph Caryl and Thomas Whitlock also selecting it as their main text. The verse itself was relatively uncontroversial, exhorting Christians to hold fast to their faith, but Whitlock, like Newcomen, expanded on the theme of Sardis, describing the city as the centre of formality and spiritual deadness – terms often used as shorthand for the human innovations of episcopal authority in defiance of Scripture.[103] Had any of these ministers so wished, they could have selected Philippians 4:9, which carried an almost identically worded exhortation, without a polemical subtext.

Broadening the scope of rhetoric to encompass royal cities such as Sardis and London had the effect of facilitating a wider debate on the nature of religious and political authority. As the departing ministers felt themselves to be orthodox members of the Church of England, it would seem natural that they should blame those bishops and politicians who had perverted the search for religious settlement into a mass ejection. However, the Act to preserve the person and government of the King gave a considerable degree of legal protection to such individuals, equating any attack on royal counsellors and officials with an attack on the King himself. But Puritan politicians and preachers were experienced circumlocutists.[104] The identification of the Pharisees of the Old Testament with the prelates of the Church of England was by 1662 such a commonplace that Thomas Lye, after deriding the Pharisees, felt obliged (perhaps with a nod and a wink) to add 'remember, I speak of the *Pharisees* all this while'.[105] Several Bartholomeans attacked the hypocrisy and human invention of the Scribes and Pharisees, John Barrett drawing from this that such 'unbelief is the root of disobedience'.[106] William Beerman warned his congregation to beware of the hypocritical religion of the Pharisees in their midst, while George Newton in drawing attention to Paul's care not to exalt himself above other men seems to have intended a criticism of episcopal government.[107] Despite the 1661 Act, the old image of a king duped by evil counsellors resurfaced repeatedly in the farewell sermons. George Thorne described how Nebuchadnezzar's jealous advisers persuaded him to legislate against Daniel's god, and how the Scribes and Pharisees had spied on Jesus in order to betray him.[108] Even the temperate Thomas Ford, in an otherwise irenic farewell sermon, discussed the conduct of Saul's evil counsellor Do'eg the Edomite.[109] It is, of course, a matter of opinion whether the priest-killing Do'eg was intended to stand for a contemporary figure, but Sheldon seems an obvious candidate. Restoration preachers had already made similar parallels – at least two sermons in 1660 had portrayed General Monck as Amasa, Saul's general who defected to David.[110]

Relatively few Bartholomeans ventured to offer direct moral instruction to those in authority. In his December sermon, Edmund Calamy gave an indication of the climate that had descended following Bartholomew's Day:

> What the Magistrate should do. I shall say but little of them, because I am not now to speak to them. They are to use their Authority for the settling of the *Ark*; for the *Ark* of Covenant will be like the *Ark* of *Noah*, always floating upon the waters, until the Magistrates settle it.[111]

Richard Fairclough, on the other hand, had earlier appeared to assume the right to lecture the King himself. Following several provocative passages where he discussed when (not if) it was permissible to disobey wicked or foolish governors, Fairclough posited a series of instructions for his superiors, concluding 'Rule not as an Executioner, but an Orator; not by force of iron, but by truth; but ever maintain the dignity of the place wherein, and the person for whom, thou rulest.'[112] The need for earthly kings to be subservient to God placed an implicit question mark over the nature of kingship. George Eubanke alluded to this in his farewell sermon at Great Ayton, saying,

It speaks Terrour to those that do their own will; such were the *Israelites*, I Sam. 8.5. They would needs have a King to rule over them, this was their will, and their will they would have, although they knew it jarr'd, and extremely interfear'd both with the will of God, and his Prophets, yet still the cry of the Rabble, and the vote of the multitude was this, *Nay but we will have a King*, ver.19.[113]

On occasion, a preacher's consideration of the relative status and power of earthly and divine authority could overlap with wider ideas of equality in the sight of the Lord. John Galpin was typical of many published Bartholomeans when he informed his congregation that 'every true and sincere believer, he is an Heir to a Crown, even a Crown of glory that fadeth not away'. He urged listeners to display their noble extraction, claiming that it was 'beneath the Children of the great King of Kings and Lord of Lords, to let their affections run inordinately after the world'.[114] Joseph Cooper declared that whilst the godly might not possess riches or honours, yet they had God, 'as a Crown of glory upon their heads'.[115] Mathew Mead noted that 'man by Grace is born to a Crown, to a Kingdom; he has a title to all the glory and blessedness of Heaven, from the first moment of his new birth'.[116] Joseph Caryl hinted that those who walked with Christ were the equal of princes and kings.[117] Just as Mead advised the godly not to envy those who possessed riches, honours, profits and pleasures, because such people had neither grace nor peace, so George Eubanke noted, 'As *Joseph* said to *Pharaoh, Without me God will provide an answer for* Pharaoh. So may I say in this case, without silver, without gold, without fair houses and rich furniture, *God can provide for the welfare of his people.*'[118] The rich and powerful, Thomas Manton noted, 'run onely for a corruptible Crown, we for a Crown that is incorruptible and glorious'. 'In other races', he continued, 'but *one* had the Crown; here all are crowned.'[119]

Even more contentious than images of crowns of glory and righteousness was the image of King Jesus – a phrase which had become all the more notorious for being heard repeatedly during Venner's abortive rising in 1661. John Wilson observes that in the 1640s references to Christ as king meant that 'the effective result was a denigration first of Charles I as the accepted king or ruler within the realm and then of a parliament composed of other than the saints'. This, he contends, 'was precisely the revolutionary import of this language, which in its effect went far beyond its explicit meaning'.[120] It is all the more interesting, therefore, that such language was to feature so widely in the farewell sermons of 1662. John Crodacot invited his congregation to 'crown the Prince of peace, the Lord Jesus Christ, in your hearts and lives; receive him as your Lord and King'.[121] John Hieron went further: 'It is to love him as our King, to submit to his Government, to be ruled by his Laws, to live according to his Gospel, to suffer no other Lord besides him, *to have Dominion over us.'*[122] George Swinnock assured his listeners that no one could arrest them without leave from the King of Heaven, and described the Gospel as 'a *royal Law, because* given to us by *God*, the King of the World, who hath Soveraignty and Dominion over all.' He went on to describe Jeroboam's innovations in liturgy of his church as high treason against the King of Heaven.[123] Philip Lamb assured his flock that Christ dictated the law, as he was the only head and king of his Church. 'Own *Jesus Christ* in all his *Offices*', he continued, 'as your *King, Priest*, and *Prophet*', 'As your *King*, let him have the Soveraignty of your Souls, that he may rule over you.'[124] That Lamb intended to throw down a challenge to royal authority was made evident from his application of Isaiah 30 (a chapter spiced with allusions to Pharaoh): '*Who say to the Seers, see not; and to the Prophets, prophecy not, & c., cause the Holy One to cease from before us?*'[125]

The tone of such a challenge was all the more strident for being combined with other metaphors recalling the armed conflict of the preceding decades. If, as Neil Keeble has suggested, the exhortation for the godly to stand fast in Thomas Manton's farewell sermon can be seen as a military metaphor, there is even more explicit imagery to be found elsewhere in the Bartholomean corpus.[126] Sharon Achinstein has found the juxtaposition of violence and grace to have been somewhat of a convention in nonconformist literature; one which may have evolved from a combination of 'Reformation apocalyptic and iconoclastic writing' and folk memories of civil war.[127] Given that the memory of civil war was still relatively fresh, it was understandable that a strain of militarism should have been evident in the farewell sermons. The purposes to which these military metaphors were put, however, appears to have varied. Given the alarming ghosts such images would have raised in the minds of older listeners, and the many occasions on which detailed military terminology was combined with other symbolism, the use of such rhetoric can hardly have reassured opponents as to the Bartholomeans' peaceful intent. Images of regimental solidarity were not simply designed to unite and energise the godly, but also to dismay and intimidate the profane. As the ejected minister Thomas Watson was later to write, 'The Earth is inherited by the meek . . . Heaven is inherited by the violent.'[128]

Several Bartholomeans pictured the invisible Church as a garrison under siege, reinforcing this image with exhortations to stand fast.[129] John Barrett regaled his congregation with examples of martyrs who had doubted their resolve in the face of a coming fight but had passed their test of courage, whilst others who had boasted of their bravery before they had put on their armour had been shamed.[130] William Bates, almost alone among the departing ministers, ventured to discuss the renewed threat of civil war. Nothing, he assured his listeners, could set off the lustre of peace more than the miseries of war; that men could make wounds, but only God could cure them. Peace came from God, whereas the counsels of war sprang 'from the devilish hearts of men'.[131] The implication of Bates's argument was that the aggression of the Bartholomeans' persecutors threatened a new civil war, whereas he and his colleagues were a force for peace. Matthew Mead was more circumspect, commenting only that 'as there can be no bitterer War than between conscience and the cure, so there can be no sweeter peace, then when mercy and peace meet together'.[132]

The military metaphors used in other farewell sermons were less irenic, many of them being used to construct the image of an army of martyrs.[133] In Thomas Lye's afternoon sermon, Joshua's invitation to his army captains to put their feet on the neck of captured kings appeared in a passage infused with a strong martial flavour: 'What a dishonour is this to a dying Saviour to see his servants flie. It was never known that men should flie before a conquered enemie, whose armes are taken away, whose limbs are cut off.'[134] John Clark mused that just as a good soldier should live and die with a good captain, so Christians should follow the 'Captain of their Salvation through difficulties and sufferings'.[135] Edward Hancock, in a sermon particularly rich in martial symbolism, reassured his flock that they were being commanded to join a successful war. He implored God to run his sword up to the hilt in the hearts of all impenitent sinners, his plea to God to make His Word sharper than a two-edged sword a provocative echo of Psalm 149, in which kings were bound in chains.[136]

Some preachers saw the war of words and spiritual conflict as a fight between opposing armies. Robert Porter spoke of the godly loosing off 'volleys of prayers', noting that,

> The Christian regiments that could joyn in Prayer, that were a Church as well as a Band, they were called *Thundring Regiments*. How it may be said of Assemblies, as of *Zion* in *Psal. 76.3. There brake the Arrows of the Bow, the Shield, and the Sword, and the Battel.*[137]

In one valediction Thomas Watson encouraged the godly to enlist ('are not we all Souldiers under one Regiment, under Jesus Christ, *the Lyon of the Tribe of Judah*, and Captain of our salvation?'), whilst in another, he cautioned against desertion ('Take heed that none of you here be found amongst the number of the *Wicked*; take heed of being of this black Regiment; beware of the Devils colours; fight not under this Banner').[138] George Swinnock advised his listeners to ignore such enemies, for, 'though their curses are like *false fire* [i.e., a misfire] which may flash a little, [they] will do no Execution'. The hardiest soldiers in God's army, he was sure, would be called upon to do the hardest service.[139] 'When the Adversary hath gotten the greatest advantage of us; of the Sun, of the Wind, of the Ground', intoned Richard Alleine, 'when he presseth with most violence, with most fury upon us, then we best know what the weapons of our Warfare are.'[140] '*The weapons of our warfare*', said Matthew Newcomen, echoing the words of Paul, '*are mighty through God.*'[141] Philip Lamb exhorted his congregation to 'keep the word, as a man keeps his Rule or the Souldier keeps his Weapon'.[142] But George Thorne urged all sides to put up the sword lest they perished by it.[143] However, Edward Hancock whilst pursuing a similarly irenic argument, still managed to introduce a element of menace by saying that,

> Prayers and tears are the Churches weapons, use no other, for those are the weapons that will fell tall and stately Cedars, those be the weapons that will scatter Kingdoms. It is said of a Queen of the Scots, that she was more afraid of *John Knox*, than of an Army of twenty thousand men.[144]

The most powerful of these spiritual weapons was unmistakably a weapon of the weak: the ability to endure persecution. 'Therefore arm your selves', said John Collins, 'with resolutions to suffer.'[145]

IV

Some years after the events of 1662, Richard Baxter admitted to the Bishop of London's chaplain that the nonconformists' interpretation of Scripture could often be interpreted as a comment against the times, as could 'all those Passages of Scripture which speak of Persecution and the Suffering of the Godly, but I hoped the Bibles should be licensed for all that'.[146] Sears McGee has argued that English Protestants, wary of endorsing Roman Catholic aestheticism, never sought affliction but rather welcomed it when it came.[147] This does not entirely accord with Matthew Newcomen's approval of Paul's eager anticipation of martyrdom, nor the contemporary report that many ministers had been preparing their followers for persecution months before Black Bartholomew.[148] Even if the Bartholomeans had not actively sought persecution, they embraced it with alacrity, as a test of faith and as a cleansing of the invisible church. Many farewell sermons contained practical advice and spiritual guidance on how to suffer patiently and peaceably. However, as one Bartholomean was to observe, the ability to endure was not a 'dull and sluggish impotency'.[149] It was, in fact, a source of considerable power.

Repeated images of incarceration, often using the imprisonment of Paul and Silas as an exemplar, suggest that many Bartholomeans anticipated a prolonged period of persecution. John Galpin urged the godly not to be afraid at the sight of their ministers suffering, nor to be discouraged by 'the backslidings of hypocriticall professors'.[150] Calamy's imprisonment for his illegal sermon at Aldermanbury seemed to fulfil predictions made in many farewell sermons that the godly would suffer in prison. William Cross attempted to comfort his more timorous followers by assuring them that

God's love would make prison Heaven.[151] Lewis Stucley said that any incarcerated for their beliefs should make their prison a palace.[152]

For Puritans, persecution was more than a transitory event; it had been an essential characteristic of Protestantism since Martin Luther. In one valediction among many featuring lengthy discussion as to why the godly should prefer suffering to sin, Matthew Mead made the astute observation that 'Persecution is the genius of the Gospel.'[153] 'We glory in Tribulations', Joseph Caryl exclaimed, recounting how Paul, Silas and other martyrs rejoiced at their imprisonment, and welcomed attempts to demean and dishonour them.[154] Several ministers held up Christ as the ultimate example of a godly man ready to embrace martyrdom and forgive his tormentors.[155] Daniel Bull called upon his congregation to '*rejoyce, in as much as ye are partakers of Christs sufferings, that when his glory shall be revealed, ye may be glad also with exceeding joy*'. Not only were the people of God apt to be troubled, Bull believed, but it was a sin for them *not* to be so.[156] Thus, as Joseph Moore observed, 'Piety hath been persecuted from the beginning of the world.'[157] Suffering was the prerequisite of godliness; without it, Galpin argued, many thousands were at that moment suffering torment in Hell because they had never been chastised in life.[158] Richard Alleine extracted a similar argument from Paul's epistle to the Corinthians, arguing that God chastened the godly in order to save them from the condemnation that awaited the world.[159] Just as God only permitted persecution for this ultimate good, so the godly by their suffering brought Him greater glory. Suffering was the paradigmatic weapon of the weak, as William Cross confirmed when reminding his flock of Paul's words to the Corinthians: '*I take pleasure in infirmities, in reproaches, in necessities, in persecutions, in distresses for Christ's sake; for when I am weak, then I am strong.*'[160]

The prevalence of Pauline scripture in the majority of printed farewell sermons owed much to the fact that the main focus of Paul's teaching had been to encourage the godly to maintain the purity of their worship and the integrity of their communion in the face of crushing persecution. The Pauline corpus thus resonated perfectly with the contemporary concerns and circumstances of the Bartholomean clergy. Like the images of kings and kingship, the application of Paul's critique of persecution was widely understood. In his sermon to the Irish Parliament on 29 May 1661, recalling royalist suffering during the Interregnum, John Parker used Pauline imagery in a fashion almost identical to that which would be employed by the Bartholomeans a year later.[161] William Jenkyn, in a valediction specifically designed to prepare his flock for the trials to come, described the anonymous epistle to the Hebrews as 'a little Book of Martyrs'. Through Hebrews Jenkyn was able to comprehend the divine purpose of godly suffering and conclude that the world was unworthy of such sufferers. William Bates drew from the same epistle an exhortation against back-sliding, seeking to inoculate his flock against the image of martyrs dying at the stake.[162] But Matthew Newcomen admitted the validity of the fears and doubts of those who had been brought up with Foxe's *Acts and Monuments*: 'Prison, and Death, and a Stake, are such Arguments, Brethren, that all the Learning and Parts of the World cannot answer, but onely Christ, and his Spirit and Grace in the Heart.'[163] John Barrett also acknowledged such anxieties, stating that 'they that decline the profession of Religion for fear of Persecution, and sufferings, are not so far from the Kingdom of God, as those who are cast off this other way' [i.e. follow false religion]. However, he also made extensive use of Pauline scripture to warn the godly to 'take heed lest by any means this liberty of yours become a stumbling block to them that are weak'.[164] It was better to suffer for a short time on earth than risk eternity in Hell. Richard Baxter challenged his listeners to prove that they were strong Christians, not weaklings who wilted at the mere threat of persecution and suffering.[165] Other ministers used a variety of approaches to both goad and comfort their listeners. Richard Alleine argued that there was peace to be found in persecution, whilst Newcomen, Watson and others offered the consoling thought that chastisement would not last forever.[166]

The ability of God to protect His children in time of trial was the recurrent theme of many farewell sermons, most noticeably those that cited the stories of Daniel's ordeal in the lions' den or the three 'children' thrown into King Nebuchadnezzar's furnace.[167] At their most basic level of meaning, these stories demonstrated that God was powerful enough to deliver the godly from the greatest peril. On the other hand, the ordeals of Daniel and the three children at the hands of Nebuchadnezzar were rare instances of Babylonian imagery in the printed Bartholomean sermons – despite the fact that Babylon had been used extensively as a yardstick of profanity during the 1640s and 1650s by preachers such as Caryl and Case, and would be appropriated in the 1660s by Cavalier writers for the same purpose.[168] William Cross, however, ventured beyond a simple message of comfort by reminding his congregation that 'the three un-martyred Martyrs encouraged themselves against the burning rage of an angry King and his fiery Fornace'.[169] Samuel Shaw made an even closer parallel between the three children and the ejected ministers.[170] The cause of the ordeal of the martyrs, Shadrach, Meshach and Abed-nego, was their refusal to participate in the idolatry and false worship ordered by the king. Annotations in both the Geneva Bible and other glossaries emphasised the fact that the three had been willing to appear before Nebuchadnezzar (a conspicuous display of passive obedience) but had suffered because they refused to obey his commands further than this, declaring that God would protect them.[171] The Book of Daniel, therefore, suggested that kings could be ungodly persecutors, that royalty could be defied, and that earthly authority was powerless to suppress the godly. Such aggressive suffering chimed with Mead's conviction that 'when Truth suffers by our silence, then we are called to suffer', and Case's assertion that, like Luther, nonconformists could be 'persecuted, but not conquered'.[172]

Underlying these discussions was a belief that persecution was ultimately self-defeating. For ministers such as John Oldfield and Samuel Shaw, the blood of martyrs was the seed of the Church. Far from requiring liberty, Shaw argued that history showed that the Gospel thrived during periods of persecution; 'even in our own Church of *England*, in the days of Queen Maryes Reign, it is observed that there grew up more good Members, than afterwards, when it had a better Head'. For Shaw, the Pauline epistles showed that when leaders were repressed followers only became more determined to spread the word; thus persecution and restraint would only produce more nonconformists.[173] Many preachers, such as John Whitlock, urged the godly to hold to the teachings of Christ despite the wiles of deceivers and the brutality of persecutors; some, such as Elias Pledger went so far as to remind listeners that 'the Believer resists unto bloud'.[174]

Warnings of imminent persecution could be combined with the sense of the eschatological moment to produce particularly powerful reasons for resistance. Thomas Brooks opined that one stage in God's destruction of Antichrist was the employment of those, like the few who had remained faithful in Sardis, willing to make any sacrifice to remain true to the Gospel.[175] The identification of nonconformists as martyrs was never far beneath the surface of such rhetoric. Richard Alleine's referral to Revelation for the image of the cloud of witnesses, and to Hebrews for that of an army of martyrs was typical of many printed valedictions.[176] If few ministers made explicit comparison between their experience and those of the Marian martyrs or the Parisian Huguenots, several ventured to offer anecdotes from the times as examples of godly conduct in the face of persecution and suffering. George Thorne, for contrast, gave an example of the dreadful fate of a Marian apostate Richard Denton, who was said to have burned to death in a house fire shortly after escaping the stake by recanting his Protestantism.[177]

The policy of religious persecution may long have been considered a popish doctrine, but – unlike in contemporaneous Anglican preaching – it was not explicitly presented as such in the Bartholomean farewell sermons. However, many Bartholomeans were willing to offer coded criticism of those they blamed for their plight. Sears McGee has discerned a contemporary consensus that a godly man could not blame his enemies for his troubles. Using the example of Joseph Caryl's extensive meditations on Job, McGee has argued that enemies were viewed simply as God's instruments of chastisement.[178] Certainly, John Whitlock urged his congregation not to 'eye man, but God in this dispensation', and Lazarus Seaman admitted that God sometimes had reason 'to let loose the Devill on his owne Children'.[179] Some ministers urged – at least, in passing – that the godly should ascribe their sufferings to their own sins, others that sufferers should not harbour thoughts of revenge.[180] However, whereas a lecture on Job would be bound to reach an irenic conclusion, meditations on persecution in the farewell sermons frequently took a more acerbic turn: Richard Alleine assured potential persecutors that 'when you have done your worst, 'twill be the better with [the godly]; though they will not thank you, yet they will thank God'. He assured his congregation that their persecutors would eventually be punished, because '*Persecution* is a black Mark of a *Son of Perdition*.'[181] Caryl explicated Revelation 6:11 by saying that it asked for godly martyrs to be honoured, when that passage of Scripture actually asked when their deaths were to be avenged.[182] Other Bartholomeans were less ambiguous in their excoriation of persecutors. Joseph Cooper remarked on the foolhardiness of all who set themselves against God's people.[183] Robert Porter believed that 'The burden that now lies upon God's Saints shall rest on the wicked in the end; God will reckon here with them.'[184] John Galpin warned that as true believers were the children of God, wicked men should take care how they meddled with them: 'little do the great ones of the world consider, what heavy reckonings will be laid to their charge one day for injuring, wronging and molesting the poor servants of God; if they did, surely, we should not have them so busily employed therein as they are'.[185]

In his farewell sermon at St Clement's, Thomas Watson painted a vivid picture of persecutors trying to defend their crimes in court on the Day of Judgement.[186] Whilst acknowledging that the sins of the godly merited punishment, Edward Hancock nevertheless cautioned potential persecutors that if they wished to damn their own souls they should not hate others that would save theirs. He was careful not to specify who these persecutors might be, but offered the opinion that 'men that have a great estate, and in great places, many times are the greatest enemies to the Church of God'. Amos 6:6, he noted, suggested that those that took pleasure in Joseph's affliction would suffer themselves.[187]

Whereas the New Testament stressed suffering under persecution, the Psalms provided useful ammunition against persecutors.[188] John Clark's citation of Psalms 37:16 ostensibly explained that 'a small thing that the righteous hath is better than great riches of the ungodly'; but the surrounding verses described how the ungodly were preparing to 'cast down the poor and needy and to slay such as are of a right conversation' and how God would break the arms of such persecutors and uphold the righteous.[189] The discussion of persecution, as with other contentious topics, benefited from the ambiguity of the follow-on tactic. Injudicious use of the Old Testament, despite the efficacy of its warnings of divine vengeance, could be provocative because it tended to name names: the slightest attempt to identify opponents – even by using Scriptural metaphor – raised questions as to the manner and timing of God's vengeance on ungodly persecutors and the identity of His agents of retribution.

Apart from attracting God's wrath, many Bartholomeans took comfort from the fact that persecution was doomed to failure. On 23 August 1662 George Latham recorded in Hunton parish register that the funeral service he had just taken was his last official act as rector. He concluded the entry with quotations from II Corinthians 6:9 and Isaiah 26:19, culminating with the words 'thy dead men shall live'.[190] Latham's sentiments resonated perfectly with the myriad images of death and dying which were at that moment saturating Bartholomean farewell sermons everywhere. The preface to Matthew Mead's *Pastor's valediction* was typical in referring to the minister's *'Civil, though Voluntary Death'*.[191]

First and foremost, such images were used to indicate the gravity of the events taking place, and the solemnity of the farewell sermons. At least one Bartholomean pamphlet referred to the author's final lecture as his funeral sermon, just as several Bartholomean compilations would include the authentic funeral sermons of James Nalton and Simeon Ashe.[192] The mood of such rhetoric was sometimes wistful, as in the case of George Eubanke's valediction:

> It's but a little, and those seats shall have other hearers, and this Pulpit have another Preacher; It's but a little that you have to hear, and I have to speak in this place, and shall not my *Dying words be Living words* to you? shall my *Farewel Sermon be a forgotten sermon*? and the last request I am like to make to you, be repulsed and slighted by you? O my dear Neighbours and Friends, *of whom I travail till Christ be formed in you*, Awake, and live.[193]

Many other Bartholomeans used the presage of civil death to great emotional effect. Thomas Jacombe informed his congregation that his farewell sermon was a duty of great importance, 'for though I speak to you as a living man, yet I speak to you as a dying Minister'.[194] Thomas Lye introduced his final morning sermon by telling his flock that he was going to speak as if he were about to die, later adding for good measure that they were unlikely to see each other again until Judgement Day. In the afternoon he assured them of his comfort, 'upon this day, that looks as like my dying day'.[195] Matthew Newcomen, after informing his flock that he was preaching his last in Dedham, measured his words carefully: 'what I would say to you, if I now lay on my Deathbed: the same I shall speak to you now'.[196]

Just as lawyers ascribed especial weight to deathbed testimonies, many Bartholomean clergy used the imminence of civil death to plead that their farewell sermons be given particular attention. Joseph Moore, after explicating the examples of Christ, Paul and Moses, urged that as the words of dying men were always highly regarded, so 'seeing in some sence we preach as dying persons, be intreated diligently to attend to dying words'.[197] 'The words of a dying friend are wont to make a deep impression', said John Barrett, 'so should be words of a departing Minister.'[198] John Galpin combined a sense of moment with the solemnity of the deathbed: 'I desire to leave a word or two with each of you, which I would have you to look upon as the words of a dying Minister, or of a dead Minister, in a civil sense; and therefore suffer them to take the deeper impression upon your hearts.'[199] The affidavit of a dying man was not simply considered significant, but was assumed to be true. Thus, by professing their willingness to embrace civil death, ministers substantiated their claims to be purveyors of God's truth. Such truth claims were often reinforced by images of purity, such as could be found in Revelation 3 ('they shall walk with me in white'); symbols of martyrdom that, as Jonathan Sawday has demonstrated, would have been perfectly intelligible to Anglicans.[200]

One effect of associating death with purity was to reinforce the equally prevalent images of martyrdom and persecution. Given that the blood of several prominent figures of the Interregnum (including the preacher Hugh Peter) had so recently stained Tyburn scaffold, one or two Bartholomeans were surprisingly daring in their rhetoric. Edward Hancock alluded to the spectacle of a public execution on the gallows, informing his flock that he was going to speak like a man preparing to die a violent death. He talked of the necessity of dying well, now that the hour had come, whilst John Clark asserted that it was a thousand times better to be hanged or burnt for Christ than to die quietly in bed.[201] Far from dying quietly, Samuel Shaw pictured himself returning as a vengeful ghost: 'How welcome do ye think a Minister rising from the dead, would be to a people, formerly it may be ungrateful to him?'[202] Ministers such as Seddon and Watson hoped that the manner of their civil death might serve as a sacrifice which would give strength and comfort to the godly.[203] Newcomen, Eubanke and Seddon all evoked the example of Samson, seeing in their imminent demise an opportunity to achieve more by a final act of faith than they had done in all their preceding years of spiritual toil: 'as *Samson* slew more *Philistines* at his *death* than in all his *life*, so I might be the happy Instrument, *to save more souls now at my departure from you, than in all my life before*'.[204]

Some Bartholomeans envisaged a more peaceful end. Richard Fairclough invited his congregation to observe 'how beautiful it is to see an old man dying, like *Jacob*' – although the bulk of his sermon revolved around the peril of dying in sin and the need for repentance.[205] The dying father was a ubiquitous metaphor, possessing both the emotional pull of a family bereavement and an assumption of hegemony. Ministers served up numerous examples of Biblical fathers giving final advice to their sons. The image of the dying father was frequently combined with an assertion that the farewell sermons were a legacy. John Crompton arranged his valediction as if it were his legal will, portraying his moral advice as a series of bequests to various sons.[206] Daniel Bull used Paul's departure from the Galatians to present images of the apostle leaving his words as a legacy to his children.[207]

The use of Pauline scripture had another implication; as John Coolidge has observed, Paul viewed death as a planting.[208] Minister after minister used their final sermons to urge congregations to contemplate the implications of death. This was sometimes presented as a warning, as when Newcomen addressed his audience as people who were already damned.[209] On other occasions, ministers simply exhorted their congregations to 'Think much of, and live in preparation for death; *walk* now and then amongst the Tombs; live every day as dying men.'[210] Baxter advice was to be 'all your life long be longing to die: let the work of your life be to learn to dye'.[211]

Civil (and even physical) death was welcome for several reasons. Firstly, it was a rejection of the world. Bull recounted the story of a child who told his bereaved mother that God was alive even though his father was dead. 'May I not say to you', Bull concluded from this, that 'though your Ministers be as it were naturally dead, yet is not God alive?'[212] Such sentiments have influenced some to argue that the events of the Restoration caused 'a redefinition of the Good Old Cause', inasmuch as nonconformists thereafter discarded any ambitions for political power in favour of an aspiration to the Kingdom of God.[213] However, the implications of the Pauline concept of Christ's death as a planting were less innocent than this. Paul's epistle to the Romans clearly implied that death was not simply a rejection of the world, but also an escape from the jurisdiction of its law ('ye also are become dead to the law by the body of Christ'), an implication made plain by the Westminster Annotations of 1657 regarding Romans 7:1–4:

> We are not onely dead to the law, but the law also is dead unto us, because it cannot thrust out its sting at us, either to curse us, or to provoke us unto sin; the law hath no more power over us than dead men in either of these respects.[214]

Civil death, therefore, handed the Bartholomeans an opportunity, in an intellectual sense, to escape the clutches of worldly authority, not that they had any intention of allowing civil death to put an end to their influence. Thus, John Crodacot was able to describe his valediction as 'the words of a dying man, yet not dead, but alive, and perhaps shall not die'.[215] Richard Fairclough hoped that when he was dead he might yet speak, while Joseph Moore prayed that the godly would let dead prophets continue to preach to them.[216] Thomas Lye emphasised that dying was not simply a matter for the Bartholomean clergy, but for all members of the invisible church: 'We live if you stand', he argued, in a conscious echo of Paul's martyrdom at the hands of Rome.[217] Dying well set a good example for the godly laity at the same time as it sent a message to the authorities – as Joseph Caryl highlighted in describing how the manner of Christ's dying impressed the Roman centurion guarding the Cross.[218] Thus, when Bartholomeans such as Newcomen and Thorne pleaded with their flocks not to weep and break their heart, they quoted Paul's words in full: '*I am ready not to be bound only, but to dye at Jerusalem for the Name of the Lord Jesus.*'[219] Civil death was not defeatist, neither was it futile; it was the ultimate expression of resistance.

V

If it was a relatively straightforward matter for the Restoration authorities to take action against ministers who openly refused to comply with the Act of Uniformity, it was much harder to control the slippery rhetoric of a competent preacher. Edmund Calamy, for example, was imprisoned for the act of unlicensed preaching after Bartholomew's Day rather than for the content of his sermon. Consequently, Biblical citations and Scriptural metaphors were skilfully deployed in the farewell sermons to circumnavigate the power of political and episcopal authority in order to posit criticism and encourage resistance.

Scripture was used because it was considered an unimpeachable source of Truth; suitably interpreted and arranged, it gave a sense of order and purpose to human existence. This was not simply a process of internal revelation, even for Puritans, but one which required external reference points in order to achieve intelligibility and coherence. In order to remain separate from the world, it was necessary to define it. On a more practical level, parliamentary legislation, a volatile political climate and widespread awareness of the radical potential of Scriptural metaphor meant that in selecting texts for a farewell sermon, each and every Bartholomean was required to make a political judgement. The saving knowledge thus expounded was, by its very nature, political advice, and the selection and application of Scripture not a sign of intellectual laziness but rigorous deliberation.

The sense of moment implicit in the rhetoric of the farewell sermons revealed a concern both with contemporary politics and wider eschatology. The tension between earthly and divine authority was brought into sharp focus, as the Act of Uniformity provoked criticism and resistance from ministers spread throughout England and Wales. The enormity of the event, combined with the experience of political defeat, encouraged many preachers to adopt an apocalyptic tone, tinged with an uncertainty borne of the vicissitudes of the previous twenty years. For many Bartholomeans, the crisis engendered by the Act of Uniformity was another episode in the unfolding role of England in God's plan. Despite an underlying belief in England's special status evident in several farewell sermons, however, no departing preacher offered a guarantee that the nation had been 'saved'; an attitude that undermined the Cavalier-Anglican trope that God had shown his favour by restoring the monarchy.[220]

The prevailing historiographical view of the farewell sermons of 1662 as quietist appears to have been predicated on an erroneous perception that the Bartholomeans were unwilling to engage with political and episcopal author-ity. However, refusal to comply with the Act of Uniformity was, by definition, criticism of and resistance to Parliament and the bishops who had authored it. Had the ejected ministers done no more than this, their actions could be (and were) perceived by contemporaries as criticism of and resistance to royal authority. As it was, despite intense moral pressure, many printed farewell sermons, which featured unmistakably critical comment on the Restoration regime and even discussed the very precepts of royal authority – albeit usually by means of Scriptural metaphor surrounded by a thickly textured and deliberately ambiguous rhetoric. Some of the rhetoric was so straightforward as hardly to be considered 'coded', such as the use of various facets of King David in reference to Charles II. References to hate figures such as Pharaoh, Ahab and Jeroboam featured in too many valedictions to be considered inadvertent embellishments. Contentious as these Old Testa-ment references were, the heavy use of Pauline scripture constituted a more fundamental challenge, namely that whilst Charles II and his ministers were held to be subject to the laws of God, the godly, in obeying the Word, were above the laws of man where these were incompatible with the Word. The rhetoric of the farewell sermons suggests that by 1662 there were deep divisions regarding the concept of monarchy. Charles II's miraculous preservation and the restoration of the Stuart monarchy after a period of unparalleled suffering and humiliation was interpreted by conformist pre-achers as conclusive evidence that Providence was on their side.[221] In the 29 May and 30 January sermons the Restoration was presented as the closure of the debate. By contrast, earthly regimes were presented in many farewell sermons to be fleeting, transitory and ultimately inconsequential. The Bartholomean image of kings and kingship had an ominous fluidity, allowing Thomas Lye to offer up prayers for Charles II as the 'nursing father' of the nation at the same time as he presented images of soldiers with their feet on the neck of a captive king.[222] Cavalier-Anglicans can hardly have been reassured to learn that supposedly moderate Puritans expressed views that amounted to a denial of the absolute power and permanency of kingship. Such views did little to resolve the morality of resisting royal authority, par-ticularly when some nonconformist preachers were able to envisage resisting even unto blood.

The ubiquitous images of persecution and suffering in the Bartholomean farewell sermons were an integral part of this negotiation of authority. Persecution was welcomed because it was held to be a confirmation of godliness. The more the nonconformists suffered, the more certainly they were children of God. By the same coin, the more their persecutors inflicted suffering, the more certainly the latter were destined for damnation. As these persecutors could hardly be construed as anyone other than the political and episcopal authorities, such rhetoric could hardly fail to be interpreted as criticism and resistance. Martyrdom in the guise of 'civil death' was the ultimate expression of such resistance, in that it was simultaneously a claim to truth and an attempt to negate the efforts of human authority to restrict the communication of God's Word.

The Bartholomeans' skilful use of rhetoric in their farewell sermons enabled them to use the valedictions not simply to provide spiritual comfort and a checklist of godly conduct, but also to foster political debate which would endure after their departure – in Newcomen's words, to make the people 'sensible' of the issues.[223] Immunity from legal retribution lay not so much in the fact that this rhetoric was encoded but that it was highly ambiguous and worked on several levels. This strength, however, was also a weakness, for the Bartholomeans would find that they were no more able to control the reception and interpretation of their exegesis than the political authorities.

NOTES

1 Watson, *Pastor's Love Expressed*, p. 14.

2 *England's Remembrancer*, p. 163.

3 Watson, *Pastor's Love Expressed*, p. 14.

4 E.g., Fairclough, *Pastor's Legacy*, p. 129.

5 A. Patterson, *Censorship and Interpretation: The Conditions of Writing and Reading in Early Modern England* (Madison, WI, 1984), pp. 10–11, 21; R. Pooley, 'Language and loyalty: plain style at the Restoration', *Literature and History*, 6, 1 (1980), p. 5; Hill, *English Bible*, p. 78.

6 Potter, *Secret Rites*, p. 38.

7 Patterson, *Censorship and Interpretation*, p. 17.

8 Pooley, 'Language and loyalty', p. 9; Morrissey, 'Interdisciplinarity', p. 1116.

9 Hill, *English Bible*, p. 337.

10 *England's Remembrancer*, p. 432.

11 Thorne, *Saint's Great Duty*, p. 5.

12 Wilson, *Pulpit in Parliament*, pp. 147–9.

13 These statistics assume that Richard Fairclough's valedictory sermons were based on the main text of II Corinthians 13:1, and those of Joseph Cooper's on Philippians 4:9.

14 Jenkyn, *Burning Yet Un-consumed Bush*, p. 16; Exodus 3:2.

15 Bates, *Peace-Maker*, pp. 1–19; Bladon, in *England's Remembrancer*, pp. 324–386.

16 Oldfield's main text was Psalms 69:6, but explicated by use of John 2:17 and Romans 15:3; *England's Remembrancer*, p. 239.

17 *Second and Last Collection*, p. 147; Jeremiah 2:11–12. Some ministers did make use of Exodus imagery; e.g., Swinnock, *Pastor's Farewell*. Deuteronomy was characterised by a discussion of the Covenant and 'preached law', binding on kings no less than subjects.

18 Lye, *Fixed Saint*, p. 11. Cf. Barrett's second sermon, in *England's Remembrancer*, p. 75; Thorne, in *Saint's Great Duty*, p. 1; Powel, in Bodl. Rawl. MS E93, fo. 43–43v.

19 DWL MS I.h.35, fo. 1; *Second and Last Collection*, pp. 159, 161–2.

20 Newcomen, *Ultimum Vale*, p. 16.

21 *England's Remembrancer*, p. 389. Cf. Joseph Moore and Thomas Bladon (*ibid.*, pp. 38, 301); Galpin, in *Third Volume*, p. 217; Oldfield, in *England's Remembrancer*, pp. 251, 257; Lewis Stucley in Bodl. Rawl. MS E93, fo. 38.

22 *Exact Collection*, pp. 109–10.

23 *England's Remembrancer*, p. 231; Matthew 3:10.

24 Slater, in *Exact Collection*, p. 128; Venning, in *Second and Last Collection*, p. 133.

25 *England's Remembrancer*, pp. 7, 10, 23, 30; Acts 14.

26 Baxter, *Reliquiae Baxterianae*, pt II, p. 384.

27 Porter, *Life of Mr John Hieron*, p. 24.

28 G. Burnet, *The History of My Own Time*, ed. O. Airy (Oxford, 1897), vol. I, p. 327.

29 *England's Remembrancer*, pp. 301–2.

30 *Exact Collection*, p. 6.

31 J. Warwell, *Votiva Tabula* (1660), p. 57.

32 Bury, *The Bow*, pp. 23–4.

33 *Second and Last Collection*, pp. 164–5; cf. Calamy's farewell sermon, in *Exact Collection*, p. 8.

34 Lye, *Fixed Saint*, p. 29.

35 *Exact Collection*, p. 12; *Third Volume*, p. 158; *Second and Last Collection*, p. 57.

36 Thorne, *Saint's Great Duty*, p. 26; Chronicles 15:2. Cf. Beerman, in *Compleat Collection*, sig. [Rr3].

37 *Exact Collection*, p. 21.

38 *England's Remembrancer*, pp. 223–4. Cf. Cross, *ibid.*, p. 162.

39 Alleine, *Godly Man's Portion*, pp. 28, 36, 38, 54.

40 Hancock, *Pastor's Last Legacy*, sig. B3; Revelation 18:4; Brooks, in *Second and Last Collection*, p. 62.

41 *England's Remembrancer*, pp. 49, 62.

42 *Third Volume*, p. 75. Cf. Fairclough, *Pastor's Legacy*, p. 66; Beerman, in *Compleat Collection*, sig. Ss2; Horton, *Rich Treasure*, sig. A2.

43 Eubanke *Farewell Sermon Preached*, p. 41.

44 *Compleat Collection*, sig. [Eeee3v–4v], [Ffff3].

45 J. Downame (ed.), *The Second Volume of Annotations Upon All the Books of the Old and Nevv Testament* (1657), II Kings 2:2 and 13:14; Newcomen, *Ultimum Vale*, p. 21; Joseph Moore in *England's Remembrancer*, p. 422.

46 *Ibid.*, p. 168; Philippians 1:12; cf. Shaw, *The Voice*, p. 187.

47 *England's Remembrancer*, p. 423 ('wonderful' here meaning 'extraordinary'). Cf. Calamy, in *Exact Collection*, p. 411.

48 M. Morrissey, 'Elect nations and prophetic teaching: types and examples in the Paul's Cross jeremiad', in Ferrell and McCullough, *English Sermon Revised*, p. 41. For discussions of England as a covenanted nation, see J. Spurr, 'Virtue, religion and government: the Anglican uses of Providence', in Harris, Seaward and Goldie, *Politics of Religion*, p. 36; Claydon, 'The sermon, the "public sphere" and the political culture of late seventeenth-century England', in Ferrell and McCullough, *English Sermon Revised*, p. 218.

49 Newcomen, *Ultimum Vale*, pp. 27–8.

50 *Exact Collection*, p. 25. Cf. Brooks, in *Second and Last Collection*, p. 56; Newcomen, *Ultimum Vale*, p. 29; Lye, *Fixed Saint*, p. 15.

51 *Third Volume*, p. 5. Cf. Case, in *Exact Collection*, p. 105.

52 *Exact Collection*, p. 30. See also Brinsley and Ludlow, quoted in Hill, *English Bible*, pp. 284, 414, and Keeble, *Literary Culture*, p. 198.

53 *Third Volume*, p. 48.

54 Bodl. Rawl. MS E93, fo. 5.

55 E.g., W. Strong, *The Way to the Highest Honour* (1647), p. 48, quoted in Wilson, *Pulpit in Parliament*, p. 212.

56 *England's Remembrancer*, pp. 314, 316; Revelation 11:7–9.

57 E.g., Alleine, *Godly Man's Portion*, pp. 101, 116; Manton, in *Exact Collection*, p. 309.

58 *Exact Collection*, p. 28.

59 Wilson, *Pulpit in Parliament*, pp. 199, 207–8, 230.

60 Quoted in Patterson, *Censorship and Interpretation*, p. 14.

61 *Ibid.*, p. 15.

62 *England's Remembrancer*, p. 309.

63 Browning, *Documents*, pp. 63–5.

64 The 29 May service was instituted by Act of Parliament, that of 30 January by a clause in the Act of Attainder (1660); H. Randall, 'The rise and fall of a martyrology: sermons on Charles I', *Huntington Library Quarterly*, 10, 2 (1946–47), p. 135.

65 E.g., Josselin, *Diary*, pp. 475, 486; E. Hickeringill, *An Apology for Distressed Innocence* (1663); Kem, *King Solomon's Infallable Experiment*; Eedes, *Great Britain's Ressurrection*; Newcombe, *Usurpation Defeated and David Restored*.

66 Miller, *After the Civil Wars*, p. 131.

67 Newcombe, *Diary*, p. 117.

68 S. Brunsell, *Solomon's Blessed Land* (1660), p. 35; Eedes, *Great Britain's Ressurrection*, p. 14.

69 J. Nelme, *England's Royal Stone at the Head of the Corner* (1660), pp. 6, 8, 9.

70 R. Mossom, *England's Gratulation for the King and His Subjects' Happy Union* (1660), p. 3. See Spurr, *Restoration Church*, pp. 28, 29; G. Sheldon, *David's Deliverance and Thanksgiving* (1660), p. 2; Josselin, *Diary*, p. 463. Earlier and later uses of the image of David are discussed by Wilson (*Pulpit in Parliament*, p. 232), McGee (*Godly Man*, p. 238), Potter (*Secret Rites*, p. 131) and Hill (*English Bible*, pp. 54, 97, 379).

71 *Exact Collection*, pp. 2, 3, 5, 12–13.

72 *England's Remembrancer*, pp. 87–8. A more subtle implication may have been intended, based on the fact that Joab's reason for murdering Abner was that he was suspicious of Abner's change of allegiance from Saul to David.

73 *Exact Collection*, pp. 70, 74.

74 E.g., Cross and Whitlock, in *England's Remembrancer*, pp. 27, 153; Eubanke, *Farewell Sermon Preached*, pp. 7, 34; Ford, in Bodl. Rawl. MS E93, fos 2–4; Alleine, *Godly Man's Portion*, pp. 13, 96; Watson, in *Compleat Collection*, sig. [Tv].

75 J. Meriton, *Curse Not the King* (1660), p. 30; Walwyn, *God Save the King*, pp. 7–8.

76 Lye, *Fixed Saint*, p. 19; Joshua 10:24 (incorrectly cited as Joshua 3:4).

77 Downame, *The Second Volume of Annotations*, Joshua 10:24.

78 Lye, *Fixed Saint*, p. 23.

79 Eubanke, *Farewell Sermon Preached*, p. 23; II Samuel 2.

80 Jenkyn, *Burning Yet Un-consumed Bush*, p. 13.

81 Fairclough, *Pastor's Legacy*, p. 83.

82 Jenkyn, *Burning Yet Un-consumed Bush*, p. 4.

83 Barrett, in *England's Remembrancer*, p. 69; Eubanke, *Farewell Sermon Preached*, p. 13; Bates, *Peace-Maker*, p. 5.

84 T. Hodges, *Sion's Halelujah* (1660), p. 7; T. Washbourn, *The Repairer of the Breach* (1661), p. 25; J. Whynnell, *England's Sorrows Turned into Joy* (1661), pp. 10–15; Meriton, *Curse Not the King*, p. 14; Sheldon, *David's Deliverance*, pp. 10–11.

85 Sheldon, *David's Deliverance*, pp. 10–11.

86 M. Henry, *The Life of the Revd. Philip Henry*, ed. J. Williams (1837), p. xxxv, quoted in Keeble, *Literary Culture*, p. 274.

87 Jenkyn, *Burning Yet Un-consumed Bush*, pp. 3, 8; Hebrews 11:25–6.

88 Alleine, *Godly Man's Portion*, pp. 54, 127, 144, 151.

89 *Compleat Collection*, sig. Aaaa; Lamb, *Royal Presence*, sig. [D2v].

90 L'Estrange, *Toleration Discuss'd*, p. 105.

91 Mead, *Pastor's Valediction*, p. 9; *England's Remembrancer*, p. 497.

92 Eubanke, *Farewell Sermon Preached*, p. 29.

93 E.g., Eedes, *Great Britain's Ressurrection*, p. 2; Kem, *King Solomon's Infallible Expedient*, p. 11; J. Parker, *A Sermon Preached at Christ-Church, Dublin* (Dublin, 1661), p. 1. Jeroboam was a traditional hate figure and example of bad kingship; Hill, *English Bible*, p. 106.

94 *Second and Last Collection*, p. 54; II Chronicles 13:9.

95 *Second and Last Collection*, pp. 55, 72.

96 Hill, *English Bible*, p. 420.

97 *England's Remembrancer*, pp. 67, 68–70.

98 Beerman, in *Compleat Collection*, sig. Rr3, [Rr3v]; Psalm 105:15; Jenkyn, *Burning Yet Un-consumed Bush*, p. 5.

99 *England's Remembrancer*, p. 310.

100 J. Douch, *England's Jubilee* (1660), p. 8.

101 Parker, *A Sermon Preached at Christ-Church, Dublin*, p. 40; C. Barksdale, *The Kings Return* (1660), p. 10; Newcombe, *Usurpation Defeated and David Restored*, p. 19. Thomas Pierce, in a sermon given at St Paul's in 1660 referred to his congregation as 'the head and heart of the Royal City'; quoted in Bosher, *Restoration Settlement*, p. 154.

102 DWL MS I.l.35, fo. 2r.

103 *England's Remembrancer*, p. 1.

104 Hill, *English Bible*, p. 246.

105 Lye, *Fixed Saint*, p. 11. For discussion of the parallel between the Pharisees and the prelates of the Church of England, see Hill, *English Bible*, p. 109. Marchmont Needham's description of the Scottish Covenanters as 'blew Pharisees' demonstrates that the term was a common term of abuse; *Mercurius Politicus*, 20–7 June 1650, p. 40 – a reference I owe to the kindness of Alex Craven.

106 *England's Remembrancer*, p. 82; Psalm 78:37; Matthew 15:7.

107 *Compleat Collection*, sig. [Rr4v], Gggg.

108 Thorne, *Saint's Great Duty*, p. 7.

109 Bodl. Rawl. MS E93, fo. 5.

110 F. Walsall, *The Bowing the Heart of Subjects to Their Sovereign* (1660), p. 3; Walwyn, *God Save the King*, pp. 1, 3.

111 *Exact Collection*, p. 28. Cf. Lye, *Fixed Saint*, p. 4.

112 Fairclough, *Pastor's Legacy*, pp. 100–2, 111.

113 Eubanke, *Farewell Sermon Preached*, p. 11.

114 *Third Volume*, pp. 182, 192 [mispaginated].

115 *Compleat Collection*, sig. [Aaaa4].

116 Mead, *Pastor's Valediction*, p. 5.

117 Caryl, *White Robe*, p. 3.

118 Mead, *Pastor's Valediction*, p. 17; Eubanke, *Farewell Sermon Preached*, p. 33.

119 *Exact Collection*, pp. 315, 325; (I Corinthians 9:25), 325 (II Timothy 4:8). Cf. Seaman and Newcomen, in *Second and Last Collection*, pp. 7, 139; Pledger and Wadsworth, in *Compleat Collection*, sig. [Fffv], Ffff2; Shaw, in *England's Remembrancer*, p. 174.

120 Wilson, *Pulpit in Parliament*, p. 232.

121 *Third Volume*, pp. 24, 26.

122 *England's Remembrancer*, p. 122.

123 Swinnock, *Pastor's Farewell*, pp. 49, 61, 62.

124 Lamb, *Royal Presence*, sig. [Cv], E2.

125 *Ibid.*, sig. [D4]; Isaiah 30:10–11.

126 Keeble, *Literary Culture*, pp. 198–9.

127 S. Achinstein, *Literature and Dissent in Milton's England* (Cambridge, 2003), p. 84.

128 Quoted in Achinstein, *Literature and Dissent*, p. 91.

129 Bull, in *Third Volume*, p. 59; Bates, *Peace-Maker*, pp. 12, 14; Barrett, in *England's Remembrancer*, pp. 107–8; Hancock, *Pastor's Last Legacy*, sig. [D4]; Swinnock, *Pastor's Farewell*, pp. 4, 44.

130 *England's Remembrancer*, p. 109.

131 Bates, *Peace-Maker*, p. 4.

132 Mead, *Pastor's Valediction*, p. 8.

133 E.g., Alleine, *Godly Man's Portion*, p. 102.

134 Lye, *Fixed Saint*, p. 19.

135 *England's Remembrancer*, p. 493. Cf. Seddon, in *ibid.*, p. 205.

136 Hancock, *Pastor's Last Legacy*, sig. [B4v], E. See also Revelation 1:16 – a reference I owe to the kindness of Roger Pooley.

137 *England's Remembrancer*, pp. 440, 445.

138 *Compleat Collection*, sig. [T3]; *Exact Collection*, p. 68.

139 Swinnock, *Pastor's Farewel*, pp. 31, 51.

140 Alleine, *Godly Man's Portion*, p. 97.

141 Newcomen, *Ultimum Vale*, p. 47; II Corinthians 10:4. Cf. Whitlock, in *England's Remembrancer*, p. 12.

142 Lamb, *Royal Presence*, sig. [B4].

143 Thorne, *Saint's Great Duty*, p. 26; Matthew 26:52.

144 Hancock, *Pastor's Last Legacy*, sig. [B4–B4v]; cf. Alleine, *Godly Man's Portion*, p. 98.

145 *Exact Collection*, p. 384.

146 Baxter, *Reliquiae Baxterianae*, pt I, p. 123.

147 McGee, *Godly Man*, p. 52.

148 Newcomen, *Ultimum Vale*, p. 5 (Acts 20:22–4); BL MS Egerton 2537, fo. 331, quoted in Spurr, *Restoration Church*, p. 42. See also Oldfield, in *England's Remembrancer*, p. 266; Pledger, in *Compleat Collection*, sig. [Ffff3]; and Watson, in *Exact Collection*, p. 55.

149 John Howe, quoted in Keeble, *Literary Culture*, p. 200.

150 *Third Volume*, p. 219.

151 *England's Remembrancer*, pp. 161–2; cf. Jacombe, in *Exact Collection*, p. 79.

152 Bodl. Rawl. MS E93, fo. 28.

153 Mead, *Pastor's Valediction*, p. 20.

154 Caryl, *White Robe*, pp. 8, 17. Cf. Moore and Shaw, in *England's Remembrancer*, pp. 169–70, 396.

155 E.g., Jacombe, in *Exact Collection*, p. 72; Alleine, in *Godly Man's Portion*, p. 101; Cross, Shaw, Seddon and Moore, in *England's Remembrancer*, pp. 165, 175, 177, 206, 219, 221, 388–9; Thorne, in *Saint's Great Duty*, pp. 49, 52; Powel, in Bodl. Rawl. MS E93, fos. 39–40; Watson, in *Compleat Collection*, sig. T2. According to Sears McGee the use of Christ as a moral example was rare in Puritan writings; McGee, *Godly Man*, p. 251.

156 *Third Volume*, pp. 36, 44.

157 *England's Remembrancer*, p. 412. Cf. John Whitlock, *ibid.*, p. 10, and Alleine, *Godly Man's Portion*, p. 9.

158 *Third Volume*, pp. 179 [mispaginated, p. 193], 211.

159 Alleine, *Godly Man's Portion*, p. 31; I Corinthians 11:32. Cf. Jacombe, in *Exact Collection*, p. 78.

160 *England's Remembrancer*, p. 165; II Corinthians 12:10.

161 Parker, *A Sermon Preached at Christ-Church, Dublin*, p. 32.

162 Jenkyn, *Burning Yet Un-consumed Bush*, p. 1; Bates, *Peace-Maker*, p. 2; Hebrews 4:34.

163 *Second and Last Collection*, p. 154.

164 *England's Remembrancer*, pp. 87–8, 89; I Corinthians 8:9, 12; Romans 14.

165 *Exact Collection*, pp. 144, 154.

166 Alleine, *Godly Man's Portion*, p. 9; Newcomen, *Ultimum Vale*, p. 57. Cf. Jacombe, in *Exact Collection*, p. 79; Watson, *Pastor's Love Expressed*, p. 19; Oldfield, in *England's Remembrancer*, p. 250; II Corinthians 4:17, 18.

167 Cross, in *England's Remembrancer*, p. 164; Eubanke, *Farewell Sermon Preached*, p. 38; Lamb, *Royal Presence*, sig. [Dv]. Jacombe, in *Exact Collection*, pp. 77, 79; Galpin, in *Third Volume*, p. 179; Swinnock, in *Pastor's Farewell*, p. 51.

168 Hill, *English Bible*, pp. 110–11, 112; Sawday, 'Re-writing a revolution', p. 183. A rare reference to Israel in bondage in Babylon appears in Watson's sermon at St Clements; *Exact Collection*, p. 55.

169 *England's Remembrancer*, p. 164.

170 *Ibid.*, p. 176.

171 Daniel 3:16–17, quoted by Galpin, in *Third Volume*, p. 179; Daniel 3:17, quoted by Cross, in *England's Remembrancer*, p. 164.

172 Mead, *Pastor's Valediction*, p. 21; Case, *Exact Collection*, p. 106.

173 *England's Remembrancer*, pp. 171, 179, 186, 243.

174 Whitworth, in *England's Remembrancer*, p. 37; Pledger, in *Compleat Collection*, sig. [Fff3].

175 *Second and Last Collection*, pp. 58, 62.

176 Alleine, *Godly Man's Portion*, pp. 101–2.

177 Thorne, *Saint's Great Duty*, p. 26.

178 McGee, *Godly Man*, p. 28.

179 Whitlock, in *England's Remembrancer*, p. 17; Seaman, in *Second and Last Collection*, p. 11.

180 Newcomen, in *Second and Last Collection*, p. 162; Thorne, *Saint's Great Duty*, p. 57; Seddon, Oldfield and Porter, in *England's Remembrancer*, pp. 220, 240, 243, 254, 468; Watson, in *Compleat Collection*, sig. T2.

181 Alleine, *Godly Man's Portion*, pp. 33, 153.

182 Caryl, *White Robe*, p. 5; Revelation 6:11.

183 *Compleat Collection*, sig. [Aaaa4]. See also Cross, in *England's Remembrancer*, p. 166.

184 *Ibid.*, p. 448.

185 *Third Volume*, p. 187. Cf. Jacombe, in *Exact Collection*, p. 80, and Lamb, *Royal Presence*, sig. [B2].

186 *Exact Collection*, p. 63.

187 Hancock, *Pastor's Last Legacy*, sig. [A4], [B3v]. See also Galpin, in *Third Volume*, p. 211.

188 Hill, *English Bible*, pp. 155, 351.

189 *England's Remembrancer*, pp. 490, 491; Psalm 37:16.

190 *CR*, p. 316; Green, *Re-establishment*, p. 155. Cf. Oldfield, *England's Remembrancer*, p. 265; Hebrews 11:4: 'though we are dead, we yet speak'.

191 Mead, *Pastor's Valediction*, sig. A2.

192 Jenkyn, *Burning Yet Un-consumed Bush*, preface. Thomas Powel described his valediction as his funeral sermon; Bodl. Rawl. MS E93, fo. 51v.

193 Eubanke, *Farewell Sermon Preached*, p. 20.

194 *Exact Collection*, p. 86.

195 Lye, *Fixed Saint*, pp. 2, 14, 17.

196 *Second and Last Collection*, pp. 159–60.

197 *England's Remembrancer*, p. 390. Cf. Hancock, *Pastor's Last Legacy*, sig. A3; Galpin, in *Third Volume*, p. 216; Lamb, *Royal Presence*, sig. E4; Lye, *Fixed Saint*, p. 14.

198 *England's Remembrancer*, p. 45. Cf. Jenkyn, *Burning Yet Un-consumed Bush*, preface, and Caryl, *White Robe*, sig. A2.

199 *Third Volume*, p. 216. Cf. Lamb, *Royal Presence*, sig. E4, and Slater, in *Exact Collection*, p. 135.

200 E.g., Brooks, in *Second and Last Collection*, p. 62, and Caryl, *White Robe*, p. 1; Revelation 3:4; Sawday, 'Re-writing a revolution', p. 182.

201 Hancock, *Pastor's Last Legacy*, sig. A2, [A2v], A3; Clark, in *England's Remembrancer*, p. 495.

202 *England's Remembrancer*, p. 179.

203 Seddon, in *England's Remembrancer*, p. 229; Watson, *Pastor's Love Expressed*, p. 2; Philippians 2:17.

204 Newcomen, *Ultimum Vale*, p. 77. Cf. Eubanke, *Farewell Sermon Preached*, p. 28; Shaw and Seddon, in *England's Remembrancer*, pp. 172, 229.

205 Fairclough, *Pastor's Legacy*, pp. 61, 49–51, 64.

206 *England's Remembrancer*, p. 198.

207 *Third Volume*, pp. 57–8; Galatians 4:11. Cf. Bull, in *ibid.* pp. 44, 64, 73–4; Watson, *Pastor's Love Expressed*, p. 7; Powel, in Bodl. Rawl. MS E93, fo. 49v. See also Clark, in *England's Remembrancer*, p. 503; Swinnock, *Pastor's Farewell*, p. 6.

208 J. Coolidge, *The Pauline Renaissance in England* (Oxford, 1970), p. 38.

209 Newcomen, *Ultimum Vale*, pp. 65–6.

210 Moore, in *England's Remembrancer*, p. 401. Cf. Baxter, in *Exact Collection*, p. 171; Beerman, in *Compleat Collection*, sig. [Rr4v].

211 *Exact Collection*, p. 175. Cf. Watson, in *ibid.*, pp. 57–8.

212 *Third Volume*, p. 44.

213 Keeble, *Literary Culture*, pp. 23–4.

214 Downame, *The Second Volume of Annotations*, Romans 7:1–4.

215 *Third Volume*, p. 15.

216 Fairclough, *Pastor's Legacy*, p. 69; Moore, in *England's Remembrancer*, p. 415.

217 *Exact Collection*, p. 338; Philippians 4:1.

218 Caryl, *White Robe*, p. 5.

219 Newcomen, *Ultimum Vale*, p. 20; Thorne, *Saint's Great Duty*, p. 30; Acts 21:13.

220 See Whynnell, *England's Sorrows Turned into Joy*, p. 22 *passim*; Mossom, *England's Gratulation for the King*, pp. 16–22; Griffith, *The King's Life-Guard*, p. 19.

221 E.g., Whynnell, *England's Sorrows Turned into Joy*, p. 22, and Mossom, *England's Gratulation for the King*, pp. 16–22.

222 *Exact Collection*, p. 327; Lye, *Fixed Saint*, p. 19.

223 *Second and Last Collection*, pp. 161–2.

Chapter 4

The public circulation of
the Bartholomean texts

The public circulation of the farewell sermons after Bartholomew's Day was to prove an even greater concern for the authorities than their exposition from the pulpit. If there were practical limits to the measures that could be taken to control private conversations and discretely circulated manuscripts, there were at the same time physical limitations to the range and impact of such media. By contrast, the legislation that by the summer of 1662 had revealed the eagerness of the Restoration regime to control the print market testified to the scope and penetration of the printed word – as Richard Baxter had already noted, 'the press hath a louder voice than mine'.[1] Thus, claims for the eloquence of the empty pulpit anticipated the continuation of the argument by other means. Some ministers were keen to contribute to the catalogue, thereby ensuring that their 'dying' words would continue to resonate. Others found their valedictions printed at the behest of interested parties. Either way, the swift appearance of so many printed farewell sermons, and their sustained production over the succeeding years, revealed nonconformity as a force to be reckoned with.

Many Bartholomeans were hopeful that reading could compensate for the loss of their public ministry: 'the less opportunity the ear hath', declared Edward Hancock, 'the more opportunity the eye should have'.[2] Departing clergy included reading lists in their farewell sermons. Richard Fairclough assured his congregation that they might find godly books in almost every house, 'and will (I hope) more now than ever'.[3] Such statements implied the existence of a widespread readership, particularly among the godly. Literacy had increased steadily during the early modern period, although it still varied widely in terms of geography, social strata and occupation. Nevertheless, the ability to read may have been reasonably commonplace, circumnavigating restrictions of social status, and gender.[4] Regular exposure had made the wider population familiar with written and printed documents, regardless of whether they themselves were fluent readers. Preachers were sensitive to these gradations of competence, although claims that this awareness enabled them to control the congregation's reading seem debatable.[5] It may have been particularly difficult to control the reading methods of groups with high levels of individual literacy. The Puritan laity were disproportionately literate: Spufford has found that the few surviving written accounts produced by writers below the status of yeoman were invariably produced by Puritans and dissenters.[6] Keeble has argued that nonconformists comprised somewhere between 12 and 15 per cent of the literate nation, and that 'no other body of seventeenth-century literature could address itself to so readily definable and so large a readership'.[7] All of which suggests that the printing of the farewell sermons had an impact far beyond the London intelligentsia.

This chapter begins by considering the context and scope of the verbal and scribal transmission of the farewell sermons, coupled with other activities likely to have promoted the image of the ejected ministers. The translation of the Bartholomean manuscripts into print will be mapped in a putative chronology of publication, leading to an analysis of the print market and the motivations of the stationers (publishers, printers and booksellers) and others involved. Never far away, however, was the shadow of government censorship, which also exerted its influence on the content and format of the Bartholomean oeuvre.

We will consider here how and why specific preachers came to be selected for publication, and whether they were able to maintain authorial control over the exposition ascribed to them. Case studies will show how at the same time publication gave the Bartholomeans greater exposure it led to a modifying of their texts. The message was further affected by the process of compilation which resulted in the production of large printed collections of sermons; developments that changed the character of the corpus, and hardened attitudes within Restoration officialdom.

With the exception of *England's Remembrancer* (reprinted in 1666), publication of the farewell sermons ended abruptly in 1664. The final task of the chapter, therefore, will be to question whether the Restoration authorities were successful in repressing circulation, or whether repression coincided with a saturation of the market and a waning of public interest. It will be argued that the natural disasters of 1665 and 1666 helped ensure that publication of the farewell sermons would not resume until the eighteenth century – proving that if the medium of print gave ejected ministers a life after their civil death, the structures of public circulation were fragile and the process finite.

I

The Bartholomeans were anxious that their 'dying' words should linger in the hearts and minds of their audiences. They were also concerned to retain as much control over their rhetoric as possible, to guard against misrepresentation and to insure that their message would be properly understood by the godly. Just as it was important for the audience actively to participate, and appreciate the finer points of the sermon in order to complete the process of encoding, so the comprehension of the message enhanced its retention in the memory. It is interesting, for example, that Samuel Pepys should record that William Bates' morning farewell sermon had 'very little reflection in it pertaining to the times', when the minister had commented on the crisis within the Church of England.[8] The listener's attention span, to which Newcomen had referred so humorously in his valediction of 19 August, had a serious subtext: memory was a factor in public circulation.[9]

Sermon repetition and catechism had always been invaluable in spreading the Word. Robert Porter noted that his friend John Hieron had always been active in teaching in every home he could.[10] In normal times, as part of their pastoral function ministers had catechised children whilst the heads of godly households had required family members and servants to recite sermons from memory in order to ensure that they would better understand the message being preached. Some Bartholomeans drew attention to the fact that these activities would soon become more important than ever.[11] Daniel Bull urged his congregation to maintain 'secret' and family-worship: 'the less preaching there is in publick, the more catechising and instructing there should be in private'.[12]

Henry Newcombe continued to catechise, repeat sermons and pray with private groups after his ejection. This came to the notice of the authorities, who in September 1662 ordered him to cease. Newcombe pleaded that he 'did not think repeating had been any offence', but the magistrate thought otherwise.[13] The continuation of such activity, therefore, if only at a local level, may have been quite influential.

Just as it was common practice for the children of the godly to memorise and repeat sermons, so it was expected that schoolboys be trained in note-taking as part of their education in rhetoric. The young Simonds D'Ewes learned to take notes at sermons, afterwards enlarging and correcting them. Pupils were required to pay attention to scriptural references, and to register pronunciation and gesticulation.[14] This would suggest that many listeners were capable of making a reasonably accurate record of pulpit-delivery, preserving scriptural citations for private contemplation. Such memoranda may thus often have preserved a more accurate picture of the sermon as delivered than the preacher's own preparatory notes. Newcomen's predecessor in Dedham, John Rogers, regretted that he was never able to recapture his original performance in writing, as his extemporaneity during the sermon had usually vastly expanded upon the preparatory notes.[15] However, a complete understanding of the encoded text required a high degree of precision and concentration on the part of the note-taker. Inevitably, mistakes occurred. Whether such discrepancies were simply errors or indicative of self-censorship is a question raised by the comparison of two surviving accounts of William Bates's closing address at St Dunstan's on 17 August 1662. Samuel Pepys' diary recorded the minister's words thus:

> I do believe that many of you do expect that I should say something to you in reference to the time, this being the last time that possibly I may appear here. You know not, it is not my manner to speak anything in the pulpit that is extraneous to my text and business: yet this I shall say, that it is not my opinion, fashion, or humour, that keeps me from complying with what is required of us; but something, after much prayer, discourse, and study, yet remains unsatisfied, and commands me herein. Wherefore if it is my unhappinesse not to receive such an illuminacion as should direct me to do otherwise, I know of no reason why men should not pardon me in this world, as I am confident God will pardon me for it in the next.[16]

The text of *The Peace-Maker* (1662), on the other hand, utilising notes taken by another member of the congregation, reported Bates' last words to be:

> I know you expect I should say something, as to my non-conformity. I shall only say thus much, it is neither fancy, faction, nor humor that makes me not to comply, but merely for fear of offending God. And if after the best means used for my Illumination as prayer to God, discourse, study, I am not able to be satisfi'd concerning the lawfulness of what is required; if it be my unhappiness to be in an error, surely *Men* will have no reason to be angry with me in this world, and I hope *God* will pardon me in the next.[17]

The implication of this comparison is that one or other of the note-takers was in error – or that Pepys deliberately omitted Bates's explanation that his refusal to conform stemmed from his fear of offending God. Certainly, the anonymous version presents a more coherent and sympathetic view of Bates's nonconformity. As the discrepancies go beyond mere abridgement or paraphrasing, the haste and secrecy with which the illegally printed farewell sermons were produced render it likely that such variations originated at the note-taking stage. The self-censorship practised by the Bartholomeans during pulpit delivery was thus also practised by note-takers. Such caution may, in some cases, have led to the deliberate destruction of sermon notes too inconvenient, or dangerous, to retain.

The widespread availability of writing manuals throughout the period indicates that there was a community of professional scribes who took notes for commercial gain.[18] Farewell sermons such as those of the Exeter ministers preserved in the Rawlinson MSS, might, therefore, have been recorded for financial rather than ideological reasons. Renowned preachers invariably attracted the attentions of note-takers desirous of selling their transcriptions to the press. But even professional scribes could harbour strong religious convictions: in a manual published in 1664, Thomas Heath exhorted his readers to support those 'Pillars left to our Nation', 'though they are the despised of Men, yet they are the Prized Ones of God, the Apples of his Eyes, which when he bindeth up His Jewels, they shall be taken into the Number'. For the profane Heath foresaw only fire and divine vengeance.[19] With phrases so conspicuously redolent of Bartholomean rhetoric, and given the fact that no such preface had appeared in the 1644 edition of the manual, the reference to the ejected ministers seems clear.[20] However, despite such empathy, there was often antagonism between note-takers who considered themselves friends of the Bartholomean preachers and those adjudged mere mercenaries. Baxter later recalled such activities with mixed feelings:

> For when the Ministers were all silenced, some covetous Booksellers got Copies of the last Sermons of many of them, from the Scribes that took them from their Mouths. Some of them were taken word by word (which I heard my self): but some of us were much abused by it; and especially my self.[21]

Tensions were also evident in the preface to *The Peace-Maker*, which declared that the printer had followed the careful transcription of the preacher's 'very good friend', and that publication was intended to forestall imperfect copies then rumoured to be in preparation.[22]

Scribal transmission achieved circulation and exposure whilst circumventing the Licensing Act. This tactic, having been used to frustrate legislation in earlier reigns, was to be employed throughout that of Charles II. Whilst there is no firm evidence that the tactic was systematically utilised by the Bartholomeans, Richard Baxter had employed scribes to copy and circulate documents during the negotiations of 1660–61. Preaching his final sermon well before Bartholomew's Day to advertise his nonconformity and encourage like-minded brethren, Baxter had both motive and means to circulate his valediction in manuscript form. The lack of a surviving manuscript cannot be taken as evidence of absence; for example, although many of Robert Atkins's sermons are known to have circulated in manuscript after his ejection, his valediction did not appear in print until 1715.[23] Thus, during the summer of 1662 it is possible that manuscript copies of Baxter's farewell sermon may have circulated among the godly, influencing the rhetorical structure of many of the farewell sermons which followed.

Considerable numbers of farewell sermons were therefore circulating even before many were committed to print, although errors, editing and self-censorship must have changed the appearance of many before they were submitted to the printers. Whatever the arguments as to the relative veracity of these various sources, it is clear that stationers soon had access to a plethora of manuscripts, and a huge demand for their publication. As the preface of one compilation explained:

> it being found too tedious a work to satisfy the desires of all by Transcriptions, some who had taken after them as followeth, by the importunity of many, have been prevailed with, for the satisfaction of their friends, to expose their Notes to publick view.[24]

II

Some farewell sermons appeared in print only weeks, sometimes days, after they had been preached. Given that these publications were illegal, few carried complete publication details. Nonetheless, it is possible to posit a putative chronology by using the funerals of Ashe and Nalton and Calamy's 28 December sermon as markers – assuming that most sermons that emerged in pamphlet form would have done so before being incorporated into the printed compilations.

The first pamphlets appear to have been produced in early September 1662, including *The Righteous Mans Death Lamented* (a transcript of Calamy's funeral sermon for Ashe, preached on 23 August) and Calamy's farewell sermon, *The Fixed Saint Held Forth*.[25] The valedictions of three other leading London ministers, Jenkyn, Lye, and Watson, may have appeared as pamphlets at around the same time.[26] All were incorporated into an early anthology entitled *A Collection of Farewel-Sermons Preached* (1662), along with sermons by Samuel Slater, Thomas Jacombe, Thomas Case, Richard Baxter and Thomas Manton.[27]

Three further pamphlets possibly followed between October and December 1662, featuring William Bates, Joseph Caryl and Matthew Mead.[28] These were immediately incorporated, along with the previously published authors, into a collection entitled *The Farewell Sermons of the Late London Ministers* (1662).[29]

The furore caused by Calamy's appropriation of his old pulpit on 28 December encouraged publishers to rush the offending sermon into print. The earliest known reproduction of the sermon, *Eli Trembling for Fear of the Ark* (1662/63) was printed sometime between January and March 1663.[30] Three more editions appeared after March.[31] Calamy's adventures gave new impetus to the paper war: the government organ *Mercurius Publicus* attacked Calamy, and applauded his incarceration. The Licenser of the Press, John Berkenhead, was sufficiently enraged to give the sermon a prominent place in his anti-Presbyterian diatribe, *Cabala* (1663) – which in turn drew an indignant response in the anonymous *A Mystery of Godliness and No Cabala* (1663).[32]

Meanwhile, other works were being added to the Bartholomean corpus. Thomas Horton's funeral sermon for the ejected James Nalton, delivered on

1 January 1663, appeared in the next compilation of the London ministers' farewell sermons, *An Exact Collection of Farewell Sermons* (1662/63), together with Calamy's Aldermanbury sermon.[33] Between the publication of *An Exact Collection* and 25 March 1663 at least two pamphlets probably made their appearance. The farewell sermon of Philip Lamb, a provincial clergyman with a national reputation, was marketed as *The Royal Presence* (1662), and would feature in several subsequent collections.[34] George Swinnock's farewell sermon, *The Pastor's Farewell* (1662), was, unusually, published openly by his agent, Thomas Parkhurst of Cheapside.[35] A further offering before 25 March may have been *Farewell to His Neighbours* (1662), by the Norfolk minister John Horne, although no surviving copy has come to light.[36]

The spring of 1663 saw a rash of Bartholomean pamphlets, as fresh offerings from the provinces arrived in London. To this period might be ascribed Cooper's *The Dead Witnesse Yet Speaking*, Eubanke's *A Farewell Sermon Preached at Great Ayton*, Fairclough's *A Pastors Legacy* and Hancock's *The Pastors Last Legacy* (all 1663).[37] Hancock had by now begun a clandestine ministry in London, and may have brought his notes from Bristol. Horton's funeral sermon for Nalton, which had first appeared in a compilation, was now published in its own right as *Rich Treasure in Earthen Vessels* (1663).[38]

Another pamphlet to emerge was Matthew Newcomen's *Ultimum Vale* (1663).[39] The frontispiece declared it to be Newcomen's final sermon, although it was not the valediction that had been delivered on 17 August, nor that given two days later. It has been suggested that Newcomen delivered this sermon in Dedham in December 1662, immediately before departing for the Netherlands.[40] However, there is no compelling evidence that Newcomen reoccupied his old pulpit, which, given his reputation and ties with Calamy, would surely have generated as much publicity as the Aldermanbury incident. Interestingly, just as *Ultimum Vale* was printed, Newcomen's farewell sermon of 19 August was belatedly added to a new collection, *The Second and Last Collection of the Late London Ministers Farewel-Sermons* (1663).

Increasingly voluminous compilations appeared over the summer of 1663. In addition to Newcomen's 19 August sermon, *The Second and Last Collection of the Late London Ministers Farwel Sermons*, for example, featured the valedictions of Seaman, Bates, Caryl, Brooks, Venning and Mead, together with a morning exercise by Lye.[41] It is difficult to ascertain whether a similar compilation, *The Second Volume of the Farwel Sermons, Preached by Some London and Country Ministers* (1663) was published by rivals or collaborators.[42] Despite some similarities, the type-setting, ornaments and fonts suggest two independent projects. Moreover, the latter collection featured a slightly different combination of farewell sermons, prayers, and rehashed material in the shape of Nalton's funeral sermon and Calamy's Aldermanbury lecture. These collections were followed by *The Third and Last Volume of the Farwell Sermons* and *The Third Volume of Farewel Sermons Preached by Some London and Country Ministers* (both 1663), the latter featuring mainly provincial sermons, although several had already been published.[43] One development was the inclusion of a sermons preached by Thomas Watson against popery.

The compilation of anonymous country sermons, *England's Remembrancer* (1663), was on sale in London streets before 14 September, as on that date L'Estrange's editorial in *The Intelligencer* railed against 'the *First, Second, Third* and *Fourth* Volumn of FAREWELL SERMONS'.[44] That the Bartholomean corpus continued to appeal to the market was demonstrated by the fact that compilations continued to be published throughout 1663. The later offerings were huge 'compleat' volumes of previous editions, featuring new authors such as George Thorne of Dorset. The Wing short title catalogue shows that there were at least five different 'compleat' editions; a flood tide so overwhelming that even the Wing cataloguers appear to have become confused.[45]

The nonconformists' critics retaliated: L'Estrange and Berkenhead were joined by writers such as William Assheton and David Lloyd in attempting to undermine the credibility of the ejected ministers.[46] But another pamphlet, ostensibly unconnected with the farewell sermons, perhaps struck a more decisive blow. *An Exact Narrative of the Tryal and Condemnation of John Twyn* (1664), described the trial of a London printer executed for the crime of printing a treasonable book, together with those of his fellow defendants Thomas Brewster, Simon Dover and Nathan Brooks. All four individuals must be considered prime suspects in the printing and distribution of the farewell sermons, as their arrest coincided with a sudden dip in the production of Bartholomean literature. The meditations of some ejected ministers continued to be published, but few works associated with Black Bartholomew's Day now appeared; two exceptions being George Thorne's valediction, now published as *The Saints Great Duty* (1664) and the valedictions of Thomas Palke, condensed into *The Loyal Non-Conformist* (1664).[47] The republication of Thorne's farewell sermon, undertaken by a self-declared friend, came at a time when the minister was particularly newsworthy, having been arrested on his return from the Netherlands in March 1664 on the charge of plotting against the Government.[48]

After 1664 publication ceased, save only for the reissuing of *England's Remembrancer* in 1666.[49] This cessation was surprising, given that plague and the Great Fire of London could easily have been appropriated as evidence of divine retribution, and given that many ejected ministers had temporarily resumed their public ministry in pulpits left vacant by those fleeing the pestilence. Production was, however, probably brought to a close by a combination of factors; many of which arose from the nature of the Restoration print market.

III

Despite Cavalier claims that the press was the 'chief ally of Dissent', the industry was politically complex.[50] In common with several ejected ministers, a number of printers and booksellers accused of seditious activities in the 1660s could claim to have aided the royalist cause during the Interregnum. In any case, no government could afford to alienate the Stationers' Company of London, whose intimate knowledge of the trade, monopolies of printing and bookselling and rights to search for unauthorised presses in the city made them necessary partners. In 1662, the company was confirmed as an integral element of state censorship by the Licensing Act. Henceforth, a new title had first to be entered into the Stationers' Register, after which the publisher was required to apply to the Archbishop of Canterbury or the Bishop of London for a licence to print.[51] Prospective manuscripts submitted after 1662 were scrutinised by a company warden acting in concert with a government representative such as Stradling, Berkenhead, or L'Estrange, or occasionally Sir Henry Bennet or Sir William Morrice.[52] Unsurprisingly, no farewell sermons appear to have been entered for registration.

In seeking to locate and seize seditious literature, the officials retained by the Secretaries of State employed much the same methods that had been followed by Thurloe's agents during the Protectorate: analysing typefaces, ornaments and watermarks and offering rewards to informants. In 1663 London's type founders were ordered to keep a proof of every letter cast, and a record of those who had purchased them.[53] However, printers attempted to evade detection by using old or foreign type, and sponsors of illicit literature habitually switched their patronage from one printer to another. Larger commissions (which, taking more time to print, were more likely to be discovered during production) would often be split into sections and shared between various printing houses.[54] In London in 1663 over 60 master printers ran such operations, employing approximately one hundred apprentices and supplying some 600 booksellers.[55]

With print runs averaging between 1,000 and 1,500 copies, even the titles registered with the Stationers' Company indicated a large and expanding market.[56] The supposed memoirs of Charles I, *Eikon Basilike*, which had run through several clandestine editions during the 1650s, continued to sell well – as did an expanding catalogue of royalist literature.[57] Nonconformist titles were equally popular: more than 20,000 copies of Baxter's *A Call to the Unconverted* (1658) were sold in 12 months, whilst a work purporting to be a true record of the Regicides' speeches on the scaffold enjoyed a initial print run of least 3,000.[58] Thomas Creake testified he had printed 2,000 copies of *A Phenix, or the Solemn League and Covenant* in 1662 at the behest of Livewell Chapman, Giles Calvert and Thomas Brewster.[59] B. J. McMullen has cautioned that a large number of editions does not necessarily equate to a huge demand, as publishers frequently tested the market with small print runs.[60] However, the farewell sermons appear to have been large print runs: in 1663, L'Estrange (who, despite his apoplectic reputation, sifted his intelligence with care) noted that there were 10 or 12 impressions of the first, second and third volumes of farewell sermons, totalling some 30,000 copies.[61] His observation that such publications were aimed at 'all humours' is pertinent in view of Neil Keeble's calculation that the production of non-conformist titles was 'comparatively far higher than the nonconformist proportion of the population would warrant'.[62]

Whatever their viewpoint, most early modern readers thirsted for news. Lois Potter has argued that readers during the Interregnum had been ready to pay a premium for illegally printed literature, which, having been produced in defiance of political authority, promised otherwise unobtainable information.[63] Religious works, which had long been a large segment of the print market, often came into this category. Whereas parliamentary proceedings had become somewhat predictable after the elections of 1661, religion continued to generate the kind of sensationalism that sold books.[64] Even before the Act of Uniformity, the reading public was being treated to gladiatorial contests which pitted Roger L'Estrange against Edward Bagshawe, and Bishop Morley against Richard Baxter in tit-for-tat pamphlets.[65] Such excitement was unwelcome to the Restoration authorities, desirous as they were of dampening public debate in religious and political affairs. But continued consumer demand for religious subject matter, and the fact that bishops had been reinstated as the chief licensers of the press, demonstrated that religion retained its prominence. The Licensing Act only served to underline this, stressing the illegality of publishing any opinion contrary to the doctrine or discipline of the Church of England.[66] Anyone publishing the works of Bartholomean dissenters, whose farewell sermons could not fail to posit opinions contrary to that doctrine and discipline, knew that they had not the slightest chance of receiving the approval of the licensing authorities.

The Restoration print market was large in terms of volume and in the extent of its geographical distribution. London, the centre of the printing trade, was predominant, and London-based ministers hugely over-represented among the authors of printed farewell sermons – their number swollen further by ejected clergy such as Baxter, who had gravitated to the capital.[67] Thus, whereas London provided just over 5 per cent of all those ejected at Fatal Bartholomew, London-based sermons would account for over 39 per cent of those in print.

However, the print market extended far beyond the gates of London. Successive members of the Brewster family commissioned London printers to produce godly works in Welsh between 1653 and 1667, and, just as L'Estrange feared, the farewell sermons themselves were quickly be translated into at least one other European language.[68] There was never any shortage of chapmen and carriers willing to convey literature into the provinces. Chapbooks and pamphlets were sold and read aloud in marketplaces and alehouses, and passed on by hand or post. Even modest print runs could achieve a circulation far in excess of the actual number of copies printed.[69]

Nonconformist literature was distributed across England via extensive networks of personal and trade contacts. A crackdown on illegal book distribution in February 1663 revealed evidence of regular transactions between Bristol booksellers and nonconformist suppliers in London: the local authorities followed Thomas Brewster around Bristol fair, whence he had gone to solicit orders from booth owners. Large quantities of unlicensed books were found in Brewster's lodgings, several of which (given the date of the operation) are likely to have been farewell sermons.[70] Bristol was one of the largest book markets outside London, with a sizeable nonconformist community. The evidence of the farewell sermons suggests that the West Country was also a rich source of information and manuscript material for nonconformist London publishers. The farewell sermons of West Country preachers were published at different times, probably as a result of being brought into London by a variety of carriers. Londoners such as Brewster would almost certainly have collected interesting material whilst on their travels, their transactions with provincial booksellers often involving payment in kind.

Nonconformist networks appear to have been heavily dependent upon the personal contacts and initiative of individuals such as Brewster, as the origins of the printed farewell sermons reveal huge disparities in frequency across the various English regions. Nottinghamshire, which statistically should have had around 2 per cent representation among Bartholomean authors, boasted no less than 13 per cent of the sermons as a direct result of the publication of *England's Remembrancer*. Other regions were strikingly under-represented: the 238 ministers ejected from Essex and East Anglia (142 forced out in 1662 alone) were represented solely by the farewell sermons of Matthew Newcomen. Of the 214 ejected ministers of northern England, only the valediction of the young and relatively obscure George Eubank was ever committed to print. Along the South coast, farewell sermons known to have been delivered in the dioceses of Canterbury and Winchester were never published, despite the fact that 62 ministers were ejected from Kent, and 52 from Hampshire.[71]

It is possible, given the rather pedestrian sermons of the unpublished manuscripts of the ministers from Exeter, that few of these provincial sermons provided enough spice to whet the appetite of London publishers. However, whilst the risks taken by publishers suggest that sensationalism could often be highly profitable, this should not obscure the fact that several factors worked against profitability. Pricing remained an important consideration – as the preface to *The Fixed Saint Held Forth* (1662) revealed, assuring potential buyers that a benefit of having Thomas Lye's farewell sermon in pamphlet form was that 'things of the greatest profit are offered at a little price'.[72] Having said this, nonconformist works often appear to have competed in a premium market. Whereas most small books of 24 to 32 pages sold for between 2d and 6d, many comparable nonconformist works retailed at around 1s or 1s 6d. Neil Keeble has discerned a gap in the market between such publications and folio collections – most of which he considers to have been Presbyterian or Congregational in nature. As these larger books tended to be priced somewhat over 15s, this would suggest that a compilation of forty-two farewell sermons such as *A Compleat Collection of Farewell Sermons* would normally have proved an expensive purchase.[73] However, the only compilation of farewell sermons known to have featured a printed price, the 326-page *The Second and Last Collection* (1663), was advertised bound for 1s 6d.[74] By contrast, a 485-page collection of Samuel Hieron's sermons had been sold unbound in 1635 for 13s 6d.[75] Given the risk and investment involved, such discounting would scarcely seem economically viable, let alone profitable; clearly, for some publishers the spiritual rewards of promoting the farewell sermons outweighed any consideration of financial gain. The frontispiece of *The Second and Last Collection* shows that the producers chose even to shoulder the burden of binding – normally the only major transferable cost. Other Bartholomean publications may even have been given away. Godly ministers had always encouraged the giving and sharing of books, and some, such as Baxter, regularly subsidised the publication of their works to ensure that they retailed as cheaply as possible and achieved optimum circulation. On occasions, Baxter bought up entire production runs in order to give them away.[76] Oliver Heywood did likewise, at considerable personal cost.[77] As relatively few ministers or stationers would have had the means regularly to have indulged in such largesse, it is possible that wealthy patrons may have underwritten the cost of cut-price godly literature, just as several provided support and employment for ejected ministers. If *The Second and Last Collection* was at all typical of Bartholomean output between 1662 and 1666, the culture of discounting godly works or distributing them free of charge is likely to have given the printed farewell sermons an even greater impact on the Restoration print market than they would otherwise have had.

IV

The furtiveness of those involved in the printing of farewell sermons was understandable. As Lois Potter has observed, whereas writers could continue to write and publish from prison, stationers stood to lose their livelihoods, or worse.[78] The public examples that had been made of leading members of the old regime suggested that there was every likelihood of physical mutilation, or even execution. Nevertheless, illegal publication continued. Most printers appear to have undertaken illicit work at one time or another, particularly when the restrictive practices of the Stationers' Company prevented most from realising a sufficient income from legitimate printing. Many organised early-warning networks among sympathetic neighbours, and maintained secret hiding places and prearranged escape routes through which to spirit offending work to safety. However, a surprise raid led by L'Estrange managed to discover a secret press in London in October 1663 – by which time he had already ensnared a printer by the name of Peter Lillicrap.

Lillicrap, one of only two printers specifically accused in connection with the printing of the farewell sermons, had an ambiguous past.[79] He was formally arrested on 23 June 1663, and his wife the day after; but his movements already appear to have been under restraint.[80] His indignant petition of 23 July 1663 stated

> That yr petitnr has been prisoner in the Messengers custody about 5 months, & for a fortnight close prisoner. Only for printing part of the farewell sermons found in my house by Mr L'Estrange, wch weere at the same time printinge in divers other houses & no man questioned for them but my selfe, who has been a man wholly affectionate to his Ma. services & a great sufferer for it.[81]

Lillicrap declared that he had served in the royalist army during the civil wars, being taken prisoner four times, and had been imprisoned in 1658 for producing a tract calling for the restoration of the monarchy. His wife and friends testified that since the Restoration he had on at least one occasion refused to reprint a book brought to him by one John Heydon, in which it was alleged that the king was a tyrant. The authorities remained unmoved, necessitating the wretched man to petition once more from his prison cell, pleading that he had 'done more to suppress seditious pamphlets than all the printers in England'.[82]

Like the unfortunate John Twynn, who in 1664 would pay with his life for subcontracting to print part of *A Treatise of the Execution of Justice*, Lillicrap was incidental to the production process. Critics of the trade suspected that printers regularly suppressed their own political or religious sensibilities when presented with the prospect of a lucrative commission. By contrast, the shadowy figures who commissioned the work, coordinated the collation and binding of the printed sheets and organised the distribution networks often appear to have acted out of acute conviction.

Bartholomean clergy themselves rarely appear to have commissioned printers directly. The wording of the preface to *A Farewell Sermon Preached at Great Ayton* (1663), suggests that it was written by George Eubanke to complement his farewell sermon, implying that he had prepared his own notes for publication.[83] George Swinnock had been more candid, affixing his name to the preface to *The Pastor's Farewell* (1662).[84]

On some occasions congregations were responsible for the publication of their minister's parting words, as seems to have the case with the printed farewell sermons of Richard Fairclough and Philip Lamb.[85] Given that these works were published during the tense period following Black Bartholomew, the readiness of these provincial congregations to expose themselves to public scrutiny is remarkable. As the events at Aldermanbury in December 1662 indicate, London congregations were no less appreciative of their ministers, and, being equally committed members of the godly, may well have sponsored works such as Edmund Calamy's *Eli Trembling for Fear of the Ark* (1663); however, they left little trace of having done so.[86] With the parishes and printing houses of the capital directly under the hand of Sheldon and L'Estrange, London's godly probably had more experience of state censorship than their West Country brethren. The confidence of parishioners in Mells and Bere Regis may therefore reflect their distance from the charged political atmosphere of the metropolis. It may also reflect a certain provincial innocence of the extent of political and religious change that had taken place between 1660 and 1662. What it does not reflect is any indifference on the part of the central authorities to dissent in the provinces. Indeed, the close interest that the authorities had so recently taken in the activities of the Nottingham ministers Barrett and Whitlock may have motivated the publishers of *England's Remembrancer* (1663) to preserve not only their own anonymity but also those whose sermons featured in the compilation. It is also understandable that unlicensed Bartholomean works published after the discovery and repression of the northern plots of late 1662 would have been more circumspect than those published before them.

It was more usual for all parties involved in the printing of a farewell sermon to conceal their identity. Apart from an occasional set of initials (themselves often deliberately misleading) the most that can normally be gleaned from the prefaces of such works is an indication where the sponsor was in all likelihood an individual operating alone, or where a group or partnership may have been at work. Certainly, individual note-takers were sometimes sufficiently motivated to sponsor publication on their own volition, as suggested by the preface to Thomas Horton's funeral sermon for James Nalton.[87]

Links between the various publications of farewell sermons are extremely difficult to verify, not least because it is apparent from their physical appearance that the same sponsors commissioned different printers for different works, and that printers routinely used a variety of typefaces, ornaments and watermarks to avoid detection. Although the preface of *The Third Volume of*

Farewel Sermons (1663), refers to 'the kind acceptance' of the two former volumes of sermons published earlier, neither the format of the frontispiece, nor the typeface, nor the ornament matches any of these earlier volumes.[88] A similar discontinuity can even be found when comparing Bates's *The Peace-Maker* (1662) with Mead's *The Pastor's Valediction* (1662), despite the fact that the prefaces, both purporting to have been written by 'N.D.', are in places identical.[89] It may not be a coincidence, however, that an 'N.D.' had been the author of *A Discovery of Some Plots of Lucifer and His Council Against the Children of Men*, which had been printed for Thomas Brewster in 1656.

Given their past involvement in publications such as *A Phenix* (1662) it seems likely that Brewster and his associates Livewell Chapman and Giles Calvert were heavily involved in the publication of the farewell sermons. The three men, labelled the 'Confederate Stationers' by L'Estrange, were well known to the authorities as sponsors of seditious publications. Chapman had been imprisoned by the Cromwellian regime in 1654, whilst Calvert had been denounced as a dangerous radical by Thomas Edwards in *Gangraena* (although he also produced Presbyterian literature).[90]

By the Restoration the trio had assembled a large catalogue and a wide network of associates.[91] If they were indeed the main figures behind the bulk of the farewell sermons, it should be noted that their activities between 1662 and 1664 were frequently disrupted by prolonged spells of imprisonment. Brewster was kept in close custody following his arrest in Bristol in February 1663, whilst Calvert was arrested and released with dizzying regularity. Chapman languished in the Gatehouse prison from November 1663 until May 1664. All three, however, had wives whose commitment mirrored their own, and whose active participation ensured that production continued. Hannah Chapman was a particular thorn in the side of the authorities: the conditions of Livewell Chapman's release bond in May 1663 also placed requirements on her good behaviour, despite the fact that the family's printing equipment and materials had been confiscated some months earlier. Elizabeth Calvert was even more active.[92] However, as none of the 'Confederate Stationers', nor their wives, nor their usual printers, were so rash as to put their name to any of the printed farewell sermons, the evidence for their involvement in Bartholomean literature, whilst likely, remains circumstantial.

A singular exception to the culture of anonymity was the prolific and prominent London printer and bookseller Thomas Parkhurst. Parkhurst had become a freeman of the Stationers' Company in 1654, and by 1662 ran a prosperous business in Cheapside, servicing several godly ministers such as Oliver Heywood and John Howe. Admitted to the livery of the Company in 1664, a former apprentice would later remember him as 'the most eminent Presbyterian bookseller in the three kingdoms'.[93] That Parkhurst was held in general respect amongst the godly was obvious, although Baxter's description of him as 'a very ingenious sober conformist' was a curious appellation in view of the stationer's brazen promotion of nonconformist publications.[94]

It was characteristic of Parkhurst that he should openly advertise himself on the frontispiece of George Swinnock's *The Pastor's Farewell* (1662) as the publisher and distributor. He even took the opportunity to advertise several other works by Swinnock listed in his catalogue. These works, together with the preface and dedication contributed by Swinnock himself, suggest a close professional relationship similar to that which already existed between Parkhurst and Oliver Heywood.[95] In 1682, the trust between Parkhurst and Heywood would be strong enough for the stationer to suggest the removal of 'some smart reflections' from the minister's manuscript for *Israel's Lamentation after the Lord*, 'thinking it was not safe to print them, being then such a hazardous time'.[96] Interestingly, the comments in question concerned the events of August 1662. Twenty years earlier, Parkhurst had clearly been less cautious in his advice to George Swinnock, for the printed text of *The Pastor's Farewell* featured several potentially dangerous criticisms of authority couched in passages borrowed from Exodus regarding the Israelites' flight from tyranny, as well as provocative references to Acts, Pauline scripture and military metaphor.[97]

Given his public association with the nonconformist cause, and the provocative *Pastor's Farewell* in particular, it is surprising that Parkhurst did not suffer at the hands of the authorities. Whereas the 'Confederate Stationers' appear repeatedly in the warrants and gaol deliveries recorded between 1660 and 1665, Parkhurst's name is entirely absent. In contrast to the mispagination and jumbled types and ornaments found elsewhere amongst the printed farewell sermons, *The Pastor's Farewell* exudes a blithe confidence and unhurried attention to detail with fastidious pagination, copious Latin and Greek type and (rare among Bartholomean works) printed marginalia. In the light of their treatment of Brewster, Chapman and Calvert, the indifference of the authorities regarding Parkhurst's activities is astonishing.

Harold Love has extrapolated from the discourse between Parkhurst and Heywood an impression that their association may have been typical of those which existed between ejected clergy and London stationers, and that as a consequence the provincial clergyman may have been 'an even more important force in the distribution of books outside London than the country bookseller'.[98] This is a hypothesis reinforced by Keeble's calculations that no less than 436 of the ejected ministers featured in *Calamy Revised* had been the author of at least one publication.[99] The printed farewell sermons reveal contacts not only between London publishers and provincial ministers, but also with provincial congregations. When placed in this context, a collection of 77 farewell sermons, delivered by 50 ejected ministers, large as it is, nevertheless begs the question as to why proportionally so few of the 1,631 ministers ejected between 1660 and 1662 had their farewell sermons published.[100] The survival of texts by Ford, Stucley, Powel and Atkins, together with references to the content of several other valedictions, suggests that many more manuscripts were available than those which eventually ended up in print. The editors of *The Third Volume of Farewel Sermons* even had access to several manuscript versions of the same sermon, declaring that their transcriptions had been compared with other copies.[101] There were, therefore, processes of selection whereby some farewell sermons, and even particular versions of sermons, were chosen for publication and others discarded.

The decision to publish depended on several factors, not least an accessible manuscript, production capacity and a saleable author or interesting content. It was important to publish the farewell sermons whilst they and Black Bartholomew remained newsworthy, particularly as it seemed likely that such literature would soon be actively repressed. It was also desirable to steal a march on commercial competitors. The speed with which an individual sermon could be translated into print is indicated by an advertisement at the end of Mead's *The Pastor's Valediction* (1662), which promised '*The Good People, among whom the Name of this Excellent man is deservedly precious, may take notice that his last Sermon upon the five a Clock Lecture at Sepulchres will suddainly be Published for their Use.*'[102] By contrast, farewell sermons from provincial pulpits took time to filter through to the metropolis. The first compilations of farewell sermons were exclusively composed of London-based ministers, the second wave belatedly included Newcomen from Essex, and not until the third was a significant contribution from the provinces evident. London stationers were perfectly willing to entertain the idea of provincial authors; in fact, the inclusion of farewell sermons preached for a country auditory served to illustrate the scope and significance of nonconformity. This was reinforced when *England's Remembrancer* was published in London in the late summer of 1663, a collection which '*some serious Christians*' (presumably from, or connected with, the Midlands) had worked hard to gather together.[103]

At the time *England's Remembrancer* was published, and even when it was reprinted in 1666, there was obviously still a market for Bartholomean literature. That even more farewell sermons did not appear in print may have been for reasons more subtle than the availability of manuscripts or the elasticity of public demand. The decision to publish was very largely dependent upon the publisher's ability to finance publication. If existing stocks of Bartholomean works were being sold at the level of discount of *The Second and Last Collection of the Late London Ministers' Farewel-Sermons* (1663) – advertised bound for 1s 6d – then budgets would have been stretched. In addition, the logistical problems faced by printing houses attempting to cope with the large and concentrated influx of work occasioned by the paper war over the Act of Uniformity should not be underestimated. The sudden rush of commissions represented by the sizeable Bartholomean catalogue may well have taxed the capacity of the presses to the detriment of other non-conformist publications, particularly if these needed to be printed secretly between legitimate projects – a problem which had occurred during the Interregnum when the overwhelming demand for *Eikon Basilike* had held back production of other clandestine royalist literature.[104]

Preachers who were also writers of repute, such as Calamy and Baxter, held a distinct advantage when their works were offered for publication, for, as Lois Potter has written, 'a work by a known author was considerably more saleable and authoritative than an anonymous one'.[105] Certainly, the printed farewell sermons did not lack for celebrities, particularly in the early compilations: Calamy and Newcomen were still notorious (from a Cavalier-Anglican perspective) as co-authors of *Smectymnuus* (1641), and, along with several others such as Lye, Case and Seaman, had had several sermons published by Parliament during the Interregnum. Fame, however, did not guarantee publication: Edward Bagshawe was one prominent author and eminent Bartholomean whose farewell sermons were never printed. By contrast, even if the anonymous ministers featured in *England's Remembrancer* had been identified at the time, few of their names or those of their Midland parishes would have been recognised by readers in London or Bristol. Yet despite this anonymity *England's Remembrancer* was a huge and expensive undertaking of 510 pages, and sufficiently saleable to warrant a reprint three years later. This, and the appearance of lesser known ministers in the later Bartholomean works suggests that some publishers may have been less preoccupied with promoting individual authors than with promoting nonconformity as an idea.

There were in many cases individual reasons and circumstances that led to the manuscripts of some farewell sermons being handed over to the press for publication. Like Mead and Bates, William Jenkyn appears to have had a committed follower who was determined to see a transcription of his farewell sermons through to print – although it is always possible that the preface was disingenuous, and that the notes were Jenkyn's own.[106] The frontispiece to Fairclough's *A Pastor's Legacy* which declared that his parishioners had themselves provided a manuscript of the farewell sermons for publication, noted that the valedictions had been taken verbatim by one of his hearers. Ironically, Fairclough had expressed a distrust of the publishing process in one of the very sermons his parishioners caused to be published: 'The world is full of Books, and I am *conscious* of a great deal of *imperfections*, else my zeal had made me Print something for my Memorial to you.'[107] This may have been the reason why Robert Atkins 'could never be prevail'd upon to print so much as one single Sermon'.[108] The parishioners who sponsored the publication and provided the preface of Philip Lamb's farewell sermons were conscious of such imperfections, and eager to ensure that the inevitable errata did not reflect upon the minister himself.[109]

The mores of selection, therefore, effectively took the Bartholomean texts out of the control of the preachers even before the process of printing began. Much of Baxter's distaste for mercenary note-takers and 'covetous booksellers' stemmed from a sense of injustice at the treatment of his own valediction;

> for they styled it *A Farewel Sermon*, and mangled so both Matter and Style, that I could not own it; besides the printing it to the offence of Governours. So that afterwards I writ out the Sermon more at large my self (on *Col.* 2. 6, 7) with another Discourse, and offered them to the Press; but could not get them Licensed, for Reasons afterwards to me mentioned.[110]

Baxter thus attempted to neuter the offending publication by producing an alternative version. However, by the time this was eventually published as *Directions for Weak Christians* (1668) it was no longer a sermon but a treatise, owing as much to an earlier work of 1658 as to his sermon of 25 May 1662. It came too late to correct the impression made by the printed text of 1662– 63.[111] In any case, despite his objections to the 'mangled' printed sermon, Baxter himself would later cite it to refute accusations that he had declared during his last sermon that the Gospel was departing from England.[112]

Thomas Manton was even more dissatisfied with the text published in his name. On 23 September 1663, in response to pressure from *The Newes* and its editor L'Estrange, he wrote:

> I do utterly disclaim the Farewell-Sermon, and Prayer, printed in my Name among other Farewel-Sermons, pretended to be Preached by some London Ministers; as being done without my privity, and consent; and indeed, as having preached no Fare-well Sermon at all at the time specified; and That which the Ignorant Publisher calls so, is strangely disguised and misrepresented, by his foolish mistakes; so much I would so ever have signified to the world, if Occasion had been offered.[113]

But Manton must have preached some sort of farewell sermon in order for him to recognise the one published as 'strangely disguised and misrepresented'. Whether he took such violent exception because the printed text was genuinely inaccurate, or whether he had been unnerved by the opprobrium the printed sermons had begun to attract, the fact that at least two leading Bartholomeans had been published without their consent was seized upon in the Cavalier press. L'Estrange had already suggested that William Bates and other Bartholomeans had also been alarmed to discover farewell sermons published in their name.[114] Fame, therefore, could often prove a curse, which in this case had led to celebrated ministers being published against their will and (allegedly) misrepresented. Publishers could scarcely plead guilty to such misrepresentation, but, as in the preface to *The White Robe* (1662), could on occasion admit that they had printed farewell sermons without the consent of their author.[115]

Misrepresentation could result from other factors than interference with the sermon itself. Except on the occasions where the minister had taken his own farewell sermon to print (and possibly even then), frontispieces and prefaces, over which he had no control, could often set the tone of the entire publication. Thus, the frontispiece to Thorne's *The Saint's Great Duty* (1664) introduced the reader to the valediction by giving a prominent place to a highly provocative quotation from Exodus 14:13 – the chapter in which the Israelites were hidden by a pillar of cloud, and in which Pharaoh and his army drowned. Thorne had indeed used this quotation in his sermon, but he had certainly not chosen it as his principal text.[116] Similarly, as the preface of *The Royal Presence* (1662) makes it clear that Philip Lamb did not control the publication of his text, it was presumably a third party who had chosen the Biblical citations on the frontispiece, and inserted 'vincenti dabitur' ('victory will be given to him') at the end of the preface.[117]

Celebrity status had rendered the ejected ministers public property, in the same way that Charles I had been made public property in *Eikon Basilike* and his son in the May 29 thanksgiving sermons. Because of this, it is little wonder that famous Bartholomeans found that they had less control over their published sermons than their more obscure brethren.

V

Less than a month after Matthew Newcomen had made his final appearance in Dedham's pulpit, a manuscript came into the possession of Robert Winter of 'Thearington' (possibly either Thorington Street, Suffolk, or Thorrington, Essex). Winter endorsed the document,

> September the 20th 1662.
> Given me by holy worshipful. Mr Matthew Newcomen.
> Written with his own hand.[118]

The manuscript, almost 100 pages long, contains a painstaking transcription of Newcomen's valedictions of 17 and 19 August, prefaced by an address. Written in a steady hand with no corrections it is possible that Newcomen produced the manuscript to give as a memento before emigrating to Leiden.[119] A comparison of the manuscript with the printed 19 August sermon reveals that much detail was lost in translation – not least the fact that the two sermons had been designed to function in tandem. The sermon printed in *The Second and Last Collection* (1663), and erroneously dated 20 August, lost much by being dislocated from that delivered on 17 August. Another significant omission was the address, in which Newcomen had commented directly on the political context of his departure:

> I suppose you have all heard of an Act of the Late Parliament, concerning the Ministry, and Preachers of the Gosple here in England, Injoyning them to the practise, and performance of certain things, or els disabling them for the future to preach; for my owne part I am not satisfied that I can doe the things there prescribed, and therefore I must fall under the penalties there imposed and before the next Lords day cease preaching.[120]

Having reminded the congregation that it was traditional for departing pastors to deliver a farewell sermon, Newcomen assured them that 'I would not willingly faile your expectation in that Particular.'[121] He cited as his mandate John 14:1, on which the Westminster Assembly had commented that Christ had not approved of 'stoical apathy' but rather expected the godly to meet trial with steadfast resolve.[122] For Newcomen, therefore, passivity was not a matter of capitulating but of holding fast. This attitude permeated his sermon on Sunday 17 August, where a warm and jovial presentation was underpinned by a resolve to 'rather leave you with a word of Exhortation, than of Reprehension'.[123] As the jokes Newcomen shared with his congregation throughout that sermon were never reproduced in print, publication gave the impression of a colder man and a more austere occasion than had actually been the case.

The printed sermon also rendered Newcomen's valediction significantly less controversial than that preserved in manuscript. Even before his ejection, Newcomen had rowed against the tide, refusing a royal chaplaincy at the same time as he had written to Baxter to propose a reprinting of the Grand Remonstrance.[124] In contrast to the published version of his 19 August sermon, the manuscript radiates defiance. Given its employment in several published sermons before Black Bartholomew, Newcomen cannot have been unaware of the rhetorical linkage between the Biblical King Cresus, Charles II and their respective royal cities of Sardis and London.[125] Thus, the selection of Revelation 3:3 as the main text of his two farewell sermons was particularly poignant. For any ignorant of the context of Revelation 3:3, Newcomen developed his 17 August sermon by drawing attention to it, linking Sardis and London as two royal cities, and describing the former as full of idolatry and uncleanness. The analogy could hardly have been more explicit. Newcomen supplemented his main text with further extracts from Revelation: Christ's warning to Sardis ('I will come upon thee as a thiefe, and thou shalt not know what hour I will come upon thee') and God's praise for the faithful few in that city who had refused to defile their garments and were destined to 'walk in white'.[126] From the explication and the juxtaposing of these Biblical images, it is abundantly clear that this exegesis and its application was intended to present a critique of the events then unfolding in England. However, whether or not printers in London had access to Newcomen's 17 August sermon, the minister's controversial explication and application of Revelation 3:3 was not printed. Thus, whilst Revelation 3:3 formed the main text of the (printed) 19 August sermon, once divorced from the explication of the earlier sermon, it became significantly less contentious. The printed sermon merely carried an explication of the actual verse ('Remember therefore how thou hast received and heard, and hold fast and repent'), and conspicuously failed to convey Newcomen's intended parallel of Sardis and London.

This was not the only item lost or adulterated in printing. Particularly significant was the treatment of Newcomen's attempt to compare the past persecutions of the godly with the events of Black Bartholomew. The printed version framed Newcomen's invitation to consider the need for vigilance in the following terms:

> If any say, No; There is not more cause; for then the Magistrate was a Mortal Enemy to the Gospel and the Professors of it, but we are (thanks be to God) under a Christian Magistrate, who doth not oppose, but countenance the Gospel and the Profession of it. If any makes this Objection, I will give you *Mr Hildersham's* Answer to it.[127]

Newcomen then outlined Hildersham's warning given in 1631, that although England lived at peace under a government which espoused the reformed religion, yet there was still a need for vigilance, due to a perceived increase in papists and the ever-present peril of 'the Fiery Tryal'.[128] The same passage in the manuscript, however, is more strident, arguing that

> If any shall say. Noe, for these were dayes of bloudy Persecutions, and of fiery tryalls, the Magistrate was a mortal enemy to Christ, and his Gosple, and ye Jewes every where incensed him against it, but we, thankes be to God, live under a Christian Magistracie, and in dayes of great peace, we have peace at home, and peace abroad, and therefore there is no such great need of pressing this Exhortation, upon People. Now this Objection I find in Mr Hildersham, and I shall give you his Answer to it, as I find it delivered by him. In the yeere 1631, just 31 years agone, and when I have done judge you whither there be not as much reason for the pressing of this duty now, as there was then.[129]

In the manuscript, Newcomen followed Hildersham's warnings of popery with images of the godly 'having fiery tryals put upon them before they knew what was happening.' It is perhaps because such images were so redolent of the Marian persecution that Newcomen felt it prudent to add that 'theise are his wordes of the times 30 years agone, not mine of these times'.[130]

It is entirely possible, given the complaints of Baxter and Manton, that the editorial process could result in a more radical message than originally intended. The case of Newcomen, however, suggests that the opposite could be true: whether or not Winter's manuscript was a factual record of the sermons delivered from Dedham's pulpit, that manuscript, being written in Newcomen's own hand, was clearly the message he wished to place on record. The omissions from the printed version show that it was neither a wholly accurate nor a complete rendition of Newcomen's preaching. The gaps and alterations presented to the reading public an image that, whilst not quietist, was certainly quieter than the man who had preached in Dedham on 17 and 19 August 1662.

VI

The farewell sermons of some Bartholomeans were published repeatedly. Some printed texts were identical: for example (allowing for differences in pagination and typesetting) Lamb's valediction as featured in *The Third Volume of Farewel Sermons* (1663) was a faithful rendition of the sermon that had first been published as *The Royal Presence* (1662).[131] Except for a missing section of two or three pages, Thomas Brooks's farewell sermon in *The Second Volume of the Farewell Sermons* (1663) was identical to that published in *The Second and Last Collection of the Late London Ministers* (1663) and in *A Compleat Collection of Farewel Sermons* (1663). Alternative published versions of other valedictions, on the other hand, reveal fundamental differences, indicating that there was often more than one version in circulation. In *The Burning Yet Un-consumed Bush* (1662), William Jenkyn's citation of I Kings 18:4 was supplemented by a reference to the Biblical Obediah hiding four hundred prophets from the persecution of his master, to which Jenkyn appended, 'I will not undertake to prophesie to you this day, yet time may come when bread and water may be good food for a faithful Prophet.'[132] The corresponding passage in *An exact collection*, by contrast, suggested that Jenkyn had gone into greater detail, describing the master in question as none other than King Ahab, 'a great *persecutor* of the *Saints*', when Jezebel had '*cut off the Prophets of the Lord*'.[133] The readiness of the editors of *An exact collection* to provide a full explication contrasted noticeably with the reticence of *The Burning Yet Un-consumed Bush*. It would be surprising if any editors had been ignorant of the fact that Ahab had served as a metaphor for Charles II during the Interregnum. The contrast becomes even more evident when Jenkyn's application of I Kings 18:4 in *An Exact Collection* is considered:

> I will not undertake to *Prophesie* to you this day, but it may come to that, *bread* and *water* may be very good *commons* for an honest *Prophet*, and *faithful servant of Jesus Christ*: for this was their condition, while the *false prophets* and *Idol Priests* was feasting at *Jezabel's* Table.[134]

The choice of punctuation preceding the word 'bread' is vital to the sense of the sentence, particularly as the use of a comma renders the sentence ambiguous. The compositor might easily have inserted a full stop or semicolon to eliminate any ambiguity. What oral punctuation by way of intonation or breathing space Jenkyn himself had actually intended must remain a matter of conjecture.

There is, however, a deeper significance in the variety to be found in alternative published versions of the farewell sermons than the expeditious pruning of contentious Biblical metaphors or the whims of compositors. A close associate of Jenkyn, Thomas Lye's two farewell sermons appeared in at least eleven different publications, including *The Fixed Saint Held Forth* (1662, Wing L3537) and *The Farewell Sermons of the Late London Ministers* (1662, Wing C242).

Although Lye's sermons in C242 form part of a larger compilation, the text is far more detailed than L3537. But where the sermons touch on the topic of earthly authority, the language of L3537 is invariably direct, whilst that of C242 is usually circumspect. According to C242, for example, Lye declared:

> If there be any of a light spirit would bear rule, that love to have preheminence, I would advise them to read two Scriptures; the first is *Luke* 22:26, the second *Mat* 26:27. [*sic*, actually Matthew 20:26–7][135]

In L3537, on the other hand, his point was made rather more bluntly:

> I would desire them that would hold authority and bear rule, to read these two Scriptures . . . The first is, *Luk* 22.26. The second is, *Matt.* 20.26–7. [*sic*][136]

Similarly, in C242, Lye's commendation of I Corinthians 8 was represented as being addressed to his fellow clergy:

> I would commend one Scripture to all my brethren in the Ministry: I *Cor.* 8:13; a Scripture that I would have writ in Letters of Gold on the lintell posts of all Ministers Doors.[137]

Whereas in L3537 the advice was aimed, rather waspishly, at those in authority:

> If men will be great Officers and talk at a rate they understand not, I commend that Scripture, which I could wish were writ upon the lintels of the Posts of the doors; the place; is I Cor. 8:13.[138]

In C242, the phrase '*Kings of the Gentiles*' was used, whereas L3537 talked of the 'Kings of the Earth'.[139] The editors (or the note-taker) of C242 appear to have been careful not to over-emphasise the concept of the godly as 'crowned', although it was not altogether expunged from their text. Thus, the phrase '*joy and triumph*' was used where L3537 instead mentioned the '*Joy and Crown of their Pastor*'.[140] And where the Lye of L3537 talked of 'my Brethren, my Joy, my Crown', the less emotive Lye of C242 simply expressed 'the terms of dearest affection, *dearly beloved*'.[141] A marked difference in emphasis is also evident in the alternative explications of the Biblical Hester:

> Oh that excellent Heroe Queen *Hester*; thus and thus I will do, *and if I perish, I perish.* [C242][142]

> Sayes *Hester*, 'I know it is death to go in unto the King, but I have sought God, and now, Come life, com death, I will go, it is for the truth, *if I perish, I perish*. [L3537][143]

C242 habitually featured the term 'Jews' whereas the compositor of L3537 inserted the specific, and rhetorically loaded term 'Pharisees'. Lye's aside, as recorded in L3537, 'remember, I speak of the *Pharises* all this while', is nowhere to be found in C242 despite its greater volume and detail.[144] The Lye of C242 was cautious when he ventured 'I hope tis not dangerous if I tell you, you are ingaged to God', whereas the preacher in L3537 stated decisively, 'you are engaged to God'.[145]

On isolated occasions C242 proved more provocative: where L3537 merely invited readers to 'remember *Zedakiah's* Cause, *Ezek*.18', C242 explained that Zedikiah '*despised the Oath by breaking the Covenant*', which caused God to declare '*as I live, surely mine Oath that he hath despised and my Covenant that he hath broken, even it will I recompense upon his own head*'.[146] Many among the congregation would have remembered that Charles II had taken the Covenant in 1650.

L3537 was the more highly charged in terms of emotion. Where C242 mentioned 'those hundreds of Ministers, that are to be plucked from their people', L3537 presented the Great Ejection as a rape of the Church, epitomised by 'the hundreds of the Ministers of the Gospel, that this day are to be ravished from the delight of their [the godly's] eyes.'[147] An easy way for Protestant preachers – and publishers – to inflame emotions was to mention the menace of Catholicism. For the most part both C242 and L3537 were equally anti-Catholic, although at one point C242 warned that 'the discords between Pastor and people have made the best musick in the ears of the Jesuits', whereas L3537 only declared that such discord 'is not the example of Christ'.[148] L3537 went much further than C242, however, when it related the suffering and temptations likely to be experienced by nonconformists to the persecution of Protestants during the reign of Queen Mary, describing how 'the bloody Papists' exploited the martyrs' concern for their wives and children.[149]

It is clear from both texts that Thomas Lye's attitude to his fellow Protestants was essentially irenic. However, in the reporting of Lye's explication of his doctrinal stance, important differences emerged which perhaps reflected as much on the predilection of the respective note-takers as anything else. In C242, Lye was recorded as criticising people who opined that,

> such a man cannot be an honest man, alas he is a Presbyterian, he's an Independent, he's an Anabaptist, &c. Now, all our great business will be, such a man cannot be good, an honest man, for he doth not *conform:* on the other side he cannot be an honest man, for he doth *conform.* These are poor things: I bless God, I lay not the stress of my Salvation upon these: tis true, I cannot in conscience conform, but I do not lay the stress of salvation on it, as I did not lay the stress of my salvation on my being a *Presbyterian;* I confess I am so, and have been; it hath bin my unhappiness to be always on the sinking side, yet I lay not the stress of my Salvation upon it.[150]

This did not accord with the version that had already appeared in L3537, however, where any potentially disadvantageous mention of Presbyterianism had been omitted:

> do not judge such a one cannot be honest, he is an Independent, and the other, for he is an Anabaptist; and the other is not honest, for he cannot conform: I bless God I do not lay the stresse of my salvation upon these; it has bin my unhappiness always to be of the sinking side, do not spend your time in censuring this man, and justifying that man, *I* do profess if I could conform without sin I would, but if *I* do it against my conscience, I should sin and break my peace.[151]

The analysis of the two versions throws up interesting indications of the attention spans of the two note-takers. It is striking that both tended to record the more dramatic passages of exegesis in almost identical terms. Phrases such as 'what, shall we prove dumb doggs!', or 'I am very sensible of what it is to be reduced to a Morsell of bread', the warning of 'a *Hurracain* a comming', and, of course, the invitation to put feet on the neck of kings, register the occasions on which Lye struck a particularly resonant chord with both note-takers.[152]

VII

If the existence of so many manuscript versions of the farewell sermons led to discrepancies, it also provided a pool which facilitated the production of something far more significant than isolated pamphlets. The concept of compiling sermons for publication was nothing new, as evidenced by the printing of Samuel Hieron's *Workes* in 1635. The reading public was also familiar with the idea that religious compilations could carry a political subtext, albeit one invariably dictated by the state in official collections of homilies.[153] The Bartholomean compilations, however, were different in that they featured works which were in themselves the central element of a political event – one that had registered widespread religious and (by implication) political dissidence. And in bringing together the voices of ejected ministers from around the country the act of compilation went beyond the promotion of dissenters to the promotion of Dissent. It was entirely understandable that the Restoration establishment should react with indignation and alarm.

Had these compilations been licensed and openly printed, their production would still have entailed logistical and commercial problems of a different magnitude to the pamphlets. Compositing, printing, storage, collation and binding each involved considerable time and expense. As many Bartholomean compilations were probably retailed at a discounted price, the income from sales may not have defrayed the financial burden of production and distribution. The need to minimise costs, together with the measures taken to ensure secrecy, resulted in a production quality low even by the standards of the day. Compilers invariably failed to include the painstaking marginalia which normally accompanied printed religious works. Entire sheets were sometimes accidentally omitted, leaving valedictions truncated and incomplete.[154] Examples of erratic or inaccurate pagination are rife, suggesting hurried collation or poor coordination between printing houses. Some compilations feature no pagination beyond the printer's signatures. It is possible that some collections were pirated, but as all save the reprint of *England's Remembrancer* appear to have been newly typeset, and most were produced from the outset in octavo, it is impossible to ascertain a precise taxonomy of production. No compilation appears to have progressed from an initial quarto to a subsequent octavo edition. None are obviously from the same press – perhaps a reflection of the disruption caused by L'Estrange's energetic policing of the industry.

Production quality, however, was less important than content. Mindful that even the godliest of purchasers would not bear an endless recycling of the same sermons, rival compilations such as *The Farewell Sermons of the Late London Ministers* and *An Exact Collection* featured slightly different combinations of ministers in a clear effort to maximise sales. Publishers of each succeeding compilation made great play of any fresh items gathered, be they prayers offered up before the farewell sermons, newly received valedictions or associated material such as Lye's final morning exercises or Calamy's Aldermanbury sermon.[155] A later edition of *A Compleat Collection of Farewell Sermons* (1663) even included Wilde's poem on Calamy's imprisonment and suffering.[156] That publishers were continually seeking ever more enterprising ways to market their compilations can be observed from the preface to *The Third Volume of Farewel Sermons*, which served not simply as an introduction, but also as a commercial advertisement and publishing offer. After listing the contents of the first two volumes in detail, the editors declared that *The third volume* was '*much more compleated than any yet extant*', and, moreover, that any customers who had already bought either of the previous volumes could request only the material they had not yet purchased, or have all three parts bound together.[157]

A fast turnover of stock was not only essential for commercial reasons: the larger the compilation the greater the risk of discovery. Increasingly complex commissions required longer periods of time to complete. Even once printed and safely delivered, booksellers and warehouse managers must have found the bulky compilations increasingly difficult to conceal. Booksellers relied upon the discretion of whole networks of printers, chapmen, employees, customers and trade rivals. Tables of contents by which publishers of compilations such as *The Third Volume* sought to advertise their wares provided more intelligence for government watchdogs than did individual pamphlets. And whilst every new compilation further raised the profile of the ejected ministers, it also served to alarm and energise the supporters and agents of the Establishment; L'Estrange was not moved to warn his readers against isolated pamphlets, but against the successive volumes of collected farewell sermons.[158] Manton's letter to L'Estrange's organ *The Newes* indicates that some ejected ministers were themselves becoming increasingly unnerved at developments.[159]

Manton's unease reflected the fact that the compilations were not welcomed by all ejected ministers, particularly if they were thereby associated with views more radical than their own. The process of compilation eroded any residual vestiges of individual authorial control, separating the Bartholomeans' public personae from the actual individuals. The sense of theatricality evident in several valedictions was reinforced every time these often unwilling actors were billed in a table of contents, bordered by a ring of their woodcut portraits. It was explicitly evoked by prefaces such as that of *The Farewell Sermons of the Late London Ministers* (1662), whose editor wrote as if he were introducing ministers to a stage audience:

> To commend them, for Non-conformity, I will not; to condemn them I dare not; but will draw the curtain from before our Subject, and present each glorious Scene: and because a Pen cannot paint out their Praise, Silence shall here be the Prologue.[160]

The publishers of the Bartholomean corpus had a variety of strategies in addition to the silent prologue for establishing the veracity of their particular publication. Some prefaces described the provenance of the text, or the status of the note-taker, describing that individual as a '*careful hand*', or as a good friend of the author.[161] The aspiration to use only the most accurate transcriptions available figured prominently in many prefaces, whilst others in admitting the possibility of the occasional error in the text implied the accuracy of the remainder.[162] Some prefaces pleaded that the reason for publication was to ensure that the minister in question be fairly represented.[163] Many publications clearly staked their credentials on the reputation of the accredited author, but on other occasions the preface specifically mentioned that the preacher had not consented to publication, or (as in the case of *England's Remembrancer*) withheld the authors' identities. By thus implying that the text was inconvenient, possibly even dangerous, for its author, the reader was expected to believe its veracity.

Texts were indeed often inconvenient for certain ministers: the decision to compile and publish printed collections resulted in a synthesis of accumulated rhetoric which produced in each case something akin to a Bartholomean meta-sermon, in which irenic and circumspect ministers were irreparably bound to divisive and outspoken ones, those resigned to their fate to those angrily defiant, those respectful of authority to others less deferential. In many cases this may have been an unintended consequence: the preface to *An Exact Collection*, for example, was a model of reticence, pointing out that, '*We conceive we need not adde any thing to take off that clamour that is cast upon them, as if out of an humour, faction, or which is worse, disobedience to Authority, they refused to conform.*'[164]

On other occasions strategies were more obvious: the compilers of *The Third Volume* chose to append an anti-popish diatribe by Thomas Watson to their collection – an item that was subsequently included in a number of succeeding compilations such as *A Compleat Collection*.[165] But this sermon was clearly distinct from Watson's valedictions, and there is nothing to suggest that it was delivered during Black Bartholomew. Furthermore, much as the sermon excoriated Catholic doctrine, it presented popery as an abstract threat from a distant foreign power, making no mention of Bartholomew's Day or an enemy within. However, by incorporating the piece within a body of farewell sermons the compilers of *The Third Volume* changed the context of both, presenting a message that, John Crodacot aside, no published Bartholomean had advocated: that Black Bartholomew was a popish plot.[166]

Equally contentious was the commissioning of woodcut portraits of ministers for the frontispieces of several compilations. In a prominent position facing the title page, the civilly dead alongside deceased divines such as Ashe and Nalton, the impact was dramatic and the purpose unmistakable. Although the departing ministers had refrained from comparing themselves directly with the Marian martyrs, the woodcuts provided a context of martyrdom even before the reader had turned the first page. Such iconography was hardly 'coded': near-contemporary hagiographies of royalist martyrs compiled by David Lloyd and William Winstanley featured portraits of dead Cavalier heroes clustered around a likeness of Charles I.[167] Just as the process of compilation helped raise the temperature of the exchanges between Cavalier-Anglican writers and nonconformists, so it appeared to indicate a hardening of doctrinal and ideological divisions which many Bartholomeans had hoped to avoid.

The production of compilations ceased as suddenly as it had begun. Given L'Estrange's estimate of the volume of Bartholomean literature in circulation, it is likely that the market had become saturated. No new publications appeared after 1664, save for a reprint of *England's Remembrancer* (1666). Over the next two centuries, only Fairclough's valedictions and Atkins's *God of Love and Peace* were published (in 1713 and 1715 respectively). An obsession with novelty evident in successive compilations suggests that publishers made increasingly frantic efforts to maintain sales. Although such activity indicated a gradual waning of public interest, nonconformist authors themselves remained popular: works such as Thomas Brooks's *Apples of Gold* (1657–1717) and *An Arke for All God's Noahs* (1662–66) continued to sell in prodigious quantities, and a compendium of ejected ministers' thoughts was published as *Saints Memorials* as late as 1674.[168] The enduring popularity of such works suggests that it might have been possible to continue with the publication of farewell sermons, had the impetus been maintained by fresh material. However between 1664 and 1666 several printers and publishers disappeared from the scene.

In February 1664 Livewell Chapman was in prison and Giles Calvert dead when Thomas Brewster, along with the printer Simon Dover and the book-binder Nathan Brooks, stood trial for seditious publishing. Brewster died in prison. At the same time Elizabeth Calvert was arrested for commissioning John Twynn to print part of *A Treatise of the Execution of Justice.*[169] Twynn's trial and execution was symptomatic of hardening attitudes to clandestine political literature – a development L'Estrange declared to be due in no small part to the circulation of printed farewell sermons.[170] This appears to have made an impression on Livewell Chapman, who following his release in May 1664 thereafter lived quietly.[171]

If governmental repression had disrupted the production of printed fare-well sermons, the Great Plague of 1665 and the Great Fire of London in the following year ended any hopes of renewed large-scale publication. It was ironic that during the plague many ejected ministers reoccupied pulpits deserted by Anglican clergy (and had to be re-ejected by the authorities), whilst some eighty members of the printing industry succumbed to the pestilence, and large numbers of their clients died or fled.[172] In September 1666 came worse fortune, when booksellers and printers, being mostly concentrated in the neighbourhoods of St Pauls and Cheapside, suffered the full fury of the Great Fire.[173] Many booksellers lost their entire stock, whilst printers, with some 1,000 to 2,000 kg of soft metal type melted beside each press, lost their livelihoods.[174] By 1668 the number of master printers in London had fallen to just 28, several of whom were still 'disabled by the Fire'.[175] Basic printing materials were scarce, and books which had cost 8s before the Fire now retailed for 20–30s.[176] Sir William Dugdale, who had lost the entire impression of his new book in the blaze, informed an acquaintance that 'there can be no thought of printing any of these for three or four years at least'.[177]

Even where businesses had survived, it seems that no publisher was willing to republish more huge Bartholomean compilations at discounted prices. Censorship, market saturation, plague, fire and fresh news (such as renewed war with the Netherlands) had all conspired to ensure that the Bartholomeans' afterlife in print was of finite duration.

VIII

Recent studies of the book in early modern England, influenced by Darnton's model of the 'communications circuit', have emphasised the distortions caused as the lifecycle of a text revolved from writing to publication, distribution and reception. Consequently, we have been urged to regard texts not simply as sources, but as artefacts: constructs characterised by inherent semiotic instability. Some scholars, in an echo of Barthes' assertion of the death of the Author, have warned against a preoccupation with authority and authorship, lest we overlook the issue of textual instability. Whilst noting the obligation that publishers were obliged to persuade their readers of the 'trustworthiness of the text', Adrian Johns has argued that 'far from fixing certainty and truth, print dissolved them'.[178] For those involved in the publication of the Bartholomean corpus the issue of trustworthiness was extremely important: firstly, being sermons, the texts were not limited to a single, linear communications circuit, but circulated simultaneously through a matrix of circuits – word of mouth, private manuscript and print – each competing with, and refining, other versions of the truth. Secondly, each printed farewell sermon reconstructed a text that had been witnessed by hundreds, perhaps thousands, of hearers, many of whom were also readers. Consequently, in order for the publishers of the farewell sermons to establish the trustworthiness of their texts, they were required not only to make plausible truth claims in their prefaces, but also to corroborate their readers' knowledge of events.

The survival of the manuscripts of Newcomen, Atkins, Ford, Stucley and Powell, together with circumstantial evidence of other unpublished valedictions, suggests that there was a considerable amount of manuscript material in private circulation. However, the public clamour for farewell sermons ensured that this medium would prove unequal to the task, and would rapidly be superseded by print. The distrust of the printed word exhibited by Fairclough and Lamb did not dampen the enthusiasm of their parishioners; indeed, the provincial material that began to proliferate in the later publications of farewell sermons demonstrates that the true significance of print at this time lay not in production figures, but in the widespread acceptance of the medium as a means of reciprocal communication between London and the provinces.[179]

The process of print circumnavigated the silencing of the pulpits (at least temporarily) and exposed the nonconformist message to a wider audience. This, however, came at a price: preachers such as Baxter and Manton observed how the processes of public circulation reshaped the message carried by the valedictions and, as a consequence, the reputation of the nonconformist clergy. Even had their sermons been faithfully reproduced, the ambiguity of the rhetoric, which had enabled preachers to protest without incriminating themselves, rendered them vulnerable to a variety of interpretations. Readers could, according to their predisposition, infer different meanings from the printed sermons, and impute various intentions to the authors. Similarly, the transition from manuscript to print could produce a misleading public image (as demonstrated by the publication of Newcomen's August 19 sermon), and competing printed versions of the same farewell sermon could lead to a variety of public faces (as in the case of Thomas Lye). Thus, what in many instances may have been intended as trenchant (albeit coded) criticism or declaration of religious conviction could by omission, addition or juxtaposition be fashioned into something altogether more menacing.

The impetus to produce and disseminate the farewell sermons came from publishers rather than printers, although profit does not seem to have been their primary motive. Evidence of retail discounting shows publishers to have taken considerable financial (and physical) risks, suggesting a high degree of religious or ideological commitment. But even the godly could not ignore commercial considerations: a sensitive pricing policy and a steady supply of saleable names, or at least newsworthy content, were all essential to success. The portrayal of nonconformist clergy as heroic martyrs was also clearly beneficial to sales. The fact that large numbers of Bartholomeans had advertised their nonconformity in terms of their 'civil death' was heavily promoted by publishers, but the loss of authorial control was apparent as Bartholomeans of all shades of opinion were conscripted into the army of martyrs. There were undoubtedly many ministers whose instinctive respect for authority made them reluctant to publish, and who were unhappy to find themselves in print. But their very selection for publication shows that publishers and readers considered their dissent (and their suffering) sufficiently controversial to be newsworthy, and the transforming qualities of print did the rest.

It has been argued above that the natural disasters of plague and fire may have been as much to blame for the cessation of publication of the farewell sermons as the efficacy of censorship and the waning of public interest. Without these calamities, and the death and incarceration of key figures in the production process, more provincial collections and even larger compilations might have appeared in print. Given the political consequences had the circulation of the farewell sermons continued to flourish and grow, it is indicative of the pre-eminence of early modern London that matters should ultimately have been decided by the chance destruction of a few streets in the locality of St Paul's and Cheapside.

The published sermons did indeed represent a louder voice than those of Baxter and his fellow Bartholomeans, even if that voice did not always reflect the message they intended. But the influence of an item of literature cannot adequately be measured either by the intention of its avowed author or the volume of its sales. 'Printed matter', as Roger Chartier writes, 'is set – always – within a network of cultural and social practices that give it its meaning'.[180] The cultural and social networks that made up Restoration England were composed of a complex and shifting matrix of agencies that included the supportive, the disinterested and the actively hostile. Lay followers, clergy, patrons and publishers, for a variety of reasons, had actively promoted the public circulation of the farewell sermons. Printers such as Peter Lillicrap facilitated that circulation, even though he and others of his trade often had no religious, ideological or emotional investment in the project. By contrast, the Bartholomeans' enemies were very much engaged, and, as we shall now see, only too eager to exploit the farewell sermons to further their own political and religious agendas.

NOTES

1 E.g., The Treason Act (13 Charles II. St I. Cap. I, 1661); The Licensing Act (14 Charles II, Cap. 33, 1662); Browning, *Documents*, pp. 63–5, 67–9; R. Baxter, *True Christianity* (1654), quoted in Keeble, *Literary Culture*, p. 82.

2 Hancock, *Pastor's Last Legacy*, sig. C2.

3 Fairclough, *Pastor's Legacy*, p. 70.

4 M. Spufford, 'First steps in literacy: the reading and writing experiences of the humblest seventeenth-century spiritual autobiographers', *Social History*, 4, 3 (1979), pp. 407–35; see also H. Brayman, 'The "great variety of readers" and early modern reading practices', in D. Kastan (ed.), *A Companion to Shakespeare* (Oxford, 1999), p. 141.

5 J. Rigney, '"To lye upon a stationer's stall, like a piece of coarse flesh in a shambles": the sermon, print and the English Civil War', in Ferrell and McCullough, *English Sermon Revised*, p. 199. Spufford, 'First steps in literacy', p. 427 successfully counters Cressy's argument that the lower social orders were invariably indifferent to such affairs. Cf. D. Cressy, 'Illiteracy in England 1530–1730', *Historical Journal*, 20, 1 (1977), pp. 8–9; K. Wrightson, *English Society 1580–1680* (1982, 1990), p. 196; Spufford, 'The importance of religion in the 16th and 17th century', pp. 65, 77; K. Wrightson, and D. Levine, *Poverty and Piety in an English Village: Terling 1525–1700* (Oxford, 1995), p. 151.

6 Spufford, 'First steps in literacy', p. 407.

7 Keeble, *Literary Culture*, pp. 136–7, 139.

8   Pepys, *Diary*, iii, pp. 166–8; Bates, *Peace-Maker*, pp. 9–10, 18.

9   DWL MSS I.l.35, fos 27v–30r.

10 Porter, *Life of Mr John Hieron*, p. 14.

11 Baxter in *Exact Collection*, p. 160; Fairclough, *Pastor's Legacy*, p. 116; Bull, in *Third Volume*, pp. 54, 70, 71; Bladon, in *England's Remembrancer*, p. 306.

12 *Third Volume*, p. 71.

13 Newcombe, *Diary*, pp. 120, 126.

14 Seaver, *Puritan Lectureships*, p. 42; Mitchell, *English Pulpit Oratory*, pp. 74, 83, 90.

15 Quoted in Bremer and Rydell, 'Performance art?', p. 51.

16 Pepys, *Diary*, p. 168.

17 Bates, *Peace-Maker*, p. 32.

18 E.g., J. Everardt, *An Epitome of Stenographie* (1658); T. Shelton, *Tachygraphy* (1668); T. Metcalfe, *Short-Writing* (1660).

19 T. Heath, *Stenography* (1664), Wing H1343, sig. [A2v].

20 T. Heath, *Stenography* (1644), Wing H1342, frontispiece.

21 Baxter, *Reliquiae Baxterianae*, pt II, p. 303.

22 Bates, *Peace-Maker*, sig. [A]. An almost identical passage appears in Mead, *Pastor's Valediction*, sig. [A2v].

23 *Account*, ii, p. 217.

24 *Exact Collection*, sig. [A2v].

25 E. Calamy, *The Righteous Mans Death Lamented* (1662), Wing C262A; E. Calamy, *The Fixed Saint Held Forth* (1662), Wing C244.

26 Jenkyn, *Burning Yet Un-consumed Bush* (Wing J633); Lye, *Fixed Saint* (Wing L3537), and T. Watson, *The Righteous Mans Weal and the Wicked Mans Woe* (1662), Wing W1141.

27 *A Collection of Farewel-Sermons Preached* (1662), Wing C5145A.

28 Bates, *Peace-Maker* (Wing B1117); Caryl, *White Robe* (Wing C789); Mead, *Pastors Valediction* (Wing M1556).

29 *The Farewell Sermons of the Late London Ministers* (1662), Wing C242.

30 E. Calamy, *Eli Trembling for Fear of the Ark* (1662), Wing C231A.

31 E. Calamy, *Eli Trembling for Fear of the Ark* (Oxford, 1663), Wing C231; E. Calamy, *Eli Trembling for Fear of the Ark* (Oxford, 1663), Wing C232; E. Calamy, *A Sermon Preached at Aldermanbury Church, Dec 28, 1662* (Oxford, 1663), Wing C267.

32 Berkenhead, *Cabala*, pp. 26 and '28' (mispaginated, p. 34); *A Mystery of Godliness, and No Cabala* (1663).

33 *Exact Collection* (Wing E3632).

34 Lamb, *Royal Presence* (Wing L207A).

35 Swinnock, *Pastor's Farewell* (Wing S6280).

36 *Abridgement*, ii, p. 485.

37 Cooper, *Dead Witnesse* (Wing C6056); Eubanke, *Farewell Sermon Preached* (Wing E3444); Fairclough, *Pastors Legacy* (Wing F106); Hancock, *Pastors Last Legacy* (Wing H640).

38 Horton, *Rich Treasure* (Wing H2879).

39 Newcomen, *Ultimum Vale* (Wing N914).

40 T. Webster, 'Matthew Newcomen (*d.* 1669)', *ODNB*, www.oxforddnb.com/view/article/19995 [accessed 26 October 2004]; T. Davids, *Annals of Ecclesiastical Nonconformity in Essex* (1863), p. 384.

41 *Second and Last Collection* (Wing S2257).

42 *The Second Volume of the Farewel Sermons* (1663), Wing S2236A.

43 *The Third and Last Volume of the Farwell Sermons* (1663); Wing T898A; *Third Volume* (Wing T914C).

44 *England's Remembrancer* (Wing E3029); *The Intelligencer*, 3 (14 September 1663), p. 23.

45 The full titles of these 'compleat' editions appear in the bibliography: Wing C243, C5638A (80), C5638A (40), C5638 (two different editions).

46 Assheton, *Evangelium Armatum*; D. Lloyd, *Cabala*.

47 Thorne, *Saints Great Duty* (Wing T1057B); T. Palke, *The Loyal Non-Conformist* (1664), P203B.

48 *CR, s.v.*

49 *England's Remembrancer* (1666), Wing E3029A.

50 Quoted in Achinstein, *Literature and Dissent*, p. 19.

51 Browning, *Documents*, pp. 68–9.

52 G. Eyre, H. Plomer and C. Rivington (eds), *A Transcript of the Registers of the Worshipful Company of Stationers from 1640–1708 A.D.* (1913–14 rpt New York, 1950), pp. 321, *passim*.

53 *CSPD* 1663–4, p. 406.

54 *An Exact Narrative of the Tryal and Condemnation of John Twyn* (1664), pp. 13, 37–9.

55 L'Estrange, *Considerations and Proposals*, quoted in Keeble, *Literary Culture*, p. 128; Plant, *English Book Trade*, p. 84; F. Siebert, *Freedom of the Press in England 1476–1776* (Urbana, IL, 1952), p. 239; D. Thomas, *A Long Time Burning: The History of Literary Censorship in England* (1969), p. 31.

56 Plant, *English Book Trade*, p. 91; Keeble, *Literary Culture*, p. 128.

57 Randall, 'The rise and fall of a martyrology', p. 157.

58 Keeble, *Literary Culture*, p. 128.

59 *CSPD* 1663–4, p. 180; 1661–2, p. 23.

60 B. McMullen, 'The bible trade', in Barnard and McKenzie, *Cambridge History of the Book in Britain*, p. 556.

61 L'Estrange, *Considerations and Proposals*, sig. [A3v]. Hetet, by contrast, derides L'Estrange's 'specious appearance of insight and authority'; Hetet, 'A Literary Underground in Restoration England', p. 11.

62 Keeble, *Literary Culture*, p. 128; see also Green and Peters, 'Religious publishing in England', p. 77.

63 Potter, *Secret Rites*, pp. 5, 25, 36; Plant, *English Book Trade*, p. 47.

64 Miller, *After the Civil Wars*, p. 61.

65 E. Bagshawe, *A Letter to the Right Honourable Edward, Earl of Clarendon* (1662); R. L'Estrange, *Truth and Loyalty Vindicated* (1662); R. Baxter, *Richard Baxter His Account to His Dearly Beloved, the Inhabitants of Kidderminster, of the Causes of His Being Forbidden by the Bishop of Worcester to Preach Within His Diocess* (1662); G. Morley, *The Bishop of VVorcester's Letter to a Friend for Vindication of Himself from Mr. Baxter's Calumny* (1662).

66 Browning, *Documents*, pp. 67, 69.

67 Seaver, *Puritan Lectureships*, p. 196.

68 E.g., R. Prichard, *Rhan o Waith Mr Rees Prichard* (1659); R. Baxter, *Galwad i'r Annychweledig* (1667); *Versameling van Afscheytspredicatien, Gepredikt van Mr Calamy, etc.* (Amsterdam, 1662).

69 J. Raven, 'The economic context', in Barnard and McKenzie, *Cambridge History of the Book in Britain*, p. 577; J. Raymond (ed.), *An Anthology of the Newsbooks of Revolutionary England 1641–1660* (Moreton-on-the-Marsh, 1993), pp. 6, 10; Spufford, 'The importance of religion', p. 65; Johns, *Nature of the Book*, p. 156; Potter, *Secret Rites*, p. 25.

70 *CSPD 1663–4*, pp. 37, 43, 297; Keeble, *Literary Culture*, p. 131; Kitchin, *L'Estrange*, p. 116. The prominence of fairs in early modern book distribution is discussed in Plant, *English Book Trade*, p. 262.

71 Kennett, *Register*, p. 743, quoted in Green, *Re-establishment*, p. 155.

72 Lye, *Fixed Saint*, sig. [A2v].

73 Keeble, *Literary Culture*, pp. 133–4; *Compleat Collection* (1663).

74 *Second and Last Collection*, frontispiece.

75 S. Hieron, *Workes* (1635); Green, *Print and Protestantism*, pp. 40, 629.

76 Keeble, *Literary Culture*, pp. 132–3J. Barnard and M. Bell, 'The English provinces', in Barnard and McKenzie, *Cambridge History of the Book in Britain*, p. 686.

77 H. Love, 'Preacher and publisher: Oliver Heywood and Thomas Parkhurst', *Studies in Bibliography* (1978), 31, p. 228; Barnard and Bell, 'The English provinces', p. 685.

78 Potter, *Secret Rites*, p. 23.

79 The other was Thomas Leach; J. Walker, 'The censorship of the press during the reign of Charles II', *History*, 35 (1950), p. 231.

80 *CSPD 1663–4*, pp. 179, 180, 213.

81 PRO SP29/77/37 (Peter Lillicrap to Sir Henry Bennet, 23 July 1663).

82 *CSPD* 1663–4, pp. 213, 230, 267; PRO SP29/78/40 (Petition of Peter Lillicrap, 4 August 1663).

83 Eubanke, *A Farewell Sermon Preached*, sig. A2.

84 Swinnock, *Pastor's Farewell*, sig. [A4].

85 Fairclough, *Pastors Legacy*, frontispiece; Lamb, *Royal Presence*, sig. A2.

86 Calamy, *Eli Trembling for Fear of the Ark* (Wing C232), preface.

87 Horton, *Rich Treasure*, sig. [A2v].

88 *Third Volume*, sig. A3.

89 Bates, *Peace-Maker*, sig. A, [Av]; Mead, *Pastor's Valediction*, sig. [A2v].

90 Keeble, *Literary Culture*, p. 121. Ann Hughes, 'Approaches to Presbyterian print culture: Thomas Edwards's *Gangraena* as source and text', in J. Andersen and E. Sauer (eds), *Books and Readers in Early Modern England* (Philadelphia, 2002), p. 104.

91 The *English Short Title Catalogue Online* reveals Thomas Brewster to have been associated with the production of 86 titles before 1662, Giles Calvert 633 and Livewell Chapman 97; http://eureka.rlg.org/ [accessed 17 January 2005]. The *ODNB* estimates Calvert to have sold or published some 475 publications individually or in partnership by his death in 1663; A. Hessayon, 'Giles Calvert (*bap.* 1612, *d.* 1663), *ODNB*, www.oxforddnb.com/view/article/39669 [accessed 17 January 2005].

92 *CSPD* 1663–4, pp. 71, 124, 297, 349, 430, 510, 581, 582.

93 *DNB*, *s.v.* J. Dunton, *The Life and Errors of John Dunton, Late Citizen of London* (1705), p. 281, Dunton, *Life*, p. 281, quoted in Love, 'Preacher and publisher', pp. 232, 234.

94 Baxter quoted in Keeble, *Literary Culture*, p. 123.

95 Swinnock, *Pastor's Farewell*, frontispiece, sig. [A4, A4v].

96 Quoted in Love, 'Preacher and publisher', p. 234.

97 Swinnock, *Pastor's Farewell*, pp. 26, 48, 58.

98 Love, 'Preacher and publisher', p. 235.

99 Keeble, *Literary Culture*, p. 144.

100 Figures extracted from *CR*, pp. xii–xiii.

101 *Third Volume*, sig. [A3v].

102 Mead, *Pastor's Valediction*, p. 24.

103 *England's Remembrancer*, sig. A2.

104 Potter, *Secret Rites*, pp. 6–7, 10.

105 *Ibid.*, p. 23.

106 Jenkyn, *Burning Yet Un-consumed Bush*, preface.

107 Fairclough, *Pastor's Legacy*, p. 122.

108 *Abridgement*, ii, p. 217.

109 Lamb, *Royal Presence*, sig. A2–[A2v].

110 Baxter, *Reliquiae Baxterianae*, ii, p. 303.

111 *Ibid.*; R. Baxter, *The Cure of Church-Divisions* (1679), quoted in Nuttall and Chadwick, *From Uniformity to Unity*, pp. 153–4.

112 Baxter, *Reliquiae Baxterianae*, ii, p. 303.

113 *The Newes*, 4, Thursday, 24 September 1663, p. 31.

114 *The Intelligencer*, 3 (14 September 1663), p. 24.

115 Caryl, *The White Robe* (Wing C789), sig. A2.

116 Thorne, *Saints Great Duty*, frontispiece, p. 20.

117 Lamb, *Royal Presence*, frontispiece, sig. [A2v].

118 DWL I.h.35, fo. 1r.

119 C. Fell Smith, 'The Essex Newcomens', *Essex Review*, 2 (1893), p. 39.

120 DWL I.h.35, fo. 1v.

121 *Ibid.*

122 Downame, *The Second Volume of Annotations*, John 14:1.

123 DWL I.h.35, fo. 5r.

124 Newcomen to Baxter, 21 May 1661, DWL *Baxter Letters*, 5. fo. 179, quoted in Smith, 'The Essex Newcomens', pp. 37–8.

125 E.g., Douch, *England's Jubilee*, p. 8; Parker, *A Sermon Preached at Christ-Church, Dublin*, p. 40; Barksdale, *The Kings Return*, p. 10; Newcome, *Usurpation Defeated and David Restored*, p. 19.

126 DWL MS I.l.35, fo. 2r.

127 *Second and Last Collection*, p. 152.

128 *Ibid.*, pp. 152–3.

129 DWL MS I.l.35, fos 64–5r.

130 *Ibid.*, fos 65r, 66r.

131 Other examples include Mead, *Pastor's Valediction*, compared with *Second and Last Collection*, and Horton, *Rich Treasure* compared with *Exact Collection*.

132 Jenkyn, *Burning Yet Un-consumed Bush*, p. 5.

133 *Exact Collection*, p. 259.

134 *Ibid.*

135 *The Farewell Sermons of the Late London Ministers* (Wing C242), sig. [T7].

136 Lye, *Fixed Saint* (Wing L3537), p. 4.

137 *The Farewell Sermons of the Late London Ministers* (Wing C242), sig. [Tv].

138 Lye, *Fixed Saint* (Wing L3537), p. 6.

139 *The Farewell Sermons of the Late London Ministers* (Wing C242), sig. [T8v]; Lye, *Fixed Saint* (Wing L3537), p. 4.

140 *The Farewell Sermons of the Late London Ministers* (Wing C242), sig. [V2v]; Lye, *Fixed Saint* (Wing L3537), p. 14.

141 *The Farewell Sermons of the Late London Ministers* (Wing C242), sig. [T8]; Lye, *Fixed Saint* (Wing L3537), p. 6.

142 *The Farewell Sermons of the Late London Ministers* (Wing C242), sig. [V4v].

143 Lye, *Fixed Saint* (Wing L3537), p. 17.

144 *The Farewell Sermons of the Late London Ministers* (Wing C242), sig. [V4v], X4; Lye, *Fixed Saint* (Wing L3537), pp. 11, 17, 26.

145 *The Farewell Sermons of the Late London Ministers* (Wing C242), sig. X; Lye, *Fixed Saint* (Wing L3537), p. 23.

146 Lye, *Fixed Saint* (Wing L3537), p. 23; C242, sig. [Xv]; Ezekiel 17:18, 19.

147 *The Farewell Sermons of the Late London Ministers* (Wing C242), sig. [T8]; Lye, *Fixed Saint* (Wing L3537), p. 7.

148 *The Farewell Sermons of the Late London Ministers* (Wing C242), sig. [T7v]; Lye, *Fixed Saint* (Wing L3537), p. 5.

149 Lye, *Fixed Saint* (Wing L3537), p. 29.

150 *The Farewell Sermons of the Late London Ministers* (Wing C242), sig. X2.

151 Lye, *Fixed Saint* (Wing L3537), p. 24.

152 *The Farewell Sermons of the Late London Ministers* (Wing C242), sig. [T8v, Vv, V2v, V6]; Lye, *Fixed Saint* (Wing L3537), pp. 5, 9, 11, 19. Cf. *The Farewell Sermons of the Late London Ministers* (Wing C242), sig. [T9v, V3v], V4, [V4v, V5]; Lye, *Fixed Saint* (Wing L3537), pp. 7, 14, 15, 16.

153 E.g., *Certain Sermons, or Homilies* [Book I], 36 editions, 1547–1640; *The Second Book of Homilies* [Book II], 20 editions, 1563–1640; Combined editions [Books I and II], at least 11 editions (1640–1726); see Green, *Print and Protestantism*, pp. 629, 630.

154 Cf. The Bodleian Library's copy of *The Second Volume of the Farewel Sermons* (Wing S2336A), sig. f–[F8v] with *Second and Last Collection* (Wing S2257), pp. 71–3.

155 E.g., *Second and Last Collection*, frontispiece; *Exact Collection*, frontispiece.

156 *Compleat Collection* (Wing C5638aA), sig. [Uu3–Uu4v].

157 *Third Volume*, sig. [A3v].

158 *The Intelligencer*, 3 (14 September 1663), p. 23.

159 *The Newes*, 4 (Thursday, 24 September 1663), p. 31.

160 *The Farewell Sermons of the Late London Ministers* (Wing C242), sig. [A4v].

161 E.g., Bates, *Peace-Maker*, sig. [A].

162 E.g., *Exact Collection*, frontispiece; *The Farewell Sermons of the Late London Ministers* (Wing C242), preface.

163 E.g., Bates, *Peace-Maker*, sig. [A]; Mead, *Pastor's Valediction*, sig. [A2v]; Jenkyn, *Burning Yet Un-consumed Bush*, preface.

164 *Exact Collection*, sig. [A3].

165 *Third Volume*, pp. 241–9; *Compleat Collection*, sig. Hhhh–Iiii.

166 *Third Volume*, p. 4.

167 W. Winstanley, *England's VVorthies* (1660); W. Winstanley, *The Loyall Martyrology* (1665); D. Lloyd, *Memoires of the Lives, Actions, Sufferings and Deaths of Those Noble, Reverend and Excellent Personages that Suffered* (1668).

168 See Green, *Print and Protestantism*, pp. 332–3, 356, 604.

169 *CSPD* 1663–4, pp. 180, 349, 430, 510; *An Exact Narrative of the Tryal and Condemnation of John Twyn*, pp. 37–42, 78; Keeble, *Literary Culture*, p. 98; Cobbett, *Complete Collection of State Trials and Proceedings for High Treason*, VII, pp. 926–59, 1111–30, quoted in Walker, 'Censorship of the Press', p. 228; Plomer, *A Dictionary of Booksellers and Printers*, pp. 32, 42–3; Kitchin, *L'Estrange*, p. 120.

170 L'Estrange, *Toleration Discuss'd*, pp. 53–60.

171 *CSPD* 1663–4, p. 581; *ODNB*, *s.v.*

172 The reoccupation was alluded to in Defoe's fictionalised, *A Journal of the Plague Year*, ed. L. Landa (Oxford, 1990), pp. 175, 235; a reference I owe to the kindness of Dr Alannah Tomkins. *CSPD* 1665–66, p. 20.

173 C. Blagden, *The Stationers' Company: A History 1403–1959* (1960), pp. 215–17; T. Reddaway, *The Rebuilding of London after the Great Fire* (1940), pp. 25, 54; W. Bell, *The Great Fire of London in 1666* (1951), pp. 129, 130, 225–6; *CSPD* 1667–68, p. 503.

174 See Gaskell, *A New Introduction to Bibliography*, pp. 37–9.

175 *CSPD* 1667–68, p. 503.

176 Bell, *Great Fire*, p. 226; Plant, *English Book Trade*, p. 34.

177 Quoted in Bell, *Great Fire*, pp. 226–7.

178 Johns, *Nature of the Book*, pp. 36, 172. See also Andersen and Sauer, *Books and Readers in Early Modern England*, pp. 1–4; M. Bell, 'Introduction: the material text', in M. Bell, S. Chew, S. Eliot, L. Hunter and J. West (eds), *Reconstructing the Book: Literary Texts in Transmission* (Aldershot, 2001), pp. 3–4; R. Darnton, 'What is the history of books?', *Daedalus* (1982), 3, pp. 65–83; Hughes, 'Approaches to Presbyterian print culture', p. 102.

179 See Barnard and Bell, 'The English provinces', p. 686.

180 R. Chartier, *Cultural Uses of Print in Early Modern France*, trans. L. Cochrane (New York, 1987), pp. 183–4, 343; quoted in Green, *Print and Protestantism*, p. 4.

Chapter 5

Polemical responses to Bartholomean preaching

As the most public manifestation of dissent from the religious settle-ment imposed by Parliament, it was inevitable that the farewell sermons would attract considerable vitriol. The polemical counterattack was not long in coming, and was made all the more ferocious because Cavalier-Anglicans were divided among themselves and fearful of the residual potential of Puritanism. Even those in power felt besieged; as Sir Henry Bennet declared, 'Now the *Press* and the *Pen* is beginning as hot a War upon us as if they intended speedily to follow it with the *Sword*.'[1] Thus, much as the ejected ministers might contend that their farewell sermons were pure transcrip-tions of conscience inspired by the word of God, the valedictions had clearly been moulded by the political context. Furthermore, as several Bartholomeans had feared, their preaching would be interpreted, and they themselves to a significant extent defined, by a largely antipathetic world. That reception can best be understood by situating it within the political culture of the Restoration establishment, and specifically in the context of the crisis of representation that was then being faced by supporters of the restored Stuart dynasty.[2] One of the consequences of this crisis was an outpouring of literature whose avowed aim was to strip Puritanism of any last vestiges of respectability. The farewell sermons provided Cavalier writers with the ideal target on which to focus their attacks. As a result, those moderate Puritans unable in conscience to comply with the Act of Uniformity came under intense moral pressure.

Considerable anti-Puritan sentiment emanated from Anglican pulpits, most particularly in sermons delivered to commemorate 30 January (Charles I's execution) and 29 May (the nativity and restoration of Charles II). Having said this, whilst many Anglican clerics sought to stigmatise and marginalise Puritans from the pulpit, most tended to avoid any direct engagement with the farewell sermons. That task was left to journalists such as John Berkenhead and Roger L'Estrange, and aspirant clerics such as William Assheton and David Lloyd. Consequently, as will be seen, the most trenchant critiques of nonconformity were motivated as much by political infighting and personal ambition as they were by the desire to defend Church and state.

The case has been made earlier that the ejected ministers did not constitute an alliance, much less a party. Nevertheless, the process of publication, particularly the process of compilation, gave the impression of unity. Writers such as Berkenhead and L'Estrange deliberately fostered this perception, portraying nonconformity as an organised and dangerous political force at the same time as they sought to divide and intimidate nonconformists. They did so by drawing from the same arsenal of rhetorical weaponry that had been deployed in the Bartholomean works – displaying an equally acute awareness of the relevance of Biblical metaphor and a greater willingness to utilise anti-popish trope. Cavalier journalists sought to dispute the very ground on which the farewell sermons had been predicated: the sense of moment, the political implications of persecution and martyrdom, and the veracity of so-called dying words. Above all they were keen to challenge the notion that earthly authority was restricted to the management of worldly affairs and consequently limited in the extent to which it could presume to intrude on religious conscience. The extent to which this avenue of attack succeeded in undermining the Bartholomean position can be measured in part by the nonconformist responses it provoked, perpetuating and sharpening the polemical debate over the Restoration religious settlement. The part played by contemporaneous Cavalier-Anglican literature is therefore no mere appendix or contextualisation of the Bartholomean corpus; it is integral to understanding how the corpus interacted with its historical moment.

I

The quest for religious settlement had been made an explicitly political process by the Declaration of Breda in 1660, when Charles II had promised that ultimate responsibility would rest with Parliament. The nature of Restoration politics, particularly the character of what might loosely be called the Establishment has excited considerable historiographical debate since the 1950s. In 1957 Robert Bosher argued that the Restoration government had been a popular and essentially unified regime with clear and coherent policies for Anglican orthodoxy in religion and politics. Sheldon and his allies he considered 'Laudians', and the gentry who ruled the provinces overwhelmingly Cavalier and Anglican, supported by large swathes of the populace, who equated religious dissent with political conspiracy and challenges to the social order. Within Bosher's model the so-called Clarendon Code was conceived and instituted by popular demand.[3]

Revisions by successive generations of historians have produced instead the picture of a fragmented and often paradoxical political establishment, within which policy emerged and dissipated in a murky fog of self-interest and expediency. Ian Green, whilst supporting Bosher's arguments that junior MPs and JPs were hot for episcopacy, has dismissed Restoration 'Laudianism' as an anachronism, and cast doubt on the notion of 'ejection from below'.[4] Harris and Seaward have shown that many moderate Puritans remained in positions of authority, with the result that there was considerable variety in official attitudes towards nonconformists.[5] John Miller has implied that Anglican clerics tried hard to persuade 'church-puritans' to remain within the Church of England (albeit conceding that their arguments 'were couched primarily in terms of obedience to authority') and that the bishops implemented 'legislation shaped by others'.[6] Even the Act of Uniformity was, according to John Spurr, 'the work of many hands, the product of parliamentary horse-trading rather than theological self-definition'.[7] The Parliament that codified the religious settlement was therefore by no means as solidly Cavalier as its nickname would suggest. However, perhaps because of this fragmentation, the two Houses, in common with the provincial gentry, resembled nothing so much as a nervous gaggle of geese, easily frightened and angered into chasing bogeymen created by activists such as Gilbert Sheldon. Sheldon and his allies, by contrast, were men who viewed the Act of Uniformity as a warrant to define and enforce Anglican orthodoxy.

For Sheldon religious orthodoxy had ideological as well as theological significance. Gilbert Burnet – admittedly no friend of the then Bishop of London – would later recall that Sheldon 'did not have a deep sense of religion, if any at all' and spoke of it 'most commonly as of an engine of government and a matter of policy'.[8] The infirmity of the aged Archbishops of Canterbury and York had effectively handed Sheldon the leadership of the Church of England at the outset of the Restoration, enabling him to influence the formulation of an exclusive religious settlement. As it became obvious that the period leading up to Bartholomew's Day 1662 would be marked by hundreds of farewell sermons, the monitoring of suspect congregations intensified, as diarists and correspondents alike brooded on the likelihood of civil disturbance.[9] Apart from confrontation in the pulpits and streets, there was concern that many disaffected clergy would lie low and avoid ejection. The survival of Josselin and others demonstrates that this did indeed occur, not least because many diocesan authorities failed to enforce the Act of Uniformity with sufficient rigour. Ian Green has suggested that Sheldon took it upon himself to act as 'a clearing house of information' in an attempt to redress such shortcomings.[10] Certainly, the Bishop of London had an extensive intelligence network, and had recruited suitably qualified and doctrinally reliable substitutes in anticipation of a mass ejection.[11] The motivation for such initiative may well have arisen from the bishop's experiences during the Interregnum, when he and other supporters of episcopacy had ministered, ordained and published under the noses of the authorities. Largely ignoring the fact that most had been infiltrated and neutered by Cromwell's secret service, the clandestine operations of political and religious royalist networks had been accorded huge credit for keeping royalism alive and ensuring the successful restoration of the monarchy.[12] Stories such as Charles II's miraculous escape from Worcester may have appealed to Cavalier-Anglican egos bruised by the experience of military defeat, but they also fuelled fears of the efficacy of political conspiracy. The fall of the Protectorate, welcome as it had been to Sheldon and his friends, appeared to show what happened to regimes that tolerated doctrinal diversity within the national church. Small wonder, therefore, that in contrast to the irenic instincts of Charles II and Clarendon, Sheldon described nonconformity as a disease to be eradicated.[13] After Bartholomew's Day, he ruthlessly enforced the Act of Uniformity within the London diocese, harassing nonconformists and moving swiftly to fill the vacant pulpits. On 30 August 1662, he attacked Clarendon over a tentative proposal to suspend the legislation, declaring soon after 'on behalf of all the bishops, that they would not comply with any resolution taken in opposition to the sense of the Act. This, with the zeal of the Duke of York, persuaded his Majesty to do nothing in prejudice thereto'.[14] Similarly, in the following December it was Sheldon who initiated the prosecution and imprisonment of Edmund Calamy following the ejected minister's sermon at St Mary's Aldermanbury.[15]

MPs, like prelates, criticised the Court at the same time as they ostentatiously declared unswerving loyalty to the Crown. In February 1663 the House of Commons rebuffed Charles's proposals to grant indulgences to peaceful nonconformists and loyal Catholics, arguing that toleration would endanger rather than promote domestic peace.[16] Their nervousness was understandable: at the same time as the farewell sermons were pouring off the presses there were signs of discontent in the country at large: from places as far apart as Southwark, Macclesfield, Ashford in Middlesex and Beverley in Yorkshire came reports of the defacing of the royal arms in churches and on proclamations. Disillusionment with the political and ecclesiastical authorities was evident in the contemporary refrain which declared that 'the bishops get all, the courtiers spend all, the citizens pay for all, the King neglects all, and the Devil take all'.[17]

By 1663 supporters of the restored Church and state were more sensitive than ever to signs of residual affection for the 'Good Old Cause'. Roger L'Estrange, for example, noted darkly that the towns of Taunton and Lyme had continued to celebrate the anniversary of royalist defeats in their respective localities during the Civil Wars.[18] In such an atmosphere, it is hardly surprising that the publication of so many farewell sermons should exacerbate Cavalier-Anglican insecurities, demonstrating by the scale of their public distribution that the crisis caused by the Act of Uniformity had not been resolved on Bartholomew's Day. It was particularly unfortunate that the period which saw the most prolific production of Bartholomean works, 1663, coincided with a perceived rise in Presbyterian activity. In October 1663, there was even a local campaign to restore Calamy to his living in Aldermanbury.[19] Several ejected ministers were rounded up as a result of the discovery of anti-government conspiracies in northern England, together with former parliamentarian soldiers and Quakers.[20]

The northern plots, such as they were, were easily crushed, just as Venner's Rising had been two years earlier. However, the trauma of the Regicide and Interregnum had ensured that the mere possession of physical power would never be sufficient to allay Cavalier-Anglican anxieties; after all, the forces of the Commonwealth had in their time dispersed royalist uprisings with ease, but military might had proved illusory. Thus, Jonathan Sawday has argued that the Restoration authorities were obliged to confront not just a political and constitutional conundrum, but also a 'symbolic crisis of representation'. The restored Cavalier-Anglican establishment was obliged to negotiate a 'new popular basis of legitimation' – a prerequisite of which was a general acceptance that the monarchical system of government had been confirmed, and the alternative rejected, by the choice of the people and by virtue of Providence.[21] This illusion required more than the policing of pulpits and printing houses, more even than the re-writing of history: it required the re-appropriation of God. As one Anglican cleric observed, 'Almighty God, in these late times, and his dreadful *Ordinances* [had] been held in a kind of *Captivity*.'[22] From this perspective, the Act of Uniformity made perfect sense.

Regardless of the intentions of the authors, the printing of the farewell sermons represented a direct and highly visible challenge to this nascent orthodoxy. As we have seen, the Bartholomean publications placed severe qualifications on the Anglican interpretation of Providence, disputing moral ownership of symbolic registers such as Scriptural metaphor, and contesting Cavalier-Anglican images of kingship. Given that they had ample warning of the nonconformists' intentions, it would have been understandable had the episcopal authorities prepared a parallel series of sermons to traduce and confute the Bartholomean valedictions. Similarly, as the Bishop of London was so obviously the main catalyst for episcopal activities, it would be logical to expect that he might have coordinated a counter-propaganda campaign from the pulpits and in print. But no such exercise was initiated by Sheldon or anyone else. We should be cautious in ascribing to pamphlets such as Sheldon's *The Dignity of Kingship Asserted* (1660) or Simon Patrick's *A Brief*

Account of the New Sect of Latitude-Men (1662) the substance of an organised campaign, just as it would be to consider the disjointed Bartholomean oeuvre in such terms.²³ However, the fact that there was no grand plan did not preclude individual Anglican clergy and Cavalier writers from attacking their moderate Puritan counterparts, before, during and after the Bartholomean crisis. In fact, as will now be shown, Cavalier-Anglican literature contributed materially to the tense atmosphere in which the farewell sermons and subsequent nonconformist literature would be produced.

II

It is possible to argue that the absence of a coordinated campaign to counter the farewell sermons bears out Bosher's impression that the Anglican clergy (unlike their lay supporters) were essentially irenic in temper and desirous of compromise.²⁴ After all, even Sheldon went to great lengths to advertise special ordination services at St Paul's as late as 21 August 1662.²⁵ These actions were not, however, engendered by a spirit of empathy, but from a desire to persuade ministers to submit to the Act of Uniformity. Gilbert Burnet wrote in his memoirs that relatively few of the 'episcopal party' were troubled by the severe treatment meted out to disaffected Puritan clergy, and that 'the blame of all this fell heaviest on Sheldon'.²⁶

At the same time there were reasons why Anglicans were unable to mount a concerted riposte. The resources of the restored Church of England were already heavily committed to reasserting episcopal authority and repairing the fabric of ecclesiastical buildings damaged or destroyed during the previous twenty years. The bishops had been obliged to prepare for the religious settlement, by conducting visitations, supervising the subscriptions of conformist clergy, and, between 1660 and 1662, managing the logistical nightmare of ejecting and replacing almost two thousand ministers. Quite simply, the bishops were already fully occupied. Individual Anglican clergy, on the other hand, particularly those occupying pulpits left vacant by the Act of Uniformity, may have delivered counter-sermons of their own volition. Charles Burke, on taking up his new living at St Margaret Moses, London, on 12 October 1662, selected Matthew 7:13–14 as the text for his first sermon: 'Enter in at the strait gate.'²⁷ The aspersion on his nonconformist predecessor, the ejected Benjamin Needler, is obvious. Far from a spirit of comprehension, a culture of anti-Puritanism had pervaded the Church of England since the Restoration, manifested not least in highly politicised Anglican sermons and liturgy.

Throughout May and June 1660, hundreds of congratulatory sermons had greeted the safe return of Charles II from exile, many of which subsequently appeared in print. Several Presbyterian clergy had initially attempted to participate in these celebrations and a number of their sermons had also been published, including those of whole-hearted conformists such as Samuel Kem, and future nonconformists such as Richard Eedes and Henry Newcombe.[28] The preface of Thomas Palke's *The Loyal Non-Conformist* (1664) made great play of the fact that his valedictory anthology included extracts from a thanksgiving sermon delivered soon after the King's return from exile.[29] This synchronicity was short lived. Behind the merrymaking was a darker agenda of blame and retribution, in which Puritan clergy were only required to play the role of accomplices to murder and rebellion. One of Sheldon's own thanksgiving sermons, published as *David's Deliverance* (1660), devoted considerable space to an aggressive political and theological critique of Presbyterianism, as did Arthur Bury's *The Bow* (1662) – Bury emphasising with heavy irony that his work had been '*Published to stop the mouth of Calumny*'.[30] In May 1660, in the midst of giving thanks for the Restoration, William Walwyn (an Anglican namesake of the notorious Leveller) condemned king-killing as a papist and anabaptist doctrine, adding, 'Nor have our Modern Puritans (call them Presbyterians if you will) lately lesse opposed the Dignity and Majesty of Kings; witness their Tenets, which will make you to Blush, Sweat and Tremble but to hear them repeated, if you have any fear for God or any honour for the King.'[31] Lori-Anne Ferrell has noted that the negative connotations of the term 'Presbyterian' in Jacobean England made it a particularly useful rhetorical device with which to stir up anti-Puritan feeling.[32] This still held true half a century later, although the connotation had undergone a seismic shift: as a consequence of 1649, Cavalier-Anglicans had come to measure the tenets of Presbyterianism against the cataclysmic events of the Regicide. Presbyterian ministers might not have swung the axe, but many Anglican clergy argued that Presbyterian preaching had nurtured Charles's executioners. The 'hunters of our Prince', declared Samuel Linch in a sermon in 1662, 'were not only Sword-men, but Gown-men, even wolves in sheep's clothing'.[33]

A prototype order of service to commemorate the death of 'Charles, King and Martyr' had been used in many churches on 30 January 1661. This, however, had been judged by a committee of bishops to be too extreme, and a revision ordered.[34] In May 1662 Charles II gave permission for the revised version to be included in the Book of Common Prayer, together with a thanksgiving service for his own nativity and restoration. The revised liturgy may have been more measured in tone, but nevertheless still demanded total obedience to royal authority and condemned the 'violent and blood-thirsty men' who had humiliated and murdered the late king. Officiating clergy were required to deliver a set homily on rebellion and obedience, or to compose an appropriate sermon for the occasion. Hundreds of ministers were only too eager to do so; by the time the farewell sermons had begun to circulate, the anniversary sermons had become an established part of the Church calendar. Nigel Yates has argued that these state services were more assiduously observed than the traditional Christian festivals.[35] The date 30 January quickly became the Cavalier-Anglican equivalent of Good Friday, and 29 May their Easter Day.

The two anniversaries were symbiotic: for every 29 May sermon that looked back in declaring that the blood of Charles I was crying out for vengeance there was a 30 January sermon that looked forward in discussing threats to the security of the restored regime.[36] Far from denying any alternative to royal authority, Anglican preachers emphasised the fragility of the monarchical system. The liturgy for 30 January stated that 'neither the greatest of kings, nor the best of men, are more secure from violence than from natural death'.[37] This was an argument for constant vigilance against sedition and disaffection, whereby Anglican preachers were able to present nonconformists and Catholics as fellow-travellers and even active co-conspirators.[38] That this was a refinement of the anti-popish trope enshrined in the traditional 5 November sermons is demonstrated by John Meriton's 30 January sermon of 1660, which invited a comparison between the unsuccessful Gunpowder Plot, the successful Regicide and the continuing danger of sedition.[39] On 30 January 1665, despite the successful ejection of nonconformist clergy and the crushing of nonconformist plots, John Twisse was still warning his congregation that 'There is no Prince can be safe, unless the Traitor in our own Hearts be first suppressed.'[40]

Even had they been free to do so, therefore, there was little need for the bishops to organise a counter-campaign against the farewell sermons. The January and May anniversary sermons already formed the centrepiece of a biannual display of ritualised hostility against Puritans in general and Presbyterians in particular.[41] The constant pressure exerted by the regular publication of anti-Puritan sermons was reinforced by a powerful and steady supply of equally hostile secular literature. Loyalist printers were hard pressed to keep pace with the insatiable public demand for *Eikon Basilike,* and there was no shortage of writers ready to complement the image of the martyred king with denunciations of his killers. The *Black Remembrancer* (1661), for example, went far beyond its stated remit of listing the Regicides, deliberately associating moderate Presbyterians with social and political radicalism.[42]

In contrast to the studied indifference to Bartholomew's Day displayed in published Anglican sermons, the Great Ejection was keenly anticipated in secular literature. The editors of the various editions of *A General Bill of the Mortality of the Clergy of London* (1662) declared that the works had been printed in anticipation of Bartholomew's Day.[43] Although these cheap diatribes were ostensibly simple lists of loyalist clergy sequestered and dispossessed during the Commonwealth, their primary objective lay elsewhere: readers were reminded that the suffering of the loyal clergy during the Civil Wars had been caused by the earnestness of '*the Brethren of the Presbytery, who now themselves cry out so much of Persecution*'.[44] The tract was itself a reworking of an earlier pamphlet written by Matthew Griffith in the late 1640s. But whereas Griffith's original tract had not mentioned Presbyterians by name, the 1662 editions repeatedly stressed the dire consequences of Presbyterian hypocrisy:

> It is much desired that some Ingenuous Persons in the several Counties of this Kingdome, will collect and present to the World in larger Characters, a Catalogue likewise of those Loyal Ministers, who in each respective County have past through the Presbyterian Furnace, which, like Nebuchadnezzar's Oven, was made seven times bitter, than that into which Gods justice, and the peevishnesse of their refractory Spirits, hath now cast their merciless Persecutors. Cursed be their wrath, for it was fierce, and their rage for it was cruell; I will divide them in *Jacob*, and scatter them in *Israel. Gen.* 49. 7.[45]

Time and again, the memory of royalist clergy ejected during the Civil Wars and Interregnum would be used to drown out nonconformist pleas for toleration, and to justify the ejections of 1660–62.[46] Edmund Calamy's sermon of 28 December 1662 (which, as we have seen, was given huge prominence in Bartholomean compilations) attracted a flood of bile and derision. The archdeacon of Suffolk, Laurence Womack, who had already published a lengthy condemnation of Presbyterian rhetoric, responded to Calamy's illegal lecture in a point-by-point rebuttal entitled *Aron Bimnucha* (1663), declaring his work to be 'AN ANTIDOTE TO CURE The CALAMITIES of their Trembling *for Fear of the Ark.*' References to ministers blowing the trumpet of sedition to mobilise the people against their lawful sovereign were interspersed with extracts from Parliamentary fast sermons published during the Interregnum. 'Tis *pride* and an *over-weening Conceit of their own worth*', concluded Womack, 'which makes men Non-conformists.'[47]

As well as being depicted as proud and conceited, Puritans had habitually been portrayed as humourless. Thus, humour was frequently offered as an antidote for nonconformist literature, eagerly administered by Samuel Butler and his imitators writing under the pseudonym of 'Hudibras'. Hudibras ridiculed nonconformist preaching when he wrote 'where had they all their gifted phrases / But from our Calamies and our Cases?'[48] Hudibras responded to Wilde's attempt to promote Calamy's cause in verse by publishing *On Calamy's Imprisonment and Wild's Poetry* (1663). Alluding to the consequences of Calamy's release from Newgate, the author warned,

> The *Cage* is open, and the *Bird* is flown;
> That *Bird* (whom though your Lordships do despise)

> May *Shite in Paul's* and *Pick out Sheldon's Eyes.*
> 'Tis he who taught the *Pulpit* and the *Press*
> To mask *Rebellion* in a *Gospel-dress.*[49]

Turning to attack Robert Wilde once more, Hudibras combined an awareness of the implications of Romans 7:1–4 ('ye also are become dead to the law by the body of Christ'), with an allegation of disunity within Bartholomean ranks:

> And now th'art *dead in Law* (though Zealots laugh)
> Impartial Truth shall write this *Epitaph*:
> This *Presbyterian Brat* was *born*, and *cry'd*;
> *Spit* in his *Mothers face*, and so he *dy'd*.
> He *dy'd*, yet *lives*; and the unhappy *Elf*
> divides *Beelzebub* against himself.[50]

Nor was this the first Cavalier verse to note that nonconformists, although living, were dead to the law, as *Iter Boreale* (1663) – another work attacking Wilde and Calamy – had already done so.[51] While this hearty diet of denunciation and ridicule was feeding into the public domain, the two foremost Cavalier journalists, John Berkenhead and Roger L'Estrange, were busily engaged in attacking ejected ministers in print and repressing the circulation of the farewell sermons. Ironically, this dual onslaught on nonconformity was made all the more vicious because the two writers despised each other even more than they did Presbyterians.

III

Although the pens of John Berkenhead and Roger L'Estrange had served a common cause during the civil wars and Interregnum, by 1662 they had become bitter rivals for the responsibility of controlling the press and supervising government propaganda. Like so many of their contemporaries involved in the interminable scramble for preferment, both had looked to powerful patrons for support, and in so doing had become embroiled in a larger political struggle between their respective mentors, Sir Edward Nicholas, Secretary of State, and Sir Henry Bennet, the future Lord Arlington. Opposites in character, outlook and faction, the mutual antipathy of Berkenhead and L'Estrange was to be brought to a head by the issue of the printed farewell sermons.

During the first two years of the Restoration Berkenhead had enjoyed considerable favour at Court. In October 1660 he had been appointed Licenser of the Press for a period of three years, and soon after had gained overall control of the official Court news-books, *The Kingdomes Intelligencer* and *Mercurius Publicus*.[52] Nicholas's influence had probably been instrumental in securing him the position of Archbishop Juxon's Master of the Faculties.[53] Through this office, Berkenhead, a former amanuensis of William Laud, had the ear of the bishops, and, with his long experience of publishing, was eminently qualified for his various duties.

Berkenhead's preferred method of controlling the press was through the agency of the Stationers' Company, a time-honoured arrangement soon to be enshrined in the Licensing Act. However, the sudden proliferation of printed farewell sermons in the summer of 1662, following the publication of several other illegal works such as *A Phenix* (1662), exposed the inadequacy of the system. The public circulation of the ejected ministers' valedictions encouraged Berkenhead's principal rival to move to the attack. L'Estrange, who since February 1662 had wielded considerably more influence after Bennet had secured him a warrant to detect and seize seditious publications, embarked on a whispering campaign to unseat his rival. Berkenhead struck back through the Court news-books. In the first week of October 1662 *Mercurius Publicus* announced that the presses responsible for printing the farewell sermons had been identified and seized. Further publications, the editorial concluded, had thereby been prevented.[54] But the editor's confidence proved premature; to L'Estrange's professed rage (but doubtless to his private satisfaction), Bartholomean pamphlets and multiple volumes of farewell sermons continued to appear in ever-increasing numbers. More ominously for Berkenhead, *Mercurius Publicus* was obliged to carry news later in October of Sir Edward Nicholas's enforced retirement.[55]

Bereft of his patron, and with his position increasingly under threat, Berkenhead attempted to cling on to power. At first there appeared no diminution in his influence: he was knighted on 14 November 1662, whilst the news-books continued to praise episcopacy, promote the Nicholas faction at court, attack nonconformists in general and castigate Presbyterian leaders in particular. The intimate knowledge of nonconformist sermons and congregations evident in *The Kingdomes Intelligencer* and *Mercurius Publicus* would suggest an extensive network of contacts and, perhaps, access to Sheldon's spies. In January 1663 *Mercurius Publicus* carried details of Edmund Calamy's imprisonment following his notorious sermon at Aldermanbury a few days before: 'we are amazed to heare how he cry'd *the Arke of God was lost*, and *the Glory was departed from Israel*, because an Act of Parliament was put into execution'.[56] *Mercurius* implied that by his actions the ejected minister had deliberately attempted to undermine the authority not only of the Bishop of London and the Lord Mayor, but that of the King himself. Significantly, the editorial message that it was morally inappropriate and politically dangerous to indulge such subversion was couched in terms very similar to those that had been used by Matthew Newcomen to conflate the royal cities of Sardis and London with the persons of their respective rulers:

for how could it stand with the Prudence and safety of the Lord Bishop of the Diocese or Lord Mayor of the City (both Members of Parliament now sitting) to see so high an affront offered to a Law made by the King and his three Estates in Parliament this very last Session, for the peace and settlement of this Church and Kingdome? And especially acted in the great City (the Chamber of the King) in that very Conjuncture when his Majesty in his Declaration promised *his particular Care to incline the Wisdome of his two Houses of Parliament at this next session for further consideration of tender Consciences*. Such Impatience (we will not say Ingratitude) just in the nick of such high Clemency and Mercy of the Gracious Soveraign is monstrously Unseasonable to say no worse.[57]

Early in 1663, perhaps mindful that he faced severe competition in his bid to seek reappointment as Licenser, Sir John Berkenhead attempted to blacken L'Estrange's reputation by alleging that his rival was a Catholic sympathiser who had written a book against the King.[58] At the same time, Berkenhead attempted to reassert his own credentials by publishing two anti-Presbyterian works. The first, *The Assembly Man* (1663) reproduced a manuscript that had originally been written in 1647 to castigate those who had colluded in the death of Archbishop Laud. Intriguingly, he alluded to the need to adapt the work to the new political climate, indicating that although *The Assembly Man* was a reproduction of his original transcript it had been lopped off in places, because '*Men and Manners are chang'd; at least they say so.*' '*Where you find no coherence*', he warned, '*remember this Paper hath suffered* Decimation: *better Times have made it worse, and that's no fault of J.B.*'[59]

The second offering, by contrast, was highly topical, coherent, and candid in its hostility to Presbyterianism. *Cabala, or an Impartial Account of the Non-Conformists' Private Designs, Actings and Wayes, from August 24 1662 to December 25 in the Same Year* was published anonymously, most probably in April 1663.[60] A satire redolent of Berkenhead's style during the 1640s, *Cabala* purported to be a transcription of the meeting minutes of a committee of leading Presbyterian clergy during the period of Fatal Bartholomew. By interweaving actual events, text from printed sermons, supposition and downright calumny, the ejected ministers were transformed into a gang of hilariously unctuous hypocrites bent on the subversion of the state. But Berkenhead aimed to do more than provide his readers with a laugh; he intended to alarm public opinion by revealing the political extremism inherent even in moderate Puritanism. In the words of Berkenhead's biographer, *Cabala* was 'astutely designed as a serious expose of potential subversion'.[61] That the Licenser regarded the farewell sermons as the principal articulation of that subversion can be seen from their prominence in the satire. The nonconformist ministers who would be caricatured were none other than those whose printed farewell sermons were at that moment providing his rival

L'Estrange with such potent political ammunition. Thus, in addition to safe-guarding Church and state, Berkenhead had a personal interest in deflating reputations that were being enhanced by the very publications which were threatening to end his career.

Berkenhead began his assault on the ejected clergy in *Cabala* by dismissing their professed piety and theological exactitude as a veneer cynically deployed to conceal political opportunism. Topical terms such as 'scruple' and 'tender conscience' were laced with an acidic irony. The fictitious meeting minutes carry a direction from the Presbyterian committee for three ministers to search through a concordance for texts that will justify the bribing of courtiers and MPs. The efficacy of such amorality was made evident a few pages later, when one conspirator reminds his neighbours at table, 'Brother *Calamy*, Brother *Ashe*, had not we become all things to all men we had gained none.'[62]

The fear of popery, as we have seen, was present but usually rather muted in the printed farewell sermons. In *Cabala*, by contrast, Berkenhead gave anti-popery full vent, portraying the ejected ministers as willing partners of scheming papists. On several occasions the Presbyterian committee is pic-tured receiving advice from '*our good friends the Catholiques*', culminating in a letter of support from the Vatican itself. In the fictitious minutes Thomas Jacombe responds to the Pope's communication by proposing 'that the fifth of *November* should be a Thanksgiving day for toleration of Popery, and all other Religions'.[63] Few of Berkenhead's readers would have been so credu-lous as to believe in the literal existence of such an alliance; nevertheless, *Cabala* drew attention to the fact that as it was so obviously in the interests of both nonconformists and Catholics to neuter the Act of Uniformity they constituted a twin threat to the common weal. Thus, by the time they had reached the page on which Berkenhead's Presbyterian caricatures order Thomas Lye to use his farewell sermon to warn of the dangers of episcopacy and popish ceremonies and then weep for a quarter of an hour, the readers had already been conditioned to view Lye as a hypocrite and fellow traveller of the very papists he had been instructed to attack.

According to *Cabala*, it was as late as 22 August 1662 when the com-mittee thought to organise a campaign of farewell sermons: 'It was agreed upon, that would be for the advancement of the Cause, if they would take the occasion of some farewell Sermons to promote it, provided, that these discourses should be very quickening.'[64] Berkenhead presented such quicken-ing as a hollow display of melodramatic emotion: after detailing Lye to weep for a quarter of an hour, the committee instructs Thomas Case to 'cry two hours together next Lords day for the abominations of the Service-book, Altar-worship, Lordly Prelacy, &c'.[65] Alluding to Presbyterian distaste for Anglican vestments and liturgy, the fictitious committee orders Joseph Caryl's farewell sermon to be based on Revelation, praising 'them that walked with the Lamb in white', whilst at the same time (Berkenhead wrote on with feigned innocence) the minister was to speak against surplices.[66] Such satire was all the more effective for the fact that Revelation 3:4 had formed the main text of the real Joseph Caryl's valediction, and that he had indeed praised those that walked in white, whilst also criticising the use of vestments and other examples of human invention.

Even the illustrated frontispieces of the Bartholomean compilations were utilised by Berkenhead to associate his nonconformist targets with the Regicide at the same time as he sought to present them as pompous, hollow and pusillanimous. The atmosphere of gravity and martyrdom these woodcuts had sought to impart is expertly twisted in those pages of *Cabala* where the fictitious committee muses 'and because the twelve Apostles are painted before the Bible, though we otherwise allow of no Images, yet it may be very convenient that twelve Reverend persons heads may be set before the sermons'. However, Lazarus Seaman urges the committee to reconsider, arguing that setting their heads up in this fashion would give detractors the opportunity to compare them to the traitors' heads at London Bridge (where in 1663 the rotting heads of Cromwell, Bradshaw and others still remained impaled on pikes), 'or to that row of heads set before the prophane book called *Montelion* last year'.[67] John Philips, a nephew of Milton, had written an almanack under the pseudonym 'Montelion' in 1662, but it is more likely that the work referred to was the comedy *Don Juan Lamberto* (1661). This play, penned a year earlier by another 'Montelion', the artist Thomas Flatman, had featured a title page faced by images of the former Cromwellian generals Desborough and Lambert, together with Richard Cromwell.[68] Despite Seaman's warning that such images might remind readers of this unsavoury past, however, the committee votes 'unanimously that they were not so fearful as not to dare shew their heads, they were ready to die, as well as to be reproached for the Truth'. But this resolve was quickly broken: 'when it was suggested that Mr *Loves* head might be amongst them, Mr *Calamy*, Mr *Case* and Mr *Jenkins* stood up, and voted it down as ominous'.[69] The Presbyterian minister Christopher Love had been executed by Parliament in 1651 for his involvement in royalist activity. Berkenhead well knew that Calamy and Case had been vociferous in their support for Love, to the extent that Case had been imprisoned. Berkenhead's readiness to use the martyred Love as a figure of fun reveals much about his regard for Bartholomean professions of loyalty to the Crown. At one stroke he sought not only to cast doubt upon the courage and integrity of the nonconformist ministers but also to discredit the protestations of passive fidelity that had been made in many of their farewell sermons.

Berkenhead suspected that the publication of the farewell sermons and accompanying devotional literature was part of a coordinated campaign to destabilise the Restoration government. Thus, immediately after *Cabala's* Presbyterian committee orders a programme of farewell sermons, its members prepare for publication:

> The same day it was Enacted, That some well-affected Stationers do gather all the Farewell Sermons in City and Country to one volum, and that they scatter them throughout the Nation for the propagation of the Gospel, the Cause will not be a little promoted by the dying words of the faithful Pastors.[70]

An integral part of this premeditated strategy, Berkenhead asserted, included an order to translate the farewell sermons into Dutch, 'for the propagation of the Gospel among the reformed Churches; and the keeping up of the dying cause in the world'.[71] He believed that the Presbyterians intended to maintain their cause in large part by publishing, as can be seen in *Cabala* by the committee's memo to Thomas Watson that if the nonconformist congregations 'cannot have their Ministers, they may yet read their books, so that if they cannot preach, they may yet live by writing'.[72] Behind all lay Cavalier fears of the spectre of nonconformist underground networks; a point made explicitly when *Cabala* pretended that William Jenkyn had received instructions that his farewell sermons were to 'perswade the people that any place is as holy as the Church, and that two or three met together in a private house might do as well as a thousand in the publick Congregation'.[73] Any reader who cared to confirm the veracity of Berkenhead's account by consulting *The Burning Yet Un-consumed Bush* (1662), or *The Farewell Sermons of the Late London Ministers* (1662), would have seen that Jenkyn's published sermons did indeed discuss the issue at some length and in such terms.[74] Berkenhead's use of the term 'private' in this context was heavily loaded, implying not simply secretiveness, but illegality and sedition.[75] Thus, when in *Cabala* it was reported that on the twenty-third day of the month 'heathenishly called *August*', Lazarus Seaman's congregation had offered to resist – although to resist *what* was left unclear – hostile readers would have been ready to believe the worst.[76]

Berkenhead had never ceased to believe the worst of Edmund Calamy, and repeatedly attacked him in the pages of *Cabala*. He implied that far from delivering the now notorious sermon of 28 December on impulse, Calamy had loitered in Aldermanbury seeking just such an opportunity.[77] Once again, the blame for this was laid on the shadowy Presbyterian committee, which in *Cabala* instructs the minister to appear in Aldermanbury once a quarter, 'and there shake his head at the times, and tremble for fear of the Ark'. Significantly, it is Calamy in *Cabala* who is ordered to guide young ministers in 'how far they may conform for the service of the cause'.[78] Berkenhead's latest offering was therefore a warning both of the intentions of those who had been exiled to the margins of Church and State and of the enemy that had remained within.

IV

If *Cabala* had been intended to bolster Berkenhead's position, it failed to save him. Since Sir Edward Nicholas's eclipse, the Licenser's situation had become increasingly untenable: Sir Henry Bennet had acquired most of Nicholas's government portfolio and had little time for an official who had so publicly supported his rival, and who, in any case, he regarded as overly independent. As one of the leading advocates of the policy of 'no compromise', Bennet must have been frustrated by Berkenhead's manifest inability to stem the flood of printed farewell sermons. At the same time, this failure had presented the Licenser's enemies with an ideal opportunity to prise him out of office. Confident that in L'Estrange he possessed a candidate more receptive to his views, Bennet's hand almost certainly lay behind his protégé's redoubled efforts to undermine Berkenhead's position.[79]

Since his tussle with Edward Bagshawe, L'Estrange had continued to batter nonconformists by resuscitating tracts such as *Presbytery Display'd* (1662) and penning new works such as *Toleration Discuss'd* (1663). It is evident, both from its content and the licence from the Bishop of London dated 16 February 1662/63, that *Toleration Discuss'd* was published at almost the same time as Berkenhead's *Cabala*. Although he did not criticise the Licenser directly, L'Estrange in his preface drew attention to the fact that the recent circulation of '*divers Virulent* Libells' had revived the nonconformists' morale.[80] *Toleration Discuss'd* took the form of a debate between three characters named 'Conformity', 'Zeal' and 'Scruple', who, as L'Estrange explained in his preface, represented the three 'grand parties', Orthodox, Presbyterian and Independent.[81] The character of Conformity is particularly revealing of L'Estrange's reception of the printed Bartholomean works. At the start of the book, Zeal loans Conformity a copy of Calamy's Aldermanbury sermon to read, suggesting that L'Estrange found nothing unusual in Presbyterians and Anglicans exchanging literature and opinions. But Conformity informs Zeal that he has seen in the pamphlet 'That Hurt that brought the *Late King* to the *Scaffold*. And (in a word) which will unsettle the Best Establisht Government in the world.' When Zeal affects not to see such ominous meaning in Calamy's words, Conformity retorts, 'it may be that you'll see better with my Spectacles'.[82] To Conformity, Calamy is 'the Mouth of the Party.' In an unmistakable reference to those publishers who had given Calamy's sermon such prominence in the Bartholomean compilations, he deprecates the seditious confidence of those who had welcomed Calamy's actions and encouraged him in his disobedience.[83] Inviting Zeal and Scruple into his parlour for further discussion, Conformity proceeds to conduct a detailed dissection of the offending text. He sees in references to Exodus, a 'direct Arraignment of the *King* and his *Ministers*', and in the bewailing of the loss of the Ark nothing less than a

'*Clamour against the Government of the Church*'.[84] Reminding Zeal and Scruple that Calamy was '*one* of the *Five* that Menag'd the Cause of the *Rabble* against *Bishops*, some Twenty Years agoe', Conformity notes darkly that then '*There* was compleyning for fear of the *Ark* too: and what Ensu'd upon it, but the *Dissolution* of the *Government*, the *Scandal* of *Religion* and the *Murder* of the *King?*' He quotes the Act for the Preservation of the King (1661) to demonstrate that Calamy is guilty of treason, just as he had been when co-authoring *Smectymnuus* two decades before.[85] Time and again nonconformity is equated with rebellion and regicide.[86] To Zeal's protestations that Presbyterians had ventured all to save the life of Charles I, Conformity scornfully responds 'Ye were *For* Him in Your *Words*, and *Against* Him in Your *Actions*.'[87]

Like Berkenhead, L'Estrange sought to present nonconformists as willing accomplices of what he termed 'the *Bloudy Design of the* Egyptian papacy'.[88] In *Toleration Discuss'd* Conformity declares that many English Catholics are better subjects of the King than nonconformists, for 'a *Presbyterian Papist* and a *Presbyterian Puritan* are Both alike to mee; and I confess, I had rather be *Preserved* by a Man of *Another Religion* than ha' my *Throat cut* by *One* of my *Own*'.[89]

The farewell sermons, together with the one delivered by Calamy on 28 December 1662 are conflated with schism, as (with a reference to Scottish Presbyterianism rare in this particular paper war) Conformity points out:

> Come, Brother *Zeal*, Your Friend of – shall pin the Basket. That Sermon of His that you wote of (at least if *His* it be, and several Impressions of it have pas'd as His, without any Contradiction) That Sermon do I take to be one of the Lewdest Requitals of the Kings Mercy and Goodness that ever – But no more, *Hee's a Son of the Kirk.*[90]

Conformity's chief concern, therefore, is not that Calamy had contravened the Act of Uniformity', but rather the dangerous scope and application of his sermon.[91] The distinction between words and actions is paramount, for whilst at one point Conformity declares that he would hang those who print such sedition, he is nevertheless minded to spare Calamy for the mere act of preaching.[92] Similarly, whilst he has little disagreement with the observations contained in the Aldermanbury sermon, Conformity is enraged by Calamy's applications.[93] The implication that words can be tolerated until and unless they precipitate action is emphasised by Conformity's explication of the Act of Uniformity: 'Your *Actions* indeed are *Limited*, but your *Thoughts* are *Free*.'[94] Replying to Scruple's question as to whether liberty of conscience cannot coexist alongside civil obedience, Conformity answers,

> Yes, Liberty of *Conscience* may, but not Liberty of *Action*, If Liberty of *Conscience* will content ye, disclaim Liberty of *Practice*; But if ye must needs have Liberty of *Practice*, speak out, and do not call it Liberty of *Conscience*.[95]

But if L'Estrange meant to imply by this that the spoken word might often be tolerated, he clearly considered the printed word to constitute action. In June 1663 he addressed the issue of the printed farewell sermons directly in a work entitled *Considerations and Proposals in Order to the Regulation of the Press*. On reporting that between ten and twelve impressions of the first three volumes of the farewell sermons had already been produced, L'Estrange estimated that the lowest print run of each had been 1,000 copies. He putatively computed the net profit from the whole enterprise to be £3,300, and proposed that this amount be levied as a fine upon those who had commissioned the printing. At the same time, he did not neglect to advertise his own prowess by reporting the recent seizure of twenty to thirty reams of unbound farewell sermons.⁹⁶

L'Estrange's principal motive in writing *Considerations and Proposals* he declared to be nothing less than the exposé of an elaborate plot against the King's life and the future of monarchical government.⁹⁷ He argued that the most compelling evidence of this conspiracy was an ongoing publishing campaign which was intended to defame the monarchy and undermine Church government, and had thus far resulted in more than one hundred schismatic titles directed against the bishops and the liturgy of Common Prayer. Those responsible for these publications – all of which either directly or implicitly charged the King with an inclination to popery – L'Estrange claimed to be ejected ministers and their allies among the booksellers and printers.⁹⁸ The scale of the campaign was truly alarming:

> it is believed by men of Judgement, and Experience, in the Trade of the Press, that since *the late Act for Uniformity*, there have been Printed near *Thirty Thousand Copies of Farewel-Sermons* (as they call them), in Defiance of the *Law*. *All which*, as they are now drawn together into one Binding (to the Number of betwixt Thirty and Forty) and represented with *Figures*, do certainly make up one of the most *Audacious* and *Dangerous Libels* that hath been made Publique under any Government; and they are now Printing it in *Dutch* too, for the greater Honour of the *Scandal*.⁹⁹

'By These *Arts* and *Practices*', he continued, 'the *Faction* works upon the *Passions* and *Humours* of the *Common-People*; and when they shall have put *Mischief* in their *Hearts*, their *next Business* is to put *Swords* in their *Hands*, and to Engage them in a direct *Rebellion*.' L'Estrange did not fail to point out that almost all the offending sermons laid stress upon the obligation of the Covenant, 'which is no other than to *Conjure the People under the Peyn of* Perjury to *Treat* your Majesty, *as the* Covenanters *did Your Father*'.¹⁰⁰ Several ministers had indeed, of course, indicated their continuing sense of obligation to the Solemn League and Covenant in their farewell sermons – and several compilers had demonstrated their awareness of Cavalier sensitivities

by editing it out. That L'Estrange was equally aware of the political significance of such rhetoric was made evident in the latter half of *Considerations
and Proposals*, which featured extracts from the seditious literature under
discussion. Works such as Calamy's Aldermanbury sermon were juxtaposed
with *Smectymnuus*, which, as L'Estrange was quick to emphasise, had been
republished in 1660 at Thomas Manton's behest.[101] Several extracts were
included to illustrate the political uses of Scripture, including a provocative
quotation from Exodus originally featured in *The Year of Prodigies*, printed for
Calvert and Brewster in 1661.[102]

L'Estrange had one further purpose in publishing *Considerations and
Proposals* besides self-advertisement: the book was not least an attack on
Berkenhead, and a refutation of the charge of writing against the King.[103]
Berkenhead had further openly advocated that L'Estrange should be taken to
Bridewell and flogged, to which L'Estrange responded by spreading rumours
that his rival had been in league with Cromwell.[104] More damaging, however,
was L'Estrange's merciless critique of the shortcomings and contradictions
of the Stationers' self-regulation under Berkenhead's management. The his-
trionics, as ever, had substance; L'Estrange's estimates of the huge numbers
of printed farewell sermons and radical titles in circulation were entirely
credible, and represented a damning indictment of Berkenhead's policies
and competence.

In August 1663 Berkenhead was ousted as controller of the Court news-
books. There can be little doubt that his failure to stem the tide of nonconformist literature had played a significant part in his downfall, and the fact
that more, and larger, compilations of farewell sermons had begun to circulate
may well have sealed his fate. Unsurprisingly, Roger L'Estrange emerged as
controller in his place, and, elbowing aside Henry Muddiman to assume the
day-to-day editing of the Monday and Thursday news-books, promptly renamed
them the *Intelligencer* and *The Newes*.[105]

L'Estrange had been confirmed as Surveyor of the Press earlier that August,
and his first editorial in the *Intelligencer* duly announced a renewed crusade
against unauthorised publication. Many printers, the Surveyor opined, were
forced to accept seditious commissions because legitimate work was distributed too thinly within an over-populated industry. Observing printers' ranks
to be cluttered by '*Foreigners*, persons not *Free* of the *Trade* and *Separatists*',
he vowed that his reformation would begin there.[106] However, as L'Estrange's
most effective ammunition in his feud with Berkenhead had been the
Licenser's failure to prevent the circulation of the printed farewell sermons,
the suppression of Bartholomean works automatically became his prime
concern. Within a fortnight, the appearance of yet another compilation of
farewell sermons received his full attention. On 14 September, the *Intelligencer*
carried news of an 'Audacious and Scandalous Pamphlet entitled, The *First*,

Second, Third and *Fourth* Volumn of FAREWELL SERMONS; which is nothing else but an appeal from *Authority* to the *Rabble*.'¹⁰⁷ L'Estrange's taste for direct action contrasted sharply with his predecessor's subtle humour:

> The Care of the *Presse* being now *my Duty*, I cannot but desire the Persons whose *Names* and *Heads* are set before the Book, either to indeceive the Multitude *Themselves*, by a Publique disclaiming of the Contrivance as a *Seditious Practice*, or to suffer *Me* to do it, by shewing under their own hands how many of those Persons, who are There Represented for the *Peoples Martyrs*, were little better in effect than the *King's Murderers*.¹⁰⁸

In the same editorial, L'Estrange did not neglect the chance to link the publication of the farewell sermons with the conspiracy he had outlined in *Considerations and Proposals*, reiterating his conviction that 'those very *Screws* and *Engines* that overturned the *Late Government*, are now Apply'd (and by the very same hands too) to the Subversion of This'.¹⁰⁹ He added for good measure that he had seized a copy of a book that had justified the murder of Charles I and had shown sympathy for two men executed *'for witnessing against the Prelats and their Superstition'*.¹¹⁰ Having established the proposition that those ejected ministers who neglected to offer a public repudiation of the farewell sermons published in their name would by their silence condemn themselves as subversives and accomplices to the Regicide, L'Estrange attempted to ferment division, declaring 'Reverence to *Doctor Bates*, whose Name (as I hear) was us'd against his Will'.¹¹¹ Crude though this emotional blackmail was, it soon yielded results.

Thomas Manton had suffered several personal attacks on his character in the preceding months, being traduced by name in *Truth and Loyalty Vindicated* (1662) and in *Considerations and Proposals* (1663). Once more berating the ejected minister for his part in the republication of *Smectymnuus*, L'Estrange had alleged that Manton had called for the total extirpation of bishops, labelling them 'Sons of *Belial*'.¹¹² It is evident that Manton, one of the more moderate of the published Bartholomeans, felt under particular pressure to respond. His letter to L'Estrange, written on 23 September 1663, utterly disclaimed the farewell sermon and prayer published in his name, declaring that it was done without his knowledge or consent.¹¹³ This public repudiation fed directly into L'Estrange's hand, who took the opportunity to remind his readers that his purpose in inviting such communications had been

> that the Multitude might not take Them to be the act of so many Conscientious Ministers, which was actually but the Imposture and Project of some Particular and Mercenary Booksellers, (however *ex post Facto* Owned and Authorised by some Few of the Ejected Clergie).¹¹⁴

The Surveyor, expressing confidence that most of Manton's colleagues would be 'equally concerned and wounded' to find their names in print, ventured to expect that they would also 'be so just both to the Government and to Themselves, as to write after so Frank an Example'.[115] When no such communications were forthcoming, L'Estrange resumed his assault. On 12 October he reported a libel seized in the act of printing, whose discovery he hoped would reveal details of the design against the King's life and the public peace. He reiterated that such plotting was 'under the mask and colour of conscience and religion', and cautioned 'all such as are Conscientious indeed, and truly Religious, that they may not be inveigled to join hands and mingle Counsels with men of such Reprobated, and Impious Undertakings'.[116] Within a page, L'Estrange reported the discovery of busy fanatics in Ipswich, declaring that,

> if you find not some of the Ejected Clergy in the Bottom of the Designe, my Intelligence deceives me ... if it may be thought worth the trouble to bring these Seditious Instruments either to shame or punishment, let me hear on't, and you shall see what pains I'll take in the discovery.[117]

The promise of reward clearly encouraged a large correspondence from a considerable number of would-be informers, whose revelations ranged from the useful to the fanciful. In sifting through various reports of plots a week later, L'Estrange confided that he was not mad enough to believe a tenth part of the information he had received.[118] However, in succeeding editions of the *Intelligencer*, he continued to demonise Presbyterians, attempting to associate them in his readers' eyes with Quakers and, particularly with Venner's Fifth Monarchy uprising in London in 1661.[119] By the time he himself fell victim to political manoeuvring and lost his monopoly of news to Joseph Williamson in 1665, L'Estrange could be satisfied that no one else had done more to demoralise the ejected clergy and disrupt the circulation of nonconformist literature. Whether his intervention achieved its aim, however, is debatable: in the 1680s, L'Estrange's erstwhile assistant, Robert Stephens, accused his former employer of being 'the great publisher of all the Phanatic Books, which are hardly known till they are mentioned in the *Observator*'.[120]

V

If the diatribes of L'Estrange had bestowed a similar saleable notoriety on the farewell sermons, he and Berkenhead were far from the only inadvertent publicists. A particularly effective and influential critique of the ejected ministers came in the form of *Evangelium Armatum* (1663), written by the then little-known William Assheton. Then aged twenty-two, Assheton appears to have had a Presbyterian upbringing, but by the Restoration had become a convinced supporter of episcopacy. The subtitle of *Evangelium Armatum* declared that its purpose was to expose several Doctrines and Positions destructive to our GOVERNMENT, BOTH CIVIL AND ECCLESIASTICAL; *Preached and Vented* by the known Leaders and Abetters of the pretended *REFORMATION*, such as Mr *Calamy*, Mr *Jenkins*, Mr *Case*, Mr *Baxter*, Mr *Caryll*, Mr *Marshall* And Others.[121]

Assheton argued that the crisis that had affected Church and state had not yet passed, despite the largely peaceful implementation of the Act of Uniformity. In the belief that Puritanism still posed a huge threat to the peace of the nation he declared that he had determined to warn the public of the true character and aims of the nonconformists. He began, as Berkenhead and L'Estrange had begun, by questioning the Bartholomeans' integrity; *'though it be* true *Piety alone that must save men'*, he wrote, *'yet it is the* shew *and pretence of Piety that governs them'*.[122] There followed an emotive description of the role of Puritan divines in the armed conflict of the 1640s, which Assheton blamed on false teachers who had supposed themselves more intimately acquainted with God. It was soon made clear in *Evangelium Armatum*, that the individuals to whom to he referred included many whose farewell sermons had recently been published:

And still they endeavour to captivate [the people's] Pity, by a bold and impudent insinuation of these two things, *That they are the People of God*, and *That they are persecuted*. For experience shews that the Opinion of Persecution naturally moves men to Pity, and Pity presently turns into Love, and whom men love, they are easily brought to defend.[123]

Assheton denied that such men could be godly, because their pretended piety involved principles and practices directly contrary to natural law and the word of God. In particular, he asserted they had preached armed resistance against their lawful king, and enshrined it in the Oath and Covenant. He wondered how anyone could imagine how such a belligerent religion could ever be thought pure, particularly when its adherents had led the common people into disloyalty and sedition, and had done *'enough to stink the* Protestant *name out of the world'*.[124] To Assheton, therefore, nonconformity was not simply a betrayal of monarchical government, but of the Reformation itself. He implied, as Berkenhead done before him, that such traitors could be all things to all men, and, indeed, that *'the only thing these thorough-paced swearers at length stick at, is the* Subscription *lately required by Law, made and enacted by Parliament, and confirmed by the Royal assent'*.[125]

By this calculation the nonconformists' pleas for dispensation and indulgence were simply strategies to buy time until they could regroup. As for Presbyterian claims that they had been instrumental in restoring King Charles II to his throne, the young writer mused that he would not feel beholden to a surgeon for setting a leg which that surgeon had himself broken. In any case, he believed that such clergy had shown little enthusiasm for the return of the monarchy until their livings had come under threat from fanatics, and '*that had not the Tythe-pig cried lowder in their ears, than either their* Conscience, *or the* word *of God, they had never been awakened to attempt that, which since it has been effected, so many of them have not obscurely repented of*'.[126]

Assheton did not fail to remind his readers that many of the Bartholomeans had collaborated with the Cromwellian regime to eject loyal clergy during the Interregnum. He saw it as a bitter irony '*that those who were partly the Authors, partly the Procurers of these hideous, remorseless Actions are those poor, gentle, suffering Lambs of Christ that now bleat out* Persecution'.[127] Such pleas of moderation irritated Assheton beyond measure, who likened such ostensibly '*pious and peaceable* maxims' to an oiled razor poised to '*cut the throat of* Majesty'.[128] He accused Presbyterians of pretending to oppose popery solely in order to gain the favour of the common people – popularity which they could then exploit by spreading sedition and disaffection against the King.[129] For Assheton, nonconformists, papists and Hobbesians were part of the same threat. Citing the Biblical maxim that rebellion was as the sin of witchcraft, Assheton observed that it was the Puritan preachers' bewitching of the people that had caused the populace to rebel:

> But I hope the World will be so far unbewitched, as to read this Collection, with their farewell-Sermons, *lately printed together and exposed to sale with so much Ostentation: Of which I shall say this, that they may very properly be called* Farewell-Sermons, *since experience is like to manifest, that their Congregations never fared so well, as when such Seducers preached their Last.*[130]

Assheton presented a collection of damning extracts from the past preaching of Bartholomeans such as Jenkyn, Baxter, Newcomen, Caryl and Slater, deliberately juxtaposing these with the writing of such Cavalier hate-figures as Stephen Marshall and Thomas Hobbes. That Assheton sought to associate ejected ministers with regicide is evident from his deployment of quotations from Thomas Case's Parliamentary fast sermons: 'he lies groveling at your feet, there wants nothing *but cutting off his head*'; 'What a sad thing is it my Brethren, to see our King in the head of an Army of *Babylonians*, refusing as it were to be call'd the King of *England, Scotland, Ireland*, and chusing instead to be called the *King of Babylon*'; '*we have no King*'.[131] Calamy, as ever, came in for particularly unfavourable treatment. In addition to quoting from a particularly incriminating Parliamentary fast sermon, Assheton reproduced extracts from a work of 1646, in which the minister had boasted of his part in the making of *Smectymnuus*, describing it as 'the first deadly blow to *Episcopacy* in *England* of late years'.[132] Even the dead Christopher Love did not escape censure, as Assheton presented extracts from Love's trial to prove that the Presbyterian had suffered for the Oath and Covenant rather than his lawful king, and moreover had declared his opposition to the King's party until the end.[133]

Assheton's diatribe was influential. It was endorsed soon after its publication by Matthew Griffiths in *The King's Life-Guard* (1665), and for many years afterwards. As late as 1683 Bishop Morley, when recalling how many royalists had been cruelly killed by Presbyterians during the Civil Wars, wrote that he could do no better than to refer his readers to *Evangelium Armatum*.[134] Assheton's distaste for nonconformity was sincere, but his polemical attack on Presbyterianism was almost certainly made with a view to furthering his career by attracting the attention of prospective patrons. Soon after the publication of *Evangelium Armatum*, he was made a Fellow of Brasenose College, Oxford, and appointed chaplain to the University's Chancellor, the Duke of Ormonde. Assheton, like Berkenhead and L'Estrange before him, exploited the alarm caused by the publication of the farewell sermons to enhance his own prospects. Neither was he the last writer to do so.

David Lloyd, appointed chaplain to the Bishop of St Asaph in late 1663, had already authored a number of works since the Restoration. He was, according to one contemporary, an impudent, plagiarising hack.[135] Certainly, Lloyd's pseudo-historical study of Puritanism, *Cabala: Or the Mystery of Conventicles Unvail'd* (1664), which was probably written in 1663 whilst he languished in prison for libel, borrowed extensively from the works of Berkenhead and L'Estrange. Published under the pseudonym 'Oliver Foulis', *Cabala* begins with a dialogue between two characters, 'Orthodox' and 'Scruple', initiated by their chance meeting in a street in Amsterdam. The vinegar-faced Scruple, complaining of persecution under the Act of Uniformity, is promptly taken to task by Orthodox and passers-by. When Scruple ventures that the nonconformist ministers are simply carrying on the work of Reformation, Orthodox explodes in anger:

> *Reformation*! It's a *dreadful word*, and in thy mouth imports no less than *ruin* and *desolation*. These are the men that propagate Religion by Warrs, force Consciences, nourish seditions, authorise conspiracies and rebellions; that put the Sword into the peoples hands; that sanctifie Tumults; preach off the heads of Kings, overthrow constitutions and Governments, undermine Lawes and settlement; that resist for *Conscience sake*, and teach others so to do for their Salvation; that make Christ a raiser of sedition and his Religion a Firebrand.[136]

A passing merchant suggests that Scruple stand trial on behalf of nonconformity, as by chance there is a historian available to act as judge. In the dreamlike court sequence which follows, Scruple presents a defence based on *Smectymnuus* and similar authorities.[137] Witnesses such as Berkenhead and L'Estrange are called for the prosecution, whilst the long-dead Calvin is summoned by the defence. The voice of the judge appears to be that of the writer himself; thus it could be argued that the judge's condemnation of Calvin's 'predestinarian way' suggests that the internecine religious struggle in Restoration England was not underpinned by a Calvinist consensus.[138] Lloyd's more immediate concerns, however, emerged in the testimony of the prosecution witnesses, when they testify to the nonconformists' use of military imagery and the Book of Exodus in their sermons, linking such rhetoric to the infamous cry of 1642, 'To thy tents, O Israel'.[139] By a carefully constructed matrix of imaginary witness statements, accusations of past treachery on the part of ministers such as Caryl, Calamy and Newcomen are interwoven with more recent activities such as Thomas Manton's endorsement of the republished *Smectymnuus* and Presbyterian intransigence at the Savoy Conference.[140] From the witness box, 'R. L.' (Roger L'Estrange) supplies information regarding underhand Presbyterian efforts to secure a majority in the 1661 elections, a prospect made all the more alarming as he discloses that radicals such as Anabaptists, Quakers and Fifth Monarchists all hide under the cloak of Presbyterianism. Thus, when Venner began his uprising, L'Estrange alleges, 'the rest were ready to fall in and improve the design, to the ruine of Church and State'.[141] Other witnesses accuse the Presbyterians of plotting with radicals, papists and even Turks.[142]

The sustenance of nonconformity was of great interest to Cavalier-Anglicans after 1662; thus Lloyd sniped at the aristocratic patronage enjoyed by many Presbyterian ministers: 'even and anon you should see a Lord drop into their Church at *Aldermanbury, Walbrook, &c*'.[143] Like L'Estrange, Lloyd clearly believed that the ejected ministers profited from publishing. In *Cabala* a witness designated 'J. B'. (John Berkenhead) informs the court that 'the brethren have the thriving way of selling their Sermons first from the Pulpit, and then from the Press'.[144] J. B. is particularly annoyed by the farewell sermons, for, he claims, at the same time their authors had pleaded for tender consciences to be respected, they had instructed the people to prepare for another Marian persecution. 'J. B.' then reveals that he has evidence that the nonconformists had conspired with papists to subvert the Act of Uniformity, but when such plots had come to nothing,

> they prepared themselves for persecution as they called it; and preached that lights were extinguished, the dear Pastors torne from their beloved flockes; then they say, *they preach their last*, and that they are *dying men*, and that this may be the *last opportunity*; Now they give their rule, one 17. another 25. another 36. All may be reduced to these six: 1. That they should not forget their faithful pastors: 2. That when they cannot hear their Words, they may read their Workes: 3. That they should take heed of whom they hear: 4. That they have nothing to do with Idols: 5. That they persevere: 6. That they hold Communion one with another.[145]

That nonconformists held secret communion with each other was a source of considerable anxiety for Cavalier-Anglicans. In Lloyd's *Cabala*, a succession of witnesses raise the spectre of trouble from the disbanded veterans of the

New Model Army, and warn the court that nonconformists are numerous, organised and their activities financed by wealthy supporters.[146] Witness after witness confirms that the main way the nonconformist cause has been maintained is through print:

> the Farewell Sermons are Printed, first singly, and then in Volums, as the dying words of the faithful Pastors, whose heads are set before their Sermons just as they looked from the Pulpit, wrapped in their reverend white and black Caps like the twelve Apostles before the Bible; *For though we worship not Images, we adore imaginations.*[147]

Thus, according to the witnesses, by continuing to spread the word outside the Church of England, ejected ministers instruct and embolden those of their brethren who have surreptitiously remained within.[148] Even the pleas of nonconformist ministers to their flocks not to separate from the Church are given a sinister construction, as it is argued that the Presbyterian 'rabbis', 'must leave the Church, lest Presbytery be swallowed up of Episcopacy; the people must not leave the Church, lest Presbytery should be brought to nothing by Independency'.[149]

In addition to the farewell sermons, it is noted by the imaginary judge that devotional works such as *Vindica Pietatis* and *A Call to Archippus* are very much in circulation, and as well as the accounts of Edmund Calamy's sermon at Aldermanbury on 28 December.[150] Despite his scaremongering, however, Lloyd ended *Cabala* on a triumphal note, expressing great satisfaction that ministers who had sequestered loyal clergy during the Interregnum 'are now silenced themselves; the Church Government is most firmly setled; the tender-Conscienced are more closely held in; and the Reformation itself become a by-word and a hissing among all Nations'.[151] He concluded with an exhortation to the nonconformists to 'Lay down your Armes and lift up your hands in Prayers for the Governours and Government of the World'.[152]

VI

As Lloyd himself had indicated by his reference to publications such as *Vindica Pietatis*, however, nonconformists appeared no more inclined to capitulate than they had been before their ejection. The response of nonconformist publishers to the growing paper war was to redouble their efforts. Throughout the remainder of 1663 ever larger compilations of farewell sermons were made available to the public, together with entirely new material in the shape of *England's Remembrancer* (1663). Previously unpublished farewell sermons appeared the following year, such as Richard Alleine's *The Godly Man's Portion and sanctuary*, George Thorne's *The Saints Great Duty* and Thomas Palke's *The Loyal Non-Conformist*.[153]

In addition to the farewell sermons, new editions of familiar devotional works such as Thomas Brooks's *Apples of Gold* and Thomas Watson's *Au'tarkia* continued to be published, despite, or perhaps even because of, their Bartholomean author's new-found notoriety.[154] For the most part, such works confined themselves to moral instruction and their prefaces avoided any direct engagement with the debate over the Act of Uniformity. However, at least one ejected minister, Thomas Cheeseman in *Via Lacta* (1663), laboured in his epistle to vindicate his ministry from detractors '*who would gladly lay hold upon any Occasion to vilify it, and load it with disgraceful Imputations*'.[155] Other Bartholomeans addressed the issue of nonconformity directly: Joseph Alleine intended *A Call to Archippus* (1664) to be a call to the ejected ministers 'to take heed of their MINISTRY, That they Fulfil it'. Defiantly, he encouraged his brethren to disregard the law and continue preaching, on the precept that they should obey God rather than man. Alleine rejected any suggestion that the Bartholomeans had separated themselves from the Church of England, asserting that the schism had been caused by those who had '*come in upon us, and have possessed our Places and Pulpits, and thrust us by the places of publick Convention*'.[156]

The Bartholomeans, as we have seen, had sympathisers in several quarters. Although the only comment the anonymous compiler of *An Exact Catalogue of Several Ministers Lately Ejected Out of Their Livings* (1663) would offer on the ministers' plight was that they had dissented out of conscience, the list of ejected ministers which unfolded upon page after page and county after county conveyed the sense of momentous loss without the need for further explanation.[157] Moral support also came tangentially from seemingly innocuous publications such as Thomas Heath's 1664 manual on shorthand.[158] Certain other attacks on the Act of Uniformity, however, such as Edward Billing's defence of Quakers entitled *A Faithful Testimony for God and My Country* (London, 1664) can hardly have been welcome, as they provided uncomfortable evidence of how much Bartholomeans now had in common with marginalised radicals.

Despite the copious amount of nonconformist literature in circulation at this time, direct engagement with specific Cavalier-Anglican diatribes was comparatively rare. One author calling himself 'R.S.' offered a point by point rebuttal of Womack's *Aron Bimnucha*.[159] A rather more significant literary riposte was *A Mystery of Godliness and No Cabala* (1663), which hit back at John Berkenhead, describing his work *Cabala* as a 'bitter and malicious' misrepresentation of nonconformity:

> When the fears and jealousies of some concerning us are so restlesse, the malice of others is so implacable, that we suffer not only for what we have done, but for what we may do, and we are not only obnoxious to Authority for those miscarriages the world hath seen us guilty of, but unto the Tongues and pens of men; for those likewise the world may imagine us guilty of.[160]

A Mystery of Godliness maintained the line that had been established by the printed farewell sermons, emphasising that nonconformists were loyal to the restored monarchy and submissive, if passively disobedient, to Authority. Particularly interesting, in view of the Cavaliers' crisis of representation, was an agreement that the King had been restored though God's Providence. The nonconformist author flattered the memory of Charles I by borrowing from *Eikon Basilike* and even expressed approval of measures to relieve indigent royalist soldiers.[161]

The author accepted that dissent would bar nonconformist ministers from public employment, but nevertheless called for Protestant unity and mutual toleration.[162] Anti-popish rhetoric, subdued in most farewell sermons but prominent in Berkenhead's literary assault, was resuscitated. The author asserted that there had been a certain amount of complacency regarding the popish threat, as many learned and godly divines had mistakenly believed that popery had made itself so odious 'by its own abominations in doctrine, worship and bloudy slaughters' that it would never again infect Protestant churches. Perhaps mindful of the provisions of the Act for the Preservation of the King (1661), the author diplomatically absolved the Government of culpability for the resurgence of popery, and blamed instead Catholic activists, sectaries and Quakers.[163] The clear thrust of his argument, however, was that disunity and error within the Restoration Church of England had resulted in the expulsion of godly ministers, to the benefit of Rome:

> And we profess sincerely, that we look upon our late miscarriages as most unhappy scandals to our Religion, and those ingaged in them so for us to persist still as Enemies to the Cross of Christ, and men born to bring our holy Christian profession into jealousie, suspition, and disgrace with the powers of the earth, and to stir up the Kings of the earth to stand up, and the Rulers to take counsel together against the Lord.[164]

When it came to fundamental and saving truths, *A Mystery of Godliness* offered no prospect of a retreat from the stance outlined in the printed farewell sermons. 'We will not', declared the author 'be carried about with every wind of doctrine'.[165] In emphasising the promise in the Oath and Covenant to 'preserve and defend the Kings Majesties Person and Authority', he indicated the impossibility of renouncing it.[166]

Berkenhead had ascribed dark imputations to remarks in William Jenkyn's farewell sermons regarding the continuance of communion in private houses. *A Mystery of Godliness* admitted that since the Great Ejection, nonconformists had held private devotions and ministers broken bread from house to house, but pleaded that 'at these our Meetings we plot nothing but the saving of souls'.[167] Although according to *A Mystery of Godliness* nonconformists had laid aside internal 'little separations and divisions', this did not mean that the establishment was threatened by an organised conspiracy:

> Whereas some have pretended that we set up a Government within a Government, and that we have an Authority among our selves, we must let the world know we are all equal, and we have no formality or Ceremony among us, but a free and voluntary entrance, left open for all.[168]

The author confirmed that in the absence of public devotions, literature had become more vital than ever in sustaining private prayer.[169] But throughout *A Mystery of Godliness*, the dilemmas facing the nonconformist clergy were still evident. They were not in conscience able to administer within the Church ('least we be defiled'), and yet were unwilling to break with it entirely ('least we be nothing').[170] Above all, in a particularly perspicacious passage, the author of *A Mystery of Godliness* summarised perfectly the impossibility of reconciling religious scruple with the stark political reality of Restoration England:

> Amongst all the strategems of Satan, whereby he would undermine Religion and pervert the souls of men, though these cannot be any more unreasonable, yet there was never any more unhappily successful than the raising and cherishing of fears and jealousies in the world, that Religion in the height and exultation of it, is an Enemy to Government; and that to be a thorough-paced, a sincere and zealous Christian, is to be dangerous to the State.[171]

VII

The polemical response to the farewell sermons confirms that they had relevance far beyond the nonconformist constituency. Because of the nature of the Restoration establishment, and the heavy workload already faced by the bishops, the Cavalier-Anglican response was not the coordinated campaign of a single mastermind. However, neither were the attacks simply the knee-jerk reaction of a few isolated Cavaliers; the reaction to the printed farewell sermons had as much to do with political manoeuvring at court as with indignation at the slighting of episcopal or parliamentary authority. In this respect, the farewell sermons became a factor in the balance of power within government itself. This gave the valedictions a more immediate political significance than many of the original authors had intended, and meant that the refutation and repression of the publications quickly became imperative for political rivals such as Berkenhead and L'Estrange. The urgent logic of political and religious orthodoxy precluded any chance of a sympathetic reading of Bartholomean literature. In contrast to Jonathan Barry's perception of a tension within the Restoration Church of England, 'between those

who wished to coerce moderate dissenters and those who wanted to con-
ciliate them', there is little ambiguity evident in the printed responses to
the farewell sermons.[172] Cavalier-Anglican writers who engaged directly with
the valedictions were those who perceived only defiance, and prescribed only
coercion.

The Cavaliers' belief in a linkage between clandestine print and political
subversion stemmed from their compulsion to proclaim the efficacy of their
own underground activity during the Interregnum. Thus, in order to per-
petuate the myth of their own potency, they were obliged to believe in the
potency of their nonconformist opponents. By the same token, they could
not afford to overlook the subversive potential of 'passive disobedience' which
had been advocated in several farewell sermons. Lois Potter has written of
the royalist response to military defeat in the English Civil Wars that 'a
defeated army naturally seeks to explain events in terms of secret purposes
which require a response of passive acceptance.' This passive acceptance, as
Potter points out, was at its most powerful when invested in the image of
King Charles the Martyr.[173] The heavy emphasis on persecution and martyrdom in so many printed farewell sermons therefore caused the Bartholomeans'
detractors great concern: firstly, as they were at that moment compiling their
own accounts of royalist martyrdom, Cavalier-Anglicans were well aware of
the hazards of making martyrs out of the ejected ministers. As William
Assheton was quick to point out, the farewell sermons, printed and distributed as the testament of persecuted moderates, could readily be construed
as a negative reflection on the Restoration establishment.[174] At the same
time, the noise of nonconformist 'lambs' bleating out persecution triggered
intense indignation, not least because, despite the Restoration, Cavalier-
Anglicans still considered themselves an embattled and persecuted people.[175]
In the 1660s Cavalier-Anglicans were undergoing a public catharsis, purging
and rationalising the memory of the Regicide with publications such as *Eikon
Basilike*, worshipping in commemorative services and composing sermons
for the anniversaries of 30 January and 29 May. They could not afford to
tolerate a representation of martyrdom which competed with their own, particularly one which presented an alternative history of the recent past and
reversed the roles of persecutor and persecuted. Neither were they willing
to allow Presbyterians to participate in their own royalist martyrology; the
sacrifice of Christopher Love in 1651 was discounted as brusquely as farewell
sermons that proclaimed loyalty to the Crown.

If the writings of Berkenhead, L'Estrange, Assheton and Lloyd confirm
that the challenge posed by the farewell sermons was very real, they also
demonstrate that the language in which the sermons had been couched was
readily accessible. Historical studies of Puritan literature before and after the
1660s often highlight contemporaneous accusations that Puritans tended to

use a coded rhetoric fully comprehensible only among themselves. 'Conformists', Neil Keeble has written, 'saw themselves as the guardians of lucidity and perspicuity against the extravagant excesses of the nonconformists' metaphysical and figurative indulgence, imprecise and obscurely evocative phraseology and wild flights of fancy'. Therefore he argues that this was presented as a debate between sense and senselessness, between a scientific conformist style and a mystic nonconformist one.[176] But such accusations were very similar to those made against religious radicals in the 1640s.[177] It is possible that such criticisms were more political than stylistic, more propaganda than substance. In the 1660s there was an acute awareness, for example, of the political applications of the Book of Exodus on the part of Anglican preachers, whose sermons paralleled Egypt with the Interregnum and the Israelites' escape from bondage with the Restoration.[178] Consequently, when writers such as L'Estrange and Lloyd saw political innuendoes in the nonconformists' use of Exodus, they were confident that they knew exactly what nonconformists were talking about.[179] Similarly, the resonance between the rhetoric of the royal city in Matthew Newcomen's farewell sermon and *Mercurius Publicus'* condemnation of Calamy in January 1663, and the use of identical imagery in both Anglican and Presbyterian sermons immediately after the Restoration, confirms the impression that Scriptural rhetoric – and therefore loyal texts with radical subtexts – was a mutually intelligible code, both amongst clerics and the educated laity.[180]

If the Bartholomeans' rhetoric was widely understood, there was nevertheless a wide gulf between Cavalier-Anglicans and moderate Puritans on the application of that rhetoric. The earl of Clarendon, for example, saw in the farewell sermons, 'all the insinuations to mutiny and rebellion, that could be warily couched in words which could not be brought within the penalty of the law, though their meaning was well understood'.[181]

Presbyterian adherence to the Oath and Covenant, alluded to in many printed farewell sermons, and discussed candidly in subsequent nonconformist works such as *A Mystery of Godliness*, might have been regarded as religious fidelity by nonconformists, but was invariably cited as proof of continuing political disloyalty by Cavalier-Anglicans.[182] It was, according to Clarendon, 'still the idol to which the Presbyterians sacrificed'.[183] The intrinsic ambiguity of Scripture, which in the artfully crafted farewell sermons had enabled Bartholomeans to square the circle of passive disobedience, left them vulnerable to the hostile interpretation of detractors no less erudite and resourceful. Thus, as the author of *A Mystery of Godliness* observed, Cavalier writers were able to use the ejected ministers' own sermons to argue that nonconformity was inimical to the state.

The archetypal enemy to the common weal was the scheming papist. Anti-popery in early modern England has been identified as a response to crisis, and a favourite tool of Puritan propagandists. The Anglican notion of Puritan conspiracy, although similar in structure, has been seen by historians as a distinct and mutually exclusive theory dating back to the 1620s. However, Peter Lake has discerned that as the seventeenth century progressed, anti-popish rhetoric was applied to new situations, informing Presbyterian attacks on Quakers and royalist condemnation of the Regicides.[184] By the Restoration, therefore, anti-popery had become a 'free-floating term of opprobrium'.[185] It was this malleability that enabled John Berkenhead to denounce a rival Cavalier as a Catholic sympathiser at the same time as he accused ejected ministers of collusion with the Pope. In contrast to the relative paucity of anti-popish rhetoric in the farewell sermons, Anglican preachers regularly accused their Puritan opponents of helping the papist cause by their disloyalty, whilst Cavalier journalists alleged that nonconformists took their orders directly from Rome.[186]

John Miller, by contrast, has argued that 'Anglican-Royalists' made *less* use of anti-popish polemic than nonconformists, not least because they had 'a plausible alternative in the idea of a "Presbyterian" (or "fanatic") plot'.[187] But the literary response to the farewell sermons shows that by 1662 Catholic and Puritan conspiracy theories were not so much 'interchangeable models of deviance' as a single synthesised matrix of subversion.[188] Berkenhead could thereby present Thomas Lye's denunciation of popery in a farewell sermon as the disingenuous cant of a hypocrite in league with the Papacy.[189] L'Estrange and Assheton in turn could supplement the traditional fears of Puritan rabble-rousing by asserting that nonconformist preachers had merely pretended to denounce popery in order to ingratiate themselves with the mob and justify rebellion.[190]

Jonathan Barry's study of Restoration Bristol has found that Anglicans and Presbyterians sometimes made common cause against local radicalism.[191] Professor Miller has opined that Cavaliers, whilst distrusting Presbyterians, considered the radical sects as the major threat to the regime.[192] But the paper war of the early 1660s reveals the true depth of Cavalier-Anglican hostility towards moderate Puritans at this time. Moderate Puritans – 'Presbyterians' in the all-encompassing parlance of contemporary Cavalier-Anglican rhetoric – were despised most of all because it was believed that they lacked the courage and conviction to be honest rebels. The menace of Presbyterianism, as writers such as Berkenhead and Assheton pointed out, was that its adherents could be all things to all men.[193] Presbyterians, *because* they were so close to religious and social respectability, were, to judge by the volume and tone of the writing against them, considered more dangerous than radicals; 'the traitor in our own hearts'.[194] For writers such as Berkenhead, L'Estrange, Assheton and Lloyd, the farewell sermons encapsulated Presbyterian hypocrisy and rationalised sedition. They sought to expose the intellectual dishonesty inherent in sermons that pleaded allegiance to the Crown at the same time as those sermons criticised and defied royal authority. They were incensed that authors who had so recently colluded in the persecution of others should now complain of being persecuted themselves.

The publication of the farewell sermons from 1662 onwards may have been aimed primarily at a sympathetic readership, but it was always liable to attract the attentions of a hostile one. Once in print, the farewell sermons provided Cavalier-Anglicans with a visible target on which to project their anger and insecurity. It was unfortunate that more and larger compilations should be published as rumours of nonconformist plots reached fever pitch in London and elsewhere. It was doubly unfortunate that this increased production should itself add to the moral panic by exposing the inability of the Restoration establishment to contain dissent. The polemical response to the farewell sermons shows that the establishment was preoccupied with the pre-eminence of secular authority. The ejected ministers' desire to remain aloof from such earthly concerns was interpreted by many in power as a desire to undermine that authority. The Bartholomeans' attempt to separate religion from politics was seen as a deliberate provocation by an establishment which believed that the two were inseparable. Despite all their efforts to remain aloof from the world, therefore, the authors of the farewell sermons were offered no alternative but to interact with it.

NOTES

1 *Calendar of the Clarendon State Papers Preserved in the Bodleian Library* vol. 5: 1660–1726, ed. F. J. Routledge (Oxford, 1970), p. 465, quoted in Greaves, *Deliver us from evil*, p. 225.

2 See Sawday, 'Re-writing a revolution', p. 171.

3 Bosher, *Restoration Settlement*, pp. 164–5, 204, 278–82.

4 Green, *Re-establishment*, pp. 22, 42, 180, 196–8; cf. Hutton, *Restoration*, p. 146.

5 Seaward, 'Gilbert Sheldon, the London vestries and the defence of the Church', in Harris, Seaward and Goldie, *Politics of Religion*, pp. 49–50; Green, *Re-establishment*, pp. 186–8. It is instructive to compare localised zeal in proceeding against those who refused the Oath of Allegiance (in Cheshire, Lancashire, Westmoreland, Wiltshire, Somerset, Oxfordshire, London, Devon and Worcestershire) as those areas where dissenters were left relatively untouched; Hutton, *Restoration*, p. 169.

6 Miller, *After the Civil Wars*, p. 134. Jonathan Barry describes alliances between moderate dissenters and Anglicans in Bristol; Barry, 'The politics of religion in Restoration Bristol', in Harris, Seaward and Goldie, *Politics of Religion*, p. 171.

7 Spurr, *Restoration Church*, p. 42; cf. Seaward, 'Gilbert Sheldon, the London vestries and the defence of the Church', p. 50.

8 Burnet, *History*, I, p. 313.

9   *CSPD 1661–2*, pp. 71, 89, 97, 111, 113, 114, 122, 125, 162, 398, 430; Pepys, *Diary*, iii, p. 183; Baxter, *Reliquiae Baxterianae*, II, p. 302; J. Evelyn, *The Diary of John Evelyn*, ed. E. S. de Beer (6 vols, Oxford, 1955), III, p. 331; Bodl. MS Carte 31, fo. 602.

10 Bodl. Tanner MS 48, fo. 69, quoted in Green, *Re-establishment*, p. 162; see also Bodl. Tanner MS 48 fos 26, 50, 51, 73v.

11 S. Parker, *History of His Own Times* (1777), p. 33, quoted in Sutch, *Sheldon*, p. 85.

12 Underdown, *Royalist Conspiracy*, pp. 332, 337, 339; Potter, *Secret Rites*, pp. 33–4; Spurr, *Restoration Church*, pp. 2–11; Sutch, *Sheldon*, pp. 26, 28–30.

13 HMC Ormonde MSS, ii, p. 97; Carte MS 45, fo. 151 (Bishop Sheldon to the Marquis of Ormonde), quoted in Bosher, *Restoration Settlement*, p. 265, and Spurr, *Restoration Church*, p. 47.

14 Bodl. Clarendon MSS C70, vol. 77 (Gilbert Sheldon to the Earl of Clarendon, 30 August 1662), quoted in Sutch, *Sheldon*, p. 86; Bodl. MS Carte 32, fo. 3 (Daniel O'Neill to Ormonde 2 September 1662).

15 *Mercurius Publicus*, 1 (1–8 January 1662/63), p. 14.

16 Hutton, *Restoration*, p. 196.

17 HMC Ormonde MSS, iii, p. 68, and PRO SP29/67/90, quoted in Hutton, *Restoration*, p. 185; PRO SP29/57/123, quoted in Greaves, *Deliver Us from Evil*, p. 88; A. Wood, *The Life and Times of Anthony Wood*, ed. A. Clark (5 vols., Oxford, 1891), I, pp. 465–6, quoted in Hutton, *Restoration*, p. 196.

18 L'Estrange, *Toleration Discuss'd*, p. 70.

19 Bodl. Rawl. MS 53, fo. 22 (Thomas Gilbert to Lord Wharton, 29 October 1663), quoted in Achinstein, *Literature and Dissent*, p. 2.

20 Nicholson, 'The Kaber Rigg Plot 1663', p. 218; *CSPD 1663–4*, p. 340 (a reference I owe to the kindness of Clark Colman); Achinstein, *Literature and Dissent*, pp. 24–5; Greaves, *Deliver Us from Evil*, pp. 101, 105.

21 Sawday, 'Re-writing a revolution', pp. 171, 172–3.

22 L. Womack, *Aron Bimnucha* (1663), p. 98.

23 G. Sheldon, *The Dignity of Kingship Asserted* (1660); S. Patrick, *A Brief Account of the New Sect of Latitude-Men* (1662). There are indications that Sheldon had organised a propaganda campaign against nonconformity by the end of the 1660s, however; Spurr, *Restoration Church*, p. 48; Sutch, *Sheldon*, p. 67.

24 Bosher, *Restoration Settlement*, p. 228.

25 *Mercurius Publicus*, 33 (14–21 August 1662), p. 554; *ibid.*, 34 (21–8 August 1662), p. 563.

26 Burnett, *History*, I, p. 329.

27 Clark Library B8535 M3, n.f. (a reference I owe to the kindness of Ann Hughes).

28 Kem, *King Solomon's Infallible Experiment*; Eedes, *Great Britain's Ressurrection*; Newcombe, *Usurpation Defeated and David Restored*.

29 T. Palke, *Loyal Non-Conformist*, sig. [A3v].

30 Sheldon, *David's Deliverance*, pp. 32–5; Bury, *The Bow*, frontispiece, pp. 36–7, 40–8.

31 Walwyn, *God Save the King*, p. 8.

32 Ferrell, *Government by Polemic*, p. 63.

33 S. Linch, *Rebellion Painted to the Life* (1662), p. 16.

34 G. Cuming, *A History of Anglican Liturgy* (2nd edn, 1982), p. 126.

35 N. Yates, *Buildings, Faith and Worship: The Liturgical Arrangement of Anglican Churches 1600–1900* (Oxford, 2000), pp. 55–6.

36 E.g., Walsall, *The Bowing the Heart of Subjects to Their Sovereign*, p. 28.

37 Order of service for 30 January, *Book of Common Prayer*, 1662.

38 E.g., Bury, *The Bow*, p. 27, and later, Griffith, *The King's Life-Guard*, p. 22, *passim*.

39 Meriton, *Curse Not the King*, p. 12.

40 R. Twisse, *England's Breath Stopp'd* (1665), p. 34.

41 An observer estimated that by 1685 that some 3,000 original 30 January sermons had been preached, and dozens published; Randall, 'The rise and fall of a martyrology', pp. 136–7; a browse of the English Short Title Catalogue online database confirms this impression; http://eureka.rig.ac.uk (accessed 16 June 2003).

42 T. Riders, *The Black Remembrancer* (1661), n.p.

43 *A Generall Bill of the Mortality of the Clergy of London* (1662), Wing G2014, frontispiece; another edition, Wing G495, frontispiece. This tract was reprinted in 1705 (ESTCT40546).

44 *A Generall Bill of the Mortality of the Clergy of London* (Wing G495), p. 6.

45 *Ibid*. Cf. M. Griffith, *A General Bill of the Mortality of the Clergie of London*, (1646/47).

46 E.g., G. Morley, *The Bishop of Winchester's Vindication of Himself from Divers False, Scandalous and Injurious Reflexions Made upon Him by Mr. Richard Baxter in Several of his Writings* (1683), p. 418.

47 Womack, *Aron Bimnucha*, frontispiece, pp. 84, 106.

48 Quoted in McGee, *Godly Man*, p. 269.

49 S. Butler, *Hudibras on Calamy's Imprisonment and Wild's Poetry* (1663), n.p.

50 *Ibid*.

51 *Iter Boreale* (1663), n.p.

52 That Berkenhead supervised the court newsbooks at this time is evident in the content of two letters written by him to Sir Edward Nicholas in October 1662; BL Egerton MSS 2538, fos 186, 189.

53 In effect, Juxon's office manager; Thomas, *Berkenhead*, pp. 209, 218.

54 Thomas, *Berkenhead*, pp. 223–4; Keeble, *Literary Culture*, p. 104; J. Williams, *A History of English Journalism* (1908), p. 187; *Mercurius Publicus*, 40 (2–9 October 1662), pp. 660–1.

55 *Mercurius Publicus*, 42 (16–23 October 1662), pp. 693–4; D. Nicholas, *Mr Secretary Nicholas 1593–1669: His Life and Letters* (1955), pp. 307–8; Thomas, *Berkenhead*,

p. 218. Nicholas informed the Earl of Winchelsea in a letter of 10 November 1662 that 'it was not my seeking or desire (as some here report) to withdraw or retire from his Majesties service'; HMC, *Report on the Manuscripts of Allan George Finch, Esquire*, 71st report, vol. 1 (1913), p. 221.

56 *Mercurius Publicus*, 1 (1–8 January 1662/63), p. 14.

57 *Ibid.*, p. 16.

58 *CSPD* 1663–4, p. 92; Thomas, *Berkenhead*, pp. 224–5. This may have been a veiled attack on L'Estrange's mentor, Sir Henry Bennet.

59 J. Berkenhead, *The Assembly-Man* (1663), facing front page.

60 According to Thomas, the attribution to Berkenhead is based on an attribution in a contemporary hand on a copy in the Bodleian Library, a close correlation between the arguments and a speech given by Berkenhead in the House of Commons in March, and on stylistic grounds; Thomas, *Berkenhead*, p. 221.

61 Thomas, *Berkenhead*, p. 222.

62 Berkenhead, *Cabala*, pp. 5, 8.

63 *Ibid.*, pp. 3, 20, 23, 25.

64 *Ibid.*, p. 6.

65 *Ibid.*, p. 7.

66 *Ibid.*, p. 6.

67 *Ibid.*, p. 7.

68 J. Philips, *Montelion* (1662); T. Flatman, *Don Juan Lamberto: Or a Comical History of the Late Time: The First Part by Montelion, Knight of the Oracle, & c.* (1661).

69 Berkenhead, *Cabala*, p. 7.

70 *Ibid.*, pp. 7, 28.

71 *Ibid.*, p. 33.

72 *Ibid.*, pp. 6–7.

73 *Ibid.*, p. 6.

74 Jenkyn, *Burning Yet Un-consumed Bush*, p. 35.

75 See Johns, *Nature of the Book*, p. 128; Hetet, 'A Literary Underground in Restoration England', p. 4.

76 Berkenhead, *Cabala*, p. 23.

77 *Ibid.*, p. 28. Berkenhead had grounds for suspicion; see *Master Edmund Calamy's Leading Case*, p. 12.

78 Berkenhead, *Cabala*, pp. '28, 25' (mispaginated, actually pp. 34–5).

79 Thomas, *Berkenhead*, p. 223; Bosher, *Restoration Settlement*, p. 257; Hutton, *Restoration*, p. 193.

80 L'Estrange, *Toleration Discuss'd*, sig. [A4v].

81 *Ibid.*, sig. [A3v].

82   *Ibid.*, p. 3.

83   *Ibid.*, p. 41.

84   *Ibid.*, pp. 55–6.

85   *Ibid.*, pp. 56–7, 59.

86   *Ibid*, pp. 14, 19, 28–9, 45.

87   *Ibid.*, pp. 24, 27.

88   *Ibid.*, p. 45.

89   *Ibid.*, p. 28.

90   *Ibid.*, p. 40.

91   *Ibid.*, pp. 40–1.

92   *Ibid*, pp. 2–3.

93   *Ibid.*, p. 55.

94   *Ibid.*, p. 5.

95   *Ibid.*, p. 6.

96   L'Estrange, *Considerations and Proposals*, sig. [a3v], [a4].

97   *Ibid.*, sig. [A2v].

98   *Ibid.*, sig. A3–[A3v].

99   *Ibid.*, sig. [A3v].

100 *Ibid.*, sig. [A3v–A4].

101 L'Estrange, *Considerations and Proposals*, p. 15.

102 *Eniautos Terastios, Mirabilis Annus, or The Year of Prodigies and Wonders* (1661).

103 L'Estrange, *Considerations and Proposals*, sig. a–[av].

104 Kitchin, *L'Estrange*, p. 91.

105 P. Fraser, *The Intelligence of the Secretaries of State and Their Monopoly of Licensed News 1660–1688* (Cambridge, 1956), p. 35; Hutton, *Restoration*, p. 201.

106 *The Intelligencer*, 1 (31 August 1663), pp. 3–4.

107 *The Intelligencer*, 3 (14 September 1663), p. 23.

108 *Ibid.*

109 *Ibid.*

110 *Ibid.*, pp. 23–4.

111 *Ibid.*, p. 24.

112 L'Estrange, *Truth and Loyalty Vindicated*, pp. 58–9; L'Estrange, *Considerations and Proposals*, p. 15.

113 *The Newes*, 4 (24 September 1663), p. 31.

114 *Ibid.*

115 *Ibid.*

116 *Intelligencer*, 7 (12 October 1663), p. 53.

117 *Ibid.*, p. 54.

118 *Intelligencer*, 8 (19 October 1663), p. 59.

119 *Ibid.*, p. 60; *ibid.*, 9, p. 81; *ibid.*, 12, p. 90; *ibid.*, 13, p. 97; *ibid.*, 14, pp. 104–6.

120 PRO SP29/424/151, quoted in Johns, *Nature of the Book*, p. 133.

121 Assheton, *Evangelium Armatum*, frontispiece.

122 *Ibid.*, sig. A.

123 *Ibid.*, sig. [Av].

124 *Ibid.*, sig. A2.

125 *Ibid.*, sig. [A2v].

126 *Ibid.*, sig. [A3].

127 *Ibid.*, sig. [A3v].

128 *Ibid.*

129 *Ibid.*

130 *Ibid.*, sig. [A4].

131 *Ibid.*, pp. 23–5.

132 *Ibid.*, p. 47.

133 *Ibid.*, p. 44.

134 Griffith, *The King's Life-Guard*, p. 22; Morley, *The Bishop of Winchester's Vindication of Himself*, p. 418.

135 Anthony Wood, quoted in *DNB*. Lloyd's *Memoires of the Lives* (1668) certainly appears plagiaristic of William Winstanley's, *England's VVorthies* (1660) and *The Loyall Martyrology* (1665).

136 Lloyd, *Cabala*, p. 3.

137 *Ibid.*, pp. 4–5.

138 *Ibid.*, p. 42.

139 *Ibid.*, pp. 42, 45.

140 *Ibid.*, pp. 44, 45, 47, 48, 49.

141 *Ibid.*, pp. 49, 50.

142 *Ibid.*, pp. 56, 60.

143 *Ibid.*, p. 51.

144 *Ibid.*, p. 53.

145 *Ibid.*, pp. 55, 56.

146 *Ibid.*, pp. 56–7.

147 *Ibid.*, p. 57.

148 *Ibid.*

149 *Ibid.*, p. 60.

150 *Ibid.*, pp. 60, 61, 63.

151 *Ibid.*, p. 91.

152 *Ibid.*, p. 95.

153 Alleine, *Godly Man's Portion* (1664), Wing A989A; J. Alleine, *The Godly Man's Portion and Sanctuary, Being a Second Part of Vindiciae Pietatis* (1664), Wing A989; G. Thorne, *The Saints Great Duty* (1664), Wing T1057B; Palke, *Loyal Non-Conformist* (1664), Wing P203B.

154 E.g., T. Brooks, *Apples of Gold for Young Men and Women and a Crown of Glory for Old Men and Women* (1665); T. Watson, *Au'tarkeia; Or the Art of Divine Contentment* (six editions published 1668–82). The 1668 publication was the thirteenth edition overall.

155 T. Cheeseman, *Via Lactea, or, The Saint's Only Way to True Blessedness* (1663), epistle.

156 J. Alleine, *A Call to Archippus* (1664), frontispiece, pp. 20, 23.

157 *An Exact Catalogue of the Names of Several Ministers Lately Ejected out of Their Livings in Several Counties of England Because They Could Not Conform for Conscience Sake* (1663), frontispiece.

158 Heath, *Stenography*, sig. [A2v].

159 R. S., *A Word to Dr Womocke* (1663).

160 *Mystery of Godliness and No Cabala*, frontispiece, pp. 1–2.

161 *Ibid.*, pp. 2–3, 4, 11, 17, 19, 20.

162 *Ibid.*, pp. 2, 3, 4–5, 18.

163 *Ibid.*, pp. 22–3.

164 *Ibid.*, p. 13.

165 *Ibid.*, p. 15.

166 *Ibid.*, p. 2.

167 Berkenhead, *Cabala*, p. 6; *Mystery of Godliness and No Cabala*, p. 3.

168 *Ibid.*, p. 8.

169 *Ibid.*, p. 9.

170 *Ibid.*, pp. 5, 9, 10, 12, 13.

171 *Ibid.*, p. 12.

172 Barry, 'The politics of religion in Restoration Bristol', in Harris, Seaward and Goldie, *Politics of Religion*, p. 171.

173 Potter, *Secret Rites*, p. 212.

174 Assheton, *Evangelium Armatum*, sig. [Av].

175 The use of persecution as a 'purifier' was common to both Anglicans and Puritans; McGee, *Godly Man*, pp. 48, 53.

176 Keeble, *Literary Culture*, pp. 242, 247, 253.

177 Hill, *English Bible*, p. 224; Keeble, *Literary Culture*, p. 247; cf., M. van Beek, *An Enquiry into Puritan Vocabulary* (Groningen, 1969), pp. 1–8.

178 E.g., Hodges, *Sion's Halelujah*, p. 7; cf. Washbourn, *The Repairer of the Breach*, p. 25; J. Whynnell, *England's Sorrows Turned into Joy* (1661), pp. 10–15; Meriton, *Curse Not the King*, p. 14; Sheldon, *David's Deliverance*, pp. 10–11; cf. the future Bartholomean Eedes, *Great Britain's Ressurrection*, p. 1.

179 L'Estrange, *Toleration Discuss'd*, pp. 55–6; L'Estrange, *Considerations and Proposals*, p. 15; Lloyd, *Cabala*, pp. 42, 45. Cf. Keeble, *Literary Culture*, p. 247.

180 *Mercurius Publicus*, 1 (1–8 January 1663), p. 14; DWL MS I.1.35, fo. 2r (Matthew Newcomen's farewell sermon of 19 August 1662); Parker, *A Sermon Preached at Christ-Church, Dublin*, p. 40; Barksdale, *The King's Return*, p. 10; Newcombe, *Usurpation Defeated and David Restored*, p. 19; Douch, *England's Jublilee*, p. 8. See also Hill, *English Bible*, p. 49.

181 Hyde, *Life*, I, p. 571.

182 *Mystery of Godliness and No Cabala*, p. 2.

183 Hyde, *Life*, I, p. 560.

184 Lake, 'Anti-popery', pp. 190, 197–8, 201, 202; Barry, 'The politics of religion in Restoration Bristol', p. 168.

185 Lake, 'Anti-popery', p. 202.

186 E.g., Berkenhead, *Cabala*, pp. 3, 20, 23, 25; L'Estrange, *Toleration Discuss'd*, p. 45; Griffith, *The King's Life-Guard*, p. 19; S. Ford, *Parallela Dysparallela* (1660), p. 10.

187 Miller, *After the Civil Wars*, p. 120.

188 The phrase is taken from Lake, 'Anti-popery', p. 198.

189 Berkenhead, *Cabala*, p. 6.

190 L'Estrange, *Considerations and Proposals*, sig. [A3v-A4]; Assheton, *Evangelium Armatum*, sig. [A3v].

191 Barry, 'The politics of religion in Restoration Bristol', p. 168.

192 Miller, *After the Civil Wars*, p. 186.

193 Berkenhead, *Cabala*, p. 8; Assheton, *Evangelium Armatum*, sig. [A2v].

194 Twisse, *England's Breath Stopp'd*, p. 34.

Chapter 6

Epilogue

In seeking to argue that the farewell sermons were not quietist admissions of defeat but highly charged political texts possessed of considerable contemporary significance, this study has concentrated on the period from 1662 to 1666: the two or three months during which the sermons were delivered from the pulpit, followed by the two or three years during which production and circulation of the written and printed texts were at their most prolific. From a high point of notoriety in 1663–64, when Bartholomean compilations were flooding the market, alarming Cavalier-Anglican opinion and fuelling fears of Presbyterian plotting, the farewell sermons began to fade into the seventeenth-century background. Several factors contributed to this phenomenon: firstly, the sermons were overtaken by events such as war with the Netherlands, the Great Plague and the Fire of London, the latter two of which impacted severely upon the lives and livelihoods of London's printers and booksellers. Secondly, the authorities were eventually to enjoy a considerable measure of success in restricting the activities of recalcitrant publishers and distributors. Lastly, and perhaps most importantly, publishers, regardless of whether their primary motivation was ideological or commercial, were under incessant pressure to satisfy the public's hunger for fresh news. The declining frequency of Bartholomean publications after 1664 was not because the issue of nonconformity became less significant politically – the Indulgence of 1672 would never have been a matter for debate had this been so – but because the farewell sermons were closely identified with a specific historical moment during which they had been rushed to press and marketed as news. That moment had now passed. By 1666 the Bartholomean corpus, like the Great Ejection itself, could be still be said to be a feature of the religio-political landscape, but it was a feature on a receding horizon.

It is evident, however, from the preface of a work such as *An Exact Collection of Farewell Sermons Preached by the Late London Ministers* (1662) that

some editors had in mind more ambitious goals than the provision of transient news, most obviously the desire to depict the Bartholomeans as a godly
community standing as one against worldly oppression.[1] Such aspirations
appear to have been short lived and uncoordinated: an impressionistic survey
of nonconformist literature published in the century after the Great Ejection
suggests that although there was an underlying awareness of the Bartholomean
corpus, and the occasional reprinting of a farewell sermon, at no point were
the collections of sermons imbued with an iconic status remotely comparable
to Foxe's memorials of the Marian martyrs. Neither is there any reason to
suppose that later nonconformist writers ever sought to promote the corpus
as a party manifesto. By contrast, the literature of their opponents continued
to reflect the line that had been taken by Berkenhead and L'Estrange: on the
occasions Tory publications carried any mention of the farewell sermons it
was in order to present them as the public face of an organised programme
of resistance, or, more ominously, as a catalyst of sedition. A particularly
blatant example of such vilification appeared in *Bishop Parker's History* (1730),
which claimed that during the crisis of 1662,

> nothing stirred up the People so fiercely, as the Volumes of Sermons, which
> the ejected Ministers preached (and afterwards published) to their Congrega-
> tions, as their *Farewel Sermons* before the Feast of *St. Bartholomew*. These
> Books, which smelt so strong of Sedition, were sold to their Party and the
> People of every Parish, from whence any Minister was ejected, being inflamed
> with Rage and Hatred, pursue with Force and Arms those who had turned
> them out, as he did of old, pursue those, who took away his Idols from him.
> By these fraudulent Artifices, they possessed the Peoples Minds with such
> implacable Aversion to the King's Government, that they took it for granted
> they should never want Volunteers when they took up Arms.[2]

In actuality the character of organised nonconformity (particularly the rebel-
lious armed host of Parker's imagination) was not defined by the farewell
sermons. It was shaped by the vicissitudes of persecution and toleration, and
through social, cultural and religious discourse within and between the nonconformist communities themselves. The farewell sermons were certainly
a feature of this discourse, along with the public (and publicised) displays of
solidarity which accompanied the burials of old Bartholomeans and other
prominent nonconformists – arenas that Sharon Achinstein has described
as 'sites for the performances of survival of an endangered community'.[3]
Indeed, the transition from farewell sermon to funeral sermon was pract-
ically seamless; as we have witnessed, the compilers of the Bartholomean
collections had from the first included funeral sermons in their publications. In 1708, whilst delivering a funeral sermon for his friend and fellow
Bartholomean John Whitlock, John Barrett reminded mourners that many
of them possessed *England's Remembrancer*, and suggested that it was worth

re-reading.[4] However, nothing preserved the vision of a Bartholomean nucleus more effectively than the initiative of individuals such as Henry Sampson, Roger Morrice, Ralph Thoresby, and, of course, Edmund Calamy III. These early historians of nonconformity each made it their business to gather together accounts of the lives of the ejected ministers, an enterprise which eventually bore fruit in the shape of Calamy's published memorials.[5] The success of the project could, as ever, be measured by the reaction of opponents such as the Anglican apologist John Walker, whose *Attempt* (1714) included a stream of sarcastic invective against Calamy's 'canonisation' of the 'Bartholomean sufferers'.[6]

The 'Bartholomean Legend', as Walker derisively dubbed it, had been given its shape by Edmund Calamy III in his account of the lives of the ejected ministers. These memorials were first published in 1702 as the famous chapter IX of the abridgement of Richard Baxter's autobiography, then expanded and supplemented by the *Account* (1713), the *Continuation* (1727) and various editions thereafter. But despite an obvious familiarity with many of the Bartholomean farewell sermons, Calamy made surprisingly little use of them in his writing. Even when revealing the identities of the preachers featured in *England's Remembrancer* in the *Account*, Calamy merely noted the new details against the relevant Midland ministers' names, with little or no embellishment. He provided an occasional brief anecdote regarding this or that preacher's valediction, but in most cases, no mention at all was made of the fact that a particular individual had featured as the author of a published farewell sermon. There is space here only briefly to reflect on Calamy's conspicuous failure to capitalise on the Bartholomean corpus in works which he intended should serve as a literary monument to the ejected ministers. It is possible that he considered the farewell sermons to be so familiar to his readers as to render an account of them superfluous. It is equally possible that the rhetorical content of the Bartholomean corpus had remained controversial – or, rather, had acquired the potential to attract fresh notoriety in a new historical setting. Taking into account the increasingly volatile political situation at the turn of the eighteenth century, with Queen Anne's precarious health and the question of the royal succession both paramount concerns, Calamy may have found it expedient not to draw undue attention to old nonconformist texts that contained criticism of government and resistance to royal authority. If anything, the fact that such criticism was coded and the resistance implicit made the farewell sermons even more of a double-edged sword: short of outright statements of treason, the enemies of nonconformity could hardly have wished for better ammunition than texts that contained such an ambiguous political message. Certainly, the passage from *Parker's History* quoted earlier, published only three years after Calamy's *Continuation*, suggests that any concerted attempt to revive interest in the farewell sermons would have provoked an extreme reaction. As it was, the circulation of Calamy's original *Abridgement* had already attracted considerable hostility. The long title to *Seditious Preachers, Ungodly Teachers* (1709) made plain its detestation of the ejected ministers of 1662, and its author's intention to refute '*Mr Calamy's Abridgement, where he has canonised them for so many saints and confessors*'.[7] It may well be significant, therefore, that on one of the rare occasions Calamy chose to quote from a farewell sermon at length in the subsequent *Account*, he selected a passage from the then unpublished valediction of Robert Atkins, in which the Exeter minister emphasised his loyalty to the monarchy.[8] That Edmund Calamy III was a judicious and deliberate editor is a matter of record;[9] given the huge influence his memorials still exert over the historiography of Restoration nonconformity, it would be prudent to remember that the treatment of the Bartholomean farewell sermons in Calamy's published writing reveals as much about the political reality of early eighteenth-century Britain as it does about the England of 1662.

Calamy's detailed knowledge of Robert Atkins's farewell sermon indicates that manuscripts as well as printed works were still circulating within nonconformist networks. Annotations within the covers of surviving publications suggest that the ageing publications were preserved and valued by succeeding generations.[10] There had even been isolated attempts to revive the spirit of the Great Ejection: Richard Baxter had rediscovered a discarded farewell sermon originally intended for his old Kidderminister parishioners in 1662 and had seen it through to print in 1683. It was reprinted after his death in 1691 and again in 1707.[11] Richard Fairclough's valedictory series, first printed in 1663, was republished in 1713 under its old title, *A Pastor's Legacy*. Two years later Robert Atkins's farewell sermon, which had been circulating in manuscript form, was finally published in Exeter. Like Calamy's hagiographies, the publishing of Atkins's valediction, under the title *The God of Love and Peace with Sincere and Peaceable Christians* (1715), may yet be shown to reveal as much about Dissent in early eighteenth-century Devon as it does about Atkins's ejection from 'East Peters' in Exeter in 1662. The second decade of the eighteenth century was, of course, a time of considerable national tension, with the Hanoverian succession challenged by the Jacobite rebellion, and with religious rioting in London and elsewhere. Dissenters' meeting houses in the West Country were attacked in 1715, just as they had been a few years earlier during the Sacheverell controversy.[12] There was also disunity within the nonconformist community in Devon itself, with internecine feuding that would eventually lead to the ejection of two ministers from their Exeter congregations in 1719.[13] After so many decades circulating in manuscript form, the decision to publish Atkins's sermon in Exeter itself during a time of such intense local and national unrest can, at the very least, be described as poignant.

After 1715, the farewell sermons suffered a century of neglect. Even the sizeable biography of Thomas Manton published in 1725 failed to mention either the farewell sermon published in the minister's name, or his public repudiation of it in *Mercurius Publicus*.[14] As it was, the next appearance of the farewell sermons in print was in the form of a collection entitled *Farewell Sermons of Some of the Most Eminent of the Non-Conformist Ministers Ejected in 1662*, published in London in 1816.[15] Surprisingly, the two hundredth anniversary of the Great Ejection in 1862 was not marked by any new compilations, although several public lectures were given. One of these papers, given by the antiquary Charles Stanford on the subject of the farewell sermons, was published as an essay entitled *The Farewell Sunday* (1862). As he had relied heavily on Samuel Palmer's 1802 revision of Calamy (together with material from the then recently published diary and autobiography of Henry Newcombe), it was inevitable that the farewell sermons would be depicted in Stanford's work as expressions of pained political loyalty and religious moderation, articulated by passive ministers loath to offend.[16] Thus, by 1913, L'Estrange's biographer George Kitchin had considerable precedent to convince him that the farewell sermons were merely 'pathetic discourses [with] very little in them beyond an exhortation to comfort'.[17] That impression was clearly still in evidence in the 1930s, as A. G. Matthews's otherwise excellent revision of Calamy's memorials, *Calamy Revised*, carried even less discussion of the farewell sermons than had appeared in the original *Abridgement* of 1702.

The three hundredth anniversary of the Great Ejection in 1962 was commemorated by articles and plays, and by the reproduction of a selection of Bartholomean farewell sermons, published under the auspices of the Banner of Truth Trust in London.[18] A facsimile of the 1816 Bartholomean compilation was published by Still Waters Revival Books of Edmonton, Canada, in the late 1990s, and the same organisation published a digital facsimile of *A Compleat Collection of Farewell Sermons* (1663) on CD-ROM as recently as 2001.[19] The SWRB website has in the past carried links to other North American sites hosted by modern Nonconformist ministers and self-styled 'paleo-Presbyterians' which have featured transcriptions of Bartholomean sermons taken from the compilation of 1816. References to the sermons currently appear in other sites dedicated to the life and works of ejected ministers such as William Bates and Thomas Manton.[20] These modern manifestations of the Bartholomean corpus, having been produced by a variety of organisations and individuals, have, predictably, been harnessed to a variety of modern agendas, ranging from the religio-political to the academic. It is beyond the remit of this present study to analyse these contemporary trends, except to observe that they appear to indicate that the Bartholomeans and their farewell sermons have entered yet another stage of an ongoing process that began with their delivery from the pulpits in the summer of 1662.

The treatment of the farewell sermons in the three and a half centuries since their initial exposition shows that they have not simply spoken to their own time and space, but have often been made to speak to other times and other spaces.[21] In the case of the Bartholomean corpus, this has resulted in an image which has at times bordered on the schizophrenic, portrayed by some as quietist, irenic and unremarkable, and by others as an articulation of religious fanaticism and revolutionary sedition. These successive layers of interpretation can, in many ways, enrich our understanding of the corpus, but they should also serve as a warning that it is all too easy to lose sight of the functioning of historical texts and artefacts in their original setting.

NOTES

1 *An Exact Collection of Farewel Sermons Preached by the Late London-Ministers* (1662), Wing C241, sig. [A3v].

2 S. Parker, *Bishop Parker's History: Or, the Tories' Chronicle, from the Restauration of King Charles II, 1660, to the Year 1680* (1730), p. 45.

3 Achinstein, *Literature and Dissent*, p. 3.

4 Barrett, *A Funeral Sermon, Preached at Nottingham*, p. 27.

5 D. Wykes, *'To Revive the Memory of some Excellent Men': Edmund Calamy and the Early Historians of Nonconformity* (1997), p. 3.

6 Walker, *Attempt*, pt. II, p. 207.

7 *Seditious Preachers Ungodly Teachers* (1709), title page.

8 *Account*, pp. 214–15.

9 Wykes, *To Revive the Memory of some Excellent Men*, pp. 5–6.

10 Witness the succession of owners' names on the copy of *An Exact Collection of Farewel Sermons Preached by the Late London-Ministers* (Wing C241), in the collection of Keele University Library; several of which relate to a family named Cranwell, who may possibly be relatives of the Derbyshire Bartholomean of the same name.

11 R. Baxter, *Richard Baxter's Farewel Sermon, Prepared to Have Been Preached to His Hearers at Kidderminster at His Departure, but Forbidden* (1683); R. Baxter, *Excellent Memorables for All Mourners* (1691); R. Baxter, *The Practical Works of the Late Reverend and Pious Mr. Richard Baxter, in Four Volumes* (1707).

12 J. Hoppit, *A Land of Liberty? England 1689–1727* (Oxford, 2000), p. 393.

13 J. Peirce, *The Case of the Ministers Ejected at Exon, by James Peirce, One of Them* (Exeter, 1719); J. Everleigh, *An Account of the Reasons Why Many Citizens of Exon Have Withdrawn from the Ministry of Mr. J. Hallet and Mr. J. Peirce* (Exeter, 1719). Several editions exist of both publications, printed in Exeter and London. I am grateful to Dr Ian Atherton for conversations on the eighteenth-century religious background.

14 W. Harris, *Some Memoirs of the Life and Character of Thomas Manton* (1725). A 1758 publication of Thomas Watson's work is sometimes listed as including his farewell

sermon as an annex, but it does not appear to have been so annexed: T. Watson, *The Godly Man's Picture, Drawn with a Scripture-Pensil* (Glasgow, 1758).

15 *Farewell Sermons of Some of the Most Eminent of the Non-Conformist Ministers Ejected in 1662* (1816).

16 C. Stanford, *The Farewell Sunday: On the Farewell Sermons of Clergy Removed under the Act of Uniformity 1662, St. Bartholomew's Bicentenary Papers* Tract VII (1862), C. Stanford, *Joseph Alleine: His Companions and Times, a Memorial of Black Bartholomew 1662* (1862); E. Calamy (1671–1732), *The Nonconformists' Memorial, Being an Account of the Lives, Sufferings and Printed Works of the Two Thousand Ministers Ejected from the Church of England, Chiefly by the Act of Uniformity 1666 [sic]*, ed. Samuel Palmer (3 vols, 1802–3); H. Newcombe, *The Diary of the Rev. Henry Newcombe, 30 September 1661 to 28 September 1663*, ed. R. Parkinson (Manchester, 1849); idem., *The Autobiography of Henry Newcombe*, ed. R. Parkinson (2 vols, Manchester, 1852).

17 Kitchin, *L'Estrange*, p. 109.

18 *Sermons of the Great Ejection: Taken from a Collection of Farewell Sermons Preached by the Late London Ministers and England's Remembrancer*, ed. I. H. Murray (1962); C. G. Bolam, 'The ejection of 1662 and its consequences for the Presbyterians in England', *The Hibbert Journal*, 60 (1961–62), pp. 184–95; R. Duce, *Beyond the Gate: A Play in One Act on the Period that Followed the Great Ejection in 1662* (1961); R. Duce, *Fire in the City: An Historical Play of the 1662 Ejection* (1961); R. Duce (ed.), *Faithful and True: A Pageant for Tercentenary Celebrations 1662–1962* (1962).

19 *Puritan Bookshelf: Vol. #17 – Sermons, Sabbath Worship & God's Promises* (CD-ROM, Edmonton, Canada, 2001). The original 1663 collection reproduced in facsimile on the SWRB CD-ROM is a variant of Wing C5638.

20 www.swrb.com [accessed 13/09/2004]; http://home.earthlink.net/~dalziell/caryls.html [accessed 19/06/2001]; www.newblehome.co.uk/bates [accessed 13/09/2004]; www.newble.clara.co.uk/manton/index.html [accessed 13/09/2004].

21 The phrase is Mary Morrissey's, commenting on Jeanne Shami's work on John Donne's 1622 Gunpowder Plot sermons; Morrissey, 'Interdisciplinarity', p. 1121.

Chapter 7

Conclusion

The farewell sermons of the ministers ejected from the Church of England in 1662 had a contemporary significance that has not hitherto been adequately reflected in modern studies of Restoration history or even in specialised studies of nonconformist literature. This oversight is surprising given the sizeable printed corpus generated by the events of 'Black Bartholomew'. It becomes astounding when we consider that, despite its size, the corpus is a comparatively small sample of the hundreds, conceivably thousands, of valedictions that were delivered over the space of a few weeks between the passing of the Act of Uniformity and its implementation. Had the farewell sermons been nothing more than notices announcing a mass resignation from the ministry of the state Church they would merit attention; but a close reading of the surviving texts, together with accounts of their reception documented in the contemporary record, reveals that they were much more than that.

In order to recover the full engagement of the sermons with their historical moment it has been necessary to do more than simply locate the corpus within the political narrative of Restoration England. Throughout this study the process of contextualisation has proceeded alongside an ongoing analysis and 'decoding' of the texts. Where, for example, cryptic references to wise serpents and innocent doves by preachers such as Thomas Watson and William Cross have shown that the valedictions were indeed encoded, an analysis of the texts has shown *how* this was done whilst the political and legislative context has indicated *why* it was necessary.[1] Thus, the intricate construction and warily couched language of the farewell sermons allowed Bartholomean authors to posit highly controversial concepts that alarmed, threatened and offended opponents, whilst generally remaining within the letter of the law.

For various reasons, contemporaries of all persuasions regarded the Act of Uniformity as an issue of pivotal importance. But where Pepys anticipated the historical implications of the Great Ejection and others such as Sheldon and L'Estrange regarded it as a religious and political watershed, the authors of the farewell sermons suspected something of far greater consequence. The imminent demise of so many ministers and the apparent eclipse of godly ideals seemed imbued with eschatological significance, leading so many in their farewell sermons to perceive a final God-given opportunity to prepare England for a time of trial that would reveal the worthiness of the chosen few and seal the eternal damnation of everyone else. That several preachers went so far as to hint that the Great Ejection might presage the End of Days demonstrates conclusively that apocalyptic preaching was a response to circumstance, not a convenient theological boundary between radical and moderate Puritans.

As representatives of moderate Puritanism, the picture of the Bartholomeans that has emerged from this study is that of a highly educated and comparatively youthful body. Close ties between the many Bartholomeans aged in their twenties and thirties and their older brethren served to foster a sense of emotional unity and continuity between the different generations. Overlapping networks embraced Presbyterians and Independents, and even moderate Anglicans. Consequently, evidence for denominational affiliation among those ejected in 1662 is so problematical that it would be an oversimplification to describe the Bartholomean corpus as 'Presbyterian'. But if most Bartholomeans chose not to define their own religious self-identity, they made it very plain that their principal opponents were 'formalists', closely followed by papists and Quakers. It is evident that by 'formalists', the departing ministers meant their persecutors within the English Church and state – enemies whose reverence for costumed ritual made them at best misguided adherents of a hollow and lifeless parody of the Protestant faith and at worst agents of Rome. In the eyes of the Bartholomeans these formalists were the true schismatics. The Bartholomeans' belief in their own orthodoxy was one of the main reasons why very few discussed the possibility of total separation from the Church of England. It was clear from the nature of the moral advice they gave to their congregations during the final weeks of their ministry that many of the departing clergy remained determined to complete the reformation of the Church of England. Thus, their resolve not to separate from the Church – and more particularly, the repeated exhortations to their followers not to separate – reflected continuing activism rather than an admission of defeat. Caution was evident on more overtly political points, for, whilst resistance to human innovation in worship was evinced in several valedictions, there was almost no direct reference to the contentious Oath and Covenant. Having said this, the silence of most Bartholomeans on this issue was in itself an answer to Parliament's demands that they disavow the Oath and Covenant. There are thus several indications that far from than pruning a stale, archaic Puritan ministry, Sheldon and his allies had attacked one that was thriving and energetic. The failed religious experiments of the Interregnum and the political reverses of 1659–62 notwithstanding, the Bartholomean response to the Act of Uniformity demonstrated that the Puritan impulse was far from exhausted.

The principal thrust of that impulse had always come from preaching. As Bartholomew's Day drew closer, growing public interest boosted church attendance, until, on the final Sunday of 17 August 1662, the farewell sermons attained a mass audience. Although their exegesis was designed to work on several levels, the Bartholomeans endeavoured to ensure that their sermons would be heard and understood far beyond the physical confines of their assemblies. Much of their message was addressed to those below the gentry, with exhortations to test the authority of incoming replacements, frequent assertions of social equality in the sight of God and the moral superiority of the godly.[2] Followers were urged to be circumspect in their relationships with worldly neighbours, and to associate (if necessary secretively) within godly networks.[3] Although revisionist historians might argue that such ministers, particularly those of a Presbyterian disposition, would never have intended their preaching to have fostered political instability, it is easy to see why opponents considered the farewell sermons to have been an exercise in seditious rabble-rousing. Despite public accusations in Parliament and elsewhere that their past preaching had encouraged rebellion and regicide, it is interesting that so many ministers persisted in using military metaphor to incite their followers to be active soldiers in the service of the Lord, to encourage them to think of Jesus as their king, and to stress that God was no respecter of rank.[4] In addition, the fact that many Bartholomean ministers declared that it was not their intention to command individual consciences but only to be 'helpers of joy' shows that they intended their sermons to facilitate dialectic discourse rather than to function as a blunt instrument of moral instruction.[5] It was not simply multivalent rhetoric that was designed to embolden and energise the laity, therefore, but the actual structure of the sermon and the theology that informed it.

The Restoration authorities had no doubts whatsoever that Puritan preaching continued to exert a significant political influence. Their efforts to monitor and control the pulpits were not primarily for religious reasons (until the Act of Uniformity made dissension from the doctrine and liturgy of the Common Prayer Book a political issue), but rather to restrict political discourse. The traditional response of preachers to such intimidation had always been to encode their comments in Scriptural metaphor, thus simultaneously evading the law and evoking the authority of the Bible. Contrary to Christopher Hill's belief that the Regicide had fatally undermined the use of Scripture to justify political actions, the content and reception of the Bartholomean texts – and indeed that of contemporaneous Anglican sermons – demonstrates that the Bible remained an important source of political inspiration after the Restoration.[6] But the patterns of Scriptural citation do appear to have been affected: the casuistry of the farewell sermons relied heavily on the scripture of the New Testament partly because the Old Testament had acquired an inconvenient association with the strands of radical casuistry that had informed and justified civil war and regicide, and partly because contemporary parallels with certain Old Testament personages and regimes were so well-known as to be considered explicit political comment. Consequently, published Anglican sermons of the period commemorating the Regicide or the Restoration appear to have been far more likely than Bartholomean farewell sermons to have taken their main text from the Old Testament. It would be premature, however, to claim that this shift from Old to New Testament marked the beginnings of a fault line between Anglican and nonconformist exegesis: it is most likely that this shift was, like the turn to apocalyptic epistemology observed earlier, a response to the political circumstances of the moment. It is evident that several sections of the New Testament contained material highly suitable for the occasion of the Great Ejection at the same time as it offered the departing ministers greater room for manoeuvre. In addition, the fact that many Bartholomeans still included some controversial citations from the Old Testament in the course of their valedictory exegesis (most particularly passages of Exodus) suggests that that shift had more to do with political expediency, rather than a repudiation of their past.

The caution of the Bartholomeans on this point is understandable not least because the need to rationalise their nonconformity necessitated a definition of the boundaries of earthly authority. Although direct references to Charles II were invariably deferential, John Collins's declaration that he feared God more than he feared the King was an acknowledgement that his nonconformity required him to defy royal authority.[7] Given the vengeful mood of many within the restored establishment, there were obvious hazards in suggesting even the most modest qualification of the power of the Crown-in-Parliament. The earnest pleas of affection and loyalty to Charles II in so many published prayers and valedictions confirm that most Bartholomeans were unwilling rebels; but at the same time, their willingness to use Scriptural metaphor to criticise political and ecclesiastical authority and to propose limits to the power of those authorities showed that they had lost none of their taste for reformation. Declarations of 'passive' rather than 'active' obedience carried their own problems: the hypothesis advanced in so many farewell sermons that the absolute requirements of salvation were entirely separate from the transient considerations of temporal politics had the effect of placing religious fidelity above earthly loyalties. The implication that governors and magistrates had no moral authority over individuals who could claim that their actions or omissions were dictated by religious conscience was not lost on Cavalier-Anglicans, for whom the very phrase 'tender conscience' had quickly become an anathema.

In the same way that the Bartholomeans did not aspire to be rebels, they had not looked to become martyrs. However, since the passage of the Act of Uniformity had made persecution all but inevitable, the nonconformist preachers quickly began to embrace the concept. The fact that Pauline scripture was the most prevalent source of sermon texts in the Bartholomean corpus did not simply reflect the suitability of Paul's farewell addresses to his various congregations, but also his endorsement of persecution as a confirmation of godliness. The Bartholomeans' self-promotion as martyrs, through farewell sermons presented as their dying words, was intended to enhance the gravity and longevity of their message. And although most were extremely careful when mentioning the Marian martyrs or any other subject likely to reflect on the Restoration authorities, it was inevitable that such images of martyrdom invited audiences to identify and condemn the persecutors. This was an unmistakable political message, which pleas of moderation actually intensified: the more the Bartholomeans attempted to portray themselves as harmless, peaceful and reasonable, the more they portrayed the political and ecclesiastical authorities as invidious, aggressive and irrational.

The translation of the farewell sermons into scribal and printed circulation moved the Uniformity crisis to a new level, increasing the cross-fertilisation of discourse between London and provincial nonconformist networks and ensuring that the debate continued long after Bartholomew's Day. Sometimes publishers (be they stationers, preachers or followers) were quite explicit in their wish to preserve a record for the judgement of posterity. In moving from the rather shadowy networks of scribal circulation to a highly visible public circulation in print, the various items of Bartholomean material quickly began to coagulate into ever larger compilations, giving an impression of unity and direction at the same time as causing new problems for the Restoration authorities. The printed word had influence in this respect not simply because the nonconformist constituency had relatively high levels of literacy, but also because, as in so many other instances, literate and oral culture functioned in tandem.

The question was raised earlier regarding the typicality of the published Bartholomean works. In fact a comparison of the demographic profiles regarding age and educational background show a close correlation between the subset of published Bartholomeans and the wider cohort. There is slightly more divergence as regards perceived denominational affiliation, but both Presbyterian and Independent temperaments were represented in the published compilations. Finally, although many of those published were already celebrities in their own right, others were not, particularly many of the

provincial preachers who nevertheless appeared in pamphlets and compilations. The published works therefore appear reasonably representative of
the type of message delivered from nonconformist pulpits between June and
August 1662.

Considering the question of typicality from another angle, it is interesting
to note that just as no farewell sermons appeared in W. F. Mitchell's 1932
listing of 'representative' early modern sermons, so none appear in Ian Green's
recent survey of over seven hundred early modern devotional best-sellers.[8]
In *Print and Protestantism* only works passing through a minimum of five
editions within thirty years were considered for inclusion. Whilst Professor
Green freely admits that this criterion thereby overlooks works such as Foxe's
Acts and Monuments, he argues that most of the remaining publications
thereby disqualified would only 'have had a localised impact.[9] However, not
only are hugely influential publications such as Thomas Edwards's *Gangraena*
thereby excluded, but also works such as William Assheton's *Evangelium
Armatum* (1663) – which was still being cited in works attacking nonconformity fully two decades after Black Bartholomew.[10] The Bartholomean farewell sermons have an even stronger case for inclusion, not least because
many of them were reprinted as many as eleven times between 1662 and
1664, albeit in different formats and under different titles. By any calculation
these were bestsellers that exerted a considerable and lasting influence.[11] In
order to assess the true contemporary significance of a publication, therefore,
it would seem fruitful to consider not merely the frequency of republication
(although at least twenty-seven Bartholomean works would qualify by this
criteria alone), but also the influence of the published responses that work
provoked. Neither should it be forgotten that censorship affected both the
language and the production of the farewell sermons. Thus, what at first glance
might appear a consensual or irenic impulse, whether in pulpit-delivery, note-
taking or in the editorial process, often turns out not to reveal theological or
ideological consensus so much as the efficacy of political repression.

A belief in authorial intention was declared at the beginning of this
book, tempered by an acceptance of the transformative potential of hearers,
editors, readers and censors. As with all such studies into encoded polemic,
it is impossible to resolve the question of how much of the authorial intention remains in the material which has survived. However, some trends are
noticeable. Firstly, the comparative case studies featuring Matthew Newcomen,
William Jenkyn and Thomas Lye suggest that the tendency of the editorial
process appears most often to have been to temper the rhetoric of any given
farewell sermon. Secondly, despite this, the process of compilation can be
seen to have begun a process by which preachers' individual public personae
were melded into the appearance of a nonconformist 'community', within
which the most irenic preacher was associated with the inflammatory language

of the most uncompromising. Thirdly, as Lois Potter has written of an earlier decade, 'whatever their original intentions, the works of victimised writers were bound to *become* subversive as a result of their punishment'.[12] As the Bartholomeans were seen by opponents as having voluntarily chosen the path of victim-hood, the farewell sermons, subversive by the very fact of their conception, were made doubly so by the process of scriptural and printed circulation.

But the farewell sermons were also subversive because it was politic for vested interests within the establishment to consider them to be so. If non-conformist literature was often predisposed to discuss eschatology and to promote the continuing quest for true Protestant reformation, Cavalier-Anglican literature was intent on re-fighting the English Civil Wars and apportioning blame for the Regicide. It has been stressed in a previous chapter how the struggle between the Berkenhead-Nicholas and L'Estrange-Bennett factions at court intensified the severity of the Cavalier-Anglican reaction to the publication of the farewell sermons. In return, the part the Bartholomean publications had played in the downfall of Berkenhead and his master proved that in a very immediate sense the farewell sermons were indeed capable of causing political instability. However, the Bartholomeans' corpus had not caused this internecine struggle, but had simply presented itself as the most obvious issue over which to pick a fight. The polemic generated by Berkenhead, L'Estrange and the other Cavalier-Anglican writers was simply a continuation of the agenda that had produced the Act of Uniformity in the first place. Whilst appreciating the threat from Fifth Monarchists, Quakers and other radicals, it is noticeable that the returned royalists' most cutting polemic was aimed at moderate Puritans. There was a constant desire both in Anglican sermons and in Cavalier-Anglican polemic to convict the 'Presbyterians' of facilitating the civil wars and, by their passivity, of allowing the Regicide to take place. The muted anti-popish rhetoric in the farewell sermons contrasted strongly with its vigorous deployment by Cavalier-Anglicans, whose polemic proceeded to synthesise the perceived threat from Presbyterianism with the more traditional fear of papist insurgency. This trope was deployed to full effect against the ejected ministers and the published farewell sermons. R. L. Greaves has argued that the biggest potential threat to the restored regime came from radical sects, rather than from moderate, respectable, Presbyterianish Puritans.[13] But simply expressing disbelief in the numerous rumours of Presbyterian plots does not preclude the potential of moderate Puritans to plot against or challenge the government of the Church or state. Many Cavalier-Anglicans within the establishment believed in such plots, and policies were formed and enacted accordingly. As the most numerous, the most respectable and the closest to political power, dissent from those of a Presbyterian persuasion could not be discounted or repressed by the authorities in quite the same way as more obviously radical religious groups such as the Quakers or the Fifth Monarchists. In addition, the royalists were required to take the potential of nonconformist networks seriously in order to give credence to their own underground past; for example, in the growing legend of the escape of Charles II in 1651 – which in the 1660s was being promoted across the nation in symbols as mundane as inn signs such as 'The Royal Oak' and 'The Black Boy'. Neither, under any circumstances, could Cavalier-Anglicans tolerate a martyrology which threatened to compete with the burgeoning cult of the royal martyr, King Charles I of Blessed Memory, at the same time as it made martyrs of those they considered accomplices to his execution.

The farewell sermons demonstrate the extent to which religion remained a central consideration in the conduct of post-Restoration politics. It was observed at the beginning of this book that although the ejected ministers went peaceably they did not go quietly. In part, this is because they were not allowed to go quietly, either by their supporters or their detractors. The more the Bartholomean clergy attempted to deny that religion and politics were intertwined, the more they highlighted the fact that it was so. Andrew Hopper has seen in the dire prophesies made by rabble-rousers during the Farnley Wood plot in October 1662 an attempt by speakers 'to restore a sense of power to their degraded position', all of which could be construed as seditious by the authorities.[14] It now seems clear that such attempts were presaged by the supposedly quietest Bartholomean farewell sermons. Indeed, far from seeking to establish some sort of post-Restoration consensus or comprehension, it is likely that the alarm and offence caused by the farewell sermons actually obstructed any chance that the Act of Uniformity might have been suspended, or the rehabilitation of nonconformists attempted.

In the course of investigating the texts and events surrounding 'Black Bartholomew', this study has challenged several received wisdoms regarding the Restoration religious settlement and the origins of organised Dissent. By bringing a well-known but hitherto largely unexplored source into sharper focus and opening up the material contained within it, the intent has been to enhance existing knowledge of the Uniformity crisis (not least to argue that it *was* a crisis), and thereby to refine the historiography of the Restoration period and to inform a wider debate on the culture of English nonconformity. A further objective has been to underline the importance of the current wave of interest in the early modern sermon. The study has challenged the simplistic preconception that historical significance must be imbued in structural change, or in political or intellectual novelty, rather than language; in doing so, it has sought to answer Lori-Anne Ferrell's call to consider how words could operate in lieu of action and the potentiality of spoken, written or printed thought to 'rescript the assumptions of religio-political culture in such a way as to transform it entirely.'[15] Finally, this re-evaluation of the farewell sermons has highlighted how much more we need to find out about the religio-political culture of Restoration communities, and particularly about the interaction between the centre and provinces with regard to the creation, reception and implementation of the Act of Uniformity. If the Bartholomean corpus signifies anything, it is that the last word has not yet been written on the nature and longevity of Puritanism.

NOTES

1   Watson, *Pastor's Love Expressed*, p. 14; *England's Remembrancer*, p. 163.

2   E.g., Collins in *Exact Collection*, pp. 380, 385; Whitlock and Bladon, in *England's Remembrancer*, pp. 24–5, 38–9, 293–4; Lye, *Fixed Saint*, p. 4.

3   E.g., Whitlock, in *England's Remembrancer* pp. 38–9; Jenkyn, *Burning Yet Un-consumed Bush*, p. 35.

4   E.g., *England's Remembrancer*, pp. 122, 293, 372; Swinnock, *Pastors Farewell*, p. 64; Jenkyn, *Burning, Yet Un-consumed Bush*, p. 8.

5   Lye, *Fixed Saint*, p. 5.

6   Hill, *English Bible*, pp. 329, 413.

7   *Exact Collection*, p. 382.

8   Mitchell, *English Pulpit Oratory*, pp. 411–52; Green, *Print and Protestantism*, appendix.

9   *Ibid.*, pp. xi, 174.

10 Morley, *The Bishop of VVorcester's Letter to a Friend*, p. 418.

11 Cf. Green, *Print and Protestantism*, pp. 173, 179.

12 Potter, *Secret Rites*, p. 210.

13 Greaves, *Deliver Us from Evil*, p. 9.

14 Hopper, 'Farnley Wood plot', pp. 287, 293–4.

15 Ferrell, *Government by Polemic*, p. 6.

Bibliography

Where authors are likely to be confused with others of a similar name (e.g. Calamy, Walwyn, Winstanley), names have been followed by the individual's dates. In view of the close similarity of several Bartholomean compilations, Wing catalogue numbers have been given. The titles of works have been shortened, except where the fuller title has been considered relevant. Unless otherwise stated, the place of publication is London.

MANUSCRIPT SOURCES

NATIONAL ARCHIVES (PUBLIC RECORD OFFICE, KEW)
State papers, SP29/54, Spies' reports; SP29/56, Spies' reports; SP29/57, Spies' reports; SP29/77/37, Petition of Peter Lillicrap, 23 July 1662; SP29/78/37–40, Documents pertaining to Lillicrap's case

BRITISH LIBRARY
Add. MSS, 37820, Personal papers of Sir Edward Nicholas

Egerton MSS, 2538, Correspondence of Sir Edward Nicholas; 2543, Correspondence of Sir Edward Nicholas; 2570, Autobiography and correspondence of Richard Baxter; 3349, Correspondence of Sir Henry Bennet, later Lord Arlington

Sloane MSS, 608, Nonconformist ministers' memorials; 4275, Nonconformist ministers' correspondence; 4276, Nonconformist ministers' correspondence

BODLEIAN LIBRARY, OXFORD
MSS Add., c 302–7, Correspondence and papers of Gilbert Sheldon

Carte MSS, 31–3, Correspondence of James Butler, Marquis of Ormonde; 46, Correspondence between Sir Henry Bennet and the Marquis and Duke of Ormonde, 1660–84; 79, Correspondence of Philip, Lord Wharton

Rawlinson MSS.E.93, Farewell sermons of Exeter ministers, 1662

Tanner MS, 48, Correspondence and miscellaneous papers

Bibliography

DR WILLIAMS'S LIBRARY, LONDON
CL MSS, I. h. 35, Farewell sermons of Matthew Newcomen, 1662; 24.7–12, Papers of Owen Stockton, 1630–1680

WILLIAM ANDREWS CLARK MEMORIAL LIBRARY, UCLA,
LOS ANGELES
B8535, M3, Notes of Charles Burke's sermon, 1662

PRINTED WORKS

BARTHOLOMEAN COMPILATIONS

A Collection of Farewel-Sermons Preached by Mr. Calamy, Mr. Watson, Mr. Sclater, Dr. Jacomb, Mr. Case, Mr. Baxter, Mr. Jenkins, Mr. Lye, Dr. Manton, to Their Respective Congregations at Their Departure from Them, to Which is Annexed, a Sermon Preached at the Funeral of Mr. Simeon Ash, Late Minister of the Gospel at St Austins in London (1662), Wing C5145A

A Compleat Collection of Farewell Sermons, Preached by Mr. Calamy, Dr. Manton etc. (1663), Wing C5638

A Compleat Collection of Farewell Sermons, Preached by Mr. Calamy, Dr. Manton etc. (1663), Wing C5638 variant

A Compleat Collection of Farewell Sermons, Preached by Mr Calamy, Dr. Manton, etc. (1663), Wing C5638aA

A Compleat Collection of Farewell Sermons, Preached by Mr Calamy, Dr. Manton, etc. (1663), Wing C5638aA variant

The Farewell Sermons of the Late London Ministers, Preached August 17th 1662 (1662), Wing C242

England's Remembrancer, Being a Collection of Farewel-Sermons Preached by Divers Non-Conformists in the Country (1663), Wing E3029

England's Remembrancer, Being a Collection of Farewel-Sermons Preached by Divers Non-Conformists in the Country (1666), Wing E3029A

An Exact Collection of Farewel Sermons Preached by the Late London-Ministers (1662), Wing C241

An Exact Collection of Farevvel Sermons, Preached by the Late London-Ministers (1662), Wing E3632

Farewel Sermons Preached by Mr. Calamy, Dr. Manton, etc., L. R. and S. N., eds (1663), Wing C243

The London-Ministers Legacy to Their Several Congregations (1662), Wing L2905A

The Second and Last Collection of the Late London Ministers Farewel-Sermons (1663), Wing S2257

The Second Volume of the Farewel Sermons, Preached by Some London and Country Ministers (1663), Wing S2336A

The Third Volume of Farewel Sermons, Preached by Some London and Country Ministers (1663), Wing T914C

The Third and Last Volume of the Farewell Sermons (1663), Wing T898A

Versameling van Afscheytspredicatien, Gepredikt van Mr. Calamy . . . (Amsterdam, 1662)

BARTHOLOMEAN PAMPHLETS

Alleine, Richard, *The Godly Man's Portion and Sanctuary Opened* (1662?), Wing A987

Alleine, Richard, *The Godly Man's Portion and Sanctuary* ([S.l.], 1663), Wing A1007

Alleine, Richard, *The Godly Man's Portion and Sanctuary* (1664), Wing A989

Alleine, Richard, *The Godly Man's Portion and Sanctuary Opened in Two Sermons, Preached August 17, 1662* (1664?), Wing A989A

Atkins, Robert, *The God of Love and Peace with Sincere and Peaceable Christians: A Farewel Sermon, Preach'd at St John's, Exon, August the 17th, 1662 by Robert Atkins* (Exeter, 1715)

Bates, William, *The Peace-Maker, or, Two Farewell-Sermons Preached at St Dunstans in the West, London, August the 17th, 1662, by William Bates, D.D., Late Preacher of the Gospel There* (1662), Wing B1117

Baxter, Richard, *Richard Baxter's Farewel Sermon, Prepared to Have Been Preached to His Hearers at Kidderminster at His Departure, but Forbidden* (1683), Wing B1266

Baxter, Richard, *Excellent Memorables for All Mourners* (1691), Wing B1261

Calamy, Edmund (1600–66), *Eli Trembling for Fear of the Ark. A Sermon Preached at St Mary Aldermanbury, Decemb. 28, 1662* (1662), Wing C231A

Calamy, Edmund (1600–66), *The Fixed Saint Held Forth in a Farewell Sermon Preached at Mary-Aldermanbury, London, August 17, 1662* (1662), Wing C244

Calamy, Edmund (1600–66), *The Righteous Man's Death Lamented: A Sermon Preached at St Austins, London, Aug. 23, 1662, at the Funeral of that Late Eminent Minister of Jesus Christ, Mr Simeon Ashe, Late Minister of the Gospel There* (1662), Wing C262A

Calamy, Edmund (1600–66), *Eli Trembling for Fear of the Ark. A Sermon Preached at St Mary Aldermanbury, Dec. 28, 1662, by Edmund Calamy, B.D., Late Minister There* (Oxford, 1663), Wing C231

Calamy, Edmund (1600–66), *Eli Trembling for Fear of the Ark. A Sermon Preached at St Mary Aldermanbury, Dec. 28, 1662, by Edmund Calamy, B.D., Late Minister There* (Oxford, 1663), Wing C232

Calamy, Edmund (1600–66), *A Sermon Preached at Aldermanbury Church, Dec. 28, 1662, in the Fore-noon by Edm. Calamy, Late Pastor of the Same Congregation* (Oxford, 1663), Wing C267

Caryl, Joseph, *The White Robe: Or, The Undefiled Christian Clothed in a White Garment; Held Forth in a Farewel Sermon Preached by Mr. Joseph Caryl, at Magnus, August the 17, 1662* (1662), Wing C789

Cooper, Joseph, *The Dead Witnesse Yet Speaking to His Living Friends: Being the Substance of Eight Several Sermons, Lately Preached by Way of Farewel to a Country-Auditory* (1663), Wing C6056

Eubanke, George, *A Farewell Sermon Preached at Great Ayton in the County of Yorkshire by George Evbanke, Chaplain to the Right Worshipful, Sir George Narwood, Baronet, at Cleaveland in York-shire* (1663), Wing E3444

Bibliography

Fairclough, Richard, *A Pastor's Legacy, to His Beloved People: Being the Substance of Fourteen Farewel Sermons. By a Somersetshire Minister. Taken from His Mouth by One of His Hearers. Now Revised, and Published at the Entreaty and Charge of His Parishioners* (1663), Wing F106

Fairclough, Richard, *A Pastor's Legacy, to His Beloved People* (1713)

Hancock, Edward, *The Pastor's Last Legacy and Counsel Delivered in a Farewel Sermon, Preached at St Philips in Bristol, August 24th, 1662* (1663), Wing H640

Horton, Thomas, *Rich Treasure in Earthen Vessels. A Sermon Preached (Jan. 1 1662/3) at the Funerall of that Reverend and Faithful Servant of Jesus Christ, Mr James Nalton, Late Minister of God's Word at St Leonard's Foster-lane* (1663), Wing H2879

Jenkyn, William, *The Burning Yet Un-consumed Bush, or, The Holinesse of Places Discuss'd, Held Forth in Two Farewel-Sermons at Christ-Church, London, August 17th, 1662* (1662), Wing J633

Lamb, Philip, *The Royal Presence, or God's Tabernacle with Men: In a Farewell Sermon Preached the 17 of August 1662 at Beere Regis in the County of Dorset* (1662), Wing L207A

Lye, Thomas, *The Fixed Saint Held Forth in a Farewell Sermon Preached at All-Hallows-Lumbard-Street, August the 17, 1662* (1662), Wing L3537

Meade, Matthew, *The Pastors Valediction, or, A Farewell Sermon Preached at Sepulchures, London* (1662), Wing M1556

Newcomen, Matthew, *Ultimum Vale, or The Last Farewel of a Minister of the Gospel to a Beloved People* (1663), Wing N914

Palke, Thomas, *The Loyal Non-Conformist* (1664), Wing P203B

Swinnock, George, *The Pastors Farewell, and Wish of Welfare to His People, or A Valedictory Sermon* (1662), Wing S6280

Thorne, George, *The Saints Great Duty in Time of the Dangerous Afflictions, Persecutions and Oppressions, They May Meet in the Troublesome and Tempestuous Sea of this World, Either by Spiritual or Temporal Enemies. Preached in a Farewel-Sermon by Mr. George Thorne of Weymouth in Dorset-shire* (1664), Wing T1057B

Watson, Thomas, *A Pastors Love Expressed to a Loving People in a Farewel Sermon Preached at Stephens VValbrook, London, August 17, 1662* (1662), Wing W1136

OTHER CONTEMPORARY PRINTED WORKS

Alleine, Joseph, *A Call to Archippus, or, An Humble and Earnest Motion to Some Ejected Ministers to Take Heed of Their Ministry, that They Fulfil It* (1664)

Alleine, Theodosia, *The Life and Death of Mr Joseph Alleine* (1672)

An Exact Narrative of the Tryal and Condemnation of John Twyn (1664)

Assheton, William, *Evangelium Armatum* (1663)

Barksdale, Clement, *The Kings Return. A Sermon Preached at Winchcomb in Gloucestershire upon the Kings-Day, Thursday, May 24, 1660. By Clement Barksdale* (1660)

Barrett, John, *A Funeral Sermon, Preached at Nottingham, Occasioned by the Death of Mr John Whitlock, sen., December 8th, 1708* (1709)

Barrett, Joseph, *The Remains of Mr. Joseph Barrett, Son of the Reverend Mr. John Barrett, Minister of the Gospel at Nottingham* (1700)

Bartholomew, William, *The Strong Man Ejected by a Stronger Man than He* (1660)

Bates, William, *A Sermon Preached at the Funeral of the Reverend and Excellent Divine Dr. Thomas Manton* (1678)

Bates, William, *The Way to the Highest Honour: A Funeral Sermon on John xii.26, Preached upon the Decease of the Rnd. Tho. Jacomb, D.D., April 3, 1687* (1687)

Baxter, Richard, *A Holy Commonwealth or Political Aphorisms* (1659)

Baxter, Richard, *Richard Baxter His Account to His Dearly Beloved, the Inhabitants of Kidderminster, of the Causes of His Being Forbidden by the Bishop of Worcester to Preach within His Diocess* (1662)

Baxter, Richard, *The Cure of Church-Divisions* (1670)

Baxter, Richard, *A Christian Directory* (1673)

Baxter, Richard, *The English Nonconformity as under King Charles II and King James II Truly Stated and Argued* (1689)

Baxter, Richard, *Reliquiae Baxterianae*, ed. M. Sylvester (1696)

Beerman, William. *Sorrow upon Sorrow: Or, The Much Lamented Death of the Worthy Mr. Ralph Venning, Being a Sermon Preached upon the Sad Occasion of His Death before His Burial* (1674)

Berkenhead, John, *The Assembly-Man* (1663)

Berkenhead, John, *Cabala, or An Impartial Account of the Non-Conformists Private Designs, Actings and Wayes. From August 24, 1662, to December 25 in the Same Year* (1663)

Billing, Edward, *A Faithful Testimony for God and My Country* (1664)

Brinsley, John, *The Christian's Cabala* (1662)

Brooks, Thomas, *An Arke for all Gods Noahs in a Gloomy Stormy Day* (1662)

Brooks, Thomas, *Apples of Gold for Young Men and Women and a Crown of Glory for Old Men and Women* (1665)

Brunsell, Samuel, *Solomon's Blessed Land* (1660)

Buck, James, *St Paul's Thanksgiving Set Forth in a Sermon Preached* (1660)

Bury, Arthur, *The Bow* (1662)

Butler, Samuel, *Hudibras on Calamy's Imprisonment and Wild's Poetry* (1663)

Calamy, Edmund (1600–66), *The Great Danger of Covenant-Refusing, and Covenant-Breaking* (1646)

Calamy, Edmund (1600–66), *A Sermon Preached by Mr Edmund Calamy at Aldermanbury London, August 24 1651* (1651)

Calamy, Edmund (1600–66), *The Godly Man's Ark* (1658)

Calamy, Edmund (1600–66), *Master Edmund Calamy's Leading Case* (1663)

Calamy, Edmund (1600–66), *Saints Memorials* (1674)

Bibliography

Calamy, Edmund (1671–1732), *An Abridgement of Mr Baxter's History of His Life and Times. With an Account of Many Other of those Worthy Ministers Who were Ejected* (1702)

Calamy, Edmund (1671–1732), *An Abridgement of Mr Baxter's History of His Life and Times. With an Account of Many Other of those Worthy Ministers Who were Ejected* (2nd edn, 2 vols, 1713)

Calamy, Edmund (1671–1732), *A Continuation of the Account of the Ministers . . . Who were Ejected and Silenced* (2 vols, 1727)

Caryl, Joseph, *The Nature, Solemnity, Grounds, Property, and Benefits of a Sacred Covenant* (1643)

Case, Thomas, *The Quarrell of the Covenant, with the Pacification of the Quarrel* (1643)

Caton, William, *The Testimony of a Cloud of Witnesses Who in Their Generation have Testified against that Horrible Evil of Forcing of Conscience, and Persecution about Matters of Religion* (1662)

Cheeseman, Thomas, *Via Lactea* (1663)

Clarke, Samuel, *A Collection of the Lives of Ten Eminent Divines* (1662)

Clarke, Samuel, *The Lives of Sundry Eminent Persons in this Later Age* (1698)

Creed, William, *Judah's Return to Their Allegiance and David's Return to His Crown and Kingdom* (1660)

A Directory for the Publique Worship of God throughout the Three Kingdoms of England, Scotland and Ireland (1644)

A Directory for the Publique Worship of God throughout the Three Kingdoms of England, Scotland and Ireland (1660)

Douch, John, *England's Jubilee, or Her Happy Return from Captivity* (1660)

Douglas, Robert et al., *A Phenix, or, The Solemn League and Covenant* (Edinburgh, 1662)

Downame, John, *The Second Volume of Annotations upon all the Books of the Old and Nevv Testament* (1657)

Dunton, John, *The Life and Errors of John Dunton, Late Citizen of London* (1705)

Eedes, Richard, *Great Britain's Ressurrection, or, England's Complacencie in Her Royal Soveraign, King Charles the Second* (1660)

Eniautos Terastios, Mirabilis Annus, or The Year of Prodigies and Wonders (1661)

Evelyn, John, *A Character of England* (1659)

Everleigh, Josiah, *An Account of the Reasons Why Many Citizens of Exon have Withdrawn from the Ministry of Mr. J. Hallet and Mr. J. Peirce* (Exeter, 1719)

An Exact Catalogue of the Names of Several Ministers Lately Ejected out of Their Livings in Several Counties of England because They could not Conform for Conscience Sake (1663)

Fairfax, John, *The Dead Saint Speaking, or, A Sermon Preached upon Occasion of the Death of that Eminent Man, Mr. Mathew Newcomen* (1679)

Feltwell, Robert, *David's Recognition, with a Parallel betwixt His and Our Present Soveraign's Suffering and Deliverances* (1660)

Ford, Simon, *Parallela Dysparallela, or the Loyal Subject's Indignation for His Royal Sovereign's Decollation* (1661)

Flatman, Thomas, *Don Juan Lamberto: Or, A Comical History of the Late Times* (1661)

A Generall Bill of the Mortality of the Clergy of London (1662)

Glover, Henry, *Cain and Abel Paralleled with King Charles and His Murderers* (1664)

Godwyn, Thomas, *Phanatical Tenderness; Or the Charity of the Nonconformists* (1684)

Griffith, Matthew, *A General Bill of the Mortality of the Clergie of London, Which have beene Defunct by Reason of the Contagious Breath of the Secretaries of that City, from the Yeere 1641, to this Present Yeere 1649* (1647)

Griffith, Matthew, *The King's Life-Guard: An Anniversary Sermon Preached to the Honorable Societies of Both the Temples on the 30th of January 1664/5* (1665)

Hardy, Nathaniel, *A Loud Call to Great Mourning, in a Sermon Preached on the 30th of January 1661* (1661)

Harris, William, *Some Memoirs of the Life and Character of Thomas Manton* (London, 1725)

Heath, Thomas, *Stenography, or, The Art of Short-Writing* (1644) Wing H1342

Heath, Thomas, *Stenography, or, The Art of Short-Writing* (1664) Wing H1343

Hodges, Thomas, *Sion's Halelujah* (1660)

Horn, John, *A Breife Discovery of the People called Quakers* (1659)

Horn, John, *The Quakers proved Deceivers* (1660)

Horn, John, *Truth's Triumph over Deceit, or, A Further Demonstration that the People called Quakers be Deceivers* (1660)

Howe, John, *A Funeral Sermon for that Faithful and Laborious Servant of Christ Mr. Richard Fairclough who Deceased July 4, 1682 in the Sixty First Year of His Age* (1682)

Howe, John, *A Funeral Sermon for that Very Reverend, and Most Laborious Servant of Christ, in the Work of the Ministry, Mr. Matthew Mead* (1699)

Intelligencer, Issues 1–18 (August–December, 1663)

Ironside, Gilbert, *A Sermon Preached at Dorchester in the County of Dorcet, at the Proclaiming of His Sacred Majesty Charles the II, May 15, 1660* (1660)

Iter Boreale, to the Presbyterian Party, or, Doctor Wildes Recantation from His Reformed Study, to Mr. Calamy in Aldermanbury (1663)

Jenkyn, William, *A Sermon Preached at Mary Aldermanbury, on the 5th day of November, 1651* (1651)

Kem, Samuel, *King Solomon's Infallible Experiment for Three Kingdoms' Settlement* (1660)

Kingdom's Intelligencer, Issues 1–24 (1662–3)

Lambert, Thomas, *Sad Memorials of the Royal Martyr* (1669)

L'Estrange, Roger, *An Interest Mistaken, or The Holy Cheat* (1661)

L'Estrange, Roger, *The Relapsed Apostate or, Notes upon a Presbyterian Pamphlet, Entituled a Petition for Peace, & c.* (1661)

Bibliography

L'Estrange, Roger, *Truth and Loyalty Vindicated from the Reproachs and Clamours of Mr Edward Bagshaw Together with a Discovery of the Libeller Himself and His Seditious Confederates* (1662)

L'Estrange, Roger, *Considerations and Proposals in Order to the Regulation of the Press* (1663)

L'Estrange, Roger, *Toleration Discuss'd* (1663)

Linch, Samuel, *Rebellion Painted to the Life in Three Choice Sermons upon the Horrid Murder of Our Gratious Soveraign Charls the I of Blessed Memory* (1662)

Lloyd, David (alias 'Oliver Foulis'), *Cabala: Or, The Mystery of Conventicles Unvail'd* (1664)

Lloyd, David, *Memoires of the Lives, Actions, Sufferings & Deaths of those Noble, Reverend and Excellent Personages that Suffered by Death, Sequestration, Decimation, or Otherwise, for the Protestant Religion and the Great Principle Thereof, Allegiance to Their Soveraigne, in Our Late Intestine Wars* (1668)

Manton, Thomas, *A Sermon Preached at the Funerall of Mr. Christopher Love* (1651)

Maxwell, John (ed. Roger L'Estrange), *Presbytery Displayed for the Justification of Such as Do Not Like the Government, and for the Benefit of Those that Do Not Understand It* (1663)

Mercurius Publicus (1662–63)

Meriton, John, *Curse Not the King* (1660)

Morley, George, *The Bishop of Winchester's Vindication of Himself from Divers False, Scandalous and Injurious Reflexions Made upon Him by Mr. Richard Baxter in Several of His Writings* (1683)

Mossom, Robert, *England's Gratulation for the King and His Subjects' Happy Union* (1660)

A Mystery of Godliness, and No Cabala; Or a Sincere Account of the Non-Conformists Conversation from the 24 of August to this Time (1663)

Nelme, John, *England's Royal Stone at the Head of the Corner* (1660)

Newcome, Henry, *Usurpation Defeated and David Restored* (1660)

Newcomen, Matthew, *The Craft and Crvelty of the Chvrches Adversaries* (1643)

Newes, Issues 1–9 (September–October, 1663)

Oldfield, John, *The First, Last, or, The Formal Hypocrite Further from Salvation* (1666)

Parker, John, *A Sermon Preached at Christ-Church, Dublin, before Both Houses of Parliament, May the 29th, 1661* (Dublin, 1661)

Parker, Samuel, *Bishop Parker's History: Or, the Tories' Chronicle, from the Restauration of King Charles II, 1660, to the Year 1680* (1730)

Patrick, Simon, *A Brief Account of the New Sect of Latitude-Men* (1662)

Peirce, James, *The Case of the Ministers Ejected at Exon, by James Peirce, One of Them* (Exeter, 1719)

Perkins, William, *The Arte of Prophecying* (1607)

Philips, John, *Montelion* (1662)

Porter, Robert, *The Life of Mr. John Hieron with the Characters and Memorials of Ten Other Worthy Ministers of Jesus Christ* (1691)

Price, William, *God's Working and Brittan's Wonder* (1660)

Riders, Thomas, *The Black Remembrancer for the Year of Our Lord God, 1661* (1661)

S. R., *A Word to Dr Womocke, or, a Short Reply to His Pretended Resolution of Mr Crofton's Position* (1663)

Seditious Preachers Ungodly Teachers, Exemplified in the Case of the Ministers Ejected by the Act of Uniformity 1662 from Their Own Printed Sermons and My Lord Clarendon's History, Opposed Chiefly to Mr Calamy's Abridgment, where He has Canonized Them for So Many Saints and Confessors (1709)

Shaw, Samuel, *The Voice of One Crying in a Wilderness* (1666)

Sheldon, Gilbert, *David's Deliverance and Thanksgiving* (1660)

Sheldon, Gilbert, *The Dignity of Kingship Asserted* (1660)

Short, Ames, *God Save the King* (1660)

Swinnock, George, *The Works of George Swinnock, M.A.* (1665)

Taylor, Jeremy, *A Sermon Preached at the Opening of the Parliament of Ireland, May 8. 1661* (1661)

Towers, William, *A Thanksgiving Sermon for the Blessed Restauration of His Sacred Majesty Charles the II* (1660)

Twisse, Robert, *England's Breath Stopp'd* (1665)

Venning, Ralph *An Elegy on the Death of that Much Lamented and No Less Wanted Industrious Labourer in Gods Vineyard, the Reverend Mr. Ralph Venning* (1674)

Walker, John, *An Attempt towards Recovering an Account of the Numbers and Sufferings of the Clergy of the Church of England* (1714)

Walsall, Francis, *The Bowing the Heart of Subjects to Their Sovereign* (1660)

Walwyn, William (1614–1671), *God Save the King* (1660)

Warwell, James, *Votiva Tabula* (1660)

Washbourn, Thomas, *The Repairer of the Breach* (1661)

Watson, Thomas, *The Godlyman's Picture, Drawn with a Scripture-Pensil* (Glasgow, 1758)

Whitlock, John, *A Short Account of the Life of the Reverend Mr. William Reynolds* (1698)

Wilde, Robert, *The Tragedy of Christopher Love at Towerhill, August 22, 1651* (1651)

Wilde, Robert, *The Tragedy of Christopher Love at Tower-Hill* (1660)

Wilde, Robert, *On the Death of Mr Calamy* (1667)

Winstanley, William (c.1628–1698), *The Loyall Martyrology* (1665)

Winstanley, William (c.1628–1698), *England's VVorthies* (n.d.)

Womack, Laurence, *Aron Bimnucha, or An Antidote to Cure the Calamities of Their Trembling for Fear of the Ark, to Which is Added Mr Crofton's Creed Touching Church Communion* (1663)

Whynell, John, *England's Sorrows Turned into Joy* (1661)

Bibliography

SOURCES AND CALENDARS

Akermann, John Y. and Guy, Henry (eds), *Moneys Received and Paid for Secret Services of Charles II and James II from 1679 to 1688*, ed. J. Y. Akerman (1851)

Baxter, Richard, *Autobiography Being the Reliquiae Baxterianae*, ed. J. M. L. Thomas (1931)

Baxter, Richard, *Calendar of the Correspondence of Richard Baxter*, ed. N. Keeble and G. Nuttall (Oxford, 2 vols, 1991)

Browning, Andrew (ed.), *English Historical Documents 1660–1714* (1966)

Burnett, Gilbert, *The History of My Own Time*, ed. O. Airy (Oxford, 1897)

Calamy, Edmund (1671–1732), *The Nonconformist's Memorial, Being an Account of the Lives, Sufferings and Printed Works of the Two Thousand Ministers Ejected from the Church of England, Chiefly by the Act of Uniformity 1666 [sic]*, ed. Samuel Palmer (3 vols, 1802–3)

Central United Bartholomew Committee, *Documents Relating to the Settlement of the Church of England* (1862)

Clarendon, Edward Hyde, earl of, *The Life of Edward, Earl of Clarendon* (2 vols, Oxford, 1857)

Defoe, Daniel, *A Journal of the Plague Year*, ed. L. Landa (Oxford, 1990)

Evelyn, John, *The Diary of John Evelyn*, ed. E. S. de Beer (6 vols, Oxford, 1955)

Eyre, G. E. B., Plomer, H. R. and Rivington, C. R. (eds), *A Transcript of the Registers of the Worshipful Company of Stationers: from 1640–1708A.D.* (3 vols, 1913–14; rpt New York, 1950)

Farewell Sermons of Some of the Most Eminent of the Non-Conformist Ministers Ejected in 1662 (1816)

Green, M. A. E. (ed.), *Calendar of State Papers, Domestic Series, 1619–62* (1858–93)

Heywood, Oliver, *The Life of John Angier of Denton*, ed. E. Axon (Manchester, Chetham Society, vol. 97, 1937)

Hines, A. B. (ed.), *Calendar of State Papers, Venetian, 1661–1664* (1932)

Historical Manuscripts Commission, *Report on the Manuscripts of Allan George Finch Esquire*, 71st report, vol. I (1913)

Hyde, Edward, earl of Clarendon, *Continuation of the Life by E. Hyde* (3 vols, Oxford, 1827)

Hyde, Edward, earl of Clarendon, *Calendar of the Clarendon State Papers*, ed. O. Ogle, W. H. Bliss, W. D. McCray and K. J. Routledge (4 vols, Oxford, 1869–1928)

Josselin, Ralph, *The Diary of Ralph Josselin 1616–1683*, ed. A. MacFarlane (Oxford, 1976)

Journal of the House of Commons

Journal of the House of Lords

Manton, Thomas, *The Complete Works of Thomas Manton, D. D.*, ed. Rev. T. Smith (22 vols, 1870–75)

Martindale, Adam, 'The life of Adam Martindale', ed. R. Parkinson (Manchester, Chetham Society, vol. 4, 1844)

Matthews, Arnold G., *Calamy Revised: Being a Revision of Edmund Calamy's Account of the Ministers and Others Ejected and Silenced, 1660–2* (Oxford, 1934)

Matthews, Arnold G., *Walker Revised* (Oxford, 1948)

Newcome, Henry, *The Diary of the Rev. Henry Newcome, 30 September 1661 to 28 September 1663*, ed. R. Parkinson (Manchester, Chetham Society, vol. 18, 1849)

Newcome, Henry, *The Autobiography of Henry Newcome*, ed. R. Parkinson (Manchester, Chetham Society, 2 vols, vols 26 and 27, 1852)

Nuttall, Geoffrey R. (ed.), *The Beginnings of Nonconformity 1660–1665: A Checklist* (1960)

Pepys, Samuel, *The Diary of Samuel Pepys*, ed. R. Latham and W. Matthews (11 vols, 1970)

Schellinks, William, *The Journal of William Schellinks' Travels in England 1661–1663*, ed. M. Exwood and H. L. Lehmann, Camden 5th series (vol. 1, 1993)

Sermons of the Great Ejection: Taken from a Collection of Farewell Sermons Preached by the Late London Ministers and England's Remembrancer, ed. I. H. Murray (1962)

Williams, W. P. (ed.), *Index to the Stationers' Register 1640–1708* (La Jolla, CA, 1980)

Wood, Anthony, *The Life and Times of Anthony Wood*, ed. A. Clark (5 vols, Oxford, 1891)

SECONDARY WORKS

BOOKS AND ARTICLES

Achinstein, Sharon, *Literature and Dissent in Milton's England* (Cambridge, 2003)

Andersen, Jennifer and Sauer, Elizabeth, *Books and Readers in Early Modern England: Material Studies* (Philadelphia, 2002)

Barnard, John and McKenzie, D. F., *The Cambridge History of the Book in Britain: 1597–1695*, vol. 4 (Cambridge, 2002)

Barthes, Roland, 'The death of the author', in *Image Music Text*, trans. S. Heath (1984), pp. 142–8

Beek, M. van, *An Enquiry into Puritan Vocabulary* (Groningen, 1969)

Bell, Maureen, 'Elizabeth Calvert and the Confederates', *Publishing History*, 32 (1992), pp. 4–49

Bell, Maureen, Chew, Shirley, Eliot, Simon, Hunter, Lynette and West, James L. (eds), *Reconstructing the Book: Literary Texts in Transmission* (Aldershot, 2001)

Bell, William G., *The Great Fire of London in 1666* (1951)

Biriotti, Maurice and Miller, Nicola (eds), *What Is an Author?* (Manchester, 1993)

Blagden, C., *The Stationers' Company: A History 1403–1959* (1960)

Blench, J. W., *Preaching in England in the Late Fifteenth and Early Sixteenth Centuries* (Oxford, 1964)

Bolam, C. Gordon, 'The ejection of 1662 and its consequences for the Presbyterians in England', *The Hibbert Journal*, 40 (1961–62), pp. 184–95

Bosher, Robert S., *The Making of the Restoration Settlement* (revised edn, 1957)

Bibliography

Braddick, Michael and Walter, John D. (eds), *Negotiating Power in Early Modern Society: Order, Hierarchy and Subordination in Britain and Ireland* (Cambridge, 2001)

Bremer, Francis J. (ed.), *Puritanism: Transatlantic Perspectives on a Seventeenth-Century Anglo-American Faith* (Boston, MA, 1993)

Bremer, Francis J. and Rydell, E., 'Performance art? Puritans in the pulpit', *History Today*, 45, 9 (1995), pp. 50–4

Brewer, J. and Styles, J. (eds), *An Ungovernable People* (1980)

Burke, Sean, *The Death and Return of the Author: Criticism and Subjectivity in Barthes, Foucault and Derrida* (Edinburgh, 1992)

Champion, Justin, *The Pillars of the Priestcraft Shaken: The Church of England and its Enemies 1660–1730* (Cambridge, 1991)

Chartier, Roger, *Cultural Uses of Print in Early Modern France*, trans. L. G. Cochrane (New York, 1987)

Chartier, Roger (ed.), *The Culture of Print: Power and the Uses of Print in Early Modern Europe*, trans. L. G. Cochrane (Cambridge, 1989)

Cliffe, J., *Puritans in Conflict* (1988)

Clifton, R., 'The popular fear of Catholics during the English Revolution' *Past & Present*, 52 (1971), pp. 23–55

Clifton, R., 'Fear of popery', in C. Russell (ed.), *The Origins of the English Civil War* (1973), pp. 144–67

Collinson, Patrick, *The Religion of Protestants* (Oxford, 1982)

Collinson, Patrick, *The Puritan Character: Polemics and Polarities in Early Seventeenth-Century English Culture* (Los Angeles, 1989)

Cragg, G. R., *From Puritanism to the Age of Reason* (Cambridge, 1950)

Cragg, G. R., *Puritanism in the Period of the Great Persecution* (Cambridge, 1957)

Cragg, G. R., *The Church in the Age of Reason 1648–1789* (1960)

Cressy, David, 'Illiteracy in England 1530–1730', *Historical Journal*, 20, 1 (1977), pp. 8–9

Cressy, David, *Literacy and the Social Order: Reading and Writing in Tudor and Stuart England* (Cambridge, 1980)

Cressy, David, 'The Protestant calendar and the vocabulary of celebration in early modern England', *Journal of British Studies*, 29 (1990), pp. 31–52

Cressy, David and Ferrell, Lori-Anne, *Religion and Society in Early Modern England: A Sourcebook* (1996)

Cressy, David and Ferrell, Lori-Anne (eds), *Travesties and Transgressions in Tudor and Stuart England* (Oxford, 2000)

Cuming, G. J., 'The Prayer Book in Convocation, November 1661', *Journal of Ecclesiastical History*, 7 (1957), pp. 182–92

Cuming, G. J., *A History of Anglican liturgy* (2nd edn, 1982)

Darnton, Robert, 'What is the history of books?', *Daedalus*, 3 (1982), pp. 65–83

Davies, Horton, *The Worship of the English Puritans* (1948)

Davies, Horton, *Like Angels from a Cloud* (San Marino, CA, 1986)

Davids, Thomas W., *Annals of Nonconformity in Essex* (1863)

Davis, John C., 'Against formality: one aspect of the English Revolution', *Transactions of the Royal Historical Society*, 6th series, 3 (1993), pp. 265–88

Dexter, Henry M, *The Congregationalism of the Last Three Hundred Years* (rpt Farnborough, 1970)

Duce, Robert, *Beyond the Gate: A Play in One Act on the Period that Followed the Great Ejection in 1662* (1961)

Duce, Robert, *Fire in the City: An Historical Play of the 1662 Ejection* (1961)

Duce, Robert (ed.), *Faithful and True: A Pageant for Tercentenary Celebrations 1662–1962* (1962)

Duffy, Eamon, 'The godly and the multitude in Stuart England', *Seventeenth Century*, 1, 1 (1986), pp. 31–49

Durston, Christopher and Eales, Jacqueline (eds), *The Culture of English Puritanism 1560–1760* (1996)

Edie, Carolyn, 'Right rejoicing: sermons on the occasion of the Stuart Restoration 1660', *Bulletin of the John Rylands University Library of Manchester*, 62 (1980), pp. 61–80

Eisenstein, Elizabeth, *The Printing Press as the Agent of Change* (2 vols, Cambridge, 1979)

Faithorn, R. H., 'The survival of Dissent in Yorkshire 1660–1780', in E. Royle (ed.), *Regional Studies in the History of Religion in Britain since the Later Middle Ages*, (Hull, 1984), pp. 95–9

Ferrell, Lori Anne, *Government by Polemic: James I, the King's Preachers and the Rhetorics of Conformity 1603–1625* (Stanford, CA, 1998)

Ferrell, Lori Anne and McCullough, Peter E. (eds), *The English Sermon Revised: Religion, Literature and History 1600–1750* (Manchester, 2000)

Finkelstein, David and McCleery, Alistair (eds), *The Book History Reader* (2002)

Finleayson M. G., *Historians, Puritanism and the English Revolution: The Religious Factor in English Politics Before and After the Interregnum* (1983)

Fletcher, Anthony and Stevenson, J. (eds), *Order and Disorder in Early Modern England* (Cambridge, 1985)

Fletcher, Anthony and Roberts, Peter (eds), *Religion, Culture and Society in Early Modern Britain* (Cambridge, 1994)

Fox, Adam, *Oral and Literate Culture in England 1500–1700* (Oxford, 2000)

Fox, Adam and Woolf, Daniel (eds), *The Spoken Word: Oral Culture in Britain 1500–1850* (Manchester, 2002)

Fraser, Peter, *The Intelligence of the Secretaries of State and Their Monopoly of Licensed News, 1660–1688* (Cambridge, 1956)

Gaskell, Philip, *A New Introduction to Bibliography* (Oxford, 1972)

Bibliography

Gee, Henry, 'The Derwentdale plot 1663', *Transactions of the Royal Historical Society*, 3rd series, vol. 11 (1917), pp. 125–42

Goldie, Mark, 'John Locke and Anglican Royalism', *Political Studies*, 31 (1983), pp. 61–85

Greaves, Richard L., *Deliver Us from Evil: The Radical Underground in Britain 1660–1663* (Oxford, 1986)

Green, Ian M., *The Re-establishment of the Church of England 1660–1663* (Oxford, 1978)

Green, Ian M., Collinson, Patrick, Walsham, A., Hunt, A. and Peters, K., 'Religious publishing in England c.1557–1695', in J. Barnard and D. Kitterick (eds), *The History of the Book in Britain*, vol. 4 (Cambridge, 1998)

Green, Ian M., *Print and Protestantism in Early Modern England* (Oxford, 2000)

Gregory, Jeremy, *Restoration, Reformation and Reform 1660–1828* (Oxford, 2000)

Hall, Basil, 'Puritanism: the problem of definition', *Studies in Church History*, 2, ed. G. J. Cuming (1965), pp. 283–96

Harris, Timothy, *London Crowds in the Age of Charles II* (Cambridge, 1987)

Harris, Timothy, 'Introduction: revising the Restoration', in T. Harris, P. Seaward and M. Goldie (eds), *The Politics of Religion in Restoration England* (Oxford, 1990)

Harris, Timothy, *Politics under the Later Stuarts* (1993)

Harris, Timothy, *Restoration: Charles II and His Kingdoms 1660–1685* (2005)

Harris, Timothy, Seaward, Paul and Goldie, Mark (eds), *The Politics of Religion in Restoration England* (Oxford, 1990)

Haycroft, Nathaniel, *Heroes and Lessons of St Bartholomew's Day, A. D. 1662* (1862)

Heywood, O., *The Life of John Angier*, ed. E. Axon (Manchester, 1937)

Hill, Christopher, *Change and Continuity in Seventeenth-Century England* (1973)

Hill, Christopher, *The World Turned Upside Down* (1975)

Hill, Christopher, *Some Intellectual Consequences of the English Revolution* (1980)

Hill, Christopher, *The Experience of Defeat: Milton and Some Contemporaries* (1984)

Hill, Christopher, *Society and Puritanism in Pre-Revolutionary England* (1991)

Hill, Christopher, *The English Bible and the Seventeenth-Century Revolution* (1994)

Hines, Thomas C., *Our Ejected Ministers: A Bicentenary Tract for AD1862* (2nd edn, 1861)

Hirst, Derek, 'The conciliatoriness of the Cavalier Commons reconsidered', *Parliamentary History*, 6 (1987), pp. 221–35

Hopper, Andrew, 'The Farnley Wood plot and the memory of the civil wars in Yorkshire', *Historical Journal*, 45, 2 (2002), pp. 281–303

Hoppitt, Julian, *A Land of Liberty? England 1689–1727* (Oxford, 2000)

Howell, Wilbur S., *Logic and Rhetoric in England 1500–1700* (New York, 1956)

Hudson, G., 'Negotiating for blood money: war widows and the courts in seventeenth-century England', in J. Kermode and G. Walker (eds), *Women, Crime and the Courts* (1994)

Hughes, Ann, '"Popular" Presbyterianism in the 1640s and 1650s: the cases of Thomas Edwards and Thomas Hall', in Nicholas Tyacke (ed.), *England's Long Reformation 1500–1800* (1998), pp. 235–59

Hutton, Ronald, *The Restoration: A Political and Religious History of England and Wales 1658–1667* (Oxford, 1985)

Johns, Adrian, *The Nature of the Book: Print and Knowledge in the Making* (1998)

Jones, James R., 'Political groups and tactics in the Convention of 1660', *Historical Journal*, 6 (1963), pp. 159–77

Jones, James R. (ed.), *The Restored Monarchy 1660–1688* (1979)

Kastan, David S., *A Companion to Shakespeare* (Oxford, 1999)

Keeble, Neil H., *The Literary Culture of Nonconformity in Later Seventeenth-Century England* (Leicester, 1987)

Keeble, Neil H., *The Restoration: England in the 1660s* (Oxford, 2002)

Kibbey, Ann, *The Interpretation of Material Shapes in Puritanism: A Study of Rhetoric, Prejudice and Violence* (Cambridge, 1986)

Kitchin, George, *Sir Roger L'Estrange* (1913)

Lacey, D. R., *Dissent and Parliamentary Politics in England 1661–1689* (New Jersey, 1969)

Lake, Peter, 'Defining Puritanism – again?', in F. Bremer (ed.), *Puritanism: Transatlantic Perspectives on a Seventeenth-Century Anglo-American Faith* (Boston, MA, 1993)

Lake, Peter, 'Anti-popery: the structure of a prejudice', in R. Cust and A. Hughes (eds), *The English Civil War* (1997), pp. 181–210

Lake, Peter, *Conformity and Orthodoxy in the English Church, c. 1560–1660* (Woodbridge, 2000)

Laurence, Anne, *Parliamentary Army Chaplains 1642–1651* (Woodbridge, 1990)

Levine, David and Wrightson, Keith, *Poverty and Piety in an English Village: Terling 1525–1700* (Oxford, 1995), p. 151

Love, Harold, 'Preacher and publisher: Oliver Heywood and Thomas Parkhurst', *Studies in Bibliography*, 31 (1978), pp. 227–35

McGee, John S., *The Godly Man in Stuart England* (1976)

McKerrow, R., *An Introduction to Bibliography for Literary Students* (Oxford, 1928)

MacLean, Gerald, *Time's Witness: Historical Representation in English Poetry, 1603–1660* (Madison, WI, 1990)

MacLean, Gerald (ed.), *Culture and Society in the Stuart Restoration* (Cambridge, 1995)

Marshall, Alan, *Intelligence and Espionage in the Reign of Charles II, 1660–1685* (Cambridge, 2002)

Miller, John, *Popery and Politics in England, 1660–1688* (Cambridge, 1973)

Miller, John, *Religion in the Popular Prints 1600–1832* (Cambridge, 1986)

Miller, John, *After the Civil Wars: English Politics and Government in the Reign of Charles II* (Harlow, 2000)

Bibliography

Milton, Anthony, 'Licensing, censorship and religious orthodoxy in early Stuart England', *Historical Journal*, 41 (1998), pp. 625–51

Mitchell, W. Fraser, *English Pulpit Oratory from Andrewes to Tillotson: A Study of Its Literary Aspects* (1932)

Morrill, John S., *Reactions to the English Civil War* (1982)

Morrill, John S., 'Between conventions: the members of Restoration parliaments', *Parliamentary History*, 5 (1986), pp. 125–32

Morrill, John S., *The Impact of the English Civil War* (1991)

Morrill, John S., Slack, Paul and Woolf, Daniel (eds), *Public Duty and Private Conscience in Seventeenth-Century England* (Oxford, 1993)

Morrissey, Mary, 'Interdisciplinarity and the study of early modern sermons', *Historical Journal*, 42, 4 (1999), pp. 1111–23

Morrissey, Mary, 'Scripture, style and persuasion in seventeenth-century English theories of preaching', *Journal of Ecclesiastical History*, 53, 4 (2002), pp. 686–706

Muddiman, Joseph G. (pseud. J. B. Williams), *A History of English Journalism to the Foundation of the Gazette* (1908)

Muddiman, Joseph G. (pseud. J. B. Williams), *The King's Journalist 1659–1689* (1923)

Nicholas, Donald, *Mr Secretary Nicholas 1593–1669: His Life and Letters* (1955)

Nicholson, Francis, 'The Kaber–Rigg plot, 1662', *Cumberland & Westmorland Archaeological Society Transactions*, 11, (1911), pp. 212–32

Nightingale, Benjamin, *The Ejected of 1662 in Cumberland and Westmorland* (2 vols, Manchester, 1911)

Norbrook, David, *Writing the English Republic: Poetry, Rhetoric and Politics 1627–1660* Cambridge, 1999)

Norrey, P. J., 'The Restoration regime in action: the relationship between central and local government in Dorset, Somerset and Wiltshire', *Historical Journal*, 31 (1988), pp. 789–812

Nuttall, Geoffrey R. (ed.), *The Beginnings of Nonconformity 1660–1665: A Checklist* (1960)

Nuttall, Geoffrey R. (ed.), *The Beginnings of Nonconformity* (1964)

Nuttall, Geoffrey R. and Chadwick, O., *From Uniformity to Unity 1662–1962* (1962)

O'Day, Rosemary, *The English Clergy: The Emergence and Consolidation of a Profession 1558–1642* (Leicester, 1979)

Oxford Dictionary of National Biography from the Earliest Times to the Year 2000, ed. H. C. G. Matthew and B. H. Harrison (60 vols, Oxford, 2004)

Patterson, Annabel, *Censorship and Interpretation: The Condition of Writing and Reading in Early Modern England* (Madison, WI, 1984)

Patterson, Annabel and Dzelzainis, Martin, 'Marvell and the earl of Anglesey: a chapter in the history of reading', *Historical Journal*, 44, 3 (2001), pp. 703–26

Plant, Marjorie, *The English Book Trade: An Economic History of the Making and Sale of Books* (3rd edn, 1965)

Plomer, Henry R., *A Dictionary of the Booksellers and Printers Who were at Work in England, Scotland and Ireland, from 1647 to 1667* (1907)

Plumb, John H., *The Growth of Political Stability in England, 1675–1725* (1967)

Pooley, Roger, 'Language and loyalty: plain style at the Restoration, *Literature & History*, 6, 1 (1980), pp. 2–18

Porter, Stephen, *The Great Fire of London* (Stroud, 1996)

Potter, Lois, *Secret Rites and Secret Writing: Royalist Literature 1641–1660* (Cambridge, 1989)

Ramsbottom, John D., 'Presbyterianism and "partial conformity" in the Restoration Church of England', *Journal of Ecclesiastical History*, 43 (1992), pp. 249–70

Randall, Helen, 'The rise and fall of a martyrology: sermons on Charles I', *Huntington Library Quarterly*, 10, 2 (1946), pp. 135–67

Reddaway, T., *The Rebuilding of London after the Great Fire* (1940)

Sawday, Jonathan, 'Re-writing a revolution: history, symbol and text in the Restoration', *The Seventeenth Century*, 7, 2 (1992), pp. 171–99

Seaver, Paul S., *The Puritan Lectureships: The Politics of Religious Dissent 1560–1662* (Stanford, CA, 1970)

Seaward, Paul, *The Cavalier Parliament and Reconstruction of the Old Regime 1661–1667* (Cambridge, 1989)

Sharpe, Kevin, *Criticism and Compliment: The Politics of Literature in the England of Charles I* (Cambridge, 1987)

Sharpe, Kevin, 'Religion, rhetoric and revolution', *Huntington Library Quarterly*, 58, 3 (1995), pp. 255–8

Sharpe, Kevin, *Reading Revolutions: The Politics of Reading in Early Modern England* (2000)

Sharpe, Kevin and Zwicker, S. N. (eds), *Politics of Discourse: The Literature and History of Seventeenth-Century England* (1987)

Siebert, Frederick S., *Freedom of the Press in England 1476–1776: The Rise and Decline of Government Controls* (Urbana, IL, 1952)

Smith, Bruce K., *The Acoustic World of Early Modern England: Attending to the O Factor* (1999)

Smith, C. Fell, 'A group of Essex divines 1640–1662', *Essex Review*, 1 (1892), pp. 107–11

Smith, C. Fell, 'The Essex Newcomens', *Essex Review*, 2 (1893), pp. 35–40

Smith, Revd. Harold, 'Sources for a list of Essex clergy under the Long Parliament and the Commonwealth', *Essex Review*, 30, (1921), pp. 170–7

Smith, Nigel, *Perfection Proclaimed: Language and Literature in English Radical Religion 1640–1660* (Oxford, 1989)

Smith, Nigel, *Literature and Revolution in England 1640–1660* (1997)

Sommerville, Charles John, 'On the distribution of religious and occult literature in seventeenth-century England', *The Library*, 5th series, 29 (1974), pp. 221–5

Sommerville, Charles John, *Popular Religion in Restoration England* (Gainsville, FL, 1977)

Bibliography

Sprunger, Keith L., *Trumpets from the Tower: English Puritan Printing in the Netherlands 1600–1640* (Leiden, 1994)

Spufford, Margaret, 'First steps in literacy: the reading and writing experiences of the humblest seventeenth-century spiritual autobiographiers', *Social History*, 4, 3 (October 1979), pp. 407–35

Spufford, Margaret, *Contrasting Communities: English Villagers in the Sixteenth and Seventeenth Centuries* (2nd edn, Stroud, 2000)

Spufford, Margaret (ed.), *The World of Rural Dissenters 1520–1725* (Cambridge, 1995)

Spurr, John, 'Schism and the Restoration Church', *Journal of Ecclesiastical History*, 41 (1990), pp. 408–24

Spurr, John, *The Restoration Church of England 1646–1689* (1991)

Spurr, John, *English Puritanism 1603–1689* (1998)

Staley, Vernon, *The Life and Times of Gilbert Sheldon* (1913)

Stanford, Charles, *The Farewell Sunday: On the Farewell Sermons of Clergy Removed under the Act of Uniformity 1662*, *St Bartholomew's Bicentenary Papers*, tract VII (1862)

Stanford, Charles, *Joseph Alleine: His Companions and Times, a Memorial of Black Bartholomew 1662* (1862)

Stewart, B. S., 'The cult of the royal martyr', *Church History*, 38 (1969) pp. 175–200

Sutch, V. D., *Gilbert Sheldon: Architect of Anglican Survival 1640–1675* (The Hague, 1973)

Swain, Margaret, *Embroidered Stuart Pictures* (1990)

Swainson, Charles A., *The Parliamentary History of the Act of Uniformity* (1875)

Sykes, Norman, *From Sheldon to Secker: Aspects of English Church History 1660–1768* (Cambridge, 1959)

Taylor, Edgar, *Suffolk Bartholomeans* (1840)

Thomas, Donald, *A Long Time Burning: The History of Literary Censorship in England* (1969)

Thomas, J. W., *Sir John Berkenhead: A Royalist Career in Politics and Polemics* (Oxford, 1969)

Turberville, A., *A History of Welbeck Abbey and Its Owners* (1938–39)

Tyacke, Nicholas, *Aspects of English Protestantism c.1530–1700* (Manchester, 2001)

Underdown, David, *Royalist Conspiracy in England* (New Haven, CT, 1960)

Underdown, David, *Revel, Riot and Rebellion* (Oxford, 1985)

Underdown, David, *A Freeborn People* (Oxford, 1996)

Vallance, Edward, 'An holy and sacramentall paction: federal theology and the Solemn League and Covenant in England', *English Historical Review*, 116 (February 2001), pp. 50–75

Vallance, Edward, 'Oaths, casuistry and equivocation: Anglican responses to the Engagement controversy', *Historical Journal*, 44, 1 (2001), pp. 59–77

Vaughan, Robert, *The Case of the Ejected Ministers of 1662: A Speech* (1861)

Walker, J., 'The censorship of the press during the reign of Charles II', *History*, 35 (1950), pp. 218–38

Walsham, Alexandra, *Providence in Early Modern England* (Oxford, 1999)

Walter, John D., *Understanding Popular Violence in the English Revolution: The Colchester Plunderers* (Cambridge, 1999)

Watt, Tessa, *Cheap Print and Popular Piety 1550–1640* (Cambridge, 1991, rpt 1996)

Weber, Harold, *Paper Bullets: Print and Kingship under Charles II* (Lexington, KY, 1996)

Webster, Tom, *Godly Clergy in Early Stuart England: The Caroline Puritan Movement c.1620–1643* (Cambridge, 1997)

Whitehorn, R., 'Richard Baxter – "Meer Nonconformist"', in G. Nuttall, R. Thomas, R. Whitehorn and H. Short (eds), *The Beginnings of Nonconformity: The Hibbert Lectures* (1964), p. 67

Williams, W. and Abbott, C., *An Introduction to Bibliographical and Textual Studies* (New York, 1985)

Williamson, George, *The Senecan Amble: Prose from Bacon to Collier* (1951)

Wilson, John F., *Pulpit in Parliament: Puritans during the English Civil Wars 1640–1648* (Princeton, NJ, 1969)

Wright, Susan J. (ed.), *Parish, Church and People* (1988)

Wrightson, Keith, *English Society 1580–1680* (1982, 1990)

Wykes, David, *'To Revive the Memory of Some Excellent Men': Edmund Calamy and the Early Historians of Nonconformity* (1997)

Yates, Nigel, *Buildings, Faith and Worship: The Liturgical Arrangement of Anglican Churches 1600–1900* (Oxford, 2000)

Zwicker, Steven, and Hirst, Derek, 'Rhetoric and disguise: political language and political argument in Absalom and Architopel', *Journal of British Studies*, 21 (1981), pp. 39–55

UNPUBLISHED THESES

Appleby, David J., 'The Culture and Politics of War Relief in Essex, 1642–1662' (University of Essex MA dissertation, 1996)

Cliftlands, William, 'The Well-affected and the Country' (University of Essex PhD thesis, 1987)

Glines, Timothy C., 'Politics and Government in the Borough of Colchester 1660–1693' (University of Wisconsin PhD thesis, 1974)

Hetet, John S., 'A Literary Underground in Restoration England: Printers and Dissenters in the Context of Constraints' (Cambridge PhD thesis, 1987)

Hetherington, Robert J., 'Birmingham and the Ejected of 1662' (unpublished essay, Birmingham Central Library, 1957)

Jackson, P. W., 'Nonconformists in Devon 1660–1689' (University of Exeter PhD thesis, 1986)

Vallance, Edward, 'State Oaths and Political Casuistry in England, 1640–1702' (Oxford D.Phil thesis, 2000)

Bibliography

ELECTRONIC SOURCES

Early English Books Online: http://eebo.chadwyck.com/home [last accessed 3 February 2005]

English Short Title Catalogue Online: http://eureka.rlg.org [last accessed 17 January 2005]

Oxford Dictionary of National Biography: www.oxforddnb.com [last accessed 26 October 2004]

Puritan Bookshelf: Vol. #17 – Sermons, Sabbath Worship & God's Promises (CD-ROM, Edmonton, Canada: Still Waters Revival Books, 2001)

Still Waters Revival Books Homepage: www.swrb.com [last accessed 13 September 2004]

Index

Note: 'n.' after a page reference indicates the number of a note on that page

Achinstein, Sharon 109, 212
Act for Confirming and Restoring of
    Ministers (1660) 2, 55
Act of Uniformity (1662) 2, 4, 18, 19, 22,
    24, 27, 28, 31, 32, 33, 35, 46, 55, 62,
    80, 81, 83, 96, 101, 102, 105, 119,
    120, 140, 148, 151, 171, 173, 174, 175,
    176, 183, 187, 188, 192, 194, 195,
    197, 218, 220, 222, 224, 225, 226
Acton (Cheshire) 74
Act to Preserve the Person and Government
    of the King (Treason Act) (1661)
    24, 36, 37, 55, 102, 107, 187, 198
Alleine, Joseph 197
Alleine, Richard 19, 32, 34, 35, 38, 40, 42,
    44, 56, 65, 70, 75, 98, 105, 110, 112,
    113, 114, 115, 196
Amsterdam 6, 194
Anabaptists 32, 156, 195
Angier, John 2, 23, 31, 39, 80
Anglicanism
    definitions of 4–5
    see also Cavalier-Anglicans
Annesley, Samuel 25
anti-clericalism 18
apocalypticism 100–1, 109, 119, 219, 221
Ark of the Covenant
    discussed in sermons 29, 98, 99, 100,
        107, 136, 179, 186
Ashe, Simeon 6, 7, 28, 40, 67, 71, 74,
    159

represented in Cavalier-Anglican
    literature 183
Ash Priors (Somerset) 37, 61
Assheton, William 25, 138, 171, 191–4,
    200, 202, 223
Atkins, Robert 2, 22, 26, 34, 38–9, 45, 46,
    47n.9, 74, 80, 135, 147, 148, 160,
    214
audience 12, 18, 56–8, 67, 220
    agency 72–4, 82, 144
    behaviour 12, 73, 74
    demographics 79
    size 57–8, 82
    intellectual capacity 67, 69–70, 72,
        73–4, 132, 133–4
    memory of 61, 69–70
authority
    episcopal 29–30, 33
    see also Bartholomean attitudes to

Bagshawe, Edward 140, 148, 186
Barksdale, Clement 106
Barrett, John 6, 23, 26, 34, 35, 47n.8, 69,
    72, 81, 99, 103, 104, 106, 107, 109,
    113, 117, 144, 212–13
Barry, Jonathan 199, 202
Barthes, Roland 10, 71, 161
Bartholomean attitudes to
    Arminians 33, 34
    authority 18, 25, 30–1, 33, 36, 41–3,
        45–6, 55–6, 62, 73, 76, 80–2,

93, 101–2, 103, 105, 106, 107–9,
113–14, 118, 120, 221–2
Catholics 34–7, 72, 98, 99, 100, 155,
159, 198, 219, 224
conventicles 31
episcopal ordination 29–30
Erastians 32
liturgy 30–1, 81
Lutherans 34
origins of term 5
Quakers 34–5, 198, 202, 219, 224
separation from the Church 31–2, 34,
37, 43, 46, 69, 197, 199, 219
social and political disobedience 41–3,
200, 201
social rank 41–2, 71, 72, 108, 220
Socinians 34
Solemn League and Covenant 28, 29
toleration 35
Bartholomeans
demographics 21, 37–8
education 19–20, 66
Bartholomew's Day
significance of 13, 97, 178
Batcombe (Dorset) 19, 38
Bates, William 11, 22, 29, 32–3, 37, 57, 60,
65, 95, 104, 109–10, 112–13, 133,
134, 136, 137, 145, 148, 149, 190,
215
Baxter, Richard 20, 33, 34, 44, 45, 60, 62,
63, 65, 69, 71, 72, 74, 78, 81, 82,
97, 111, 113, 118, 131, 135, 136, 139,
140, 142, 145, 148, 149, 151, 152,
213, 214
represented in Cavalier-Anglican
literature 192, 193
Beere Regis (Dorset) 38, 73, 144
Beerman, William 60, 72, 106
Beeston (Nottinghamshire) 92
Bellarmine, Cardinal Robert 35
Bennet, Sir Henry, Secretary of State
(later Lord Arlington) 139, 171,
180, 181, 186, 224
Beresford, John 40
Berkenhead, Sir John 5, 136, 138, 139, 171,
172, 180–7, 189, 191, 192, 194, 195,
197, 198, 199, 200, 202, 205n.52,
206n.60, 212, 224
Billing, Edward 197
Billingsley, John 80

Bladon, Thomas 23, 29, 35, 41, 42, 43, 59,
68, 70, 71, 72, 76, 95, 97, 100, 102,
106
Book of Common Prayer 2, 5, 30, 42, 56,
58, 177, 220
Bosher, Robert 8, 46, 79, 172–3, 176
Boxted (Essex) 21, 57
Braddick, Michael 55
Breadsall (Derbyshire) 38
Bremer, Frank 64, 70
Brewster, Thomas 138, 139, 141, 145, 160,
167n.91, 189
Bristol 21, 58, 73, 80, 137, 141, 145, 202
Brooks, Nathan 138, 160, 197
Brooks, Thomas 72, 73, 98, 105, 114, 137,
153, 160
Bull, Daniel 41, 62, 70, 99, 100, 112, 118,
133
Bunyan, John 82
Burghal, Edward 74
Burke, Charles 176
Burke, Sean 10
Burnet, Gilbert, Bishop of Salisbury 97,
173, 176
Bury, Arthur 97, 177
Butler, James, Marquess (later Duke) of
Ormonde 3, 42, 79, 194
Butler, Samuel 179

Calamy, Edmund III 5, 6, 18, 60, 213–14
Calamy, Edmund, the elder 3, 7, 22, 24,
25, 26, 27, 28, 29, 40, 50n.68, 56,
57, 62, 67, 71, 73, 74, 75, 77, 79,
97, 98, 99, 100, 103, 107, 111, 119,
136, 137, 144, 148, 174, 175, 179,
180, 181
represented in Cavalier-Anglican
literature 183, 184, 186–7, 189,
192, 193, 195, 196, 201
Calamy Revised 57, 215
Calvert, Elizabeth 145, 160
Calvert, Giles 139, 145, 160, 189
Calvin, John
represented in Cavalier-Anglican
literature 194
Cambridge
University of 2, 20
Emmanuel College 20
Carmarthenshire 21
Carr, Nathaniel 57

Carsington (Derbyshire) 11
Caryl, Joseph 27, 28, 59, 67, 106, 108,
    112, 113, 114, 115, 118, 136, 137
  represented in Cavalier-Anglican
    literature 183–4, 192, 193, 195
Case, Thomas 25, 26, 27, 28, 35, 40,
    47n.9, 59, 61, 70, 96, 113, 114, 136,
    148
  represented in Cavalier-Anglican
    literature 183, 184, 192, 195
catechising 133
Catholics
  represented in Cavalier-Anglican
    literature 174, 178, 183, 187, 195,
    201–2
  see also Bartholomean attitudes to:
    Catholics
Cavalier-Anglicans
  anxieties 21, 24, 41–2, 46, 55, 74, 76–7,
    81, 105, 139, 171, 173, 174–5, 177,
    178, 184–5, 188, 195, 202, 211, 220
  definitions of 5
'Cavalier' Parliament 2, 79, 173
Cavendish, William, Duke of Newcastle
    72
censorship
  self-censorship 134
  state censorship 12, 132, 133, 139, 140,
    143, 144, 162, 180–1, 188–90,
    223
Chapman, Hannah 145
Chapman, Livewell 139, 145, 160
Charles I 97, 102, 103, 108, 139, 159, 171,
    178, 186, 187, 190, 198, 200, 225
  execution of 37, 97, 103, 171, 175, 177,
    178, 179, 187, 190, 200, 220, 221,
    224
Charles II 1, 24, 25, 27, 36, 98, 101, 102,
    103, 104, 106, 120, 153, 171, 172,
    174, 176, 177, 181–2, 198, 221, 225
  taking the Covenant, implications of 27,
    28, 102, 155
Chartier, Roger 10, 163
Cheeseman, Thomas 197
Cheshire 21, 74
Chesterfield (Derbyshire) 80
Church of England 2, 4, 5, 18, 19, 20, 27,
    31, 33, 34, 37, 43, 46, 55, 106, 107,
    133, 140, 173, 176, 196, 197, 198,
    199–200, 218, 219

circulation
  printed 13, 136–40, 143, 146, 147, 161–2,
    180, 188, 189, 211, 222–4
  scribal 13, 132, 135–6, 147, 150–1, 161,
    214, 222
Clarendon, earl of see Hyde, Edward
Clark, John 61, 63, 105, 110, 115, 117
Clark, Samuel 67
Claydon, Tony 9, 83
clergy
  demographics 37–8, 219, 222
Cleveland (Yorkshire) 40
Colchester (Essex) 57
Collins, John 26, 30–1, 57, 65, 72, 73, 111,
    221
Collinson, Patrick 4
Commonwealth regime 25, 179
Compton, Henry, Bishop of London 37
Congregationalists
  demographics 21, 33
Cooper, Joseph 3, 5, 62, 80, 105, 108, 115,
    137
Corporation Act (1661) 2, 31
Cragg, G. R. 7, 8, 60, 61, 66
Cranwell, Luke 47n.8
Creswick, James 62
Crockett, Bryan 11
Crodacot, John 25, 34, 35, 57, 60, 68, 73,
    76, 77, 100, 108, 118, 159
Croft, Herbert, Bishop of Hereford 27
Crompton, John 56, 74, 118
Cromwell, Oliver 78, 105, 184, 189
Cross, William 28, 30, 92, 111–12, 113, 218

Darnton, Robert
  communications circuit 161
David
  images of, in sermons 69, 102–3, 107,
    120, 124n.72
death
  discussed in farewell sermons 44, 71,
    74, 96, 100, 116–19, 132, 159, 162,
    172, 219, 222
Dedham (Essex) 6, 20, 38, 58, 70, 96, 116,
    137
Dell, William 25
Derbyshire 6, 11, 23, 31, 38
Devon 21, 81, 214
Directory for the Publique Worship of God
    (1644) 64, 67, 71, 76

Index

Dr Williams's Library, London 6
Dodd, John 67
Do'eg the Edomite
    images of in farewell sermons 69, 100, 107
Dorset 38
Douch, John 106
Dover, Simon 138, 160
Durham, William 80
Durston, Christopher 47

Eales, Jacqueline 47
Eastington (Gloucestershire) 2
Edward VI
    cited in farewell sermon 98
Edwards, Thomas
    Gangraena 223
Eedes, Richard 25, 103, 177
Egypt
    images of in sermons 35, 94, 96, 98, 103, 104–5, 108, 109, 146, 150, 186, 187, 195, 201, 221
Engagement (1650) 27, 97
England
    as a saved nation 99, 100, 120
England's Remembrancer (1663, 1666) 6, 21, 33, 132, 138, 141, 144, 147, 148, 159, 180, 196, 212–13
English Civil Wars 21, 24, 58, 82, 109, 179, 180, 194, 200, 224
Essex 2, 6, 57, 80, 141, 147
Eubanke, George 35, 40, 61, 63, 65, 77, 99, 104, 105, 107, 108, 116, 117, 141, 143–4
Euripides
    cited in farewell sermon 65
Evelyn, John 73
Exeter 2, 21, 22, 38–9, 74, 97, 141

Fairclough, Richard 5, 6, 21, 22, 30, 38, 42, 44, 62, 63, 67, 70, 75, 80, 104, 107, 108, 116, 117, 131, 144, 148, 160, 214
Fairclough, Samuel 67
Farnley Wood plot (1663) 42, 225
Ferrell, Lori Anne 8, 9, 11, 13, 177, 225
Fifth Monarchists 224, 225
Finlayson, M. G. 7
Flatman, Thomas 184
Ford, Thomas 5, 22, 69, 107, 147

formalists
    images of in farewell sermons 33–4, 106, 219
Foucault, Michel 10
Fox, Adam 11, 65, 71
Foxe, John
    Acts and Monuments (1563) discussed in farewell sermons 97, 98, 113, 212

gadding 57, 78
Galpin, John 37, 47n.9, 60, 61, 64, 108, 111, 112, 115, 117
Gauden, John, Bishop of Exeter 39
Germany
    discussed in farewell sermons 70
Gloucestershire 2, 22
godliness
    discussed in farewell sermons 43–4, 70, 83
Golden Legend, the, 66
Grand Remonstrance (1641) 45
Great Yarmouth (Norfolk) 5
Greaves, Richard 8, 21, 224
Greek
    used in farewell sermons 20, 64–5, 67, 146
Green, Ian 79, 80, 173, 223
Griffiths, Matthew 179, 194
Gunpowder Plot
    discussed in sermons 35, 178

Habermas, Jurgen 83
Hackett, John, Bishop of Lichfield 80
Hampshire 62
Hancock, Edward 22, 31, 43, 57, 58, 63, 73, 78, 98, 110, 111, 115, 117, 131, 137
Hardy, Nathaniel 25
Harris, Tim 7, 37
Heath, Thomas 135, 197
Hebrew
    used in sermons 20
Henry, Philip 80, 105
Herring, John 22
Hertfordshire 21
Hetet, John 8
Heywood, Oliver 23, 47n.8, 74, 80, 142, 145, 146
Hieron, John 23, 38, 65, 68, 108–9, 133
Hildersham, Arthur
    cited in farewell sermons 152

Hill, Christopher 8, 36, 68, 220
Hobbes, Thomas 193
Holles, John, earl of Clare 40
Homer 64
Hooker, Thomas 64
Hopper, Andrew 225
Horn, John 34, 137
Horner, Sir George 22
Horton, Thomas 40, 55, 60, 136–7, 144
House of Commons 1, 173, 174
House of Lords 173
Howe, John 32, 145
Hudibras 179–80
Hughes, Ann 18
Hyde, Edward, earl of Clarendon 3, 24,
    76–7, 174, 201

Independents 1, 32
Indulgence, Declaration of (1672) 33
Interregnum 18, 19, 23, 24, 58, 77, 93,
    105, 112, 148, 175, 179, 180, 193,
    196, 200
Intelligencer, The 138, 189
Ipswich (Suffolk) 191

Jacombe, Thomas 32, 34, 65, 67, 68, 103,
    116, 136
  represented in Cavalier-Anglican
    literature 183
Jenkyn, William 7, 30, 41, 45, 95, 104,
    105, 106, 112, 136, 148, 153–4,
    223
  represented in Cavalier-Anglican
    literature 184, 192, 193, 198
Jesus Christ
  portrayed as king in farewell sermons
    25, 108–9, 127n.155, 220
Johns, Adrian 10, 12, 161
Jollie, Thomas 59
Jones, J. R. 7
Josselin, Ralph 2, 5, 31, 173
Juxon, William, Archbishop of Canterbury
    181

Keeble, Neil 8, 19, 109, 132, 139, 142, 146,
    201
Kem, Samuel 25, 29, 177
Kidderminster (Worcestershire) 214
Kingdomes Intelligencer, The 180
King Jesus, portrayals of *see* Jesus Christ

Kingstone (Dorset) 38
Kirk Langley (Derbyshire) 11
Kitchin, George 215
Knight, Sir John 80

Lake, Peter 4, 36, 41, 47, 202
Lamb, Philip 38, 43, 68, 72, 73, 75, 98,
    105, 109, 137, 144, 149, 150, 153
Lancashire 2, 21
Latham, George 116
Latin
  used in farewell sermons 20, 64–5, 67,
    146
Laud, William, Archbishop of Canterbury
    181, 182
L'Estrange, Sir Roger 5, 6, 41, 105, 138,
    139, 140, 143, 144, 149, 157, 158,
    159, 160, 171, 174, 180–3, 185–91,
    192, 194, 195, 199, 200, 201, 202,
    212, 215, 219, 224
Licensing Act (1662) 135, 140, 181
Lillicrap, Peter 143
Linch, Samuel 177
literacy 11, 70, 131–2, 222
Lithuania
  cited in farewell sermons 70
Lloyd, David, canon of St Asaph 27, 138,
    159, 171, 194–6, 200, 201, 202,
    208n.135
London 3, 21, 22, 24, 38, 39, 58, 73, 78,
    79, 99, 106, 138, 140, 141, 146,
    147, 151–2, 160, 161, 163, 181
  Great Fire of 35, 132, 138, 160, 211
  Great Plague of 132, 138, 160, 211
Long Parliament 1
Love, Christopher 25, 26, 58
  represented in Cavalier-Anglican
    literature 184, 193, 200
Love, Harold 146
Lye, Thomas 7, 27, 28, 32, 33, 34, 36, 41,
    44, 45, 47n.9, 57, 58, 59, 60, 65,
    68, 71, 72, 78, 96, 98, 103–4, 107,
    110, 116, 118–19, 120, 136, 137, 142,
    148, 154–7, 223
  represented in Cavalier-Anglican
    literature 183, 202
Lyme (Dorset) 174

McCullough, Peter 9, 11
McGee, Sears 4, 111, 114

magistrates
  interventions in preaching 78, 80–1, 83,
    133, 173, 203n.5
Manchester 80
Manchester, earl of *see* Montagu, Edward
Manton, Thomas 26, 38, 40, 44, 47n.9,
    60, 65, 108, 109, 136, 149, 152,
    158, 189, 190, 215
  represented in Cavalier-Anglican
    literature 195
Marian martyrs
  discussed in sermons 77, 97–8, 114,
    155, 159, 212, 222
Marshall, Stephen 192, 193
martyrdom, discussed in farewell sermons
    77, 79, 83, 109, 111–13, 114, 117, 121,
    172, 200, 222, 225
Mary I, discussed in farewell sermons
    98
Maurice, Henry 80
Matthews, A. G. 21, 215
Mead, Matthew 65, 77, 108, 110, 111, 114,
    116, 136, 137, 145, 147, 148
Mells (Somerset) 5, 81, 144
Mercurius Publicus 136, 180, 181, 201,
    215
Meriton, John 178
Mew, William 2, 5, 22
Miller, John 7, 35, 36, 102, 173, 202
military metaphors
  used in farewell sermons 109–11, 120,
    146, 220
Milton, John 8, 184
Mitchell, W. F. 8, 19, 60, 64, 66, 223
Monck, George, Duke of Albemarle 107
Montagu, Edward, 2nd earl of Manchester
    40, 79
Moore, Joseph 23, 44, 72, 75, 99, 112,
    116–17, 118
Morley, George, Bishop of Worcester 41,
    80, 140, 194
Morrice, Roger 213
Morrice, Sir William 139
Morrissey, Mary 9, 64, 82, 93, 99
Moseley (Worcestershire) 3
Mossom, Robert 103
Muddiman, Henry 189

Nalton, James 6, 22, 25, 60, 136–7, 144,
    159

Narwood, Sir George 40
Needler, Benjamin 176
Nelme, John 103
Netherlands 137, 138, 211
  printing in 6
networks
  clerical 20, 22, 23, 46, 146, 174
  nonconformist 20, 21, 46, 141, 146, 163
Newcombe, Henry 25, 38, 47n.8, 60, 80,
    102, 106, 133, 177, 215
Newcomen, Matthew 6, 23, 34, 36, 38, 45,
    59, 61, 70, 71, 72, 73, 77, 91n.192,
    95, 96, 98, 99, 106, 111, 113, 116,
    117, 118, 119, 133, 137, 141, 147, 148,
    150–3, 181, 201, 223
  represented in Cavalier-Anglican
    literature 193, 195
Newes, The 149, 158, 189
Newgate prison 3, 179
New Model Army
  veterans 42, 175, 195–6
Newnham, Thomas 39
Newton, George 37, 47n.9, 107
Nicholas, Sir Edward, Secretary of State
    77, 180–1, 186, 205n.52, 206n.55,
    224
nonconformists
  demographics 37–8, 41, 58
  geographic dispersal 37
Northumberland 21
note-taking 133–5, 144, 148, 155–6
Nottingham 23, 81, 144
Nottinghamshire 6, 141

Oath and Covenant *see* Solemn League
  and Covenant
O'Day, Rosemary 20
Oldfield, John 11, 20, 26, 30, 114
O'Neill, Daniel 42
oral culture 11, 70, 222
Ormonde, Marquess of *see* Butler, James
orthodoxy, discussed in farewell sermons
    32–3, 219
Oxford
  Bodleian Library 6
  University of 2, 20
    Exeter College 20
    Magdalen College 20
    New Inn Hall 20
    Wadham College 20

Palke, Thomas 138, 177, 196
Palmer, Samuel 63, 215
Papists *see* Catholics
Parker, John 106, 112
Parker, Samuel 212, 213–14
Parkhurst, Thomas 137, 145–6
passive obedience 26, 45, 79, 198, 200,
    201, 221–2
Patterson, Annabel 92, 93, 102
Paul 55, 60, 71, 77, 107, 112, 118, 119, 222
Pauline scripture
    deployed in farewell sermons 35, 55, 74,
        94, 95–6, 99, 103, 105, 111, 112,
        113, 114, 118, 120, 146, 222
Pentrich (Derbyshire) 6, 31
Pepys, Samuel 1, 3, 42, 57, 67, 82, 133,
    134, 218
Perkins, William 65
    Arte of Prophesying, The 63, 64
persecution, discussed in farewell
    sermons 77, 79, 96, 111–16, 117,
    121, 172, 200, 202, 210n.175, 219
Peter, Hugh 25, 117
Philips, John 184
Piedmont
    cited in farewell sermons 70
Plato
    cited in farewell sermon 61
Pledger, Elias 38, 77–8, 114
Pliny
    cited in farewell sermon 65
Plumb, J. H. 7
Pooley, Roger 93
Post Office 78
Porter, Robert 6, 23, 31, 44, 59, 69, 70,
    94, 97, 110, 115, 133
Potter, Edmund 78
Potter, Lois 8, 9, 64, 93, 140, 142, 148,
    200, 224
Powel, Thomas 5, 22, 43
preachers
    Anglican 19, 97, 102
preaching
    Anglican 19, 33, 37, 56, 58, 66, 97, 104,
        114, 175, 176, 178, 201, 202, 221,
        224
    audiences 18
    techniques 60, 75, 82
    emotive aspects 59–61, 64, 74, 82
    extempore 62, 63–4, 133

humour 61, 62, 65, 151, 179
'plain style' 64, 65, 82
scripted 62
target audience 63, 67, 69–70, 140
theatrical aspects 59–60, 64, 65, 82,
    158
Presbyterians
    alleged conspiracies of 3, 23, 77, 184–5,
        188, 191, 192, 195–6, 198–9, 202,
        212, 224
    cooperation with Independents 1
    definitions of 4, 18, 19, 21, 177, 202,
        219
    Scottish 187
print culture 10
printers 138, 139, 141–3, 162, 178, 188,
    211
printing industry 6, 131, 132, 138, 139–48,
    157–8, 160–1, 162, 189, 211
Privy Council 3, 57, 78
Protectorate regime 1, 139, 174
Puritan gentry 40–1, 46, 59, 79, 142
Puritanism
    definitions of 4, 177

Quakers 34, 71, 74, 175, 191, 195, 225

radical sects 1, 202, 224
regicide 18, 27, 220, 221
    see also Charles I: execution of
Repton School (Derbyshire) 23
Reynolds, William 23
rhetoric
    training in 20
Rogers, John 58, 133
Russell, William, earl of Bedford 40
Rydell, Edward 64, 70

Sampson, Henry 213
Sardis, discussed in sermons 73, 106, 114,
    151–2, 181
Saul, discussed in farewell sermons 69,
    100
Savoy Conference (1661) 1, 195
Sawday, Jonathan 117, 175
Schellinks, William 74
Scripture
    as political comment 68, 69, 76, 92–4,
        96, 102, 111, 119, 180, 186–7, 188,
        195, 200–1, 220–1

Index

'run-on' technique 67–9, 94, 115
  use of 64, 67–9, 93, 94–6, 111, 119
Seaman, Lazarus 57, 114, 137, 148
  represented in Cavalier-Anglican
    literature 184
Seaward, Paul 79
Seddon, Robert 11, 23, 26, 47n.8, 96, 98,
  117
Seneca
  cited in farewell sermon 65
sermons
  29 May 25, 57, 58, 76, 83, 102, 103, 120,
    124n.64, 171, 177–8, 200
  30 January 25, 37, 58, 76, 83, 97, 102,
    103, 120, 124n.64, 171, 177–8, 200,
    205n.41
  authorship of 10, 11, 12, 132, 135, 148,
    151–7, 158–9, 161, 223
  duration 61–2
  funeral 6, 7, 23, 26, 60, 136, 212–13
  parliamentary fast 25, 93, 94, 101, 148,
    193
  political significance of 8, 9–10, 11, 22,
    24, 29, 41, 47, 55, 58, 64, 67–9,
    70, 75–9, 81, 82, 83, 92–4, 98,
    102, 134, 171–3, 177–80, 181–7,
    190, 192–3, 195, 198, 199, 201–3,
    211–12, 213, 218, 220, 224, 225
  provenance of 12, 135
  reception of 12, 61–2, 75
  rhetorical structure of 12, 13, 28, 58, 59,
    64, 66–9, 71, 93, 201, 220
  see also preaching
Shaw, Samuel 23, 99, 113, 114, 117
Sheldon, Gilbert, Bishop of London,
  (afterwards Archbishop of
  Canterbury) 5, 78–9, 80, 104, 107,
  144, 172, 173–4, 175, 176, 177, 180,
  181, 204n.23, 219, 220
shorthand manuals 135
Shrewsbury (Shropshire) 80
Silas 77, 111
Slater (or Schlater), Samuel 38, 96, 136,
  193
Smectymnuus (1641) 77, 148, 189, 190,
  193, 194, 195
Smith, Bruce 11
Solemn League and Covenant 2, 21, 25,
  27, 29, 45, 189, 193, 198, 201, 219
Somerset 5, 21, 22, 37, 38, 61

spies 23, 40, 78, 173, 181
Spira, Francis 70
Spufford, Margaret 43, 58, 69, 132
Spurr, John 4, 8, 173
Staffordshire 6
Stanford, Charles 215
Stationers' Company 139, 143, 181, 189
Stephens, Robert 191
Still Waters Revival Books 215
Stradling, George 139
Strode, William 77
Stucley, Lewis 5, 22, 66, 112, 147
Suffolk 21
Swinnock, George 20, 30, 40, 65, 109,
  110, 137, 144, 146

Taunton (Somerset) 37, 174
Taylor, Jeremy, Bishop of Down and
  Connor 79
Thoresby, Ralph 213
Thorne, George 26, 43, 44, 67–8, 74, 94,
  98, 107, 111, 114, 119, 138, 150, 196
Thurloe, John 78, 139
Tookie, Job 5
Treason Act see Act to Preserve the Person
  and Government of the King (1661)
Twisse, John 178
Twynn, John 138, 143, 160

Underdown, David 19

Vallance, Ted 28
Venner's Rising (1661) 42, 108, 175, 191,
  195
Venning, Ralph 20, 21, 33, 44, 68, 96–7,
  137
Vincent, Thomas 73
Virgil 65

Wadsworth, Thomas 32, 59, 70, 78, 99
Wales 21
Walker, John 5, 60, 213
Walter, John 55, 69
Walwyn, William (1614–71) 177
Ward, Seth, Bishop of Exeter 39
Warwell, James 97
Watson, Thomas 7, 25, 26, 28, 31, 35–6,
  40, 65, 67, 68, 74–5, 92, 109, 110,
  113, 115, 117, 136, 137, 159, 197, 218
Wharton, Lord Philip 40

Whitlock, John 6, 20, 30, 31, 40, 42, 44, 62, 73, 75–6, 81, 96, 97, 106, 114, 144, 212
Whitlock, Joseph 23
Wilde, Robert 7, 78, 157, 179–80
Wilkins, John 65
Williamson, Joseph 191
Wilson, John F. 64, 71, 94, 101, 108

Winter, Robert 6, 151
Womack, Laurence, archdeacon of Suffolk 179, 197
Worcester, battle of 27
Worcestershire 3

Yates, Nigel 177
Yorkshire 40

Lightning Source UK Ltd.
Milton Keynes UK
UKHW051323230522
403391UK00012B/89

9 780719 087806